STARS AND SILHOUETTES

Contemporary Approaches to Film and Media Series

A complete listing of the books in this series can be found online at wsupress.wayne.edu.

GENERAL EDITOR

Barry Keith Grant
Brock University

STARS AND SILHOUETTES

The HISTORY of the CAMEO ROLE in HOLLYWOOD

JOCELINE ANDERSEN

WAYNE STATE UNIVERSITY PRESS
DETROIT

© 2020 by Wayne State University Press, Detroit, Michigan 48201. All rights reserved. No part of this book may be reproduced without formal permission.

ISBN 978-0-8143-4691-4 (paperback)
ISBN 978-0-8143-4690-7 (hardcover)
ISBN 978-0-8143-4692-1 (e-book)

Library of Congress Control Number: 2020938731

Wayne State University Press
Leonard N. Simons Building
4809 Woodward Avenue
Detroit, Michigan 48201-1309

Visit us online at wsupress.wayne.edu

CONTENTS

Acknowledgments		vii
	Introduction	1
1.	Worthy of Recognition: The Cameo as Portrait	29
2.	Familiar Faces: Ensemble Cameos in the Studio Era	61
3.	Inside Laughs: Comedians and the Casual Cameo	101
4.	The Ambassadors: Cameos Transformed through Television	133
5.	Author Signature: Directors On-Screen and the Celebratory Cameo	163
	Conclusion	195
Notes		209
Works Cited		253
Index		285

ACKNOWLEDGMENTS

During the long process of researching and writing *Stars and Silhouettes*, I benefited from the valuable insights, contributions, and encouragement of many individuals along the way. Prominent among them was my thesis supervisor at McGill University, William Straw, whose important work pointed me in the direction of cameos in the first place. His unfailing support and guidance have been extremely valuable to me throughout the duration of this project.

I would like to thank the Social Sciences and Humanities Research Council of Canada (SSHRC) for supporting my research through the Joseph-Armand Bombardier Canada Graduate Scholarship and the Michael Smith Foreign Study Supplement. I also thank Media@McGill for awarding me an Advanced Dissertation Grant.

I am especially grateful to Keir Keightley at Western University and Ernest Mathijs at the University of British Columbia for their engaging feedback and mentorship as I worked to refine my manuscript towards its final form.

In addition, I am indebted to Vanessa Schwartz for welcoming me at the Visual Research Institute at the University of Southern California during the winter of 2014–15 as well as for sharing her insights on Mike Todd as a key figure in the evolution of the cinematic cameo. Anna Luise Kiss of Film University Babelsberg provided me with a valuable forum for exchanging ideas on the cameo and other underexplored film roles.

Among the many people who helped me with my research, I would like to thank Jenny Romero and the staff of the Margaret Herrick Library at the Academy of Motion Picture Arts and Sciences; Peggy Alexander at the UCLA Library Special Collections; Ned Comstock at the USC Cinematic Arts Library; Dace Taube at the USC Doheny Memorial Library Special

Collections; John Cahoon at the Seaver Institute of the Los Angeles Natural History Museum; and Jennifer Garland at McGill's McLennan Library.

Marie Sweetman, the acquisitions editor at Wayne State University Press, played an enormous role in helping bring this project to fruition. I am grateful to her and the rest of the WSU Press team for their hard work in guiding me through the complicated process of book publication.

Throughout the writing of this book, I have been enriched by the friendship of Elyse Amend, Li Cornfeld, Paul Fontaine, Dylan Mulvin, and Vicki Simon. I could not have written this book without their encouragement, curiosity, and thoughtful commentary. I also appreciate the help of Barbara and Nathan Laurie in proofreading my manuscript.

Great thanks are due to my parents, Robin Andersen and Michèle Mitchell, and the rest of my family for their love and support. Last but not least, I would like to thank my husband Mark Laurie for his careful reading and constant willingness to act as a sounding board, and more generally, for being with me on this journey.

INTRODUCTION

As the final credits roll in *Tropic Thunder* (2008), an additional scene unfolds. The scene shows a minor character, the producer of the beleaguered action flick whose production the movie follows, as he boogies in his office, hamming it up for the camera. Like many codas in contemporary comedies, this non sequitur scene sits somewhere between impromptu, are-we-still-rolling blooper and orchestrated bonus content. In the film, the producer is tough-nosed, canny, and given to obscenity; in the coda the actor's dancing is a silly spectacle far outside of the character the audience has become familiar with after ninety minutes of screen time. Who exactly are we watching getting down, the producer or the actor? The credits give the audience a further clue, as they reveal that the role of the producer is not just any actor's performance in a minor role, but a cameo by perennial leading man Tom Cruise, made unrecognizable by a bald cap and fatsuit (fig. 1; fig. 2). The reveal is twofold: first, the movie breaks the spell of narrative by slipping into pure performance, then, second, the carpet of recognition is pulled out from under the audience as they turn their attention not to the character but to the actor who plays him. With this dancing cameo, audience members

Figure 1. Tom Cruise clowning around as Les Grossman in the credits for *Tropic Thunder* (2008).

Figure 2. Leading man: Tom Cruise in *Mission: Impossible* (1996).

are asked to reevaluate their relationship to the film and its filmmakers and yet also to reaffirm their deep participation in film culture and its system of stars. This is the work a cameo does. Cameos destabilize the relationship of a film's fictional premise to the world's nonfictional reality, but they also leverage the audience's investment in the personas of stardom to fulfill their moviegoing experiences. Cameos create a space in the movie, a break in the narrative, that is filled by the audience's extratextual knowledge.

Cameo roles are usually defined as small roles where people play themselves, or, as Ernest Mathijs writes, "a short appearance by a publicly known person who is instantly recognizable, which makes them harder to accept as a character than as the public person they are."[1] The specific qualities that make a person publicly known and instantly recognizable depend, as Mathijs suggests, on the audience. A cameo may be visible or invisible depending on what audience is watching, transforming performers masquerading as nobodies into recognizable figures. Scholars and journalists writing about movies use the term *cameo* to describe roles that run the gamut from Tom Cruise's unexpected turn as the boogying agent to Buster Keaton's late career bit parts[2] to a college professor's extra role in *Lincoln* (2012).[3] All of these are small roles that rely on the audience's extratextual knowledge to set them apart from other characters in the film, whether they know Tom Cruise as matinee idol, Buster Keaton as slapstick king, or the extra as the instructor of a history class. Cameos can fall out of view, while new ones emerge from old footage. An audience in the twenty-first century might not recognize comedian Red Skelton get shut out of a casino in *Ocean's 11* (1960), but an audience in 1960 was sure to laugh at the irony of the regular-joe treatment Skelton receives. Cameos can be built into films as publicity stunts, in-jokes, or tributes by the director, producer, or writer, but they can only be affirmed by the audience's power of recognition. Cameo roles are transformative, creating an active role for the audience in watching.

Movies ask a lot of their audiences. Usually, they ask that audiences suspend their disbelief and use their imaginations to fill in the details that movies exclude: multiplying crowds, transforming known locations into other worlds, trusting that actors and actresses are the characters they say they are. Thanks to the suspension of disbelief, movie reality and real-world reality are two separate realms that often bear only a slight resemblance to each other. There are genres that cross this threshold, such as documentary film that purports to record life as it really is or experimental film that distorts and plays with vision. However, Vivian Sobchack suggests that within fiction films, there can be moments of documentary space that are created when the viewer acknowledges that the world on-screen is contiguous with the viewer's lifeworld.[4] Cameos point toward this real world, but it is up to the viewer to recognize the cameo as a documentary space that accesses the world outside the film. This space invites audiences to examine how the real world and the movie world overlap, potentially exposing the actors, directors, writers, and technicians who create the movie for who they really are, or at least, who they might be in real life. Like a cinephilic moment where the viewer is prodded into private reflection by a cinematic image,[5] documentary space asks audiences to exit the diegesis of the film.

Once considered, the borders of documentary space in cinema seem hard to pin down, especially where the cameo is concerned. Film, by its nature, cannot help but reveal documentary space as it records and manipulates images of the real world. At what point in a performance are audiences supposed to draw the line between real and make-believe? When should the audience consider Tom Cruise as Tom Cruise, and when should they let him be Les Grossman, movie producer? The cameo calls special attention to the audience's task of attending to or ignoring documentary space. In a film, challenges to the coherence of the fictional world are constantly ongoing, especially as movie actors are among the most recognizable private individuals of our time. As brief, small roles, cameos that explicitly draw on real world personas and fictional characters both contain and focus the conflict of fiction and reality.

For Victor Burgin, a pure cinephilic moment is based on private memories, yet the reflection the cameo produces is grounded in a very public and mass culture. In order to recognize a cameo, the audience needs to recognize the person on-screen as a person in the real world.[6] In this highly visual age, who we recognize has extended beyond people we have met to include people we have only seen in media images.[7] These celebrities may be famous for their achievements; they may be famous, as Nathalie Heinich suggests, only because of their continued visibility.[8] Celebrity emerges from recognition while also making recognition likely. Stars, on the other hand, as Richard deCordova points out, are recognized for their achievement as performers, as they at once embody a series of character roles, a set of skills as a performer, and a real-world persona.[9] Celebrity and stardom increasingly overlap, as scholars like Joshua Gamson have pointed out, as celebrities appear in film, television, and online images, and stars develop real-world personas that overshadow their body of work as an actor. Overwhelmingly, those recognized in cameos are celebrities.

Like the star, the celebrity's own image in the increasingly manipulated world of publicity often relies on the interplay between a public and private persona, enlisting fans to assemble and assess the available information to determine the real nature of the celebrity they only know from afar.[10] This "play of surface and depth" is an integral part of star discourse, says deCordova, where "behind the image, this discourse constantly tells us, lies something more real."[11] The obsession with uncovering an individual's innermost reality that drives fans has been linked by Foucault to a post-Enlightenment culture of confession. The confession, which establishes subjecthood for the person confessing as he asserts an inward life while placing himself at the mercy of the confessor who now knows his secrets, links the knowledge of a person's private life with power.[12] The cameo's momentary reveal of the celebrity as he supposedly is stands in as a confession, exposing the deeper reality behind the surface illusion. Yet, rather than a private reveal, this confession is delivered to the entire viewing public. This contradiction between public and private discourse, and its promise of power for both fan and star, underpins our fascination with celebrity.

Celebrity culture challenges fans to uncover celebrity secrets, asking, how familiar can audiences really become with someone they recognize but do not and cannot know? A fan's interest in the cameo as documentary space reflects their excitement about a celebrity encounter and the private information that encounter could expose, but any recognition of that documentary space depends on the machinery of celebrity culture that has made the celebrity visible. Even when recognizing a celebrity on-screen, audiences are reminded of the limits of the documentary space that is opened up to them, in that it is contiguous with their own real world while remaining separate. Following quickly on the demystification of the industry's secrets that Hollywood so often dangles in front of its viewers, the reinstatement of illusion reasserts a balance of power in favor of the culture industry.[13] Each cameo reaffirms celebrity culture, allowing viewers to momentarily reflect on their investment in celebrity culture before the cameoist's exit artfully returns audience attention to the narrative.

The cameo exists at the intersection of celebrity culture and participative audience practices, where audiences recognize documentary space and eagerly seek out revelation. Cameos allow audiences to participate actively in the construction of the story on-screen as they identify cameos by weaving their own extratextual knowledge of the celebrity into the diegesis, knowledge derived from other confessions made by celebrities across the media landscape. Cameos expose the audience to documentary space but rely on the audience to fill that space, offering up a potentially private cinephilic moment that is nevertheless built for a mass audience. As it has evolved over the last century, the Hollywood cameo has reflected changing perceptions of celebrity as fans have sought to become more and more intimate with the stars who are the object of their interest. Cameos, like celebrities, depend on visibility for their existence, and some cameos are more visible than others. Ultimately, the cameo positions audiences not only as consumers of celebrity and mass culture, but also offers them the opportunity to participate in the making of meaning by recognizing and reflecting on who is celebrated and why.

What Is a Cameo?

Critics and scholars refer to many different types of roles as cameo appearances, often using other labels like *guest appearance, guest star,* or *bit part* interchangeably.[14] These cameo roles include celebrities playing an ordinary person, the celebrity as another celebrity, the celebrity as him- or herself, and the nonactors and noncelebrities who nevertheless appear in cameos as celebrated figures in the real world. Ultimately, recognition and brevity are the clearest criteria for identifying what is and is not a cameo. Frank Sinatra in *Around the World in 80 Days* (1956), playing the piano in the background of a saloon and finally revealed in a silent close-up is appearing, as Dyer notes, in a cameo; Frank Sinatra playing organizational whirlwind and criminal mastermind Danny Ocean in *Ocean's 11* is just acting (fig. 3). Cameos occur when audiences recognize and celebrate the performer despite their brief appearance on-screen, whether that performer is a world-famous crooner or a writer escaped from behind his typewriter. While celebrity once stood for achievement, the cinema age and its valuation of the visual has meant that a celebrity's ability to be recognized is an achievement in itself. The cameo is an important symptom of this changing visual celebrity culture, where the mere circulation of one's image is worthy of note.

Most cameos are celebrity cameos. When celebrities appear in small roles as other people, they are subverting the movie star hierarchy. Reacting against the dominant logic whereby major roles are reserved for stars, and those who play the smallest roles are unknown, celebrity cameos provide an element of surprise.[15] They create an incongruity between what the savvy audience, well-versed in the celebrity- and image-manufacturing process, expects from the conventions of casting.[16] By appearing in a small role, the star flouts expectations. *The Film Encyclopedia*'s disparaging entry on the cameo as "publicity gimmick"[17] suggests that the disparity in star status and

Figure 3. Frank Sinatra as a saloon piano player in *Around the World in 80 Days* (1956).

role length in the cameo largely results from the astronomical rate per minute that stars command. If studios are paying for the time of the star in promoting the film as much as the minutes of on-screen performance, cameos become an economical way of attaching star endorsements to films, and thus "'guarantee' audience purchase of tickets to the celebrity's vehicle."[18] The cameo is no new gimmick; marketing for films such as *A Man's Man* (1929), where repurposed newsreel footage of Greta Garbo and John Gilbert attending a premiere allowed the stars to be credited in the film to much fanfare,[19] indicates that studios have long traded on star aura. More recently, Brad Pitt's well-publicized cameo as an exceedingly moral itinerant laborer in *12 Years a Slave* (2013), a film which he coproduced, certainly helped to draw multiplex audiences to a "less multiplex-friendly film."[20] Perhaps cameo roles permit celebrities to trade long hours of labor on set for a comparatively less taxing but equally valuable talk show sound bite publicizing the brief appearance, but small roles have value in and of themselves. Often minor characters are allowed to have alienating qualities that major characters who must carry the affection of the audience for the duration of the film cannot risk. Such small roles are sometimes publicized as exercises in humility and commitment to acting. Indeed, while Pitt's *12 Years* cameo reinforces his humanitarian brand, many cameo roles allow celebrities to play counter to type, like Tom Cruise in *Tropic Thunder*. Although celebrities are not playing themselves, these roles nonetheless are couched in the terms of their stardom.

Another common cameo type is the celebrity stand-in. Graeme Turner points out that celebrities are essentially interchangeable commodities created by entertainment industries and recognized for their visibility rather than any achievements that are manufactured, consumed, and ultimately disposed of.[21] If audiences recognize celebrities as interchangeable but for the smallest details of biography, then it makes sense that one celebrity should represent another on-screen. Reality TV feeds this logic, bringing together season after season groups of different yet similar celebrities in camera-rigged compounds that show them interacting in the imagined wild of an *MTV Cribs* episode. Braudy tells of an encounter between Jacqueline Kennedy and Elizabeth Taylor in the 1970s, two celebrities who had never met before that occasion, and the air of disbelief with which this fact was reported in celebrity tabloids.[22] If cameos call on performances that tie together the diegetic and real world, then the celebrity is uniquely poised to play a famous personage. Celebrities as celebrities include pop star Gwen

Stefani as Jean Harlow in *The Aviator* (2004; fig. 4) or comedian David Cross as Allen Ginsberg in *I'm Not There* (2007). Celebrity is Turner's infinitely reproducible personified commodity, and therefore, naturally, any celebrity can replace any other.

Director Alfred Hitchcock's cameos in his films are often so brief as to be unnoticeable. Hitchcock's cameos are not speaking roles, but momentary glimpses: disembarking in *Strangers on a Train* (1951), scurrying down the hallway in *Marnie* (1964), or exiting the elevator in *Spellbound* (1944). These brief cameos appear almost as if Hitchcock does not want to be recognized but instead lost as a mere nobody among the extras (fig. 5). Of course, if that is the case, why appear in the first place; extras were in no short supply in Golden Age Hollywood. For Straw, "The film extra belongs both to the domain of mise-en-scène, of the filmic ornament and detail, and to the realm of performance, of the acting body,"[23] both set dressing and performer. Hitchcock's cameos link an extraordinary and ordinary persona, as he is celebrated enough to be recognized, yet outside of the regular constellation of film faces. By relegating himself to the background, Hitchcock joins the masses; as Regourd suggests, attention to the groups in crowd scenes is a populist action that reflects the image of the people back to the audience who it comprises.[24] The celebrity cameo thus becomes paradoxically truly ordinary. After all, the extra is the absolute noncelebrity. However, the appearance of Hitchcock, as emphasized by the *Spellbound* trailer that trumpets this otherwise hidden moment to the audience with a freeze frame and voice-over, makes the anonymous crowds

Figure 4. Gwen Stefani as Jean Harlow in *The Aviator*.

Figure 5. Alfred Hitchcock could be mistaken for an extra in this still from *Rebecca* (1940).

of the film noteworthy. The ordinary thus becomes worthy of note, and the people milling in the background become the subject of interest. The kind of minute attention that Hitchcock prided himself on is thus cultivated in the audience with the cameo as an "ironic wink to the viewer from the director-demiurge who banished the coincidental or accidental from his films."[25]

Set within the image-making industry, backstage comedies frequently feature celebrities playing themselves as extras, combining verisimilitude with the affective jolt of celebrity sighting. In the black comedy *This Is The End* (2013), which follows a group of comedians trying to reach heaven following the Rapture, the extras in the initial party scene are so thoroughly seeded with celebrities that when the heroes finally reach their ultimate destination and throw another party, the crowd of somewhat awkward-looking extras becomes the subject of unusual scrutiny. Placed under close attention, extras appear "forced, wooden and unreal."[26] Willemsen suggests that "what distinguishes an actor from an extra is a form of orientation . . . through anticipation and interaction within a broader whole whose final crystallized form is still hidden at the moment of shooting."[27] Unlike standard extras, celebrities as extras are oriented toward a broader performance: that of their own persona. While both are "indifferent to the directing,"[28] which is focused on the major roles, the celebrity performance suffers less because of his internal sense of direction. They can be neglected without succumbing to the boredom and surly lack of conviction of the extra who is meant to disappear rather than be discovered.

Sometimes the celebrity plays himself in a major or starring role. This is the case in *This Is the End*, where all five major roles are played by comedians as themselves. In *Jack and Jill* (2011), Al Pacino, playing himself, falls in love with Adam Sandler, who is playing a woman. These large roles partake in some of the confusion and tension of the cameo, as they combine both the register of reality—Al Pacino is a real person—and tenuously distinguishable flights of fiction—Al Pacino is not in love with Adam Sandler, nor is it likely he thinks Adam Sandler is actually a woman. However, unlike the bite-sized cameo roles that serve to suggest both the celebrity as real person and performer, larger star-as-self roles undermine the intimacy and contingency of the celebrity sighting even further. Unlike brief cameos, where the celebrity may not be identified by name, the work of fan recognition is already done for the audience by the clearly defined celebrity character of these larger roles. Played for the duration of a feature film, the fictional character-space (where Al Pacino and Adam Sandler as Jill are united in true love) supplants the real world character. To the dismay of fans who seek accidental hints of the real alongside the constructed celebrity persona, the major star-as-self role creates an alternative character that is populated purely with fictional details.

To the audience of today, Hitchcock's cameo refers to a readily recognizable image: the beaky nose, the large head, and the larger belly. His image, although already a publicly self-referential act, as evident in the *Spellbound* publicity, was made ubiquitous through the abstract silhouette that began the television series *Alfred Hitchcock Presents* in the 1950s and 1960s, transforming in the opening credits from sketch to shadow to the photographic image of the man himself introducing that evening's episode. Hitchcock built celebrity around his image, despite participating behind the scenes of film production as a director. In large part, his image is celebrated because of his cameos. Yet even Hitchcock's early appearances in the 1920s and 1930s are cameos, because he has the potential to be recognized. Although not yet a celebrity, he is celebrated within his own film as its creator. These cameos of celebrated figures who are otherwise not widely known have a cultish appeal. Because they restrict their possible audience to those who can celebrate them and why, they further divide an audience. The earliest filmgoers who appreciated Hitchcock's appearance as cameo would have been restricted to people working in the film industry, personal acquaintances, or perhaps eagle-eyed readers of film magazines. Such cameos for a restricted or minority audience of fans continue, creating distinction around those who take part in a community that can identify the images as belonging to a celebrated figure rather than a celebrity.

In the early days of cinema, movie stars were anonymous but known by their image. Celebrated figures may be known to many but their physical appearance recognized by few. Unlike celebrity cameos, these cameos often consist of faces that are not famous, although the names attached to them might be. Performing the star-making process, these cameos of celebrated figures, or celebratory cameos, reward the ability to validate an image with a name. An audience can perceive almost any performance as a cameo if the figure appearing in a cameo can be celebrated on some scale as they are elevated from the background of nobodies. For example, upon the release of *Lincoln*, local newspapers separately profiled local extras, like a college professor and an "Allentown native," for appearing in what they called cameo roles.[29] Sometimes, the celebrated person is not the actor but the character portrayed. Kate Masur, a scholar of American history, writes about the characterization of mulatto housekeeper Lydia Smith in *Lincoln* as a cameo.[30] For Masur as audience, the recognition of an extradiegetic performance is for a little-known historical figure rather than the little-known actor who plays her. While studios may cast stars in cameos to draw audiences to the box office, ultimately audiences decide who is worthy of their attention.

Like other cameos, celebratory cameos reveal the unseen labor behind the film, bringing to light faces other than those of the star. When artists of the sixteenth century first celebrated the importance of their roles as creator of an image of power, they turned to their own self-portraits, including themselves alongside saints, heroes, or their patrons, like Dürer in the *Altarpiece of the Rose Garden* or Velázquez in *Las Meninas*;[31] writers, illustrators, and directors perform the same self-referential attribution through cameos. Yet, while the creative minds of the sixteenth century were using their appearances to establish themselves as individual authors of their work, film cameos celebrate the multiple authors of a movie. Usually these celebratory cameos are extremely brief, even by cameo standards, and appear among the extras, like Hitchcock or baroquely costumed director Peter Jackson in his *Lord of the Rings* trilogy or comic book writer Stan Lee in the Marvel movie adaptations. The celebrated cameo has the advantage that they may appear as themselves while also being ordinary. To those who are not aware of the reasons for which the person is celebrated, they are merely another extra. Straddling this line, they have a less recognizable image and persona than the celebrity, and the line between fiction and reality, ordinary and extraordinary, somebody and nobody, is effectively blurred. In *Barfly* (1987), where Charles Bukowski, the film's screenwriter, appears at the local bar, is he appearing as the notoriously down-and-out author or is he merely playing a drunk? Because only some audience members will recognize him as Charles Bukowski, he can play both. However, like Hitchcock's increasingly publicized cameos, the recurrence and recognition of a celebrated cameo helps them make the transition to celebrity cameo. In *Fantastic Four: Rise of the Silver Surfer* (2007), the ninth Marvel film in which he appears, Lee insistently plays himself rather than a bystander, a point driven home when he is refused entry to a celebrity event despite insisting, "Don't you know who I am? I'm Stan Lee!" Because celebratory cameos are exclusively by nonactors, they frequently suffer from the wooden acting that Regourd laments in the extra. Thus, every small badly acted role can suggest either poor casting or a hidden meaning, allowing for a cultish appreciation of the "seams, gaps, and shiftings"[32] of the film that allow audiences to become more fully involved in the production of the film's meaning.

Examining the Cameo

Cameos have been a marked presence in film culture for as long as the movies have feted their stars, but there have been few critical examinations of the cameo's function in popular cinema. Existing scholarship on the cameo focuses primarily on roles in Hollywood-set movies where Hollywood plays itself. While not explicitly examining the cameo, much of this literature addresses the cameo in passing as a symptom of Hollywood-set films. Cinema scholars began to show an interest in films that take Hollywood as their setting and the industry as their milieu in the late 1970s, producing encyclopedic works like Alex Barris's *Hollywood According to Hollywood* in 1978 or

James Parish's *Hollywood on Hollywood* that same year, which included synoptic entries on everything from animated renditions to X-rated films.[33] Rudy Behlmer and Tony Thomas's *Hollywood's Hollywood: Movies about the Movies*[34] from 1975 is a broad examination of the overarching genre that groups films into themes from cowboy westerns to Baby Vamps, providing anecdotes about their production alongside lists of which industry professionals played themselves. Patrick Donald Anderson's *In Its Own Image: Hollywood's Cinematic Vision*, also from 1978, examines movies set in Hollywood as exploring the dichotomy of illusion and reality, tracing three cycles of self-reflection from the rough-and-tumble unskilled days of early Hollywood to the deep nostalgia that he sees exemplified by Hollywood in the 1970s.[35] Anderson identifies cameos as allowing studios to serve audiences who "enjoyed seeing their favorite stars as 'themselves'"[36] as well as to make use of actors who were under contract and "readily available to do the kind of brief walk-on parts these appearances entailed." Anderson asserts the cameos offered publicity and exposure for star and studio alike.[37] In *Movies about the Movies: Hollywood Reflected* from 1997, Christopher Ames characterizes the genre as both celebrating and critiquing the idealized Hollywood of the American Dream, where cameoists are little more than "living set decoration."[38] For Ames, cameos are part of the challenge of "what to reveal and conceal,"[39] not only revealing Hollywood movies themselves as movies but also exposing acting ability as an ability to pretend.[40] Anderson and Behlmer and Thomas trace the origins of the Hollywood-playing-itself genre back to the Vitagraph two-reeler *Making Motion Pictures: A Day in the Vitagraph Studio* from 1908, set in the same New York Vitagraph studios that a few years later would produce the first cameo of studio executives appearing as themselves.[41] More recently, Steven Cohan in *Hollywood by Hollywood* has explored how cameos in the backstudio picture authenticate Hollywood as a location, where real stars mingle with fictional characters.[42] Identified by scholars of the genre as both a celebration of their milieu and a practical use-what-you-got strategy, cameos in Hollywood-as-Hollywood movies are predicated on the recognition that the star system had already built for its celebrities.

More recent interest in the cameo has radiated from attention to the small part. Scholarship into the cameo has been primarily the ground of those interested in film acting as a reflection of a society, where extras stand in for the ordinary masses, and, according to Georges Didi-Huberman, relegate them to invisibility.[43] Conversely, Serge Regourd suggests that the extra in prewar French cinema was an appreciative reflection of the common man and thus the common filmgoer, a reflection that has increasingly gone out of style.[44] While Regourd's extras belong to the larger whole of French society, for Paul Willemsen the extra is disconnected even from the society of cast and crew, existing in his anonymity as a cipher for meaning without orientation toward the plot.[45] The cameo seems to reconcile these two visions of the extra, rarely oriented toward the plot yet never melting into the background, calling out for the audience's recognition as part of their everyday lives yet apart from their ordinariness. Unlike the extra, the cameo is never an "empty signifier."[46] The nobody that is the extra is transformed into a recognizable somebody. Will Straw has demonstrated how actors considered exemplary of social types were often recirculated as extras in Hollywood's Golden Age in B films where "every role was a familiar face."[47] While early film actors like Anna Q. Nilsson and Buster Keaton may have evaded the obscurity of Straw's perennial extra Bess Flowers, one can witness their increasingly small roles in the period that Straw documents, culminating most famously in their roles as the silent bridge partners to Gloria Swanson's fading silent star in *Sunset Boulevard*. However, even in the background, Nilsson and Keaton were never absorbed as extras. Because of their former fame and the sensational stories of their rise and fall, their roles are consistently credited in catalogs like those of Behlmer and Thomas or Barris due to the awestruck recognition accorded them by a dwindling number of older patrons and film buffs.[48]

While I have addressed the cameo as a moment of Sobchack's documentary space, it should also be considered in relation to cinephilia. As a mode of film appreciation, cinephilia is subversive and nonstandard because it is a refusal to devote one's attention to the resolution of the film's plot; it is, as Mary Anne Doane writes, "a love that is attached to the detail, the moment, the trace, the gesture."[49] Classical Hollywood movies march inexorably toward resolutions where wayward behavior is punished and characters are recuperated into the bosom of dominant ideology. The cameo diverts the viewer's attention from this impulse, encouraging viewers to engage in cinephilic reverie about autobiographical details about the cameoist, and, by extension, the audience's own autobiography.[50] That the sudden appearance of a star can act as a cue for personal memory suggests the audience's relationship to celebrity has an important place in the story of our contemporary lives.

As celebrity culture has become a central concern of modern society, the notion of celebrity has been an important subject for scholarship. Leo Braudy identifies in his history of celebrity a centuries-long shift in popular fascination from the seat of power to its image and image-makers, beginning with artist-patron relationships of the Renaissance, developing through the popular theater of the eighteenth century, and ultimately creating a nineteenth-century public invested in the idea that the appearance of power was as important as its reality. Achievement was made all the more compelling by its visual portrayal, and admiration transferred to those imitators who were only portraying success.[51] By this token, Braudy suggests that a nineteenth-century focus on outward appearances spread the fantasy that any ordinary person could take up the trappings of power. Braudy asserts that "fandom mediates the disparity between the aspirations fostered by the culture and the relatively small increments of personal status possible in mass society."[52] For Richard Dyer, stars fascinate audiences within a mass society because they enact the conflicted experience of individuals who must conform to the roles ordained by dominant ideology.[53] Over and over again in the movies, stars negotiate and resolve the disparity between their real selves and their on-screen roles. At the same time, these stars reflect an aspirational origin myth of the ordinary person bestowed with special talent.[54] This dream is one of the enduring myths of Hollywood stardom, taken up regularly if sometimes critically in the Hollywood-as-Hollywood genre.[55]

Whether this dichotomy of real self and on-screen role can ever really be resolved is another question that theorists of celebrity culture and stardom address. For deCordova, the accretion of roles and performances onto the actor's biography means that a star "cannot be viewed simply as a real individual."[56] Marxist theorists of stardom suggest that the star biography is mobilized as a commodity. King situates the star as a reflection of the process of commodity creation, where their personal attributes are openly commodified. While King asserts that workers usually deny their individuality in order to fit interchangeably within a system of work, stars "profit from the sale of their own personae."[57] Turner modifies this claim to suggest that the star in fact does locate himself within a system of roles, occupying a position somewhere between the repeatable standard and the unique individual.[58] In the age of what Barbara Klinger calls "replay culture,"[59] where media products are preserved and repeated on multiple platforms, actors are continually represented in their past roles, making it hard to separate

Arnold Schwarzenegger from *The Terminator* (1984) or Al Pacino from Michael Corleone in *The Godfather* (1972). Lusted has suggested that stars often enlist these past roles as a record of their labor, reinscribing the star as an ordinary worker among the working masses. Indeed, audiences are increasingly aware of and in awe of the labor that ostensibly, following Dyer's model, transforms an ordinary but talented person into the extraordinary star. Gamson counters that audiences are not charmed by celebrities as former everymen but embrace them as entertaining products of an industry.[60] For Gamson, cued by "the visibility of glamour production,"[61] fans find pleasure in unraveling the manufactured elements of celebrity identities in a quest not merely for their true identities but for the seams of their construction.[62]

For popular audiences to be interested in picking at seams only confirms that modes of viewing associated with cult film have become mainstream. Umberto Eco identifies the cult film as allowing the spectator to "break, dislocate, unhinge it so that one can remember only parts of it, irrespective of their original relationship with the whole."[63] By turning attention to celebrity, cameo roles allow just such a dislocation, as they offer up a juncture to the audience's lifeworld through documentary space. The cameo induces a cultish breakup of a film's content where background becomes foreground, and nondiegetic information overtakes the diegesis. For many authors, the exemplar of cult film is *The Rocky Horror Picture Show* (1975), which induced particular behaviors and rituals from the audience linked not only to scenes but also to specific lines and appearances on-screen.[64] Cult viewing is participative, as viewers participate in the breaking up of a film as a contained whole. According to Eco, Hollywood narratives increasingly take advantage of "a 'Casablanca universe' in which cult has become the normal way of enjoying movies"; the frequency of the cameo in new films is evidence for this shift. Barbara Klinger supports this assertion, while Thomas Elsaesser sees these new narratives as taking the form of "game logic,"[65] noting that filmmakers are purposely disrupting their films by "disorienting or misleading the spectator"[66] to create narrative puzzles that need to be solved. The cameo is one such narrative puzzle or game. While cult may privilege the contingent and the happenstance,[67] narrative logic can also purposely be broken. Writing about audience reception, Henry Jenkins confirms that "texts play central roles in shaping the terms of their reception, even if they do not totally control their meanings."[68] For Klinger as well, cult digression can allow a kind of audience-led "re-narrativizing,"[69] but nonetheless this "difference in viewing . . . is not necessarily alternative or oppositional."[70] Audiences are increasingly drawn toward interpreting and commenting on the images they receive, taking on roles as what Gamson calls "artifice detectives,"[71] or assembling details as evidence of a fan mastery that rivals that of its authors.[72] Studios have recognized and adapted to this need. Reality TV and puzzle films are two such concessions; the cameo, I suggest, is another.

Although the cameo has existed in film culture for over a century, there are many questions about cameo roles that have yet to be answered. Why do audiences react to and recognize so many different kinds of small roles as cameos, from almost hidden sightings of famous heartthrobs to movie debuts of local boys made good? The breadth of roles journalists and scholars assign the name of cameo suggests that the cameo role cannot be strictly defined, but exists as a constellation of interactions between duration and recognition, dependent on who is watching and when. Even audiences of the twenty-first century who are inundated with the details about the lives of movie stars and habituated to images of their personal friends on screens continue to find cameos surprising and engaging. Cameos reveal the links between our obsession with celebrity and our desire to participate in the powerful cultural industries within contemporary society and expose how we value, understand, and assert our part in the labor behind our popular culture.

A Century of Cameos

While the notion of the cameo has clearly developed its own complex constellation of meanings and associations in the last one hundred years, the idea of the cameo as an artwork that provides the minimum detail by which a person can be recognized as himself has been around for much longer. The cameo as a concept begins with the decorative art of antiquity as "a precious stone having two layers of different colours, in the upper of which a figure is carved in relief, while the lower serves as ground"[73] (fig. 6). The silhouette, conveying the barest outline of a likeness, became a popular decorative item in the nineteenth century, where it so thoroughly entered popular culture that it gave metaphorical meaning to all things brief and biographical, from theater performances, literary sketches, and, later, to the vignettes of the emerging film art. In film, like this ornamental miniature, cameos are usually small roles that convey the outline of a character, for minutes or even seconds, without fully involving them in the film's plot. For the first half of the twentieth century, the term *cameo* described brief performances that stood out for their quality; in Edmund Crispin's 1950 crime novel *Frequent Hearses*, set in a London studio, the cameo is a small role by a rising young actress, "something just a little more important than walking on."[74] By 1956, producer Mike Todd added the dimension of recognition associated with stardom by using it to advertise the small roles in which he had cast actors like Frank Sinatra and Marlene Dietrich. While Todd firmly united the cameo and the celebrity in the popular imagination, he gave name to a phenomenon that was already recognizably present in film culture.

Call it a *cameo role, true-life casting, guest appearance,* or a *celebrity flash*,[75] the cinematic history of the cameo role begins with the history of film stardom. Leo Braudy has traced the growth of the culture of celebrity by looking at how power has been represented in theater and painting. According to Braudy, modern celebrity, untethered from political or religious power, emerged when power and performance became inseparable, uniting the act of being made visible with power itself. The photographic image, as a semiotic index that provides evidence of the real world it represents, served to strengthen the link between representation and reality, making claims for the power of visibility while remaining rooted in a real world subject. Movie stars owe their fame to the photographic image, both as the medium by which they make their performances visible, but also because of the medium's complex claims to express power, performance, and reality. For Barthes, the specifically cinematic allure of the star is caused by the realization of the essential qualities of a type in the existential qualities of a real person.[76]

The story of film stardom begins with silent film star Florence Lawrence and her transformation from the anonymous girl in pictures produced by Biograph, the so-called Biograph Girl, to recognizable name, a metamorphosis credited to the publicity genius of her new employer Carl Laemmle, who in 1911 spread rumors of her death and then staged her miraculous reappearance.[77] Other studios followed suit, transforming their roster of picture players into stables of star personalities. Before the rise of photography, Braudy notes, portraits of famed people had been used not to convey unique features but to emulate the faces of other

Figure 6. Roman cameo, c. AD 40. gallica.bnf.fr / Bibliothèque nationale de France.

famous figures, creating a genealogy of greatness; portraying well-known men with the features of Lord Byron was one such established trope.[78] While advertisements and fan magazines had begun to describe favorite actresses by attributes such as The Girl with the Curls or studio affiliations such as the rotating Biograph Girl,[79] until cast lists appeared in the 1910s film stars were "anonymous celebrities."[80] Unlike writers or politicians who were known through deeds, film celebrities of the early silent era did not broadcast their biographies or even their names, but became known initially only by their images.

When studios recognized the allure of their newly minted film stars, suddenly it became as important to groom screen personalities when they were off-screen as when they were in front of the camera. Studio publicists honed the ideal screen star image, which developed from democratic royalty to a more mundane lifestyle in the 1930s, developing the myth of the ordinary star with the singular talent that has, according to Dyer, continued to be the most relevant metaphor to the making of celebrity, even as audiences recognize that the ordinary star is yet another carefully constructed presentation.[81] By the 1930s, fan magazines had begun to make fans savvy to the teams of studio publicists and employees that surrounded these stars, perfecting the projection of their glamorousness.[82] The desire to unmask the real person and uncover her/his secrets has driven much of the fascination with and demand for celebrities' increasingly intimate revelations. Publicity has struck back, with occasions of "predictable spontaneity"[83] through vetted performances, interview locations, and the rehearsed candid reveal of talk show appearances. Well versed in the tactics of modern publicity, audiences are "neither completely gullible nor completely postmodern, but somewhere in between,"[84] content to assess the appearances of their favorite celebrity for potential correlations with the tantalizing hidden self.

These voracious fans were fed on films like Vitagraph's *Making Motion Pictures: A Day in the Vitagraph Studios*, a 1908 two-reeler that documents the process of movie-making from writing the scenario to shooting with actors, then follows that document with the film recorded in the preceding shots.[85] However, scholars trace the first cameo back to the first fiction film that re-creates studios representing themselves, the 1912 Vitagraph two-reeler *A Vitagraph Romance* that briefly features Vitagraph studio executives and the Vitagraph Girl as themselves.[86] These "first" cameos help underscore the evolution of the growing film industry, demonstrating an attempt to fight against the hierarchies of visibility that place actors before the camera and producers behind it. In this case, those behind the scenes are made visible for the benefit of their audiences, both contemporary and present. The fact that scholars like Behlmer and Thomas writing sixty years after the fact can identify these images suggests that, it is obviously easier to identify long-standing executives than local and largely unskilled crewmembers. The stage for the cameo is set, therefore, with the inclusion of real-life personages in fictional environments.

The ability to parse reality and illusion weighs heavily on these Hollywood-set films, which Behlmer and Thomas assert exploded after the appearance of *A Vitagraph Romance*.[87] These films that exposed the filmmaking industry warned audiences not to be drawn in by the "confusion of reality and cinematic illusion of reality."[88] The "venerable tradition in which the humor derives from a hayseed's naiveté in his first encounter with the filmic medium"[89] has been revisited from the very beginnings of the medium, beginning with the apocryphal story of the frightened spectators in front of the filmic train and one-reelers like Porter's *Uncle Josh at the Moving Picture Show* (1902). Uncle Josh dances and cowers alongside the actors he sees on-screen, unable to distinguish what is happening in his immediate surroundings from what is occurring on the screen and by extension, many months and miles away. This quaint bumpkin, an uninitiated spectator, is reborn consistently on-screen alongside the cameo, offering to the audience the opportunity he has bungled: the ironic potential to recognize a cameo for what and who it is. In *A Vitagraph Romance*, the senator fears for his daughter's life and rushes to find her at the film studio. Chaplin makes the same mistake when he sees Mabel Normand in distress in *A Film Johnnie* (1914). Later films would follow this genre, as in the lost film *Hollywood* (1923), where the heroine seeking stardom in Hollywood fails to recognize star after star as she bumps into celebrities all over town. The same hayseed, in different clothing but with the same spirit, refuses credit to Red Skelton in *Ocean's 11*, denies Stan Lee admission to a Marvel-brand wedding in *Fantastic Four*, and steals Mike Tyson's tiger in *The Hangover* (2009). The cameo serves as evidence against this naivete, allowing the audience to assert that they, on the contrary, are no bumpkins. Audiences that recognize the cameo assert that they are not merely being taken for a ride through movieland, but are seizing on the cameo as a moment of documentary space where they can assert their own Bourdieuian cultural competences to distinguish themselves against the poor, unenlightened bumpkin.[90] Set against the bumpkin, recognition becomes an act of distinction for audiences within the otherwise common experience of mass entertainment.[91] While early cameos were often framed as spontaneous celebrity sightings, even from these early moments audiences practiced their recognition while asserting that they, unlike Uncle Josh, were fully aware of the mediating screen.

While early film cameos often featured glimpses of stars arriving at train stations or leaving the studio gates, emphasizing the spontaneity of the encounter, fans could enter the movie theater with a clear idea of what roster of stars might appear on-screen. Studio affiliations are at play in even the earliest cameos. According to James Naremore, Chaplin as the Tramp appears in a cameo role in 1916 Broncho Billy movie *His Regeneration*, and "in the same year [Broncho Billy] Anderson reciprocated by doing a walk-on as 'himself' in a Chaplin short," both while at the Essanay Studios.[92] During his earlier time at Keystone, he and Fatty Arbuckle had traded appearances much the same way.[93] Just as Vitagraph naturally called on its own executives and studio to portray the essence of the film industry in their own films, studios would begin to call on their increasing stables of stars to market their films, as actor contracts were not merely on a film-by-film or film-per-year basis, but required that actors be available and on set whenever the studios demanded. As Ames writes, "the use of self-referential star cameos to add verisimilitude to the representation of Hollywood . . . is especially prevalent in films from the studio days, where contract players could be trotted out en masse for self-promoting films such as *Hollywood Canteen*."[94] Paramount films showed a Hollywood populated with studio loyalists like Cecil B. DeMille, while MGM showed hopefuls swooning over contract stars like Marion Davies and John Gilbert in *Show People* (1928). The vision of what "candid cameos"[95] in Hollywood looked like depended on the studios that backed the movie.

The cameo continued in this vein with Michael Todd's 1956 film *Around the World in 80 Days*. If the cameo were meant purely to ensure the continued visibility of a studio's stars, Todd, an independent producer funded by his own fortune, would have had little to gain because his affiliation with the stars in his film was temporary. Yet, Todd, who had a reputation as an extravagant theater producer with an eye for the marketing gimmick, embraced the cameo head on, proposing a film that was almost entirely composed of cameos. According to his biographer Art Cohn, he brought the term *cameo* into popular usage, defining it as "a gem carved in celluloid by a star."[96] While differing from Crispin's usage only half a decade before to define any small role, Todd's film straddled both definitions of the cameo, casting many actors, stars or otherwise, in small vignettes that took place across the world, and then using the star power of a few like Frank Sinatra and Marlene Dietrich to vault the other respectable but hardly stellar actors into the same level of regard. The term *cameo*, although it may have begun as a small part, was thus elevated by Todd into a type of celebration in keeping with the roles of celebrities as themselves that studios had been using for decades to promote their films. Todd's knack for publicity combined with his supposed evaluation of the marketing potential of his own outrageous life story positioned him to transform the cameo from easy cross-promotion to marketing idea par excellence.[97] The term grew to encompass roles by actors, directors, and others.

Cameos quickly took on a new association with not only stardom, but intimacy as well. As film studios finally permitted their contractees to appear on the small screen to promote their films, cameos began to appear on television. The intimate space of television added a new dimension to the cameo, presenting not only a candid space but also juxtaposing multiple visual texts from movies to advertising and variety shows to create a complex vision of celebrity. Cameos showed down-to-earth celebrities who were not afraid of a little light self-mockery, while introducing stars to potential audiences through cross-media marketing. By publicly identifying the audience-drawing benefits of the cameo, Todd set the stage for viewers to become wary of its overuse as stars became visible at the expense of performance. The 1970s saw a dearth of cameos, as tastes in realism changed in both film and television, but by the 1990s, cameos reappeared for an audience well-versed in the strategies of celebrity-making. Self-reflexive cameos promised not intimate glimpses of celebrity, but a critique of image-making itself.

On-demand viewing and home video in all its digitally enabled permutations has transformed the cameo over the last thirty years, as minute details of scenes can be watched, and fans devoted to the pursuit of small moments of cinephilia have recognized and fetishized previously unappreciated stretches of celluloid. The visual encyclopedia of recognition has expanded, so that fans can recognize authors, illustrators, and other elements of the moviemaking machine. Sharing on the internet has likewise increased the visibility of these cameos, as fans use video-sharing and forums to demonstrate a deep pool of fan knowledge by discussing and identifying cameos. Cameos, small and large, are circulated as a testament to fans' mastery of pop culture.

As evidence of the explosion of the visual image as an important aspect of identity, the cameo exposes how audiences negotiate images and their relation to reality. Whether audiences and fans can encounter a celebrity's real self or not, they are nonetheless fascinated by how celebrities harness images to create identity. For audiences, cameos and the act of recognition allow the chance to participate in the expansion of a film's meaning outward into the real world by exposing a documentary space. As the nature and function of the cameo has changed over the last century, it has reflected an evolution in who is celebrated and recognized in popular culture, growing from favorite characters to celebrities and their manufactured personalities to stars of sports, politics, and reality TV shows. The cameo reflects the transformation of moviegoing and the visual culture of the cinema as it calls on specialist and repeat viewers to create a relationship to films that is both mass and intimate. The cameo allows and encourages a kind of audience participation across media landscapes, manufacturing the possibility for fan digression and control while ensuring continued and long-term publicity as celebrity images live on outside of the film. Yet, this participation is in service of the culture industries it celebrates, rewarding the labor of accumulating fan knowledge with an illusion of power that has little value outside of the consumption of mass media. The cameo and its reception demonstrate how people negotiate a mass culture that insists that celebrities are real people and that real people can be celebrities. Cameos promise to provide clues for mastering that transformation.

This book traces the history of the cameo as it emerged in twentieth-century cinema, beginning in chapter 1 with the cameo's precedents in visual culture and the portrait in particular. Like cameos, portraits depend on the powers of recognition of the viewer to acknowledge the subject depicted. Portraits have been used for centuries to express power, authority, and allegiance, and portraitists have long mixed reality and fiction, placing their subjects within tableaux that tell stories about mythology, religion, and science using visual clues to express layered meanings to a variety of audiences. Portraiture thus provides a precedent to the cameo's engagement with audiences through the promise of both realism and intimate access, whether defined as fifteenth-century allegory or nineteenth-century photographic document. In particular, the Victorian attitudes toward collecting, nostalgia, and the miniature created an environment where the mass-produced cameo object became a popular form in decorative art and jewelry. The miniature became a substantial and intimate mark of tribute, setting the stage for the brief filmic cameo. While early cameos such as that of the Vitagraph executives in the 1910s act as tributes that emphasize creators behind the camera, the emergence of actors as movie stars shortly after would ensure that they would be the primary subject of the cameo for decades to come.

Turning from audiences, chapter 2 explores the evolution of the cameo under the control of the studio system as a marketing technique that harnessed cinephilic viewing. Beginning with the emergence of star cameos as indicators of studio affiliation, I examine the cameo trades in Charlie Chaplin's work at Keystone and Essanay that publicized the sought-after star's affiliation with each studio. Production files and movie reviews for *Hollywood*, *Souls for Sale* (1923), and *Show People* reveal cameos that reflected the consolidation of stars under studio ownership while speaking to a fan culture established by fan and trade magazines that valued the ability to recognize stars and their stories. The emergence of fan magazines legitimized fan culture while encouraging detailed, cinephilic viewing that focused on extratextual knowledge. Fan appetites for behind-the-scenes visions of Hollywood accounted for the success of these cameo-laden, Hollywood-set films, and the many similar films that followed as autocratic studios used cameos to make their glamorous lineup of stars as visible as possible. As studios declined and their control of stars and their images relaxed, independent producers perceived the value of cameos as a marketing tool. *Around the World in 80 Days*, *Pepe* (1960), and *It's a Mad, Mad, Mad, Mad World* (1962) essentially took cameos as their subject. While studio ensemble cameos were largely interchangeable, reflecting the aura of stardom without referencing individuals, these latter-day cameos directly referred to past roles and current biography. Forgotten stars, revived on television through reruns of their older works, also made appearances in these cameo extravaganzas. Yet cameo spectaculars became the victims of their own success, as once-eager fans were jaded by the constant parade of stars, old and new, presented to pique their interest at the expense of the story world. As audiences became more knowledgeable about stars, their lives, and their personas, the filmic moments that could be counted on to conjure cinephilic responses evolved along with their reserve of knowledge.

Chapter 3 traces the development of the cameo in comedy, where cameos began to show not only glimpses of celebrities at their best but also views of celebrities at their worst. Alongside the studio ensemble cameo films, a parallel trend in the cameo of the 1940s and 1950s involved comedians and disruptive, self-reflexive references to Hollywood and its stars. Comedy duos such as Bob Hope and Bing Crosby and Dean Martin and Jerry Lewis invited extradiegetic appearances and cameo trades that poked fun at their acts, their personalities, and their home studios. Disruptive and comedic, these cameos broke down narrative space in a way that encouraged a viewing experience that kept one foot in the real world of Hollywood gossip even as viewers committed to the film's characters and plot. The casual, leisurely attitudes that Hope, Crosby, and their colleagues struck in their cameo trades would influence the function of the cameo and its reception by fans, transitioning the cameo's function away from providing polished views of celebrities and stars to revealing more unflattering glimpses of the famous. Unlike the stylized presentation of earlier cameos that reflected glamorously on studio networks, these casual cameos were touted as spontaneous, unorchestrated, and natural, representing networks of high-profile friends doing favors rather than studios trading star property. As casual cameos became common in the 1950s, hand in hand with the popularity of cameo spectaculars, audiences became more knowledgeable about star lifestyles apace, thanks to television and uncensored gossip magazines. Using the same tactics as independent producers churning out nostalgic cameos in the 1950s, many studio-affiliated networks turned to established if declining movie stars for starring roles, with more high-profile stars filling in small roles to entice viewers and give credibility to the new medium. At the same time, television experienced its own cameo boom. Yet as the New Hollywood welcomed a new type of realism in the late 1960s, audiences became less excited about these supposedly unmediated encounters with quipping celebrities. This chapter examines the poststudio trajectory of comedy duos and friendship groups from the first loosening of studio power in the 1940s to the mid-1960s, tracking their public image and behind-the-scenes compensation and working schedules to examine how co-marketing became an important part of comedy.

On television, comedic cameos take a slightly different form than in film. Chapter 4 examines the television guest spot. Cameos on television quickly became an important way for stars and studios to market both their films and stars from other media like music in trades that reflected an increasingly integrated mediascape. Thanks to television, cameos became the links that tied together different media rather than consolidating star images. When comedic film cameos reared their heads again in spoof comedies of the late 1970s and 1980s, cameos were rarely about affirming personal relationships.

Instead, they created absurdist and anarchic juxtapositions that placed stars in situations that were ridiculously outside of the bounds of their star image. Television's expansion into the multichannel format with its need for constant content, much of which is supplied as celebrity-driven infotainment, embroiled audiences more and more deeply into star images. Responding to the interests of the media-savvy viewer, cameos have come to reflect and critique star image-making rather than promise unmediated or natural views of unscripted celebrity. Yet as twenty-four-hour TV and the internet have transformed access to celebrity lives in a way that mirrors the changes of the 1950s, cameos have again ricocheted to present friendship groups that are inseparable from fame and multimedia networks. Rather than affirming those claims through casual cameos, these bad cameos seem to outdo celebrity gossip by disrupting celebrity image with the kind of boundary-pushing absurd situations seen in spoof comedies, while embracing a wider range of pop culture figures into their networks. This chapter explores a cross section of television cameos in sitcoms from the 1950s to the 2000s, examining a transition in the cameo's role from confirming to undermining star images as audience demands changed while still keeping stars and their multimedia networks visible.

In chapter 5, I examine auteur cameos and the cameo as a sign of authorship. While Christopher Ames suggests that in the studio era, writers were so embarrassed by their participation in the mass culture movie machine that they refrained from presenting themselves on camera, directors seem to have had no such qualms. Author, and auteur, is often synonymous with director, links that the cameo established. Like the producer cameos of pre-star-system Hollywood, director cameos created recognition and reputation for those behind the camera. The author cameo came into its own in the films of Alfred Hitchcock and the publicity surrounding them. Like comedian cameos, the director cameo owed its changing importance to the decline of the studio system in the 1940s. Director cameos reaffirm the fan's interest in the film not just as a stage for actors, but as a forum for the visibility of the director. Other directors followed in Hitchcock's authorial wake: Woody Allen, Martin Scorsese, Quentin Tarantino, and Peter Jackson took up the portmanteau of auteur, using cameos of not only their own but also of other prominent figures—philosophers, authors, and writers—to emphasize the extent of their control. Not only do they appear as the author looking back at the audience, but they also appear as the hand behind the scenes paying tribute to favored icons. Fans who can identify these references participate alongside the author in a process of detailed viewing. In this chapter I review production files and scripts as well as contemporary and retrospective press reviews to explore the importance of the author cameo in establishing and consolidating authorial power in Hollywood. I examine cameos as a participative moment, rewarding attentive viewers while establishing author images that are as important in the establishment of reputation as craft or originality.

Cameos have had a lasting influence on cinema because they lay bare the fundamental documentary power of the film image, where the onus is on the viewer to judge which characters and character traits belong to the real world and which belong to fantasy. Yet, as cameos have evolved over the last century to reflect different demands on audience powers of recognition, the type of recognition the cameo encourages has continued to change. Audiences tuned in to celebrity image-making have turned to internet forums and video-sharing platforms where they share, identify, and critique cameos as well as their function both within the diegesis and as part of larger narratives of friendship and affiliation within star culture. As what Jenkins, Green, and Ford call spreadable media, cameos are a transferrable currency of distinction for fans as they affirm visibility for both stars and nobodies.[98] Fans collude with the celebrity machine even as the cameos they clamor for appear to critique it. The ever-expanding network of media is reflected in the growing kinds of recognition celebrated in and reduced to cameos—take, for instance, the reel of President Trump cameos on YouTube. The popularity of this video exploded in the lead-up to the presidential election of 2016 as his political policies were weighed alongside and even viewed through the lens of his appearances in movies such as *Home Alone 2* and 1990s sitcoms. Cameos demonstrate who media industries represent as deserving of recognition, whether movie stars or business tycoons, and a study of their history illustrates the strategies that film and television has used to encourage and reward the attention of curious audiences to people they want to celebrate as stars.

1

WORTHY OF RECOGNITION

The Cameo as Portrait

A cameo in a film is essentially a portrait. When a fifteenth-century donor to a Florentine church sat for a portrait in the guise of a saint to be included alongside the Virgin Mary and Jesus in the church's decorative altarpieces, he was commissioning an artist to demonstrate his power and wealth dressed up as decoration and benevolence. When the executives of the Vitagraph Company, one of the most prolific film producers of the early twentieth century, posed in front of their own cameras in 1912 for a scene in *A Vitagraph Romance*, a two-reel tale of a runaway daughter made good in the movies, they were likewise making portraits that acknowledged them as both part of the entertainment and its source. While J. Stuart Blackton, Albert E. Smith, and William T. Rock were playing the anonymous characters of powerful movie executives in the short film, they were also simultaneously posing for a photographic portrait that would be used to identify them specifically by name in a trade magazine that their production company controlled. Seated in a dark wood-paneled room overstuffed with club chairs and settees, the variously bearded and bespectacled men recline and converse in a staid manner that acts as a counterpoint to the earlier frenetic face-pulling and excited flapping of the young ingenue and her husband, who, as the film's stars, are trying to secure their big break (fig. 7). The executives are the vision of respectability; in fact, their scene is so static and so solemnly dark that it stands out from the otherwise busy film narrative and film actors. And yet, conversely, we know effort was made to capture their performance: to light and prepare this office, to make up the faces of the executives so that their features are visible, to turn the camera, to cut the film. Like the patron sitting for his artist, the executives have carefully committed to their presence in the film in return for recognition.

Drawing from life, artists have long sought to make the subjects of their portraits instantly recognizable, whether they are kings, gods, philosophers, or friends. How someone is made recognizable has changed. Photography offers one way of accessing the familiar, cinema another. If, as Mathijs suggests, the brief role of the cameo presents a subject who is both instantly recognizable and publicly known, then the cameo acts as a portrait.[1] However, while kings and gods have a historical claim to being recognizable, with the advent of cinema, the list of people appearing for recognition in cameo roles expanded to include actors, writers, directors, producers, and even extras. Multifaceted like the celebrity image, the cameo presents brief snapshots of a range of private and public roles, where celebrities and celebrated figures can play themselves, others, and others like them while drawing on references from real and narrative worlds. Ultimately, these roles are tied not only to the fact that their players are publicly known and instantly recognizable, but also to the inability of celebrities to shake their real-world identity for the purpose of performance. Cameos are acted portraits, and as such they bear the imprint of the history of portraiture, not only in their form but

Figure 7. Vitagraph executives play themselves in *A Vitagraph Romance* (1912).

also in the name they carry, the cameo. Like portraits, cameo roles follow in a long line of celebrity representations that call on the visual fluency of the viewer to assert power, authority, and allegiance.

The legacy of the portrait defines the cameo. In fact, what makes the Vitagraph cameo unique, and perhaps what marks it definitively as a cameo role in the eyes of scholars like Anderson and Behlmer and Thomas, is that it exists not only as a cameo in a motion picture film but also as a photographic portrait that was circulated as part of publicity about the Vitagraph Company. This dual usage allows us to make several points about the cameo as a portrait. Undoubtedly, part of the reason why this frame translates to a still image is because the scene itself is staged like a portrait, with all three men stiffly facing the camera rather than acting as a mobile group. And because this scene is also a portrait used in print, we can infer that in the film, it is asking the viewer to do the same work toward recognition that a portrait commands. While ostensibly other real people may be playing their real-world roles in this studio-set film, like the cameraman and director who bob in and out of several scenes, the alternate usage of this cameo appearance as a portrait shows that the cameo is not merely a side effect of the collaborative nature of early film. After all, a film needs bodies for its drama in the same way that a church needs saints for its decoration. The question that is posed to the viewer by both kinds of portrait is, why these bodies? Enlisting the viewer to perform that act of recognition, the cameo as portrait makes itself visible for recognition and remembrance. The matching of the Vitagraph portrait in the film suggests that both versions were marked to serve the same purpose, ensuring by the fact of their visibility, the potential for the recognition of the Vitagraph executives not only in their lifetime but also in ours.

Portraits, and cameos, do not just ask to be recognized. They give their viewers work to do, involving them in the process of recognition in a way that gives them agency. And like portraits, cameos play games with recognition, disrupting expectations as they ask the viewer not only who is recognized but also why, linking faces to the source of their power, whether that is wealth and its attendant fame or fame and its attendant wealth. Cameos reinforce visibility, as viewers recognize the faces that stand out from the crowd. Cameos also reveal public personas apart from the characters portrayed in each role. Recognizing a cameo means recognizing a desire to be visible. Visibility once meant political power, as in the case of wealthy Florentines, yet in the twenty-first century, visibility is a means to the end that is celebrity, and the cameo is one tool in consolidating and reaffirming that power while likewise placing its validation in the hands of the viewer.

A History of the Portrait

As an image of a person who is to be recognized, the concept of the cameo has its origins in portraiture. A portrait is made to outlast the sitter; it transforms a momentary reflection into an enduring legacy. For Emmanuel Levinas, the face indicates an encounter with an individual, a not-I who resists possession.[2] The portrait does the same. Portraits attempt to reconcile the individual likeness of a person with a generic type to which they belong. Portraitists, suggests Shearer West, have the task of balancing the images they produce between the idiosyncratic likeness and the ideal.[3] The poses and trappings of the body belong to that ideal while the body itself belongs to an individual. In portraiture, says Richard Brilliant, "resemblance is the willed connection between the portrait image and the person or persons to whom it refers."[4] The viewer is thus important in confirming a portrait as having an "acceptable relationship"[5] between the real world and the representation. In fact, most viewers will never see the subject of their portrait, so the believability of the representational quality of the subject is as important as actual resemblance. However, the viewer's expectation of the image to adhere more or less strongly to likeness and ideal, and his ability to read the poses and objects of power, can influence the reading of the sitter's identity. A portrait is a depiction of a person, rather than an inanimate object or an animal,[6] and it expresses the authority of the subject as a person who is worthy of having his reflection preserved. However, how that authority is most powerfully conveyed is dependent on the context of the artist's visual language and the viewer's visual vocabulary.

It is not the depiction of a face alone that makes a painting a portrait. Unlike studies or landscapes, portraits indicate that their subjects are meant to be recognized. While West does not illuminate what about the portrait begs the viewer to recognize it, Brilliant suggests that the neutral expression defines the portrait. The portrait bears a generic expression in order to convey the essence of a person rather than what could be characterized as fleeting emotion.[7] This lends what Brilliant calls "a formal stiffness, a heightened degree of self-composure"[8] to the image that identifies it as a portrait, even when its resemblance is no longer identifiable. West uses a similar argument to suggest that the anonymous *Portrait of a Young Man* by Botticelli must be a portrait "because of its descriptive specificity and contemporary air,"[9] and Ann Jensen Adams likewise uses her "eye" to parse Dutch *portraits historiés* that depict real people in historical roles from mere history painting.[10] Drawing on Barthes's concept of the punctum, where the image adds the memories of the viewer to the extant image, Brilliant suggests that this timeless expression creates a punctum in all portraits. Like the cameo, the portrait has a formal aspect that demands recognition.

Portraits have long been associated with the power of the celebrity. While portraits of mythological or governing figures within typical scenes have existed since classical times, freestanding portraits of individuals have existed in European art since the fourteenth century.[11] In the late medieval period, important contemporary celebrities of note, such as royalty or wealthy noblemen, had appeared primarily within religious paintings that they had commissioned to decorate a church or other religious site. These images not only provided a visual record of the generosity and piety of the donor but also served as a documentary confirmation of political ties to the powerful Catholic church, and the attendant right to direct clerical appointments that accompanied such donations. Donor portraits pictured the donors in contemporary dress at the margins of the religious scene depicted, usually in miniature.[12] Donors also appeared as witnesses or bystanders to important religious events such as the Crucifixion or the martyrdom of saints.[13] Placed in the background, these portraits affirmed their importance by association with the foundational myths of Christianity while indicating by the disparate size of their portraits that their appearance was only secondary to those of the saints and martyrs. That the donors were only performing a supporting role, albeit one that buttressed the power of the Church, was expressed by the physical scale of the painting. Yet, although reduced, these roles were brought into relief by the composition of the painting, which connected patron and saint across the painting's surface through the meeting of gazes or the direction of hand gestures.[14] Additionally, Jill Burke suggests that Florentine donor portraits of this period create intertextual references to other donations likewise commemorated in altarpieces or other decorative art, making donors recognizable across oeuvres not only because of physical likeness but also by portraying them in the same religious roles.[15] Small yet expressive of power, donor portraits provide a precedent for attention to detail and context in cameos.

Hand in hand with the donor portrait is what Adams calls the participant portrait.[16] In this case, the painter himself appears within the work. Braudy notes the increased importance of the artist as creator of the public image in the Renaissance, to which this trend can be attributed. The appearance of Velázquez looking out from a canvas in the corner of the royal drawing room in *Las Meninas* from 1656 is perhaps the most famous example, alongside that of Jan van Eyck reflected in the mirror behind the married couple in the *Arnolfini Portrait* from 1434. Adams notes these portraits appeared most often in public works, often in *portraits historiés*, scenes that evolved from the donor portraits to seamlessly incorporate biblical and contemporary persons to commemorate real events such as christenings.[17] Ultimately, Adams suggests that the artist included himself as a type of testimony "to increase its veracity as an historical event witnessed by the artist."[18] Looking out at the audience, the author offers himself up for recognition. In artworks for a public audience who are not necessarily acquainted with the subject, the appearance of the creator gives the audience a link between the depicted image and its depiction. Rather than give the credit for the powerful image to the subject alone, the artist reminds the audience of his presence as author in the transaction. For studio executives hoping to present themselves, the participant portrait was an important precedent.

Whether an audience perceived a resemblance as good was also dependent on the conventions of the period, and on an audience literate in those conventions, whether they were the characters of biblical stories or the language of flowers. Until the fourteenth century, identity was not linked inextricably to distinctive facial features but could be visually represented by symbolic means such as heraldry.[19] Drawing on Aristotelian teachings that a person's moral failings are visited as imperfections on the body, Renaissance portraits of those in power whose continued influence depended on political strength rarely displayed anything less than perfection.[20] Portraits needed to convey a recognizable image of that person in order to establish the links between the trappings of power and their bearer: the power to commission an image and to circulate that image. What it meant to be recognizable depended entirely on the context of the period in which the portrait was commissioned, and physical features could be deemed secondary to conveying the ideal qualities for which a person was known. For example, paintings of Elizabeth I relied on poses, settings, and the repetition of elaborate objects that were appropriate for her type to convey her identity yet present a face that is flat and empty in its vagueness.[21] In the twentieth century, Picasso's well-known portrait of Gertrude Stein was based on the stoic stone faces of Iberian statues rather than her own features.[22] Yet, lifelikeness was also valued as a sign of painters' skill, and the perfection of mirrors during the Enlightenment revolutionized relationships to visual representation, allowing portraitists to not only paint themselves but also encouraging experiments with perspective and vision. As a new standard of verisimilitude, the mirror as metaphor and tool encouraged portraiture to develop away from creating idealized images toward reflecting eccentricities and individual quirks, a movement that was in full storm by the seventeenth century.[23] In the nineteenth century, an accurate resemblance entailed not only reliable likenesses but also quotidian settings like drawing rooms, positioning the informal portrait as best expressing a sitter's identity.[24] While informality was the standard by which likeness was determined, as a convention it too formally controlled the expression of sitters' identities.

While the portrait may have been used to establish the authority of individual sitters, portraits could be repurposed and assembled to create new meanings for subsequent viewers. Beginning in the fifteenth century, collectors began to amass single portraits into pantheons of celebrity.[25] Sets of important geniuses, political figures, and beautiful women were sought after by collectors who even reassigned anonymous portraits to known personages in order to complete their collections. The work of owning, organizing, and professing recognition of these images of great personages shows these collectors engaging with a kind of early modern fan culture, creating new meaning by sharing the celebrity image in new contexts. The Renaissance's new emphasis on the alignment of the great personality and the image maker emphasized that the power to make a figure important was also in the eyes of the beholder. The links between resemblance and recognition were playfully expressed in the Renaissance novelty for paintings that represented two things at once, such as the portraits by Arcimboldo where faces were assembled out of inanimate objects.[26] Late medieval paintings were often inscribed with words and devices that could be deciphered only by intimates and "served as a test of iconographic knowledge, allowing members of a court to gauge each other's degree of access to their lord's identity."[27] Painters like Holbein and van Eyck conveyed secret meanings with astrological and alchemical symbols as well as hidden texts.[28] Other recognition games, such as guess-who-style games assembled from drawings of important contemporaries, often after extant portraits, show how official images were repurposed for the pleasure of viewers.[29]

Many of these uses were made possible by the reproduction of portraits. Portraitists kept copies of their commissions to reproduce them for other parties, where they became part of the workshop's stock.[30] Members of the courts had portraits of rulers copied on furniture and personal objects such as fans and game boards, juxtaposing the image of authority with commonplace and even trivial objects. While portraits were usually resurrected because of the status of the sitter, sometimes they were reproduced because they had become anonymous, separated from their contexts altogether. A number of rulers appear in the background of large group paintings of the Renaissance, featured because their old-fashioned images could be easily copied from the stock of old workshop drawings.[31] Although this repurposing of portraits is specific to the Renaissance, it demonstrates that, dating from the emergence of the stand-alone portrait, viewers incorporated images of authority into their own visual landscapes; the images occupied personal and playful spaces that belied the portrait's authority. Important faces, worthy of note, appeared not only in authorized images but were also reproduced in unexpected places and ways that undermined the formal roles these sitters were meant to occupy and suggested a temporal ebb and flow to their authority.

Cameo as Jewelry

A cameo has historically meant a distinct kind of portrait. Dating back to antiquity, the cameo as an art object refers to miniature silhouettes carved in relief into two-toned stone with limited detail, often worn as jewelry.[32] Likenesses limited by the material in which they were carved to an "elegant simplification,"[33] cameos portrayed celebrities and celebrated scenes—classical gods and heroes, exotic rulers, and contemporary monarchs. The cameo is therefore defined by its limitations as a portrait—small, simple, yet nevertheless minutely worked to represent a recognizable figure, even if only on close inspection. At the same time, the miniature calls attention to itself as an object, because, as Susan Stewart suggests, it requires the viewer to consider its context—the context in which it is a miniature thing, and the real world context from which it is miniaturized.[34] It distills the portrait to the minimal elements needed for recognition. What the cameo as an art object does with form, a cinematic cameo does with duration, representing the public person in a brief flash.

Cameos have long been collected, commissioned, and worn by the powerful elite, as both jewelry and devotional objects. Ancient cameos were sought after as historical objects in the Renaissance, and the form saw a swell in popularity beginning in the nineteenth century as cameos were appropriated to indicate new sources of power as well as aspirations to its trappings.[35] In the early nineteenth century, Napoleon and his court instituted a vogue for the cameo and the wearing of cameo jewelry, featuring multiple cameos of classical and Napoleonic subjects worn as a set, presenting many images of power in a way that made them interchangeable rather than exceptional.[36] As a miniature, the cameo conveys power as it puts its real-world referent within the grasp of the owner; as a less complex and manageable form of the original, the cameo presents "a diminutive and thereby manipulatable version of experience, a version which is domesticated."[37] This assembly of many small cameos had historical precedents in an "age-old practice of incorporating cameos into objects of greater size and complexity."[38] That these cameos were worn on the body indicates how closely identified the wearer was with the small portrait that helped to complete his/her self-presentation. Displayed together, these cameos provided a multiplicity of references to antique and modern ideals and exemplars of power that surround and include the wearer, as one visage among the idealized many (fig. 8). Owing to their size, these collections of cameos were inscrutable to all but the most intimate viewer, requiring a familiarity with the person who was wearing them in order to recognize and assess their subjects. These cameo sets thus enticed a viewer to a closer, intimate encounter with the wearer, and one that associated these miniature images, and their idealized images, with the wearer herself.

Cameos followed in the sentimental Victorian trend of wearing "jewellery of remembrance,"[39] of which the jewel called the miniature was another example. Miniatures, which unlike the cameo were painted rather than carved portraits, were likewise worn on the body as a brooch or a bracelet, often in mourning.[40] Cameos and miniatures sometimes were fashioned with lockets to hold locks of hair to aid this remembrance.[41] The strict mourning that Queen Victoria followed for her husband Prince Albert ennobled the passion for remembrance in the Victorian age, but fashion

Figure 8. Cameo brooch featuring the likeness of a family member of the original owner. Walters Art Museum, Baltimore, Gift of Mrs. Frederick B. Adams, 1972.

outgrew this obsession as the queen and population aged. Indeed, it seems as if the fashions of that time were themselves associated with death and the macabre. By 1885, cameos, which had been popular since the 1830s, were no longer among the most common pieces of jewelry.[42] Flower quotes a fashion editorial of the 1880s that called out the dead and abandoned state of the cameo, stating that some wearers had revived "neglected cameos exhumed from jewel-cases" as clasps for gowns.[43] Even later in 1910, the *Daily Star* in

Brooklyn reports that "cameos, those attractive specimens of carved jewelry, are being brought to light by women fortunate enough to possess grandmothers." Cameos were not only jewels but were also linked to the bodies of subjects they represented, either through indexical references such as hair or iconically through representation of their portraits. The concept of the cameo retained these meanings of remembrance, preserving in its filmic guise both the iconic and indexical relationships of the image to the original. By the twentieth century, there was something nostalgic about the cameo as well, imbued not only with its own memorializing impulse, but also with a sentimentality surrounding the impulse itself.

Photography and Portraits

Like the mirror in the Renaissance, photography in the nineteenth century set a new precedent for resemblance and verisimilitude, feeding a Victorian mania for realism and truthfulness that reflected a desire to see objects as they truly were.[44] Photographs, introduced in 1839, were seen as authorless works, produced by the sun, the sitter, and the photographer, where the photograph was examined for its subject rather than appreciated as a medium in itself, a habit that, according to Barthes, continues to govern our relationship to photographs.[45] Whereas painted portraits may ask the viewer to appreciate the skill of the artist, photographs, according to Barthes, command the viewer to observe the subject.[46] Photographs allowed viewers to study, compare, and contrast their subjects at leisure and intensely. However, despite its referential immediacy the photograph is, as West points out, no less composed than the painted portrait.[47] Yet, Barthes counters, the photograph can never be as entirely composed as the painted portrait, as some of its details escape the control of the photographer.[48] For the viewers of the late nineteenth century, this intervening influence was invisible or at least negligible, and contrary to the nature of photography. In the 1860s, the use of photographs in dramatic tableaux composed by Pre-Raphaelite photographers caused an outcry as an abuse of the medium.[49] Yet, while Barthes concedes that a photograph is only a partial representation of its subject and therefore can never be an entirely true representation because it records only one "anecdote" of a person's life,[50] Victorian images were seen to represent a standard that captured essential elements of a person's physiognomy and thus their character.[51] This perceived transparency encouraged institutional use of portrait photographs alongside exact measurements of body parts to document norms and aberrations in features, eventually resulting in the standard identification portrait photograph that was used in combination with vital statistics to establish legal identity by the end of the nineteenth century.[52] This transparency is the ultimate realization of physiologies that accepted outward appearances as the true sign of one's character. If one had seen a person, one could judge and know him, and no medium, not even the presence of the person himself, allowed for better contemplation of his features than the fixed stillness of the photographic portrait. Compared with the properties of the photograph as Barthes identified it, the miniature shares much of the same potential for nostalgia and memory, all under the control of the viewer. The photograph is a kind of miniature in itself, freezing and transforming people into objects that require a viewer's context to make them come alive.

Photography put the portrait in the hands of the middle and lower classes, allowing members of these groups access to their own likenesses as well as to the mass-produced likenesses of celebrated political and cultural figures. Following closely on the announcement of the invention of photography in 1839, the initially expensive and tedious process saw innovations that reduced costs by decreasing exposure times and replacing the tintype with glass plates.[53] While photographic studios were open to the middle classes, the camera's increasing portability allowed itinerant and single-operator photographers to spread the photographic portrait among the lower classes. Photographs were used to memorialize likenesses of people of all walks of life. Duplication was another important milestone for the spread of portrait images; until the 1850s, the tintype was a "personal and private keepsake,"[54] kept behind glass in velvet and leather cases. When the introduction of glass plates into the process made photographs reproducible, wealthy sitters ordered copies in the hundreds, distributing them to friends for albums.[55] Photographic studio portraits of actresses and actors were printed with magazines and sold individually and made available to a wide array of classes, drawing on earlier traditions that had reproduced engraved portraits for mass consumption.[56] Photographers retained the proceeds of these photographs, while actors were seen to benefit from their increased visibility to potential paying audiences.[57] Initially accompanied by biographies, these inexpensive photographs were traded and collected much as the portraits of rulers had been reproduced and flaunted by admiring members of court in the preceding centuries.⁵⁸ As photography progressed to depict mobile subjects and momentary poses, informal representations of people in all classes were taken to new heights, mirroring developments in painting toward informal settings and intimacy.

Photography was born amid the cameo fad, providing a much less expensive form of portraiture that worked against the simplification of the cameo form by offering replicas of the living rather than idealized likenesses. In fact, the cameo's heyday mirrors that of the photographic cartes de visite, which permitted portraits of the self, acquaintances, and the famous to mingle in cherished albums.⁵⁹ As if reflecting this new access to the personal image, the vogue for cameos among wealthy women grew to include not only classical and royal subjects but also self-likenesses. With the advent of early plastics such as celluloid in the 1870s, cameos were mass produced for middle-class audiences, featuring idealized images of an anonymous middle-class woman.⁶⁰ Where women had worn cameos to associate themselves with classical precedents, these cameos represented a different kind of ideal and aspiration to generic respectability. Photographic portraits that mimicked the small, simplified portrait of the cameo would come to bear that name of *cameo*.⁶¹ The cameo as an art object thus documents the transformation of celebrity in the years that preceded the film star, as these new technologies of image making and duplication allowed members of the middle class to be celebrated as both collectors and subjects of the art.

With the popularity of the cameo object came the popularity of the cameo as concept, extending beyond its obvious parallels in portrait photography to other media. The term was adapted in the 1850s to mean a brief literary sketch or biography, such as those in *Cameos from English History* that would "give the spirit of real events" and allow its readers to "be struck with characters and scenes presented in some relief."⁶² While this book of cameos is not illustrated, similar biographies, as miniature as their glyphic counterparts, were circulated as an accompaniment for the popular photographic cartes de visite. While cameo art objects attested to the physical features of a person or personage, these short biographies conveyed in brief the stories behind the images. The cameo-biography supplemented the cameo-object, providing the information that the memorializing image only alluded to and assembling a whole that referred one to the other. Cameos were established as fragments to be supplemented with text, images, or (in the case of remembrance jewelry) bodily remains, much in the way that cinematic cameos would call on fans to supplement their brief appearance with information gleaned from their films and fan magazines. A cameo offered a striking proof of identity, if not a complete one.

The photographic portrait set the precedent for the viewer's recognition of the cinematic cameo. The more accessible photographic portrait meant that bourgeois and working-class people had a model for seeing representations of themselves, an honor originally reserved for aristocracy. Ordinary faces caught by the camera became a commonplace that could thus be translated to the cinema screen, although unlike the limited access provided to the nobleman's personal portrait, the images of film stars would be available for mass viewing. Intimacy, distance, ordinariness, and extraordinariness are all combined in this understanding of the portrait. Photography brought many of the conventions of court painting to a popular audience. Staged photographs that adopted the classical and mythical references of studio painting ensured that audiences also had a complex sense of how to look at portraits: as direct representations of self, as allegories of power, as people who were simultaneously one thing and another. While the secret language and the hidden meanings within Renaissance portraits made for the wealthy middle classes were far removed from the audiences of twentieth-century nickelodeons, they provided a model of special access and intellectualization of images that cinema would draw on as some of its fans matured into cinephiles. Providing visibility that was fleeting rather than fixed, the cinema presented images like photographic portraits that were an invitation to look, to identify, and to recognize the subjects for their persona outside the studio. If the major difference between a portrait on- and off-screen was their brevity, the cameo provided the perfect metaphor for the representations cinema offered.

Stardom and Visibility

Who is celebrated and why has changed wildly over the millennia. From the Florentine donor to the successful movie star, there is a long chain of reevaluations of power.[63] Leo Braudy discusses the history of the famous as beginning with rulers like Alexander, Caesar, and Charlemagne, whose feats were synonymous with the states they helped found. With the rise of Christian spirituality in the West, the selflessness of saints, martyrs, and desert-bound hermits became the models for a new intellectual power, inspiring meditative writers like Saint Augustine to praise the famous in texts that are foundational to Christian thought.[64] Gradually, the heroism of the great personality and the model of the reflective hermit fused in the Renaissance into admiration for the artist and intellectual who helped record and broadcast the might of their rulers, compounding and creating new myths of empire through iconic artist-patron relationships such as Holbein and Henry VIII or Velázquez and Phillip IV.[65] Braudy emphasizes the role that theater and acting held in the transfer of importance from the seat of power to its image, as performances in British theater especially demonstrated that power was constituted purely by its trappings and postures.[66] The eighteenth-century audience that emerged from the theaters took these lessons to heart, creating a society that "instead of passively responding to its idols, takes an active role in defining them."[67] Attention to the attitudes and trappings of greatness grew alongside mass culture, coalescing in fandom that allowed ordinary people the small consolation of defining the successful, extraordinary few who best mimicked the powerful. Film, as the inheritor of the theater that first exposed greatness as one among many poses a person can adopt, has become a site where the actor is visible in many guises, as both familiar face and removed idol.

While it may have centuries-old precedents, celebrity culture as we know it today emerged with film stars in the 1910s, linking image, persona, and power in a new and powerful way. In the early twentieth century, film actors were transient, employed as day players by emerging film companies to work with their permanent cameramen. Actors played in single-reel films with simple narratives, and they were filmed in public celebrations, stage shows, and everyday life.[68] Audiences watched films that reflected what Miriam Hansen calls a "primitive diversity" of early cinematic viewing positions, troubling the relationship of the film image to the real world and generating pleasure through disjunction of fact and fiction.[69] Whereas early filmmaking was a collaborative partnership where joint responsibility was taken for camera operation, direction, story, and acting, in the first decade of the twentieth century hierarchies and specializations began to emerge that separated extra from star and director from actor.[70] As narratives became longer and more complex, actors were hired as stock players for the film companies to draw on, and so they appeared interchangeably in roles that ran the gamut from what we would now think as an extra to a featuring role.[71]

Theatrical stardom provided an important precedent for cinematic stars. For deCordova, stardom began in 1908 when famous stage stars began to reprise their signature theatrical roles on-screen.[72] While deCordova points out that many of these actors were not necessarily household names, they were presented in advertising to the moviegoing public as potentially recognizable.[73] Recognizing or attempting to recognize these foreign, largely French names, though not necessarily their faces, was set as a mark of Bourdieuian distinction in the ongoing campaign to make film a bourgeois art rather than a working-class entertainment.[74] Famous Players, established in 1911, capitalized specifically on this intellectualizing trend, advertising itself as the home of the industry's "best thought and genius."[75] DeCordova suggests that studios tried to extend the value of the name-brand actors they hired from the theater beyond the productions they were actually in by refusing to release the names of the actors in any one production so that audiences might anticipate their presence in any of the films on offer.[76] If a star could be in any film, all films would draw equally on the perceived talent of the star. In this way, audiences were being trained to recognize faces and to look for the famous among the merely on-screen before names were used to signal their presence.

While theatrical stars were lauded for their talent and performance, film stars had an unusually intimate relationship with the audience. Even before the close-up was introduced, film actors could be seen at a very close proximity on the magnified cinema screen, a proximity unimaginable in the theater.[77] This close proximity meant unprecedented confrontation of the audience with the actor's face and intimate familiarity with their features. These faces were then projected endlessly, playing across screens as their one- or two-reel exploits were presented in looped programs that audiences could see again and again and again for a single admission.[78] Although they might be looking for legitimate theater stars, audiences knew these nameless faces like their own. To achieve something like this familiarity, theater stars like Sarah Bernhardt and Geraldine Farrar had allowed their faces to be distributed in cartes de visites,[79] but moviegoing created that intimacy without the intermediary. Cinema multiplied the potential for visibility, not only by making the screen image larger than life but also by making it accessible simultaneously across town and across the state. Cinema created the potential for visibility for a film actor that far exceeded that of the theatrical actor.

Audiences struck by these faces gave them names based on studio affiliations or popular characters they had played, such as the Biograph Girl or

Vitagraph Betty, and studios soon followed suit by advertising films based on their inclusion of their trademark actress.[80] Theater and vaudeville acts that toured on certain circuits such as Keith's or Belasco theaters were similarly linked to those chains.[81] Producers did not release cast lists, keeping early film stars as "anonymous celebrities"[82] whose identities were solely tied to the film company they worked for. Any attractive face could take up the mantle of stardom simply by being named the company's new star. There were two faces known concurrently as the Biograph Girl, as film producers outbid each other for the favored but still-anonymous Florence Lawrence and Mary Pickford, and those actresses moved from studio to studio. Emphasizing the face as produced by the film company, rather than as belonging to a person, the Vitagraph Girl and the Kalem Girl were faces without biographies.[83] Soon film companies realized that audiences wanted to know more about the people behind the faces, faces with whom they were as intimately familiar as people a generation before had been with the faces of no one but their own family, altering recognition from the local and the personal to the mass and the public.[84] This explosion of mass visual culture was unprecedented. While studios tried to maintain complete control over their stars as a product rather than a person, attempting to promote a new hierarchy that ignored the precedent of theatrical stardom and made faces synonymous with a brand name rather than a personal one, the reality of competition eventually brought this attempt to failure.[85] When Carl Laemmle initiated a press tour that revealed the Biograph Girl as Florence Lawrence in order to make it known that she had moved to his own IMP group, soon to be Universal, in 1910,[86] stars had to be acknowledged not merely as characters in the film but as real-life persons as well. Their identities were no longer entirely linked to the studios they worked for and the characters they played. Lists of players began to regularly accompany plot summaries, eventually including images of the stars.[87] Unlike the Bernhardts and other French names first introduced as stars to film, these stars had simple names like Fatty, Mary, and Mabel.[88] IMP even used a cameo-portrait of Lawrence as their trademark, signaling the precedence of star visibility above all else.[89]

The visibility of film stars made them recognizable, and, as Nathalie Heinich writes, it is visibility in which celebrities trade.[90] For Heinich, in a visual culture, power and importance is judged by visibility. Visibility and recognizability are two sides of the same coin; being visible is not simply being seen but the accumulation of many instances of being seen.[91] It is the accumulation of visibility that makes a person recognizable. If I see my neighbor once, he is a stranger. But if I see him many times, he becomes familiar to me. That does not, however, make him a celebrity. The second element of Heinich's visibility as traded in by the celebrity is its inverse relationship to the seer.[92] A celebrity is a person visible to many people, fans or otherwise, yet to whom few of those people are visible. For Dyer, the star is ordinarily hardworking yet extraordinarily talented; this talent that sets them apart is precisely the talent for being visible.[93] The inequality of this relationship is resolved not simply by making fans visible to celebrities. In fact, Kerry Ferris suggests that many fans, when they experience an actual chance celebrity encounter, may attempt to minimize the extent of the interaction because of its unusual and uncomfortable reversal of visibility and distance.[94] Rather than make themselves visible to the object of their interest, fans make the object of their interest more visible, uncovering as many details of the image and its composition as possible.[95] Movie stars became famous simply because they were visible to more fans than any person had ever been before. Audiences affirm stars as they recognize them in multiple ways. The increased and long-term visibility of the actor in multiple roles as a public persona, set of characters, and professional performer is what, for deCordova, defines stardom's emergence.

The public reaction to Lawrence's dramatic death and rebirth in 1911 testified to her visibility in the eyes of audiences, and is credited as the catalyst for studio support of the transformation of film actors from cast members to marketable personalities.[96] The role of the star grew to include performing outside of the film, in events in support of the film and interviews for the new film fan magazines.[97] These fan magazines, directed entirely at fans rather than exhibitors, were themselves overwhelmingly created and edited by studio and distribution groups, and they reflected their affiliations by excluding discussion of films produced by rival groups.[98] *Motion Picture Story Magazine*, launched in 1911 by one of the owners of Vitagraph, was funded by members of the Motion Picture Patents Company, and *Photoplay* was established in 1910 to promote independent productions.[99] Both magazines, as their titles suggest, mostly provided short stories that supplemented the scenes on-screen, providing detail both seen and unseen. These magazines grew from detailed retellings of the photoplays currently in theaters to include reviews and articles about celebrities, all within the boundaries of studio affiliation.[100] Yet, Abel insists that the inclusion of full-page photographs of the studios' "picture plays" in *Motion Picture Story* from its inception incited an important shift in the invention of the movie star in 1911.[101] Rather than promoting the stories their films told, studios began to market the stars their films featured.[102] Writing to these magazines, fans were not afraid to ask for the particulars of the faces they were so familiar with from the screen. Writers answered some but not all questions about film stars' private lives, keeping details like marital status from the public.[103] Studios became more and more involved in promoting the business of star visibility; in 1914 Theda Bara toured the United States before she had released "a film of note."[104] Studios were profitably selling picture personalities as much as pictures. However, the reservations that studios had held in making their stars more important than the productions they were in were realized. Unlike the generic and interchangeable nicknames of a few years earlier, stars now could move from offer to offer and studio to studio while ensuring that their public persona moved with them.

Early stars were kept largely nondescript, embracing the ordinary within the extraordinary that Dyer suggest draws the adulation of fans. As Abel notes, through the late 1910s they were portrayed as hardworking and independent.[105] Florence Turner, the Vitagraph Girl, proudly admitted she was a regular jack-of-all-trades behind the scenes.[106] Even Bara, the famous vamp, distanced herself in fan magazines from the vamp character she portrayed.[107] While Studlar suggests that Bara represents a shift away from a publicity tactic that equated actors directly with their characters, as if Mary Pickford was Little Mary or Kathlyn Williams was a real-life heroine, audiences were well versed in the premise of acting. The blandishment of *Vitagraph Life Portrayals* in 1910 that suggests of their actors, "they act like real people doing what real people do" nevertheless insists on these people as actors, undertaking labor.[108] Stills from the action accompanied plot summaries in this trade paper before the regular appearances of tiny cameo portraits of those same actors were introduced in 1911 to distinguish actor and character.[109] These cameos appear around the same time that Florence Turner was gaining notoriety as the Vitagraph Girl. If, as Braudy suggests, fans of mass culture assert their agency in bestowing notoriety on someone otherwise just like them, these children of immigrants who contributed to the many practical facets of studio labor—sewing costumes, preparing meals, and building sets—were made entirely relatable. However, the collaborative atmosphere these articles describe in 1910 and 1911 was made obsolete by the very articles that describe it. The power of visibility established a hierarchy that placed the pictured above the producer. Although exhibitor magazines like *Vitagraph Life Portrayals* included articles by the company's executives and sometime-directors, fan magazines were filled with the particulars of actors and actresses rather than the behind-the-camera producers of the film. Who the public at large valued was defined by visibility. As these personas were built, audiences expected certain people to be increasingly visible, and the studios obliged them.

Cameos on Stage and On Screen

How then did the term *cameo* come to be used in the cinema? Beginning in the 1910s, small roles were described as cameos as authors drew on all the connotations of the art-object namesake: the play between background and foreground, the purity of the miniature image, and its true-to-lifeness. Most notably, the phrase "stand out like a cameo" appears occasionally in early newspaper reviews of vaudeville and cinema from the turn of the century to the 1920s to describe distinctive or especially noteworthy performances by individuals within larger acts that offered performers the chance to "cameo" themselves.[110] Small character roles were most often described in this way, like fortune-tellers, maids, and worried mothers.[111] The purity of the miniature was reflected in the term "cameo-like," which could mean the physical perfection of a beautiful "cameo face"[112] or a perfect figure like that of swimming star Annette Kellerman, or it could mean being perfectly true to life in a role that was "cameo like in its fidelity,"[113] or as in the case of Hitchcock's 1928 *Blackmail*, a "clear cameo" of working-class London. The term continued throughout the 1950s to indicate small roles in which players distinguished themselves.[114] From the cameo of antiquity, the idea of the cameo appearance borrows the ability to depict a person with a minimum of detail, as a simple image animated by the knowledge of its historical precedents as well as its association with a removed yet well-elaborated ideal. Distinctive, perfect, miniature, and yet also true to life, the cameo as it was discussed in the early twentieth century adopted a particularly photographic concept of the portrait.

Even while the concept of the movie star was still young, "cameo" was used to signal the presence of a remarkable performance that was at least one-half of the hallmark of stardom (fig. 9). Identifying actors by name in recognition for their performance, those performances cited as "cameos" in the 1910s and 1920s were marked to recognize and distinguish between the actor and the role. In these cases, we witness actors in small roles being offered up as potential stars by suggesting latent talent or strong effort, identifying the elements of hard work and natural ability that have defined the celebrity persona in the twentieth century.[115] Being recognized for a cameo hints at this potential to be outstanding. In a review of the 1910 play *The Wife Tamers*, the author makes special notice of the actor who "plays the role of the maid with a piquancy and a cleverness that make her work stand out like a cameo."[116] Remarked on as an actor playing a role, and playing it well, the acknowledgment by the reviewer of a "cameo" performance is a step toward building the public persona that was the hallmark of the star. Actors were being noted for reversing the expectations of who stands out in a film as reviewers expressed curiosity about the performer while commending a job well done. The term *cameo* recognized someone who stood out despite her small role, yet who made the viewer aware that there was a person behind the performance. As stars increased their monopoly on audience attention and recognition, stars would eventually become linked with the concept of the cameo. However, these celebrity cameos were so identified because the public persona of the star reflected on the performance rather than performance on the public persona.

Cameos as portraits are sites for memory and reflection, and the popularity of the cameo as a motif and metaphor in the earliest years of cinema means the term carries nostalgia related to the past. In the 1910s and 1920s, short films occasionally referred to themselves as cameos, as in Mutual's 1914 *Cameos of the Yellowstone* or Educational's Cameo Comedies from 1923.[117] The adoption of this phrase was in line with the new industry's attempts to borrow for itself the classical associations that were nevertheless familiar to a popular audience, a role that the mass-produced decoration with Greco-Roman roots, and its bourgeois cousin the popular biography, filled exactly. As serials fell out of fashion, *cameo* as a term continued to be associated with individually striking episodes within a larger narrative, sometimes to criticize the kind of disjointed breaks with narrative that Susan Stewart suggests is intrinsic to the miniature and that Umberto Eco locates as the site of cult.[118] While not exclusively devoted to short films, a number of movie palaces in cities from Pittsburgh to San Francisco dating from the

Figure 9. The cameo came to signify stand-out performances, like that of the Cameo Girl in this 1919 ad in *Variety*.

mid-1920s were named Kameo and Cameo, especially new Universal palaces.[119] However, this name was not given to new theaters after 1928, as the famous Broadway-based Moss's Cameo fell into decline and the Cameo in San Francisco was renamed, suggesting that the name *cameo* quickly became an old-fashioned term as short films and views became less and less a mainstay of popular cinema.[120] The idea of the cameo motif, like the forgotten jewels of a half century earlier, was a relic of early cinema.

Early Cameos: Set Apart by a Portrait

From the anonymous player to millionaire movie star, the second decade of the twentieth century witnessed an important change in celebrity culture. While actors like Mary Pickford or Colleen Moore became the most visible celebrities of their time, in the early twentieth century other players in the film industry were making bids for the type of visibility that has since been seen as the sole province of film actors. If the modern celebrity is built on the suggestion that stars are just like us, it was perhaps most true in the early days of cinema, when pioneers quickly established themselves as the aristocracy of the new and almost unimaginably profitable industry.[121] But it was not just for movie stars. Photography had created the myth of the authorless image, and the labor behind moviemaking was likewise perceived as invisible, suggesting that there was little art to the transformation from idea to film reel. Going Hollywood was not merely a pipe dream for beautiful people but a reverie that held in its thrall storytellers of all types, hardworking or otherwise. While performers were definitely made the most visible, the fan magazines that emerged in the mid-1910s also profiled directors and writers.[122] By the end of the decade fan magazines offered not only popularity polls for favorite stars but also contests promising contracts for surefire story ideas as well as beguiling faces.[123] Even today, the embellished biographies of these pioneers are appealingly melodramatic, like that of screenwriter Anita Loos, who apocryphally began her long and successful career in 1912 as a preteen (give or take a decade) sending story ideas to D. W. Griffith.[124] Although stars were definitely the most visible in the marketing of films, writers, directors, and producers were also made the subject of scrutiny.

However, outside the developing star paradigm, certain types of labor were more visible than others. Vitagraph founders J. Stuart Blackton and

Albert E. Smith had gotten their start in cinema as a camera-operator/director pair, and when Vitagraph developed its publicity machine, it acted in favor of making directors and producers visible alongside actors. Adopting the legacy of showmen like Barnum or Belasco, the producer was already recognized as an important figure who outlasted the popularity of that season's assembled acts.[125] Early trade publications suggested a more traditional ascription of visibility and recognition along these lines of power. Before the fan magazines, which were so instrumental in consolidating the star's visibility, the industry communiqués of the early 1910s were trade publications distributed to provide information to exhibitors and producers on upcoming releases, new equipment, company mergers, and international acquisitions.[126] From 1912, Vitagraph's exhibitor journal *Vitagraph Life Portrayals* gradually included press announcements and advertising copy about their regular players. This new format that followed the original and much more perfunctory synopses of the *Vitagraph Bulletin* punctuated its pages with anecdotal "Purely Personal Puffs" about the foibles of actors and other studio employees but also prefaced the publication with a full page of "Heart to Heart Talks" authored by Vitagraph's founder.[127] While exhibitors might be expected to be more interested in the advice of fellow businessmen rather than the gossip on actors, the changing format and cute subheadings suggest that the journal was no longer made purely for reference or reprinting but for browsing by eager fans. *Vitagraph Life Portrayals* distinguished producers as those with agency from actors as those without. Portraits were an important part of the campaign for visibility of off-screen roles. Executives appeared at the front of the magazine with their byline, while the actors were presented in grids of studio portraits in the back. By ascribing to themselves authorship of the production of films, producers and directors sought to make themselves as visible as their actors. Including their portraits in print was one way to accomplish this visibility; including their portraits in films, as part of their own Life Portrayals, was another. This style of campaign appeared in other venues. Advertisements and editorials authored by Vitagraph's presidents Blackton and Smith in related publications sponsored by their distribution group likewise featured large portraits of the men as the locus of power. In a full-page 1915 advertisement for Vitagraph's *The Goddess* in the *New York Evening Journal*, Blackton, Smith, and director Harry Ince are pictured in large portraits as "the Company producing The Goddess"[128] (fig. 10). An image of the exterior of the Vitagraph studios is also reproduced, showing the site of their film factory. While the film star may already have been established, the still-young industry was imagining, or perhaps seeking, other ways to curtail costs and promote their films.

Whether as potential employees or as burgeoning fans, moviegoers were curious about film production, and films documenting the process of moviemaking even predated the birth of fan magazines. Vitagraph's *Making Motion Pictures: A Day in the Vitagraph Studios*, a 1908 two-reeler that documents the process of moviemaking from writing the scenario to shooting with actors, follows that documentation with the film recorded in the preceding shots.[129] While this film straddles documentary and fiction, it demonstrates how early film workers likewise straddled many roles, transitioning within a single day from actor to director to grip and costumer and back to actor again. There are many people playing themselves, as film workers in this short film, thus referencing a public persona that exists in the real world. Of course, film's relationship to its referent means that few if any films escape the reference to the real world. For the viewer, film as a medium with an indexical reality represents what Vivian Sobchack identifies as narrative space that is confined to the screen and also documentary space that is contiguous to the viewer's own world.[130] Yet none of these films ask the viewer to recognize a public persona, presenting its subjects in long shots that emphasize the collaborative nature of their group work rather than isolating individuals for recognition. Ultimately, these people, although playing themselves, are not made visible for recognition; they are merely documenting.

It is because of its dual status as a portrait that scholars identify the appearance of Vitagraph's founders in *A Vitagraph Romance* as the first cameo. Importantly, this cameo also appears in what Behlmer and Thomas identify as the first fiction film that is Hollywood-set (or, technically, as it was shot in that other East Coast hub of production before the exodus to Los Angeles, Brooklyn-set).[131] It is only when this type of film is established as fictional that we can clearly see the cameo at the intersection of public persona and fictional narrative space. Rather than existing purely on-screen, the still of the three executives hobnobbing in a wood-paneled office was also used in a 1916 article in the exhibitor's journal *Moving Picture World* about their status as pioneers[132] (fig. 11). At its release, *Moving Picture World* described *A Vitagraph Romance* as featuring three of the studio's executive members, including Smith, Blackton, and president William T. "Pop" Rock, in roles as the producers of a Vitagraph picture.[133] A backstage romance about a senator's daughter who willfully marries young and then

Figure 10. A series of ads for *The Goddess* (1915) in the *New York Evening Journal* culminated in these images of the film's producers and director.

joins the film industry, *A Vitagraph Romance* features Vitagraph's Brooklyn studio as well as studio hands, crew, and otherwise nameless actors milling about the set.[134] While *Vitagraph Romance* is a fiction film, the interplay of documentary and narrative space demonstrates how difficult it is to parse fact and fiction in this era where staff worked in multiple roles. For example, James Young playing the young lover was actually the director of this film, rather than the unidentified yet recurring cameraman-director team he meets at the studio, and the senator was heroine Clara Kimball Young's real-life father. The question of visibility and public persona is relevant in this film. Like *Moving Picture World*, scholars writing about the Hollywood genre mention the executives by name as being those who play themselves in the film.[135] Yet, Vitagraph itself in its monthly publication only states that the actor meets "the heads of the company."[136] That we recognize Blackton, Smith, and Rock relies on the preservation of their portraits and names in other media. They had a visibility that lived on outside of the film. While the cameraman-director duo may also have been reprising their real-life roles, unrecognized, their roles are not cameos. When the three appear together in the scene that would be lifted for their portrait, their limited movement means that viewers have nothing to do but contemplate their images rather than the temporarily arrested narrative. Although only the keenest fans may have recognized these captains of the film industry, they are presenting images that are synonymous with their public persona as a kind of portrait.

This public persona had been well curated in the previous decades. *A Vitagraph Romance* was not Blackton and Smith's first bid for visibility. Both men exemplify the entrepreneurial spirit of the early cinema, developing not only successful production companies but also distribution networks and their attendant publicity machines. Blackton and Smith had been unsuccessful vaudevillians who nevertheless managed to obtain an Edison camera with which they started their first film company at the end of the nineteenth century.[137] Shooting as a team, they gradually built up their production company to have its own studio, expanding from a rooftop location in Brooklyn to larger and larger complexes at the outskirts of New York. Vitagraph became one of the most important early film companies, making bids for Pickford, training such stars as Mabel Normand, and founding the formidable independent-busting trust of the Motion Picture Patents Company, until an ill-suited merger and poor management of money drove Vitagraph into bankruptcy in the late 1910s.[138] Despite their rise to industry

O NE of the earliest exhibitors of motion pictures was William T. Rock, better known to the trade as "Pop" Rock, who was for years the president of the Vitagraph Company of America, but who has now retired from active participation in the manufacturing business. It was out at his delightful summer home at Oyster Bay, Long

THE ORIGINAL VITAGRAPHERS,
"Pop" Rock, Albert E. Smith and J. Stuart Blackton.

Island, that "Pop" related the story of his beginning in the picture business a few weeks ago to a representative of the Moving Picture World. We relate it here as nearly as pos-

Figure 11. The portrait appearing in *Moving Picture World* is a still of the executives' cameo in *A Vitagraph Romance*.

prominence and wealth, both of these men retained a hands-on role in their filmmaking enterprises, returning periodically to directing after 1910.[139] Photographic portraits of the pair accompanied both advertisements for the films they produced and the regular editorials they published in the publications they founded to publicize their films. Blackton and Smith were powerful men, eager to establish their legacy. Certainly they made a stronger bid than president Rock, who eschewed publication and whose biography is largely lost to time.[140] Despite the fact that they were working in what seems like the very early days of filmmaking, by the 1910s they were harnessing the language of nostalgia and memory to discuss their roles as pioneers and old-timers. In 1915, Smith describes himself as an "old fossil" of filmmaking whose stars, employees, and technicians have been stolen from him.[141] In 1913, *Moving Picture World* lamented the lack of films by the "old-time Vitagraph Girl" so familiar to the "old-time picturegoer."[142] Consolidating this power and history in a portrait follows old precedents. Like the cameo jewel, nostalgia and memory are tied to the portraits of stars and public personages in cinema.

Like art historians who claim to be able to see the qualities of a portrait in unrecognizable faces, it is hard not to want to read into this scene something distinctively cameo-like. Like portraits, cameos present their subjects for recognition. Barthes discusses the photograph's command to the viewer to look, and the cameo offers some of these same qualities. The Vitagraph cameo offers us a narrative break. While earlier scenes showed Blackton and Smith hiring the young hopefuls, the appearance of all three of these men together after the Vitagraph setting has been well established with intertitles, extensive views of the studio, and previous scenes in the executive offices, is superfluous. As such, there is something undeniably awkward about their scene that cannot be explained by their nonactor status alone; after all, two of the three had been actors in the shuffle of vaudeville and early cinema. For their portrait, they appear in the dark office, in contrast to earlier scenes that show the bustle of large groups of extras and grips in the busy courtyard of the studio, carrying scenery and lining up for roles. They are presenting themselves, like a portrait, to be admired and acknowledged. Like a princess depicted wearing copious amounts of jewels or a merchant portrayed with a globe on his desk, they are not acting powerful, they are merely being powerful. The awkwardness comes from performance. Jacqueline Nacache suggests that film performance is about appearing as close to performing an action without crossing the border into simply doing that action as natural;[143] the three executives fall on the wrong side of that border. On the other hand, Florence Turner's extremely brief cameo, which is also singled out for mention by *Moving Picture World*, is a much better performance: she strides toward the newcomers purposefully, she greets them with open arms and an expression of consternation. She gestures, wrinkles her brow, and laughs. While we linger with the Vitagraph three in their office for almost thirty seconds as they sit, stiffly allowing themselves to be captured, Turner appears for far fewer seconds. However, it is the executives who stand out to Behlmer and Thomas, and not Turner, whose appearance is not mentioned. If they stand out, it is only because of their stiffness; they seem to not belong to the film world that they have created. Whether their scene was ideal as a portrait because of its static framing, or it was static because it was also framed as a portrait, their cameo stands out from the film narrative.

These "first" cameos help underscore the evolution of the growing film industry. While in 1908, roles were less defined—studio owners might work as directors or actors, or a player might work in wardrobe, and actors were not yet credited by name—by 1912, an executive in front of a camera is a statement of tribute, a peek into the studio and behind the screen. By this time, the division between illusion and reality is more strictly if playfully guarded. *Making Motion Pictures* presents its first reel as documentary of what produces the second reel of fiction, firmly dividing what is real and what is not, while the 1912 film intercuts actuality of the studio at work with the fiction of the senator's daughter run amok. For scholars, it is obviously easier to identify long-standing executives than local and largely unskilled crewmembers. Yet, just as Blackton and Smith presented their faces in portrait photographs to exhibitors and fans in magazines, here they were presenting their faces in the setting of the films they were making, asking for recognition as their off-screen public personas. Such appearances, relying less on convenience (as in the early film period) and more on establishing the power of visibility, created a precedent for appearances by film authors other than actors in films. Given the history of the portrait and the influence of the businessmen behind the screen, as well as the predilection for showmanship of not only Blackton and Smith but also many other production pioneers, it is not surprising that such producers and directors would present themselves for acknowledgment. Florence Turner had already become a star; her appearance in the film studio as a helpful colleague is perhaps less surprising. Alongside their product, these producers struggled to maintain a public persona that if not rivaling at least echoed that of the stars they created.

Making the Cameo Cinematic

While the cameo clearly has its precedents in the fine and decorative arts, when it transitioned to the moving image, the cameo took on a life of its own. Unlike the cameo jewel, a cameo role is not a keepsake, although it can nevertheless accumulate memory and provoke study. Instead, the cameo is an experience limited by screen time. Writing about cinematic time, Deleuze suggests that some images promote more reflection than others, prompting viewers to reflect on these "time-images" as they exist in the present and the past rather than being propelled through the narrative, a task that falls to the "movement-image."[144] For Deleuze, the time-image is not stagnant but allows the viewer to reflect on how the image could and has changed from its past iterations. When dealing with a public persona, the cameo as time-image aptly allows the viewer to reflect on prior cinematic roles and extracinematic details that the viewer recollects.[145]

Viewed on a cinema screen, a cameo is gigantic. While the cameos in *A Vitagraph Romance* are not close-ups, composed mostly in medium shots, the close-up would become an important part of the presentation of the cameo, allowing the dual experience of both whole and part at once. Mary Anne Doane notes this contradiction between totality and detail as "crucial to the ideological operation of the close-up, that which makes it one of our most potent memories of the cinema."[146] For Stewart, the face in a gigantic close-up is a synecdoche for the even larger body. Presented with the grotesque face, the viewer alone must flesh out the absent parts to make sense of the experience. Fan magazines provided the necessary material, filling the whole out with other images, interviews, and biographies with which the fan could complete the image supplied by the cinematic part.

The need for reflection and assembly the cameo offers the fan is important: both Marshall and Gamson agree the opportunity to participate in the construction of the celebrity from incoherent images is what keeps fans fascinated.[147] While the viewer can possess the images surrounding the performance with stills ripped from fan magazines or purchased portraits, until relatively recently with the development of home viewing, the sequence of the performance existed exclusively in the movie theater. Its gigantic and time-dependent nature meant that the cameo could not be carried home or possessed like a portrait or carte de visite; instead, the fan had to return to the theater to see it again and again. Even if, as in the early days of continuous running programs, that revelation occurred every hour or so, the encounter was continually marked by its brevity, and by its position within the accumulated images of the film. Collected or copied outside of a film, the cameo is simply a fragment, a portrait that loses its playfulness when it no longer occupies an outsized position within the narrative.

Split from the film as a still or even a video clip, the cameo loses its impact; the cameo is surprising because it challenges the narrative form of the film it is part of. Small roles on-screen, like those onstage, are usually miniature in relation to the other supporting and starring roles that surround it in the film. While we can define these small roles by the time they take up on screen, small roles are not simply defined by duration, but by the purpose they serve. Alex Woloch examines the relationship between major and minor roles in literature. For Woloch, small roles present an empty character-space, devoid of history, that provides a stark contrast for the detailed character-space of the major character.[148] Usually innocuous minor characters make way for major characters, existing only to provide interactions that help to fill out the biographies of main roles and shrinking from view even as they propel the progress of the story.[149] Yet, refusing to step aside like meek minor characters, cameos reverse the character-system that Woloch documents. When actors began standing out like a cameo, as the phrase was coined in the 1910s, they were standing out despite their small roles. Cameos take minor characters and create a character space that is fuller than it should be, causing reflection where there should be none. Whether because of a particularly eye-catching performance or an existing celebrity persona, the cameo challenges the dominance of major characters in the story, asking fans to look outside narrative convention to the new rules of cinematic visibility. Cameos, like portraits, ask the question, who am I? It is a question that only the initiated viewer can answer. The more viewers became initiated into movie fandom in the early twentieth century, the more they delighted in solving the riddle.

2

FAMILIAR FACES

Ensemble Cameos in the Studio Era

Sitting amid a group of stars and starlets in a well-appointed dining room doing duty as the star's commissary in the 1928 movie *Show People*, Marion Davies is treated to a kind of stilted talent show from the most famous stars of the day: Douglas Fairbanks stands up from the table to do a flip and William S. Hart throws out a few lassoes toward the camera. The more decorous celebrities without characteristic gags stare out from along the long narrow table as the camera slowly pans across the group, seated singly as if at the head table of an honoring banquet. The camera stutters along from face to smiling face. Each halt gives the audience the chance to recognize film stars such as Leatrice Joy and Mae Murray, and the intertitles follow to make sure there are no cases of mistaken identity. While Davies doesn't play herself, but Peggy Pepper, aspiring starlet, her famous lunch mates appear as themselves. Why they might be performing for Davies, who is playing a newly risen ingenue on the MGM lot, is only clear in the context of the lavish luncheons that the real Marion Davies was known for serving in the stately dining room of her MGM bungalow, a perk bankrolled by the special funds available to her as the consort of newspaper magnate millionaire William R. Hearst (fig. 12). Of course, the luncheon is only a pretense to have the stars performing for the audience, making sure that there is no mistaking them for anyone but their famous selves. Even in these short roles, these celebrities were made to be instantly recognizably, because it was for celebrities that audiences came to see films. While films set in movie studios had featured what we might call cameos from the invention of the movie star, usually they featured stars who were working at a single studio. Davies's assemblage of celebrities from disparate studios has a laboriously presentational style that, while spectacular, is in keeping with the parodic tones of the rest of the film's rags-to-riches Hollywood-set story. Throughout the 1940s and 1950s, as studios ceased to command actors, directors, and producers to appear on set at will, the parades of celebrity cameos began to include not only the current film and television stars of the day but also some of those same faces of the silent era that had graced Davies's dining room, made biddable and inexpensive by the intervening years of decline. Returned to visibility, they retained some of the striking glamour, or at least the nostalgia for it, that was present in that long-ago luncheon, and for a very cheap price.

In the period from the 1920s to 1950s, cameos reflected the rise and decline of the studio system. Cameos initially advertised studio ownership of a carefully managed hierarchy of stars, both old and new, but gradually grew to reflect a shattered star system and increasingly interchangeable industry affiliations that positioned any and all recognizable faces in cameo roles. The initial surprising appearance of big actors in small roles as early as the 1910s in the case of Chaplin and the Keystone regulars fascinated fans, establishing the cameo as a potentially cinephilic moment that studios could

Figure 12. Marion Davies and other famous guests at a working luncheon in *Show People* (1928), republished in a program from an AMPAS Screening of *Show People* in Honor of *The Artist*.

exploit to engage audiences. By the end of Hollywood's Golden Age, the brief cameo had become so thoroughly associated with stardom that the label of cameo alone warranted the fame of its player. The elevation of peripheral show business figures playing small roles to the status of star grated on fans for whom the cameo had rewarded their attention to celebrity culture, eventually inciting negative reactions about the cameo as a lazy marketing gimmick. Cameos began by advertising studio affiliations and making use of excess star power, but as studio control of stars past and present and their appearances weakened, other less remembered actors were used to supplement and ultimately degrade the audience's enchantment with the cameo's cinephilic power.

The earliest cameo of the Vitagraph executives was about publicly claiming authorship and ownership of a film production, and in the 1910s and 1920s cameos continued to be about indicating studio affiliations. Cameos ask for recognition and visibility beyond the norm, so they emerged only after moviemakers were established in distinct roles behind and in front of the camera. While Blackton, Smith, and Rock appeared in front of the camera for recognition of their power within the studio, both real and narrative, making the complementary claim that the studio and its performers, crews and product belonged to them, cameos were often used to illustrate who the studio owned. In the 1920s, cameos quickly became importantly tied to publicity, as they showed who was on set at any one time. Feeding fans who clamored for behind-the-scenes looks, Hollywood-set films such as *Show People* were filled with cameo after cameo, presenting stars, directors, and writers for recognition by their audiences, while indicating who worked with whom in Hollywood. Cabals and allegiances were represented through cameos, whether they presented stars-in-training as part of a marketing sweep of several films or established stars who had deigned to make one or two movies on the studio lot that year. Cameos showed who was already on set and who could be summoned to shoot a small part that, although without the prestige of the starring role, nevertheless fulfilled the fan desire for star visibility.

Yet it was not only current stars that studios used to advertise their films but old and half-remembered stars as well. Nostalgia had a strong hold on audiences, reflecting the legacy of the sentimental remembrances of Victorian fashions and values of which the cameo jewel was one symptom. Audiences thrilled to see the return of out-of-the-limelight faces as early as the 1910s. In 1912 Florence Turner was pointed out as the "old-time Vitagraph girl,"[1] while in 1923, a disgraced Fatty Arbuckle appeared as an out-of-work extra in *Hollywood*. Unlike cameos of current stars, who were well profiled and extremely visible, these nostalgic cameos asked viewers to reach back into their memories, although they were heavily abetted by press releases applauding the studio's use of great actors of an earlier age. This tactic can be seen as actively cinephilic moviemaking, embracing a gamelike interaction that mimicked the type of interaction found in the contests and quizzes of fan magazines. Cinephilic viewing was thus very early on tied to the cameo. Fans steeped in the short history of the movies were thrilled to see their early heroes and heroines once again on-screen, after a hiatus however brief. Cinema provided an indexical record of times gone by, and so it could show its fans exactly who they were no longer.

As studios lost control of stars, nostalgic cameos engineered for recognition became more and more popular. Whether studios felt responsible for the sometimes ignoble fate of their high-grossing stars of the 1910s and 1920s, these forgotten stars came cheap. As the stable of stars became less and less biddable, faces from the past were available for a pittance. Of course, by the 1950s independent producers had also realized this availability: actors with full character-spaces yet empty pockets who could fill roles and be billed as stars. Independent films such as *Around the World in 80 Days* (1956), *Pepe* (1960), and *It's a Mad, Mad, Mad, Mad World* (1963) unearthed some of these forgotten faces in the name of spectacle, allowing them to be named as stars alongside some of the most famous and greediest stars of the day.

Stars, unhitched from studios and masters of their own production companies, became free to appear in roles of their choosing. The term *cameo* as introduced in *Around the World* negated difference between stars of yesterday and today, merely asserting that they all stood out in small roles. Cameos were for stars, therefore any cameo players were repeatedly identified to audiences in posters, programs, and other publicity as bona fide stars, regardless of the nuances of the billing they currently commanded in Hollywood. Where studios had guarded their stars to prevent too much visibility, newly freed stars had no such limitations, dropping in for single days or even hours of shooting and collecting, and in addition to their official day rate, gifts in kind and reciprocated publicity that made the hassle worthwhile. Cameos broke away from representing studio affiliation, but they were still tied to publicity, for television shows, upcoming movies, or nightclub acts. Audiences, who had demanded nostalgic faces and views of stars off duty, were jaded—when star billing didn't guarantee anything more than a brief appearance, or any appearance at all, and actors appeared ad nauseum in cameo roles, visibility became overexposure, and what had seemed like a cute reveal was reviled as a cash grab. Cameos offering Hollywood realism no longer stood out to the audience as worthy of special recognition; there was no cinephilic frisson of discovery. While cameos since the studio days had become more sophisticated in the extent of recognition they demanded and rewarded, the star as actor cameo had become less compelling to fans the more visible it became.

Early Cameos and the Celebrity Sighting

The act of recognition that occurs in the cameo mirrors the experience of the celebrity sighting. For Kerry Ferris, the celebrity sighting creates a special type of work for the fan, as it is an encounter with a stranger about whom they know details as intimate as those shared with a close friend.[2] In the real world, fans will often avoid celebrities in a chance encounter for fear of crossing boundaries of personal and public interactions. As part of a film audience, no such negotiation is necessary. Early film fans were enchanted by the seemingly chance encounter of the celebrity sighting in Hollywood-set films. Just as they collected magazines to delve into intimate details of star lives, from which words stars lisped to actors' favorite meals,[3] fans went to the movies to encounter the stars. Cameos doubled up on the kind of personal information that sold popular publications such as *Photoplay*, making the films satisfy desire not only for an escapist story but also offering a look at the star's personal life. If the fascination with stars is a "fascination with a concealed truth"[4] where fans attempt, as deCordova suggests, to parse screen performance and actor's identity, then cameos of celebrities as themselves offered audiences a view of the celebrity where performance and identity were ostensibly one and the same. Hollywood-set films were populated with these types of cameos, where stars appear on set and at leisure, and scholars indicate their presence is ostensibly to accurately represent the movie colony.[5] Yet, the number of films from the 1910s to the present day that represent a perfectly recognizable Hollywood without cameos suggests that cameos are not merely convincing set dressing. Cameos, briefly presenting their subjects to be recognized, call on fan knowledge of the type that moviegoers stored up in spades in the 1920s while offering the kind of extraordinary experience that makes a moment memorable.

Like the etiquette for encounters with celebrities, an etiquette for interaction with cinematic illusion was already established in the 1910s. Early cinema audiences derided the "buttinski"[6] who insisted on acknowledging the camera with suspicious glares or repeat viewings. The buttinski had a parallel character in the cinema: the bumpkin. Where the buttinksi did not respect how one should act in front of a camera, the bumpkin did not know how to act in front of the screen. For Robert Stam, the spectator both derides and admires the bumpkin, because while he is on the one hand "so naive as to take image literally for reality,"[7] he also believes in the film as fantasy in a way the savvy spectator cannot. When encountering a cameo, the fantasy of the celebrity encounter and the familiarity with the paradigm of film production conflict within the savvy fan. Anderson suggests that Hollywood-set films are predicated on this desire, examining the bumpkin's failure to acknowledge cinematic illusion within the context of an increasingly sophisticated Hollywood film industry while simultaneously exploring fans' "confusion between the screen's image and reality." While the excitement that accompanies a cameo may belong to the fantasies of the bumpkin, the recognition of a celebrity cameo reconfirms the audience's position as savvy viewers. Like privy courtiers who recognize the meanings of symbols that represent the king, audiences who recognize cameos assert their initiation into film fandom, affirming their own Bourdieuian cultural competences to distinguish themselves against the bumpkin.[8] Audiences that recognize cameos know how to process the intersection of documentary and narrative space, and to interpret cinematic illusion.

While cameos may not occur in Hollywood-set movies for convenience, as Ames writes, "the use of self-referential star cameos to add verisimilitude to the representation of Hollywood . . . is especially prevalent in films from the studio days, where contract players could be trotted out en masse for self-promoting films."[9] Just like Vitagraph naturally called on its own executives and studio to portray the essence of the film industry in their own films, studios would begin to call on their increasing stables of stars to market their films as actor contracts were not merely on a film-by-film or film-per-year basis, but required that actors be available and on set whenever the studios demanded. The vision of what "candid cameos"[10] in Hollywood looked like depended on the studios that backed the movie.

The power of the individual connection to the star was harnessed early on by studios as a way of ensuring viewership and generating profits.[11] Cameos could not have existed until stars were made distinct from bit players in terms of their billing and the publicity that surrounded them, becoming images to be recognized for the biographies that had accompanied them in fan and trade magazines. Early cameos of the owners of Vitagraph, an important early production company, in *A Vitagraph Romance* (1912), straddle the line between the simple convenience of having these ex-actors turned owners fill these roles to save the expense of pulling stock players out of rotation, and on the other hand the desire to present their images for recognition as portraits for adulation.[12] At the same time, these cameos, which include an appearance by Vitagraph Girl Florence Turner, forged a brand identity for the studio that included the faces of its stars and its authors, reinforcing their value as a group. Similar cameos by newly contracted stars in Keystone and Essanay films reinforced the relationships between star and studio and confirmed which stars found their homes where.

Key among cameos that indicated studio affiliation were the appearances of Charlie Chaplin. James Naremore and Harry Geduld identify Chaplin as appearing in several early "cameos."[13] As an early distinctive star who nevertheless moved studios several times during his early career, Chaplin's cameos indicate which studio he was working at when. Making clear who was producing legitimate Chaplin shorts was not as easy as it might seem. In the mid-1910s, Chaplin imitators were numerous, as studios tried to take advantage of Chaplin-mania that had his face plastered not only in magazines but also on goods of every kind.[14] Juvenile Film Corporation even presented a film of young Chaplin look-alike retreading well-known Chaplin gags.[15] Cameos established a visual link between Chaplin and the other well-known members of his current studio. This linkage was established when Chaplin, strictly a star player, appeared in small roles within his colleague's films.

Chaplin's iconic character the Tramp first emerged at Keystone in 1914 in what Naremore calls a candid-camera-style appearance, building his performance in *Kid Auto Races at Venice* (1914) from mere curious onlooker in the crowd to spectacularly misbehaved center of attention.[16] Emerging from the conventions of actuality, *Kid Auto Races* subverts the already established etiquette of the real-world encounter with the camera and belies the supposed naturalism of such recordings.[17] This double register of the commonplace and unusual is where ordinary subjects are made exemplary thanks to the presence of the camera and its record. Geduld also agrees that *Kid Auto Races* is "one of the first-self-reflexive films in the history of the motion picture" as Chaplin "relegates the event to the inferior status of 'background,'"[18] refusing to become part of the organized mass. The Tramp, sighting the camera, initially tries to feign nonrecognition, but he gradually progresses to more and more open acknowledgment. When the cameo emerges with Chaplin as its subject, it continues Chaplin's conversation about naturalism and performance by examining the transformation of the real world when its people encounter the camera.

Given his popularity, Chaplin's cameo not only served to remind audiences whose studio he was contracted at but also increased the draw for other films as other stars' movies could become Chaplin films. Beginning at Keystone and then at Essanay, Chaplin traded cameos with his colleagues. At Keystone, stars were not mentioned by name, but that changed with Chaplin's arrival as first he and then others were billed as stars.[19] Although Chaplin was a star, he appeared in several small roles or slight appearances in films that were vehicles for other stars at his current studio. In *A Film Johnnie* (1914), a Chaplin picture, movie fan Chaplin tries to avenge the abuse of Minta Durfee in a Keystone film by showing up at the studio to rescue her. He is surprised to meet Durfee, Fatty Arbuckle, and Mack Sennett at the studio gates, out of makeup and decidedly out of danger. Geduld notes that *A Film Johnnie* marks Chaplin's first lead in a scripted, pre-planned film, where many comedic films were shot without a scenario and completely improvised.[20] While on the one hand this means that Chaplin was not merely improvising with whoever was at hand, it also means that this film was crafted by the studio to showcase not only Chaplin but also to place him among their other leading actors. In some ways, the scenario apes that of *A Vitagraph Romance*; indeed, the idea of the hayseed who mistakes narrative space for real-world space was a running gag in the cinema, beginning with poor Uncle Josh who makes eyes at an on-screen dancing girl then attempts to fight off on-screen attackers.[21] Earlier that year, Keystone followed in the footsteps of Vitagraph by producing a behind-the-scenes film called *How Motion Pictures Are Made* (1914), which featured the Ince Studios and "typical Keystone buffoonery."[22] While critics feared that revealing the labor behind the illusion would tarnish the reputation and glamor of the studios,[23] *A Film Johnnie* uses the cameo instead to assert the prestige of its own players, as Chaplin, their new star, is shown in awe of Keystone's more established cast. While the cameos in this film are by Durfee, Arbuckle, and Sennett, among other Keystone players, the strategy plays with narrative and documentary space in a way that Geduld identifies as characteristically Chaplinesque in its refusal "to accept cinematic objectivity."[24] The counterpart to this cameo trade at Keystone, where Chaplin appears briefly as a referee to a boxing match Fatty can't possibly win in *The Knockout* (1914), is perhaps more cameo as actor than cameo as celebrity. Chaplin cannot help but stand out as the world's biggest comedy star in a very small role as the chief abider-of-rules and keeper-of-order.

Chaplin established that films were not only about entertainment but also about informing a presumably interested audience about his movements within the film industry. His first film for Essanay was what Stam calls a studio tour appropriately titled *His New Job* (1915).[25] He soon appeared in another boxing film as a spectator, *His Regeneration* (1915), starring studio owner and cinema's first cowboy star Broncho Billy Anderson.[26] Anderson likewise appeared in *The Champion* (1915).[27] In the Essanay cameos, both actors appear as little more than extras. Naremore identifies the 1916 reciprocation of cameo roles in two Essanay pictures featuring Chaplin and studio co-owner and star Broncho Billy Anderson as the first self-conscious instance of "true celebrity characters."[28] Of course, sometimes these performances were more impromptu: Buster Keaton claims he was roped into playing an extra in a Fatty picture for Paramount when the crew chanced on him out hunting in the Mojave Desert.[29] Comedic performances such as those of Keaton or Chaplin owe their popularity to the disruption of coherence, firmly establishing the difference between an anarchic narrative space and real-world documentary space. However, drama asks that the suspension of disbelief that unites the two not be disturbed, and sharing the dramatic narrative space with a famous comedian undoubtedly taxed the Broncho Billy film's claims to verisimilitude.[30] The fact that Anderson welcomed Chaplin into his films despite the narrative perils reinforces the importance of these cameos as a tactic of visibility, as insistence on the demonstration of their business affiliation trumped any desire for narrative continuity.

Chaplin's comedy plays with the boundaries of the frame that separate performance from real life.[31] The cameo likewise depends on exploring the limits of reality and illusion. Rather than merely stand out in these small roles, Chaplin's participation is notable specifically because, as the biggest movie star on earth in the 1910s, he could undoubtedly command a much larger role. Chaplin's films, which often play with the apparent objectivity of the cinema, gave rise to one of the earliest associations of the cameo: not just a portrait for recognition, but recognition despite the desire of the narrative space to control its own characters. Chaplin's innovative use of self-reflexivity and his positioning of a recognizable character at the intersection of narrative and documentary space would be a legacy of the cameo beyond his use of it as one of the many ways that cameo roles could stand out to audiences.

Consolidating Studio Ownership of Celebrities

The explosion of Hollywood-set films in the 1920s made the cameo as self a recognizable phenomenon. Hollywood-set films reflected an indefatigable fan interest in celebrity lives and their labor in the movie colony, self-consciously exploring the new industry and its nascent mythology.[32] The sheer mass of print information ensured the visibility of Hollywood celebrities; as Leo Rosten wrote, "if four hundred columnists and feature writers were assigned to Detroit or Pittsburgh and were charged with the sole responsibility of writing daily stories about the foibles, diet, and libidinous acrobatics of automobile magnates or steel monarchs, the public would have a different set of stereotypes about these men, and about the circles in which they move."[33] For many fans, the most authentic star images were those produced by the studios, and so audiences clamored for Hollywood-set films.[34]

Hollywood-set films provided a basis for the inclusion of cameos of celebrities appearing as themselves, presenting noted personalities from journalists and directors to socialites and actors for recognition. There was much for fans to see, and many faces to recognize. The mass of stars was an important part of the marketing of the film; a proposed trailer for Hollywood-set rags-to-riches tale *Souls for Sale* (1923) promised "the most dazzling cast ever assembled in one picture."[35] These films, as Anderson suggests, corralled together players already under contract who were "readily available to do the kind of brief walk-on parts these appearances entailed, and they provided good free publicity (and exposure) for the star, and hence, the studio."[36] While displaying those on contracts to eager fans, such films also offered studios the chance to establish and consolidate their associations among different actors and social groups, presenting gossip columnists, preachers, and even independent stars such as Mary Pickford for recognition. The brevity of cameos made economical use of the time of in-demand stars, while new stars could be shown hobnobbing with old, establishing who might appear in upcoming features while assuring continuity of star power. *His Regeneration* and *A Film Johnnie* are precursors to this method, using brief star appearances within films that were billed as part of the repertoire of another star to advertise studio affiliation. In the 1920s, the same kind of thrilling intersection of cinematic illusion and reality was unleashed in Hollywood-set films that deployed celebrity cameos to increase their visibility. While, as Ames notes, there were many Hollywood-set films released in this decade, only a few used cameos in strikingly large numbers. *Hollywood* (1923), *Souls for Sale* (1923), and *Show People* (1928) are the best examples of this adoption of the cameo in Hollywood-set films.

While nominally cautionary tales inspired or even commissioned to warn audiences about the perils, the Hollywood depicted in these three films is pretty forgiving. Each film tells the story of a young woman, a typical "Hollywood Extra Girl"[37] who arrives in Hollywood to seek her fortune as a movie actress, with eventual happiness in the movies or otherwise as her reward. As Behlmer and Thomas note, this "very simple but exceptionally effective formula would be repeated with minor variations over and over into the 1940s and beyond."[38] Although warning about the difficult path to stardom, backstudio films make Hollywood seem, as Cohan writes, "at once loathsome and irresistible."[39] Tales of the success of lucky stars led to a massive influx of vulnerable young women to the movie capital, which, although a phenomenon of newly won autonomy and mobility for women, had serious social consequences.[40] Thousands who arrived in the city weekly looking for jobs working at even a fraction of the astronomical salaries of up to $10,000 a week that stars commanded found themselves unemployed and destitute.[41] Movies that showed stars as extras and extras hoping to be stars, and campaigns that publicized such a film with claims to show the "dozens of screen celebrities that she meets in her work"[42] could not help but confirm small roles as providing access to glamour.

Hollywood, a lost film from Paramount, follows the story of Angela, a wannabe actress who leaves her backwater town to find fame in Hollywood, chancing on celebrity after celebrity while accidentally fixing her own family up in the business as they arrived one at a time to save her from Hollywood's corrupting influences. It was perhaps the earliest major use of cameos, indicating the division of documentary and narrative space was a real concern for those casting this film. Behlmer and Thomas assert that "in order to avoid confusion with the real actors playing themselves, it was decided the leading players in the story would be virtual unknowns."[43] A *New York Times* review of *Hollywood*, the first film to unleash a parade of cameos, explained the cameo phenomenon was a "production in which noted pantomimists appear as the extras," assuring audiences that it "can be seen more than once and enjoyed."[44] No doubt the opportunity to recognize scores of celebrities, many of them appearing on-screen at the same time, was part of the draw of the film. (It is perhaps for this same reason, their relevance to movie fans of that decade, that both *Hollywood* and the extended luncheon scene in *Show People* have not been preserved.)

In Goldwyn's *Souls for Sale*, the heroine Mem escapes a murderous husband and ends up getting a big break when she chances on a studio crew shooting on location. As Mem soars to success, her biggest problems are the admiration of both her director and her leading man, as well as the skullduggery of her husband, problems that are resolved during a studio accident where suitable partners are found for everyone. Behlmer and Thomas suggest that the cameos in *Souls for Sale* were an "afterthought" as director Rupert Hughes copied *Hollywood*, resulting in what they suggest are cameos "arbitrarily dragged in by the gross,"[45] although early story synopses named stars such as Chaplin and Pickford at the Hollywood soirees where Mem dances the night away.[46]

By the end of the decade, Goldwyn's *Show People* takes the elements of the tale of the overwhelmed movie star wannabe in Hollywood and turns them to parody. Featuring Marion Davies, *Show People* shows Peggy Pepper, a Southern belle who finds success first as a comedienne and then as a dramatic actress, eventually abandoning the glamorous company of costars with questionable royal titles to return to her true love, comedy and her comedic partner. This entry, coming at the end of a decade, punctuates the end of the cycle with a transformative satire. *Show People* features many cameos as Peggy aimlessly stumbles into famous actors, writers, and directors, including Davies as herself in a double role (fig. 13). Satirical or otherwise, their cameos served much the same purpose: showing audiences the star power that a given studio commanded at any one time, and which fans were clamoring to see.

Figure 13. Peggy Pepper is nonplussed by Marion Davies's cameo role in *Show People*.

Films with cameos allow the audience both the fantasy of the manufactured story and the chance to encounter the supposed real persona behind them. Like deCordova, Gamson suggests that fan behavior is fueled by fascination with the truth behind the image, as audiences try to piece together as complete an image of the celebrity as possible.[47] The myth of the ordinary star with the singular talent has continued to be relevant to the making of celebrity,[48] even as audiences recognize that the ordinary star is yet another carefully constructed presentation. Even in carefully stage-managed cameo groups, fans were promised they were seeing beyond the persona to the private image as studios marketed cameos as reflections of star identity rather than roles or labor. Publicity for *Souls for Sale* promises it is a "smashing bit of realism . . . makes you feel as if you actually knew all those stars. It leads you up to shake hands with them, as it were, and then leads you into their world. . . . And yet it pokes gentle fun at the movies, too, at moments, making them all the more real and delightful."[49] Realism and celebrity encounters were what cameos promised for fans. The press account of the luncheon that Marion Davies threw for stars before filming the stars' commissary scene in

Show People suggested the mixing of documentary and narrative space, as if the luncheon perhaps just leisurely continued into the hours of the shoot with the headline "Film stars volunteer aid in Show World."[50] Whether or not MGM stars such as Eleanor Boardman (who as a new face had played the heroine in *Souls for Sale*) were in fact volunteering their time rather than abiding by the terms of their contract, many of Davies's guests were not studio contractees. Yet production photographs of this same scene show how much of a production this luncheon was, including an impressive lighting setup that belies the bright windows behind the stars, a massive half-moon table engineered to display the lunching faces to the camera tracking in front of it while placing the people lunching together at opposite ends of the room, and the crew in its unfinished center surrounded by a mess of papers, tools, and camera equipment.[51] As a marketing strategy, studios suggested cameos were capturing stars at ease in a documentary space, suggesting real insights into the private lives of stars. At the same time, they were manufactured and managed in the same way as other narrative events within the film.

While the Vitagraph cameos, followed closely by the Chaplin cameo trades, mimicked the formula of the portrait, as cameos became more closely aligned with the marketing strategy of the studio they took on a specific cinematic form. Overdetermination was the first strategy. While Chaplin or Broncho Billy might be readily recognized, studios took steps to ensure that those who they were marketing were recognized by the audience, introducing their name in the intertitles of silent films. In *Souls for Sale*, the titles are expository. When the heroine enters the commissary, a situation that "terrified her to see about her so many famous faces," the heroine "encountered T. Roy Barnes and Zasu Pitts," and then five consecutive titles provide exhaustive identifying lists of twenty names from Kathlyn Williams to Blanche Sweet[52] (fig. 14). In *Hollywood*, the cues for celebrity identity were more cleverly incorporated into the narrative, as celebrities or fans greeted the featured celebrity by name in written dialogue, or in other props, such as addressed letters, pay stubs, dance cards, and even golf scores featured in close-up to convey the names of those featured celebrities. On the one hand, this need to cue fans for recognition suggests that cameos were not necessarily directly arising out of fan desire to see certain stars. Rather, stars were being prodded into visibility by suggesting that they were worth recognizing. Recognition was being mobilized as a strategy for star-making.

Figure 14. A crowded table of stars at the studio commissary in *Souls for Sale.*

Often these celebrities were presented in groups that emphasized their star power rather than their own star personas: lunching at the commissary as in *Show People*, dancing at the Hollywood Hotel as in *Souls for Sale*, loitering at the studio mailboxes as in *Hollywood*. Celebrities were presented as a dazzling mass. The credits for *Souls for Sale*, after listing six principals, reduce the rest to "thirty-five famous stars."[53] These celebrities were largely interchangeable, as evident from the scripts of *Hollywood*, for example, where Gloria Swanson's role cruising up to an opening in a chauffeured car became Lois Wilson's.[54] While Swanson's glamorous worldly image was far from the down-to-earth Lois Wilson, they were scripted to play the exact same scene, each ostensibly as herself.[55] As a note in the *Hollywood* scenario draft suggests, "almost any stars or directors can be used in these various episodes—unless there is something specially written characteristic of the individual."[56] Likewise, the early draft of *Souls for Sale* has a theater scene begin with Al Jolson "or any well-known musical stag."[57] The identity was not important; what was crucial was the sense of celebrity, ease, and glamour intertwined with only the barest hint of labor and art. The point of the cameos was the mass of star power, rather than the individual and their biography. Gamson suggests that marketing in the 1920s aimed to present stars as a kind of democratic royalty, untouchable and glamorous, rather than the ordinary joes made good of the late 1930s and 1940s.[58] In the late 1910s and early 1920s, the ordinary lifestyles stars were supposed to lead were further and further removed by their extreme wealth.[59] While Hollywood-set movies claimed to make the everyday lives of their stars visible, allowing audiences a closer look, these lives as represented were a far cry from ordinary. Like fan magazines, which balanced the stories of family life and early struggles with glamorous images to present a carefully orchestrated view of the star, the cameos that were featured in Hollywood-set films were no closer to exposing real-world lives of celebrities. Exceptions such as *Hollywood*'s ejection of a disgraced Fatty from a casting queue are remarkable enough to deserve special "surprise" mention.[60] Their interchangeableness suggests these early cameos merely communicated the aura of visibility rather than actual characteristics of public persona.

Despite the fact that changes could and would be made, stars were scripted by name into each film quite early in the process, indicating a pool of stars from which studio writers knew they could draw. For these films, elaborate scenarios were drafted that include painstaking lists of celebrity names. Who was featured depended on the type of relationship that the studio had with a star. Stars currently on Goldwyn sets in 1923 such as Zasu Pitts and Blanche Sweet, for *Greed* and *In the Palace of the King* respectively, would replace proposed roles for Mary Pickford and Doug Fairbanks, upholding the idea that real-world relationships trumped fiction.[61] These demonstrate that cameos depended on the relationships that studios could reliably draw on, whether business or social, and served to reinforce these relationships.

Studio affiliations were not the only considerations. *Show People* was a Marion Davies vehicle undertaken by Goldwyn with the financing of her lover, newspaper magnate W. R. Hearst. Davies, backed financially by Hearst, created her own production unit under Goldwyn and later MGM. Early drafts of this story from 1926 featured Davies in the role of the benefactress to Peggy Pepper, and were littered with characters from the Hearst empire rather than the studio, including society writer Cholly Knickerbocker and gossip columnist Louella Parsons.[62] The writers knew that they could guarantee the participation of public figures associated with Hearst for the Davies's film. As such, that version of the film documents Hearst's power. The final version, which featured Davies, emphasized the relationships that Davies had secured socially as a hostess with the ear of the Hearst gossip columnists. Other relationships from outside studio confines were reflected in cameos from actors Douglas Fairbanks, Charlie Chaplin, and William S. Hart, who as a result of being executives of their own production companies under the UA umbrella had control of their own appearances.[63] In fact, Davies's custom-built Hearst-financed and jealously coveted Spanish-style bungalow on the Goldwyn lot was regularly used for this and frequently other "lavish luncheons."[64] These cameos indicate the burgeoning independence of some stars, liberated from studio control.

An important aspect of the Hollywood-set film's claim to verisimilitude was behind-the scenes access to studios, sets, and the unseen moviemakers. If actors and actresses were shown at leisure, filmmakers were shown at work. While filmmakers and writers had been visible in fan magazines, movies gave them a chance to be seen in action. In *Hollywood*, Alfred Green and Cecil B. DeMille were shown on set in the middle of shooting. DeMille and his assistant Jeannie Macpherson then reappear in a confrontation with the aspiring starlet's grandmother, who ends up in the DeMille film after all.[65] With this role, DeMille began a long venerable tradition of cameos that has perhaps contributed to his continued visibility. *Souls for Sale* showed Chaplin, Fred Niblo, and Erich von Stroheim directing. Behlmer and Thomas suggest that these directors were in fact filmed in the production of real films; rather than being assembled on set to make a show of directing, they were actually working.[66] Of course, they are appearing to advertise their films, a fact the intertitles make clear as they name the heroine's supposed extra roles in the actual films *Greed* and *The Famous Mrs. Fair* that were currently in production.[67] In fact, the proposed trailer introduced only a series of directors among the real stars the heroine meets, although Ernst Lubitsch and Marshall Neilan replaced Chaplin.[68] Directors and their personas were linked with their labor, unlike actors, whose work was intrinsically tied with visibility.

Despite claims to the contrary, cameos were about respecting and emphasizing relationships rather than merely providing realistic interludes for studio-set films. Cameos that were written as tributes could outlive their usefulness as markers of verisimilitude. In *Hollywood*, a note mentions that the role of minister at the Hollywood Bowl's Sunday service should be given to a certain preacher as a "well merited compliment."[69] When this scene was cut, the force of the compliment outweighed the reverend's value as set dressing. Instead of adding authenticity to the Bowl scene, the reverend appeared, somewhat out of place, in the background in a studio scene, where he was, of course, mentioned by name.[70] Not just everyone on the studio lot could be written into a cameo because some potential cameoists preferred to leave visibility to the stars. For example, what began as a role for studio head Jesse Lasky in early drafts of *Hollywood* became simply a studio executive in final drafts. While Vitagraph executives may have preened in front of the camera, the extraneous notes the *Hollywood* scenario writer included belie unease about the inclusion of the head of Paramount in the film. As the note goes, "[Lasky] thinks it is all right if we feel we want to show the mechanics of picture-making in a scene—in fact, he says that we should not have any rule to go by, but merely keep story value in mind."[71] In the long run, story value alone did not guarantee Lasky's appearance in front of the camera. Cameos were not purely about verisimilitude but about demonstrating loyalty, power, and allegiance in a visible manner.

In these films of the 1920s, the playful interjection of narrative and documentary space that Chaplin had pioneered became a hallmark of cameos. Where there were cameos, there were bumpkins to misrecognize them. Angela, the heroine straight from the sticks in *Hollywood*, bumbles past a score of celebrities at the Los Angeles train station.[72] In *Show People*, Marion Davies as Peggy, on her quest for fame, pushes past Chaplin at a screening of her latest comedy. Each heroine is a fan who is drawn to the movies no doubt because of the images they have seen on-screen and in magazines. Yet they are initially remarkably unsophisticated in their ability to recognize film stars. Unlike Uncle Josh and Chaplin's film johnnie, who confuse narrative space for documentary space by imagining what they see on screen to be real, Angela and Peggy fail to recognize the movie idols around them who are drawing on documentary space within the narrative world. While they are prepared to swoon at star characters such as the dashing leading man or the mesmerizing count turned actor, they are less able to immediately recognize stars who do not exist firmly within the film's established character system. Instead of Charlie Chaplin, Peggy sees a kind gentleman in a theater. Instead of Mae Murray, Angela sees a well-dressed career girl rushing to work. Cameos surprise and confound them. Having outgrown the buffoonery of earlier bumpkins, these clueless ingenues show audiences in their failure how and when stars can be recognized. Even they can learn; Davies's performance in *Show People* reveals the scriptedness of the cameo interaction when, in a shot reverse shot sequence, Davies as Peggy Pepper gives passing screen actress Marion Davies, on her way to a tennis date, a skeptical double take. Naremore identifies this cameo as a moment of sophisticated performance, as narrative and documentary space come up against each other unavoidably.[73] Notably, Davies is one star that Peggy can easily identify, and from this point on, she is able to recognize other celebrities. Cued in to this new type of role, where narrative space and documentary space collide, and stars surprise the viewer in small roles, Peggy represents not only the success story that fans longed to emulate but also a knowing cameo etiquette for the savvy fan.

Sophisticated Viewers and Cinephilic Details

By the 1930s, twenty years of fan magazines had produced audiences well versed in the workings of the studio system. Reflecting the same fan consciousness that pushed the cameo's popularity, fan magazines served fans who were proud to demonstrate that they knew how movies were manufactured and stars were built. As active viewers, they were encouraged to be part of the system through the magazine, participating in contests to pick and choose new stars, film titles, and stories. Like spectators who had clamored to see the sideshows of P. T. Barnum's circus, these fans were caught up in an operational aesthetic, marveling in how the ruse worked as much as the product itself.[74]

Thrilled by the aesthetic mastery and complex networks of the studio system, audiences never tire of uncovering the reality behind the smoke and mirrors of production magic through opportunities like the cameo. Audiences look past what is presented for easy viewing to uncover the seams of the production with a cinephilic attention to detail. Cinephilia is unique to the viewer, yet this unique moment can only be found within the mass-produced art of cinema.[75] The cinephilic detail is a strategy that allows viewers to "customize industrially produced pleasures."[76] Both intensely personal and generic, belonging to narrative and documentary space, the double-edged cinephilic moment accounts for the thrill of the cameo. The cameo, while visible to all audiences, is striking only to those who have begun to uncover the behind-the-scenes operations of studio ownership. Memory, too, weighs heavily on the cameo and cinephilia. As remembered film images mix with and stand in for important images from our real lives, conflating reality and narrative,[77] film stars of a certain era with their ubiquitous faces likewise become tied to memories of a person's real life. Cameos harness memory that is both private and bound up in the history of the film industry.

The viewer of the 1930s already had developed a nostalgic relationship to the faces of the 1910s and 1920s. Films had long appealed to the memories of their fans for stars of yesteryear, steeping themselves in history before it had duly passed. As early as 1914, a letter from a representative of former Vitagraph Girl Florence Lawrence to Vitagraph requested that the company stop referring to the twenty-eight-year-old as an old-timer.[78] In the 1930s, there were many silent stars who had dropped from minor roles to bit parts on their descent to the low-paid ranks of extra thanks to studio reorganization. At the same time, older stars, some less than five years out of the limelight, gained value as nostalgia became an important strategy for the cameo. While certain cameos may appear like extras to the uninitiated, an extra is merely a part of the setting, set aside from the center of the action and attention.[79] As Rosten writes, "extras are important en masse, not as individuals."[80] Roles that stand apart from the background are no longer extras, and many formerly famed actors persisted in standing out from the crowd for audiences. Studios were quick to capitalize on these remnants of recognition: down-on-his-luck star Buster Keaton made a late career of showing his face in overlooked corners of the set in wordless roles such as a waiter or train conductor.[81] Actors like Keaton were playing small roles often populated by another recognizable type, the character actor. When character actors are recognized, it is not primarily for their persona outside of movies, but for their persona within other movies that they carry with them from film to film, small part to small part. The character actor through cumulative roles becomes representative of a generic type, whereas a cameo serves the opposite function by carrying the baggage of a specific biographic reference that exists in the real world.[82] Those actors such as Keaton who have descended from some stardom to small roles can't quite become character actors as they bring to each role references to their more illustrious pasts. As Will Straw suggests, they "come already laden with cultish appeal."[83] Even in the background, they are never quite extras, either, because they are sure to be recognized by audiences, even if only those with long memories. Although audiences and filmmakers reported being chagrined to see fondly remembered yet now archaic works from the 1910s or 1920s through "the eyes of 1935"[84] or later,[85] seeing those same actors in new films, especially if only briefly, offered the chance to reflect on those remembered films while positioning them within a more contemporary aesthetic. However, cameos included to ignite the memories of filmgoers of the day run the risk of escaping the attention of later viewers. *Souls for Sale* is full of these composed frames of expectant figures waiting to be recognized.

The cameo, because it is linked only tenuously to the narrative and thrives instead on diversion and reverie, is an ideal cinephilic detail. It asks viewers to reach back in their memories of public and private life and make the connections between real and narrative space, promoting active viewing through reflexivity. While cinephilic viewing acknowledges the potential for individual reflection within films geared to the mass audience of cinema, ultimately, active viewing is limited by the film text. By the 1930s, cameos had already been routinely used to trot out up-and-coming stars and studio assets. As the maturing film industry and its fans began to share a mutual history, cameos presented a new opportunity for studios to channel audience memory and reflection in order to imbue a film with personal resonance through cinephilic detail.

New Nostalgia: Hollywood Cameos in the 1930s

In the 1930s, the optimism of Hollywood-set films of the 1920s began to dissipate. Even a film with a title that oozed skepticism at the fate of many Hollywood hopefuls such as *Souls for Sale* was less a story of failure than one of triumphant pluck. The stock market crash had much to do with it: in 1927, 743 feature films were made in Hollywood, while in 1937 only 484 feature pictures were produced.[86] Anderson notes that the initial excitement about making it in Hollywood as a "new gold rush" had begun to settle, Hollywood itself tried to stem an alarming influx of young hopefuls tracing the cross-country journeys fictionalized in *Show People, Hollywood,* and *Souls for Sale* in hope of the same results: fame.[87] If *Show People* sowed the first seeds of skepticism, the 1930s continued it. Central Casting tried to dissuade young women from mimicking their on-screen counterparts in the hopes of meeting the new stars of the 1930s on their home turf. Hollywood-set movies reflected the end of this golden age, as tales such as *What Price Hollywood* (1932) and *A Star Is Born* (1937) reflected a more mercenary Hollywood that made stars and threw them away. In writing about the production of *A Star Is Born*, producer David O. Selznick indicated his desire to show Hollywood without bowdlerizing or idealizing it—to show a true Hollywood.[88] Interestingly, in both films, this was done without recourse to cameos. Hollywood had a history, and while that history could be bittersweet, a new type of cameo emerged not just to present celebrities of the moment for adulation, but to acknowledge the has-beens of Hollywood past. Stars, even half-forgotten ones, even if they could no longer carry a film, could be reliably trusted in small roles, like cameos.

Perhaps emulating Poverty Row films that benefited from the wealth of discarded silent stars in the early 1930s, a picture by a Big Five company such as Paramount's *Hollywood Boulevard* (1936) used a different strategy to bring the sting of the real to these unflattering depictions of Hollywood machinery. *Hollywood Boulevard* presented the swan song of a former silent star deep in alcoholic decline who publishes his memoirs, embroiling his former costars and lovers as well as his daughter, a Hollywood hopeful herself, in romantic and commercial troubles as the past is dredged for excitement. Rather than promoting a current stable of stars, former silent stars in small roles were used to convey a type of pathos. By the 1930s the Hollywood narrative of success and failure had matured to include the cautionary tale of the has-been. These aging stars were only half-remembered yet still "familiar to the generation which went to pictures nightly some years back."[89] The cameo and the Hollywood-set film were likewise the subject of this cynical attitude. While *Show People* was hailed in 1928 as offering the "greatest assemblage of talents ever photographed,"[90] *Variety* labeled the group assembled in *Hollywood Boulevard* less enthusiastically as "20 former stars who are still interesting to many a picture goer."[91] *Variety* sourly makes note of the benefits to exhibitors in "many a sales angle that should appeal to the fans who have a yen for Hollywood info and would like a glimpse of this Bagdad."[92]

These stars were relics not only of another era but also of another mode of celebrity. As Gamson notes, "pushed by the development of sound and film realism . . . the presentations by the 1930s had become more and more mortal."[93] To forge a connection with the masses of moviegoers, film stars were portrayed as ordinary people in extraordinary situations: when not swanning around on set, they cooked their own meals, visited the lunch counter, or played baseball on the lot. At the same time, fan magazines had begun to make fans savvy to the teams of studio publicists and employees who surrounded these stars to perfect the projection of their glamorousness.[94] These cameos were not just about cross promotion; they presented a sophisticated use of cameos to invoke the memories of fans for the recent, carefree past when these stars were at the height of their fame.

Unlike previous films, the has-beens were hailed as "this picture's dependable interest creating assets."[95] Admittedly, the film offers a typical shout-out to studio affiliation as the has-been greets Paramount star Gary Cooper at a bar populated by other silent-era stars, naming him, but only by his first name. Elsewhere, the presentation of each star is more subtle than the intertitled introductions in *Show People*, relying purely on audience recall of the old-timers to the point where even *Variety* thought the stars were too difficult to recognize.[96] The cameos of fallen stars were not mentioned by name. Instead, they depended on the audience's powers of recognition, which were actively cultivated with promotions for the film such as the "Old Time Stars Recognition Contest."[97] While these actors were paid as bit players, as former stars they were instrumental in the film's marketing. Print ads for *Hollywood Boulevard* in 1936 framed the image of top stars and the title credits with little stars containing the names of the former stars briefly glimpsed in the background[98] (fig. 15). Press book copy saluted the number of remembered faces in *Hollywood Boulevard*. While left to audience recognition within the film text, these names were frequently mentioned in reviews and press releases, actively encouraging the kind of paratextual relationship to the film that Barbara Klinger associates with cinephilic digression.[99]

Like many earlier cameos, these roles were written for an interchangeable group of silent stars. Among the "fellow has-beens" who meet the tragic hero at the bar, the script names "three or four actors of former prominence.... Such persons as Jack Mulhall, Gaston Glass, Frank Mayo, etc. are recognized."[100] Several names of such former stars would be added and dropped to the cast list during production. Eventually the roles were filled by romantic leads of the silent era, Creighton Hale, Jack Mulhall, and Frank Mayo, star of *Hollywood*, each of whom who had continued to work on Poverty Row. As Read remarks, the decline of Mulhall had been documented in the smaller roles and poorer quality productions that he worked on, as he appeared in "more and more lowgrade programmers," making nine features between 1931 and 1934 that, while maintaining visibility, did so in a way that was "serving only to highlight his outmoded and antiquated screen persona."[101] Mayo's and Hale's filmographies follow a similar trajectory. Both actors were visibly declining: decline was part of their public persona. As big studios "were waxing nostalgic over the disappearance of stars from the silent cinema,"[102] the continued visibility of these stars in Poverty Row meant that their reappearance in studio films was all the more poignant. This sophistication points to a viewer who is not

Figure 15. At left, a dozen tiny stars contain the names of cameoists in this lobby card for *Hollywood Boulevard* (1936). Press image.

only able to recognize stars but also recognizes other signifiers of the film business: production values, studio affiliations, all of these indicators of star status. That being said, *Hollywood Boulevard* was far from a prestige picture, and cameos came cheap.

Hollywood was undergoing a period of transition in the 1930s with respect to its relationship to stars. Perhaps in light of the way that unfashionable stars had been cast off with the excuse of the advent of the sound era, many actors began to demand more power within their productions to decline roles in certain studio films, to refuse trades to other studios for large payments of which they saw minimal amounts, and to escape the claustrophobic hold of the traditional seven-year contract.[103] With the oversight of a new, semi-independent breed of agents, as early as 1935 many major stars were working in nonexclusive contracts.[104] The studios faced other challenges in the 1940s, including antitrust legislation that put an end to block booking that guaranteed the distribution of studio product, good and bad, into studio-controlled theaters, and gave them incentive to "amp up their efforts to establish some equity in the industry's working conditions."[105] Stars such as Bing Crosby and Frank Sinatra took control of the films they appeared in with shorter contracts and eventually their own production companies under the aegis of larger studios who served as distributors, where they were guaranteed not only their own salaries but also the profits from their own films.[106] Importantly for the cameo trend, these new agent-negotiated contracts also included provisions to avoid overexposure.[107] Perhaps reflecting this instability, Warner's *Hollywood Hotel* (1937) limited the appearance of movie stars to a literal parade of placards that call them out by name in the film's opening, using instead radio hosts, musicians, and writers in its ensemble cameos. Longtime free agents such as Chaplin and DeMille had made it their business to appear in cameos since the 1920s, benefiting from the visibility that these nods to their stardoms offered. Like the financial need of older stars contributed to their presence in cameos, financial and contractual independence was also a limiting factor.

In the 1940s, the last gasp of prestige studio ensemble cameos was completed under the united front of the war effort, as studios such as Paramount, Warner Brothers and MGM mobilized their stars in films for the troops that harkened back to the Hollywood-set glamour of the 1920s. In *Follow the Boys* (1944), Eddie Cantor even did a double role as himself and a lookalike GI who ends up embroiled in a show for the troops. Bumpkins, such as *Hollywood Canteen*'s (1944) serviceman-on-leave Slim, chat with stars Barbara Stanwyck and Jane Wyman "doing their bit to entertain the home front and servicemen based all over the world"[108] as they wait tables and run through nightclub acts for the troops. The soldier in question carefully verbally identifies even the most prominent stars by name, with a soft-focus close-up, often set up as a double take on behalf of the poor confused soldier, that establishes the star through their portrait (fig. 16) Despite their number, these star roles were interchangeably filled by any star who could sing, dance, and express a little sympathy for the boys over there in each studio's take on the genre. These cameos are barely more than portraits, standing out for recognition but offering a character-space that is only marginally infringed on by the narrative. Several studios had their own version of this kind of wartime Hollywood-set film, a spectacular send-off for the genre and the last time that bona fide stars could be mobilized en masse at studio command.

Figure 16. Slim is oblivious to Joan Crawford's charm in *Hollywood Canteen* (1944).

Sunset Boulevard

Sunset Boulevard is perhaps one of the most beloved Hollywood-set films of the twentieth century. The story of a declining silent film star seeking a personal and professional comeback through the energy of a young screenwriter, it owes much of its charm to its careful casting and ingenious mixing of the real and narrative space. Real-life movie screen siren Gloria Swanson plays the former silent star who imagines a return from her mansion to the Paramount soundstage under the direction of DeMille. The enigmatic silent film master Erich von Stroheim is her former director and husband turned zombie-like butler, and among her friends are the Waxworks, a trio of former silent stars. Grayson Cooke suggests that *Sunset Boulevard* is about the face presented for recognition, where "the face presents us with a scenario in which to examine the mechanisms of stardom and highlights the importance of youth and beauty to the star system."[109] While the main face is Gloria Swanson, the Waxworks likewise present their faces for recognition, comparison, and remembrance. Following Mathijs's definition, and considering the interplay of Woloch's character-space and character-system, the roles of Stroheim and Swanson cannot be considered cameos; as Swanson would lament, in the wake of *Sunset Boulevard*, she was associated more with the foibles of the disturbed, aging Norma Desmond than her own esoteric past and moderately successful present as TV personality and businesswoman.[110] The roles small enough to maintain their integrity as cameos, however, provide a good cross section of the type, including celebrities such as DeMille and Keaton but also less celebrated figures such as songwriters Livingston and Evans, who sing along to one of their hits during a party held at the lower end of the Hollywood social spectrum.

Sunset Boulevard was marketed as an insider look—one poster tag line read "Hollywood from the Inside."[111] Fans of the 1920s delighted in unspooling the Hollywood roman à clef, and fans of the 1950s were no different. While chroniclers of the film's history claimed that casting the Waxworks was part of Wilder's attempt to introduce "documentary realism," and "pseudodocumentary illusion,"[112] Wilder admits to a more fluid adherence to reality by suggesting the Waxworks add "a genuine flavor"[113] to the film. Rather than in documentary, its precedents are clearly in the Hollywood-set films of the 1920s and the adoring cameos of that era. Publicity surrounding the cameos pointed to the film's bids for realism, such as the use of real Paramount production stills of Swanson to decorate Norma's home. A 1949 article about DeMille's appearance before the cameras noted that the film had "more realism than is usual."[114] Audiences and fans of the film were likewise enthralled. Staggs points out that the Waxworks had in fact worked together, while Sikov recounts how DeMille changed his lines to make them more like himself, tying these cameos to the real world once again.[115] Even stars were not immune to the blending of fact and fiction that *Sunset Boulevard* gave. Nancy Olson, who plays the love interest of Norma's live-in screenwriter in the film, said of Hedda Hopper's cameo, "she appears in the sequence, but I had a feeling that she would have been there anyway."[116] The idea that Hopper belonged on set in the way that the Waxworks belonged at Norma's side indicated the way these cameos operated in both documentary and narrative space.

While the Waxworks have been written about extensively as exemplars of the nostalgic cameo, a brief look at their form within the movie helps to examine how the cameo was used to play on nostalgia and cinephilic detail. As Norma's hapless live-in assistant Joe, the narrator, introduces the Waxworks as her bridge group, a medium long shot shows a group of stately gray-haired players from behind, seated around the central Norma (fig. 17; fig. 18). Unlike earlier cameos, from *Show People* to *Hollywood Boulevard*, that presented subjects in long shots and primarily in groups, the scene breaks to close-ups of the individuals, revealing the Waxworks to be Buster Keaton, former DeMille leading man H. B. Warner, and Swedish-born silent star Anna Q. Nilsson, who made her own rounds in Hollywood-set films such as *Inez from Hollywood* (1924) and *Souls for Sale*. As Joe intones, they were "dim figures you may remember from the silent days."

There were undoubtedly many "dim figures" to choose from at the time, eager for work. The identity of the Waxworks in *Sunset Boulevard* was not integral to the film; the shooting script names the group only as "three actors of her period,"[117] although other proposed cameos of current figures such as humorist Abe Burrows and columnist Sid Skolsky are mentioned by name.[118] Many names appeared again and again in small roles of the time. Keaton writes that by 1951 there was new interest in once-forgotten stars, suggesting that

Figure 17. The Waxworks surround Norma Desmond in *Sunset Boulevard* (1950) . . .

Figure 18. . . . as their morose faces are revealed one by one.

"between one thing and another I was pretty much in business as an actor once more,"[119] not only in movies but also television guest appearances. Keaton may have been satisfied, but not all actors were as thrilled with the scraps the studio offered. Behlmer and Thomas quote the 1951 complaint by Elmo Lincoln, the original Tarzan, when he spoke bitterly about being feted at tributes and premieres for films that followed in the wake of *Sunset Boulevard* to the tune of hundreds of thousands of dollars of publicity, while even those with dialogue were often paid for at most the day player's rate of less than $60.[120] Among the Waxworks, Nilsson made $1,000 less than H. B. Warner for the same screen time.[121] These former stars knew exactly how they were being used. As Keaton wrote about a cameo as a waiter in a 1940 film, "the producer wanted a familiar face in that little bit and picked mine as the movie face hardest for fans to forget."[122] Warner had found similar character roles in the Capra films of the 1930s and 1940s.[123] The brevity of the cameo conjured all of the aura of the cinephilic detail, guaranteeing a nostalgic reaction from the audience, and all dividends of a long-ago investment in the star persona of a decade or more ago.

Sunset Boulevard reflects a weakened studio system in the type of actors it is content to represent as emblems of cinematic history, allowing other networks to be displayed. While Paramount's publicity department for the film prided themselves on returning stars such as Swanson who had excelled under their banner to the limelight, they were just as happy to sing the praises of longtime MGM star and, in more troubled times, employee, Keaton. While it has been reported that Swanson used her personal connections when she "coaxed" DeMille to appear as her former director, DeMille, "the story's one lasting success,"[124] did well by the arrangement.[125] The difference between the cameos of the forgotten and the remembered was marked in the payment of DeMille, who received $10,000 a day and then demanded a new limousine when additional close-ups were required,[126] while Nilsson received $200 for her work.[127] While Sunset Boulevard referred to networks outside of the studio, it was also building intermedial networks. Hopper, who made $5,000, wrote about the shoot in her column,[128] while rival columnist Sid Skolsky gave the film bad reviews after his cameo was cut.[129]

Carefully chosen or not, like the fading stars of Hollywood Boulevard, the Waxworks' aged faces were important to the publicity of the film; indeed, still photographs of Swanson with the almost-silent foursome were included in the press book, and their floating heads appeared in some versions of the print ad in miniatures descending in size from the prominent portraits of Swanson to Stroheim through less players[130] (fig. 19). Sunset Boulevard used the strategy of naming cameos in releases while not in the film, as in the case of the Waxworks. DeMille and Hopper insisted on billing above the three characteristically wordless silent stars, although all were credited "as themselves" in ads produced by Paramount. Strangely, Franklyn Farnum, an early two-reeler western star similarly credited, played the undertaker, a role he did not reprise from real life.[131] Obviously, whether Farnum appeared in a fictionalized role or not, he was enough of a kind with the silent stars to be recognized for his public persona rather than the bit part he was cast to play. In the Sunset Boulevard program, framed as a gossip magazine, one "item" cited these actors as "stars we all remember, from what seems like a thousand years ago,"[132] and, in a selection of photographs illustrating the film synopsis, a single close-up appears among the group shots. Transformed from the static scene where Keaton breaks the silence with a single word into a portrait,

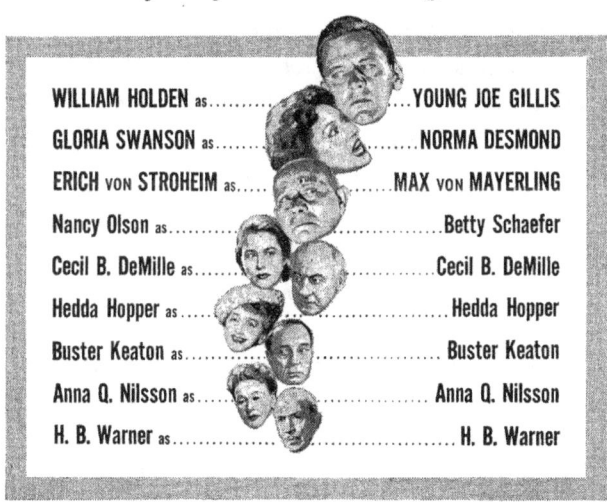

Figure 19. The Waxworks' half-remembered faces feature prominently alongside the film's stars in this ad from the *Sunset Boulevard* press book.

as a cameo so easily is, Buster Keaton's unattributed face is captioned with an echo of the film's script that identifies him only as one of the "dim figures you might remember from *Broken Blossoms* or *Ben Hur*."[133] While still a portrait, this less obvious nostalgic cameo represents a change in the work of recognition, the level of familiarity with the workings of Hollywood, and the relationship of fans to movie history.

Star Studded: The Cameo Fad

In the 1950s, there were more and more opportunities for forgotten faces to be unearthed and re-recognized. Television made old movies visible again as studios' back catalogs were handed over en masse to studio-owned stations and affiliated networks to fill out empty broadcast time, bringing even the most ephemeral stars such as *King Kong*'s (1933) Fay Wray back into the public eye.[134] *Sunset Boulevard* seemed to mark the end of glamorous, unproblematic cameos, as the cameo transitioned out of the ensemble portrait, at least in the hands of the studio. The film saw a wake of imitators such as *The Star* (1952), starring Bette Davis, and the Judy Garland remake of *A Star Is Born* (1954) documenting the decline of stars as a reflection of the decline of the star system. It sparked a "rash" of raw Universal behind-the-scenes pictures such as *Hollywood Story* (1951) with ensemble cameos that featured only the forgotten and the fading.[135] Yet, while studios no longer "trotted out"[136] their stars, producers trained in the studio system who operated outside of the newly humbled studios saw a use for the latest nostalgic iteration of the cameo as a reflection of power and influence at a cheap cost.

Cameos were ideal for independent producers who were looking to keep costs low. While many productions would eventually be distributed by major studios, a film's financing was the responsibility of the producer. Divorced from studios as free agents and producers in their own right, stars were mobile and for hire. For established or even declining stars, the investment in publicity had already been made by the studios at the height of their power, and now independent producers could reap the benefits without the high price tag. Cameos were acknowledged as good publicity, as evidenced by their recurrent mention in film press books throughout the 1950s, from Keaton in *Sunset Boulevard* to Chester Conklin in *Son of Paleface* (1952) through to Jimmy Durante in *Pepe* in 1962. As publicity for *It's A Mad, Mad, Mad, Mad World* noted, the film was "populated with a cast which reads more like the roster of a major studio than the cast of a picture."[137] What's more, stars were willing to appear in cameos, and not just the old-timers. Newly independent stars wanted to promote their own images and collect their own earnings without the input of the studio. Freed from the bonds of studio, in control of their own bookings and their own earnings, the biggest stars made some interesting choices in the 1950s and 1960s in terms of capitalizing on their visibility. Independent producers took advantage of this unstable state of affairs by billing stars, new and old, alongside one another in cameo blockbusters of the 1950s and early 1960s. If there was no need for stars to reflect on the studio, there was the sense they were present to the personal glory of the producers. Mike Todd, George Sidney, and Stanley Kramer had seen critical and box office success in theater and under the studios, and now in their own films "only the big names were invited."[138] Indeed, publicity for a spate of independently produced films, *Around the World in 80 Days*, *Pepe*, and *It's A Mad, Mad, Mad, Mad World*, made liberal use of the cameo and adopted the leveling tactic of advertising forgotten stars as if they were current ones.

In the wake of television and loss of studio power, the 1950s saw the emergence of spectacular touring road-show movies such as DeMille's *The Greatest Show on Earth* (1952) and *Oklahoma!* (1955). These special films toured like a stage production, traveling town to town, commanding special prices and featuring a large fanfare with associated events at each special screening.[139] Vanessa Schwartz positions producer Mike Todd's travelogue *Around the World in 80 Days* within this tradition. Based on the Jules Verne tale of an English gentleman who takes the bet that he can get around the world and back to London in just eighty days, picking up a French butler, an Indian maharaja, and a private detective, the film offered the opportunity to present itself as a travelogue populated with colorful characters, and filmed in a special wide-screen 70 mm format called Todd-AO. These small vignettes featured "world-famous faces that peek out everywhere in bit parts."[140] *Around the World* was a spectacle whose note began in production with a cast that grew daily and a budget that doubled to $6M during production.[141] It had its own lavish televised premiere with flowing champagne and live animals, "the last time a network picked up the tab for a publicity party,"[142] a commemorative program, and copious rounds of publicity that were as much about the exotic locales visited by the crew, the new ultra-wide screen format, and Todd's Odyssean task of casting the film as the film itself.¹⁴³ Monumentalism would become a common tactic in marketing these films, as the sheer number of stars provided the precedent to beset potential audiences with lists of other amazing expenditures and compendiums.

The term *cinema cameo* was used to refer specifically to the casting of major actors such as Frank Sinatra and Marlene Dietrich in small, non-starring roles, yet also carried the old-fashioned quaintness of two-reelers and grandma's jewelry box that could reflect on the roles taken on by languishing stars with nevertheless recognizable faces such as Buster Keaton and Beatrice Lillie. Todd harnessed the concept of the cameo, adopting the parameters of brevity, recognition, and reversal of the expected division of character-space; he made a lasting impact on the use of the term *cameo* by insisting that all of his cameos were stars. While until this point the term *cameo* had been reserved for performances that were outstanding because of their ability to fill small roles with the nuance and authenticity usually reserved for larger ones, these small roles were about harnessing the public personas of Keaton, Lillie, and Sinatra rather than having them develop complex character-spaces within the character-system of the film. Todd's publicity campaign inextricably linked star power and small roles to the word *cameo*. Every small role in *Around the World* was played by a star, even if in name only, because in press releases and interviews surrounding the film, cameos were linked irrevocably with stars. Todd insisted that if they were playing a cameo, they had to be a star. Todd linked cameos purely with stars in the same way that portraits were once purely the province of kings, reinforcing the relationship between visibility and celebrity but using a term and concept that predated his marketing campaign. In this way, the cameo came full circle.

Todd actively cultivated the idea that each role was cast based entirely on the public persona of a star, where "each star fit the part of the story."¹⁴⁴ Todd directed the audience to find the 'real' in the public persona of the celebrity, the public face and attendant biography instantly recognized by fans. Like his insistence on on-location shooting, Todd's cameos were part of his quest to share documentary and narrative space on-screen.¹⁴⁵ In Sinatra's Barbary Coast scene, Marlene Dietrich mashes up some of her most famous caricatures as the saloon girl marooned in the Orient while Sinatra plays the piano and her boyfriend, George Raft, does his best tough guy impression, coin toss included. Todd has Sinatra play a musician "not because he's Sinatra but because when he sits down at that piano, a bowler on his head and garters on his sleeves, he's for real."[146] Taking up where *Sunset Boulevard* left off, these cameos are not mentioned by name. They are melding the traditional cameo as a stand-out role with the idea of the star cameo, finally fulfilling Mathijs's definition as their universally recognized public persona makes them recognizable despite the narrative space they live in.

Todd's cameo, "a gem carved in celluloid by a star,"[147] builds on precedents in film and theater. There are even more direct linkages: the 1923 film *Souls for Sale* includes in its opening a prominent and lingering close-up of a cameo pin as it is stolen from the hapless heroine on her journey to Los Angeles, a piece referred to as "homely" in the original intertitles.[148] This homely jewel befits the wide-eyed bumpkin the heroine proves herself to be as she stumbles into fame, echoing the cameo's changing position in pop culture from the merely antique to the antiquated. With the decline of the two-reelers sometimes called cameos by the end of the 1920s, the cameo stood for the old and the passé in film form as well as fashion, and, in a few short decades, was resurrected as an emblem of nostalgia and fond remembrance. Show business continued to use the term for small parts, as exemplified in continued use of "stand out like a cameo" in the 1940s as well as the identification of "cameo roles" in the 1951 British-studio-set Crispin novel, *Frequent Hearses*.[149] When producer Mike Todd popularized the term *cameo role* in 1956, he reunited the industry use of the term *cameo* with the nostalgia recalling the early days of film-going culture in name and form, for the kind of short two-reelers in which his oldest stars appeared. Recalling the early days of film-going culture in name and form, as Schwartz writes, "winking at the early days of the movies" in sequences that homaged the western, the adventure rescue film, and slapstick as well as the inclusion of the Méliès film *A Trip to the Moon* (1902).[150] In fact, the marketing for the film draws explicitly on the associations of cameos with the past, echoing not only the more recent idiom but also he fashions of the 1880s that brought the cameo to popularity. In the commemorative program that accompanies the film's release, all roles are listed alphabetically in the back of the book, complete with an illustrated portrait in profile and a brief biography that mimics the aesthetic of the cameo in its nineteenth-century incarnation. Indeed, following in the steps of the studios, this film revived a few old-time stars such as Beatrice Lillie and the ever-present Buster Keaton, calling on nostalgic viewing.

The brief vignettes of *Around the World* mean that there were many, many cameo players. As a result, all cameo players were lumped together as being of one order, a fact that did not sit well with current stars who found themselves in parts comparable in size to older has-beens. Lists of cameos were circulated to the press with claims that from Mike Mazurki to Sir Cedric Hardwicke to John Carradine, the cameos featured "44 well known film stars"[151] (fig. 20). The alphabetical program listing gives some indication of the mixture of stars and plebeians; obscure British stage actors, lesser silent stars, character actors, and major box office draws are all jumbled together democratically. Todd explained away this strategy with the insistence that "only a real top name could afford to take alphabetical billing,"[152] although this would cost him the participation of Maurice Chevalier. MGM refused to release both Elizabeth Taylor and Alec Guinness for cameo roles, fearing that the appearance of these top-billed stars in small roles would undermine their stature. Following the logic that stars played feature roles and extras or character actors played bit parts, MGM did not want to damage their assets by billing them alongside older or little-known actors such as Bea Lillie and Sir Cedric. Loaning out stars was usually a profitable enterprise, but in this case, Todd's often impoverished production offered the studio a day player's rate, wooing instead the stars themselves with gifts in kind.[153]

Carefully grooming their stars was part of the studio guarantee, whereas these one-off collaborations with independent producers such as Todd did not need to protect or preserve the star as an investment. Todd was concerned with one-time visibility, and rather than reflecting on the studio brand, he reflected that glory on this film and himself. Studios may well have worried about the damage done to their stars, as the leveling seems to have succeeded almost too well. Schwartz reports the *Los Angeles Times* commenting about the ensemble nature of the performance, disappearing into the film "so perfectly do they lend color, vitality, and authenticity to Mr. Todd's mighty spectacle."[154] The biography written with Todd's blessing during this marketing tour crows about how he "sweet-talked the women and fast-talked the men and conned them all"[155] into working for a pittance, an exercise in egotism to which other cameo directors would fall prey. He even joked about taking advantage of an old-time western star who "so believed the part I just paid him off with a campaign medal."[156] Cameo producers made sure that audiences knew that each star face briefly appearing

CAMEOS

CHARLES BOYER (M. Gasse, Clerk, Thomas Cook, Paris). Born in Figeac just before the turn of the century, Charles Boyer was educated in Paris at the Sorbonne and the Paris Conservatory. He made his stage debut in 1920 in *Jardin des Murcie* and for the next fifteen years his professional activities alternated between the French stage and screen. His Paris plays include *L'Homme Enchaîné* and *Galerie des Glaces Melo*.

In 1935 Mr. Boyer went to Hollywood where he quickly became one of the most popular leading men. Among his more memorable pictures are *Mayerling*, *Back Street*, *Love Affair*, *Algiers*, *Hold Back the Dawn*, *Arch of Triumph*, and *The Earrings of Madame de—*.

He made his Broadway bow in 1948 in *Red Gloves*, has since appeared with the First Drama Quartet in *Don Juan in Hell* and in *Kind Sir*. Boyer has also been seen in many television programs.

JOE E. BROWN (Station Master, Fort Kearney). A native of Holgate, Ohio, born in 1892, Brown ran away to join the circus at the age of nine. After playing professional baseball for several seasons, he entered show business in earnest, touring in *Listen, Lester*, then in vaudeville and later starring on Broadway in such productions as *Greenwich Village Follies*, *Betsy Lee* and *Captain Jinks*.

Brown went to Hollywood in 1928 and has been making pictures ever since. For three years he was one of the top ten box-office stars. His movies include *Burlesque*, *On with the Show*, *Hold Everything*, *Elmer the Great*, *A Midsummer Night's Dream*, *The Daring Young Man* and *Showboat*.

Some years ago he returned to the stage to play *Harvey*. In 1953 Brown was tapped for TV's "This Is Your Life" program.

MARTINE CAROL (Girl in Railroad Station, Paris). The epitome of French femininity, Mlle. Carol was born Maryse Maurer in Biarritz in 1924. She attended schools at Pau and Neuilly-sur-seine, studied piano and painting. In 1941 she made her stage debut in Paris.

Two years later her phenomenally successful cinema career began with *La Ferme aux Loups*. Since then she has appeared in some thirty films. She quickly became the highest paid actress in France. In recent years she has starred in *Wedding Night*, *Love and Desire*, *Lucrezia Borgia*, *Adorable Creatures*, *Darling Caroline's Caprice*, *Madame du Barry*, *Nana*, *Lola*, and *The Diary of Major Thompson*.

In 1946 Mlle. Carol appeared on the stage in a French production of *Tobacco Road*.

JOHN CARRADINE (Colonel Proctor, San Francisco Politico). A native New Yorker, John Carradine was educated at the Episcopal Academy and Graphic Art School in Philadelphia, Pennsylvania, and at the New York Art School.

His dramatic career began at the age of nineteen in *Camille* at the St. Charles Theater, New Orleans, in 1925. Mr. Carradine then became a marine artist and portrait painter and subsequently a designer for Cecil B. de Mille.

In 1928 he launched his career in Hollywood, and subsequently appeared in the widest span of pictures, from Westerns like *Stagecoach* to musicals like *Alexander's Ragtime Band* and spectacles like *The Ten Commandments*.

Carradine returned to the stage in 1941. He toured with his own Shakespearean repertory company, and in 1946 made his first appearance on Broadway in *The Duchess of Malfi*. His other New York roles included Voltore in *Volpone*, Nyunin in *The Wedding* and the Ragpicker in *The Madwoman of Chaillot*.

CHARLES COBURN (Clerk, Hong Kong Steamship Office). Though born in Savannah, Georgia, in 1877, Charles Coburn more often than not has been mistaken for an Englishman. He attributes this to the fact that he received his training in Shakespearean drama and that he made his biggest hit on Broadway playing a British tommy in *The Better 'Ole* for two years during and after World War I.

He began his career as a program boy at the Savannah Theater at the age of fourteen. He first appeared on the New York stage at the Fourteenth Street Theatre in 1901 in *Up York State*. Several years later he organized the Coburn Shakespearean Players, which he and his wife, actress Ivah Wills, maintained for many years.

Mr. Coburn moved to Hollywood in 1938. Since then he has contributed many notable cinema characterizations, especially his role in *The More the Merrier* for which, in 1943, he won the Academy Award as the best supporting actor.

In 1946 he reappeared on the stage, touring for the Theatre Guild as Sir John Falstaff in *The Merry Wives of Windsor*. He has supervised the annual Mohawk Drama

51

Figure 20. The program for *Around the World in 80 Days* (1956) illustrated the cameo's fusion of ostensible star power and nineteenth-century decorative art.

on-screen, new or old, pointed back to the power of the filmmaker in a way that it had once reflected on the studio.

Around the World in 80 Days was a hit, and the cameo fad was born. Admittedly, cameos were just one part of the film's marketing success; the new super-wide screen Todd-AO process, the charismatic Todd's relationship with Elizabeth Taylor, and then his astonishing death all helped to keep the film popular as it toured in the years following its production. However, there is no doubt that other films that modeled themselves on *Around the World* took the cameo as the hallmark of its success. Yet there were doubts whether the supposed prestige of the cameo as defined by Todd was universally accepted. Follow-up films took the idea that stars could appear in small roles while still being stars rather than taking the first steps in a slide down the Hollywood hierarchy that had already been completed by Buster Keaton or Joe E. Brown. While Todd cast his roles as written, *Pepe*, a more typical Hollywood-set rags-to-riches story starring Mexican comedian Cantinflas, the valet sidekick from *Around the World*, as a star-blind bumpkin, indicated that "individual stars were approached for specific characterizations created for them in the story."[157] The emphasis on story above cameos set a pattern for marketing to come. *It's a Mad, Mad, Mad, Mad World*, a road-trip picture that followed a cast of comedians on the hunt for buried treasure, would reassure audiences that, alongside scores of smaller roles by actors of the past "who once shone as bright as the novas"[158] such as Zasu Pitts, Edward Everett Horton, and the 3 Stooges, "15 brilliant comedy virtuosos were signed to portray them . . . no cameos or vignettes these; every one a starring, picture-length characterization."[159] Yet publicity also emphasized the nostalgic cameos as belonging to a comedy paradigm that was antithetical to feature-length narratives, advertising the film as "a resumé of references to the comic tradition" and "an album of comic players . . . homage to classic American comedy"[160] (fig. 21). Keaton's *Mad World* cameo as a boat captain was cut down to non sequitur brevity and, once again, to characteristic silence, but he was featured in many press photos with the cast, including those for scenes in which he did not even appear.[161] The final knell for cameo films came in the reception of the star-studded 1965 film *The Greatest Story Ever Told*, where cameos such as that by John Wayne broke with the story in a way that was "shattering and distasteful."[162] In these final iterations, ensemble cameos were seen as drawing attention away from the narrative, switching out character spaces developed within the narrative to

Figure 21. Buster Keaton's face appears alongside both stars and cameoists on the cover of the *It's a Mad, Mad, Mad, Mad World* (1963) program.

the greater good of the story for the ready-made character spaces of public persona and pop culture appeal.

Like earlier Hollywood-set studio films, *Around the World*, *Pepe*, and *Mad World* tried to astound with the number of stars in each film. Posters for both films featured large illustrated masses of star caricatures, tumbling over each other in a confusing melee of action.[163] As with *Around the World*'s sets of cameo illustrations, the *Pepe* program is punctuated by pages of yearbook-style headshots, while those of *Mad World* are laid out in groups of descending size.[164] The number of cameos, made possible by their brevity and the independents' creative system of payment, meant that many stars could be used in a single film. Rather than thrilling at the brief encounter, critics and audiences had turned against the cameo as a simple portrait of their favorite stars. Instead, they saw the brevity and the "surfeit of celebrities"[165] as "embarrassing,"[166] especially when, as with the Voice of Judy Garland in *Pepe*, it didn't even guarantee their actual presence in the film. Numbers may have astounded in *Show People*, but by the 1960s there was a glut, lining up the same old-timer faces for a nostalgic appeal that began to harken back not to the ever-more-distant era of the silents, but only as far as the most recent cameo film. Where cameos had fed a desire to see stars in their natural habitat in the 1920s, and thrilled at their return to visibility in the 1940s and 1950s, by the 1960s audiences were increasingly savvy to the manufacture of stardom and the economic conditions driving the appearance of their beloved stars. Audiences were no longer dazzled by stars' visibility, and when cameos entirely overwhelmed a film's narrative, the opportunity to exercise their powers of recognition provided little in the way of cinephilic reflection for fans.

3

INSIDE LAUGHS

Comedians and the Casual Cameo

In the 1960 Hollywood-set rags-to-riches film *Pepe*, crooner Bing Crosby drives out of a nameless studio and into a cameo. Idling at the arches of the studio entrance, he is met by the title character, a Mexican peasant played by the popular comedian Cantinflas who is adrift in Hollywood in search of his best friend. As Crosby launches into a somewhat lackadaisical medley of his favorite hits while waiting for the porter to bring him his mail, he proceeds to harmonize with Pepe on "South of the Border" (fig. 22). Despite his ability to pick up on the tune from Crosby's few mumbled lyrics, Pepe has no idea who Crosby is, and is more angered than honored that a generous Crosby has signed his proffered tortilla. Even more perplexed is Crosby himself, as Pepe proceeds to eat up his valuable signature. The

Figure 22. Bing Crosby sings along with Cantinflas in *Pepe* (1960).

unrecognized Crosby drives off, only one in a string of celebrities that Pepe the bumpkin fails to acknowledge as unmistakably famous.

Crosby's puzzlement is understandable. During his encounter with Pepe, Crosby drops a series of references to the trademarks of his star persona. Talking with the porter, he reveals he might have a part in his next movie for poor, struggling Bob Hope, the other half of his comedy duo that performed in the *Road* series in the 1940s and 1950s. This seven-film series featured Hope and Crosby as vaudevillians traveling the world through mishaps that pitted them against exotic evildoers with designs against their perennial love interest, Dorothy Lamour. The *Road* films pioneered a style of comedy that placed Hollywood as the butt of its own jokes, with specific callouts of contemporary actors, directors, and producers in gags, wisecracks, and a series of prominent cameos. At the same time, this partnership began a series of cameo trades that resulted in Crosby's appearance in Hope's films in sequences full of mutual derision. Seen as witty and unprecedented insiderisms in the 1940s, by the 1960s the cameo trades had lost their steam. This Crosby cameo in *Pepe*, which did not include Hope, was panned as one more excessively bad performance in a poor and long-winded film stuffed with lazy cameos. Yet, it has all the ingredients of a successful Crosby cameo of the earlier period: a famous star playing himself in a comedy, inside Hollywood references, the nonchalant air of improvisation, and, of course, a zinger at the expense of Hope. The laid-back air that was cultivated in Crosby cameos in Hope films in the 1950s was lazy and "just plain embarrassing"[1] in the *Pepe* appearance. How did these cameos, which were so enthusiastically received by audiences in the 1940s, go from inciting audience to "howls of glee"[2] to having critics bemoaning another installment of yet more "dreary inside japes?"[3]

Bob Hope and Bing Crosby used the casual cameo to establish their double act in the 1940s in much the same way that Chaplin and Broncho Billy had traded cameos in the 1910s. Unlike Chaplin cameos, their partnership exceeded studio bounds, with Crosby appearing in Hope movies made for rival Goldwyn Productions as well as their home studio of Paramount. The strength of their partnership trumped studio ownership of their comedy act. These 1940s cameos transformed Hope's and Crosby's work as actors under the control of big production companies into unalienated labor that transcended studio ties, an important signal in the disintegrating studio system. Later double acts, such as Martin and Lewis and larger groups such as the Rat Pack, emulated these cameo trades, appearing in diegetically disruptive roles that called attention to the partnership and away from the plot. The loose narratives Hope and Crosby as a former radio MC and a singer appeared in allowed plenty of room for jokes, gags, and musical acts rather than character development. Cameos were just one of the ways in which what Seidman calls comedian comedies broke with the norms of classical Hollywood film by calling attention to the comedian's public persona, emphasizing performance above narrative.[4] Beginning with Hope and Crosby, but continuing into comedies of the 1950s and 1960s, these cameos were billed as afterthoughts, inside gags, and jokes at the expense of the director, the production, and, by extension, the studio.

With the advent of television, the movie theater was no longer the only place where audiences were promised movie star sightings. As gossip magazines uncovered lurid details about stars in the 1950s, and television talk shows featured interviews with celebrities promoting their upcoming films, audiences were treated to new takes on the Hollywood star beyond the cinema screen. Hollywood struggled with the question, why would audiences continue to go to the cinema? Casual cameos competed with television access by providing performances that disrupted the status quo of scripted film appearances, showing intimate, seemingly spontaneous, and often unflattering depictions of celebrities that were nevertheless carefully controlled. Unlike cameos that presented movie stars in appropriate roles, the casual cameos disrupted the plot to encourage an engaged, cultish relationship between viewers and the moving image. Films are embraced as cult because they are narratively unstable, allowing audiences to repeat and assimilate the film's nonstandard elements for performative pastiche and parody.[5] Movies that present disruptive moments ready-made for cinephilic contemplation, such as the cameo, undermine their own structure, reconciling nominally private instances of cinephilic reflection with the mass viewing practices that create a cult object. While cinephilia depends on memories of the viewer's private world, cult emphasizes a shared fictional world, where, as Eco writes, "adepts of the sect recognize through each other a shared expertise."[6] Adept moviegoers no longer stopped at simply identifying favorite stars; instead, they could use the casual cameos of double acts to learn more about the film industry and its partnerships and peccadilloes. Cameos created a cultish experience for viewers.

While these casual cameos were surprising and thrilling in the 1940s and 1950s, the easygoing attitude these cameos professed was problematic for viewers. Press that emphasized cameos as marks of friendship rather than pure publicity and gave misinformation about how cameoists were remunerated shows the industry's conscious decision to make cameos seem less like part of the film business and more like favors among friends. As the 1960s dawned, cameos, whether casual and irreverent or nostalgic and laudatory, came to be characterized as laziness on behalf of actors, directors, and producers cashing in on their cultish thrill. Perhaps the originators are to blame: Crosby, the "effortless" crooner, struggled with public perception of his laziness based on his underdressed, easygoing persona and love of leisure pursuits like golf and horse racing.[7] Yet, undoubtedly the question of acting as labor is wrapped up in the 1960s cameo fatigue. In film, the labor of acting is often invisible by design. Thanks to the camera's ability to represent documentary space, film acting is sometimes transparently reduced to simple presence. The performance of ease, such as that of Crosby in his laid-back cameos, was often read by audiences as easy work, or no work at all.[8] To these audiences of the 1960s, casual cameos were no longer a challenge to the status quo. More revealing views of stars could be had elsewhere, and as actors became free agents, building a stand-alone persona outside of the old studio system became a normal part of the new economics of the film industry. Those following in the footsteps of Hope and Crosby found that the kind of cameos that had been marketed under the umbrella of friendly impromptu kidding eventually crossed a threshold where they were panned by critics as lazy, easy, and, sometimes, too much fun.[9]

Casual, comedic cameos depended on their disruptive power to engage audiences eager to participate in the construction and deconstruction of star personas. When they ceased to be groundbreaking, comedic cameos experienced a backlash against the happy-go-lucky lifestyles they supposedly revealed. Freed from the oversight of studios, actors such as Crosby and Frank Sinatra became serial cameoists, driving widespread fatigue with roles that newly clued-in audiences had recognized as little work for welcome perks and enormous marketing potential. In 1960, Bing Crosby, whose initial cameos had thrilled audiences and critics, discovered that performances along the same lines, such as his cameo in *Pepe*, no longer resonated with viewers. Cameos were seen as symbols of decadence in a filmic landscape that was turning toward new standards of narrative and of acting as the New

Hollywood redefined performance and realism in fiction film. Without its claim to insouciant insiderism or the power to disrupt and reveal the Hollywood machine, the cameo had no attraction for savvy audiences.

Just Friends: Selling Comedy Duos with a Casual Cameo

The belief that film can represent the world as it really is depends on obscuring acting as labor. While the mannered acting of Lillian Gish or Mary Pickford may seem far removed from effortlessness to viewers today, as Nacache notes, what is perceived as natural is culturally and historical contingent.[10] Early twentieth-century film acting reflected the training of theater actors who were initially recruited to bring their skills to the screen as both stars and extras. Typecasting, where theater actors were assured of continued work based on a protectionist specialization in certain roles for which they owned costumes and scripts, was a guarantee of skilled experience. Yet, according to the fan magazines of the day, narratives of luck and perseverance were all that separated the film actor, and especially the star, from the ordinary person.[11] The natural endowments of expressive eyes or vampy looks were described as doing the acting as much as the actors themselves, and the star "appeared to be chosen quite randomly."[12] Naturalistic acting helped to conceal the labor of the actor, instead transferring the audience's attention to the intricacies of the drama.

Naturalism was sought off-camera as well. When cameos shifted away from perpetuating the glamour of early Hollywood, they were responding to the first swells in a "rising economy of realness."[13] Studio publicity machines turned away from ideal images of stars in an attempt to connect with skeptical audiences who had been cued in by fan magazines to the work of professional publicists.[14] As early as the 1930s, this realness was reflected in both the official and unofficial marketing of star personas, as new stars such as Judy Garland were photographed with baseball bats rather than the tennis whites donned in *Show People*,[15] and more sensational stories replaced innocuous biographical details in fan magazines and their gossip progeny. To make their lifestyles appear more typical, stars asserted their performance as a kind of labor. While the unique gifts of the star set them above the masses, their hard work is an experience to which ordinary people can relate. David Lusted suggests that, in order to reveal their ordinary labor, stars undermine their own performances by participating in "regular demystification of the process"[16] of entertainment. At the same time, the unequal relationship between feted celebrity and mass audience is checked by the claim that fame is bestowed by the audience, asserting audience participation and control.[17] Cameos are never naturalistic, nor can they ultimately be subversive in their demystification of Hollywood because the spectator's attention is always returned to the narrative above all else.[18] However, the cameo calls on the intersection between narrative and documentary space, exposing film performance as a record of labor defined most obviously by presence and its visibility. Audiences contribute their labor too, working to fill in the details of character-space that surround the cameo's brief performance.

Audience labor is at the heart of cult appreciation, as fans seek out opportunities to interact with the on-screen world.[19] Mathijs asserts that the cameo has "high cult potential," especially when it is recurring, presenting a "cult supertext stretched across films."[20] Cult exists in dialogue with other texts in different media, encouraging intertextuality that shapes reception beyond the limits of the movie,[21] where audiences "break, dislocate, and unhinge" elements of the film from their moorings within the diegesis.[22] The cameo is intrinsically intertextual, drawing on movies or studio and fan publications to allow the audience to fill out the cameoist's character-space. In fact, the cameo as a kind of role was first established through metatexts that commented on the film, such as reviews and publicity that notified audiences of the stars they were about to see in publicity campaigns from *Hollywood Boulevard* to *It's a Mad, Mad, Mad, Mad World*.[23] Cameos demand the response of recognition from the audience, encouraging their participation in becoming adept fans. Cameos, both disruptive and for a mass audience, exist at this intersection of cinephilia and cult.

If cult is bumpy and unhinged, then comedy is a natural home for cult, especially the disruptive comedian comedy in which cameos abound. Steve Seidman positions the comedian comedy as a genre that centers on an "already recognizable performer with a clearly defined extrafictional personality"[24] who appears within a fictional universe in which he must confront and attempt to adhere to social norms and boundaries. Comedians like the Marx Brothers, Lewis and Martin, or, more recently, Jerry Seinfeld or Jim Gaffigan, work in this genre. Drawing from the off-screen star persona of the comedian, comedian comedies owe more to the nonnarrative comedy routines of vaudeville than classical narrative film, and they largely abandon causal motivation.²⁵ Comedian comedies unite both performing and acting, a dichotomy that Nacache establishes based on whether or not the actors in a diegesis address themselves to the audience or work to construct a fictional world that excludes viewers.²⁶ Indeed, comedian comedies reflect the performing codes of early cinema based on gags, jokes, and the jolt of the cinema of attractions.²⁷ Comedian comedies are perfect sites for the cameo and its disruptive power, thriving on the art of distraction as they play with the norms that would make the star the center of attention, cueing audiences to watch the background for comedic details.²⁸ Like cameos themselves, the genre fell in and out of favor with audiences; after their anarchic zenith in the 1930s, comedian comedies experienced a crash when they were characterized as lazy in comparison to the more genteel narrative comedies.²⁹ Comedian comedies were seen as clowning, the antithesis of work, an accusation that would eventually be leveled at casual cameos as they migrated from comedian comedies to more staid narratives in the 1950s and 1960s. Within comedian comedies, the cameo used antinarrative and extradiegetic tactics to communicate the studio and performer affiliations that were their message.

Perhaps the best-known comedian comedies of the 1940s and 1950s are those of Bob Hope and Bing Crosby in the *Road* series. Beginning with Paramount's *Road to Singapore* in 1940, the series ended with a seventh and final installment, *The Road to Hong Kong*, produced in 1962 by both United Artists and the two stars. The series followed Hope and Crosby as two vaudeville entertainers who found themselves down on their luck in far-flung parts of the globe, invariably digging themselves even deeper into misfortune with their attempts to rescue an heiress, princess, or otherwise wealthy woman, usually played by Dorothy Lamour. As entertainers, they played characters not that far removed from their star personas as laid-back crooner and neurotic lothario, respectively, and their dialogue was peppered with jokes not only about their own achievements (Academy Awards) or lack thereof (Academy Awards) but also Hollywood quips of all kinds, from name-checking off-duty star eatery the Brown Derby in *Road to Bali* (1952) to calling out the politics of billing order in *Road to Hong Kong* (1962) (fig. 23). Hope and Crosby were among the top box office earners of the 1940s, and both were signed to Paramount, the studio behind almost all of the series. Not only their style was edgy. They were also on the forefront of star autonomy from studios in the 1940s. Beginning with their second picture together, both Hope and Crosby had special contracts that allowed limited nonexclusivity, including the right to make another picture outside of Paramount in the 1940s.[30] Following the success of the *Road* movies, Hope and Crosby used this option to make their fifth movie together, *Road to Rio*, in 1947, benefiting from Paramount as coproducers rather than employees.[31]

As performers, both Hope and Crosby came from a milieu outside of cinema. Their performances were heavily influenced by the platforms of radio and vaudeville where they had found their start. Hope in particular persisted with the style of direct address to the audience that had been a hallmark of the vaudeville performance.[32] In vaudeville, performance was more important than character and narrative.[33] The comedies made by double-acts such as Hope and Crosby and the duo of crooner Dean Martin and zany Jerry Lewis inherited vaudeville's antinarrative impulse, where a loose narrative linked together variety show spectacles.[34] Hope's trademark radio patter not only involved jokes about the stars and their private lives, introducing unusually prescient commentary on the real world as recognized by the audience,[35] but he frequently also laughed at his own jokes, a move that biographer Lawrence Quirk suggests encouraged an empathic relationship through a kind of "winking at the audience, as if to tell them he was enjoying

Figure 23. Typical Hope-Crosby ribbing in the title credits for *The Road to Hong Kong* (1962).

it as much as they."³⁶ Rather than creating a character who wisecracked about his imaginary life, Hope ribbed the celebrities that he and audiences knew.³⁷ In the 1940s, Hope was edgy, and his jokes were thought by many reviewers to make too many clever references to Hollywood insiders. Critics worried that the "close-in satire on Hollywood itself" was "likely to miss with Mr. and Mrs. Average Audience."³⁸ Irreverent and contemporary, his jokes about Hollywood movie stars and their private lives helped establish the trajectory for a new kind of comedy, delivered in a spontaneous style. As comedian comedies, Hope's movies were written around this style of direct address and interaction with real-world Hollywood as the audience knew it. In filmic terms, the direct address was translated into camera asides, but also diegetic rupture.³⁹ Cameos were the perfect extension of this style into the visual language of film, presenting the real-life stars that Hope was poking fun at as not only visible but also visibly complicit in the comedic reframing of their persona undertaken by Hope and his audience.

If audiences loved them, it may have been because Hope and Crosby were opening their movies up to cultish fan interactions. The combination of direct address and frequent industry jokes emphasized Hope and Crosby not only as film insiders but also as appreciative spectators, name-checking contemporary culture to demonstrate to the audience that they were not only movie stars but also movie fans.⁴⁰ In *Road to Rio*, the pair even champion cultish, antinarrative modes of viewing a screening onboard the ship that is carrying them to South America. There, they encourage Dorothy Lamour to attend not to the main action in the movie screened as the ship's entertainment but rather to the extras, among whom can be spotted Hope and Crosby in what are ostensibly their own cameos as moonlighting musicians. As in musicals, which confuse the production and consumption of entertainment, Hope and Crosby revealed the labor behind the film throughout the series, making references to the terms of their contracts, frequently chastising the studio they were working for, and taking every opportunity to illustrate that their far-flung locations were nothing more than studio soundstages. In *Road to Hong Kong*, they cry out for special effects to get them out of sticky situations, or even out of conspicuous clothes; in *Road to Utopia* (1946) they wax poetic about the famous Paramount mountain. They were undertaking the labor of skeptical spectators, who wanted to see through the images. In their performances, Hope and Crosby continually acknowledged the spectator. While "most actors must act unaware of the spectators in movies,"⁴¹

Hope and Crosby constantly referred to the audience, their performance, and the Hollywood movie industry. Their movies were "shot through with references to other movies (and to themselves *as* movies)."[42] Although Hollywood reviewers were themselves unconvinced that fans could have absorbed enough of the details that Hope and Crosby had been throwing at them to have a real familiarity with Hollywood, the duo and their writers were sure that audiences were interested in behind the scenes and beyond. Instead of leaving audiences to pick apart the production themselves, Hope and Crosby participated in the action, doing some of the work to make their inside jokes more accessible.

While their performances assured audiences that Hope and Crosby were laughing along with spectators at the Hollywood machine, their publicists were quick to confirm that the curtain was well and truly pulled back to reveal the industry at its most vulnerable. To do this, they made an effort to broadcast that while the sets were manufactured, and the plots prewritten, the laughs were real and the jokes spontaneous. Critics claiming to have made visits to the studio breathlessly reported the fun the two had on set,[43] perpetuating the story of Hope and Crosby as inveterate ad-libbers.[44] The identical accounts from journalists make it clear that the shenanigans were vetted if not entirely fabricated by Paramount publicists who recognized the value of the ad-lib anecdotes. Seidman has noted that the comedian comedy relies on both the recognizability of the comedian persona on- and off-screen and the assurance that the comedian's comedic energy is not only part of his public persona but his private persona as well.[45] The appeals to documentary space in the comedian comedy are meant to confirm for the audience that the comedian's impulse for zaniness has been subdued by the studio, if only briefly, for the audience's viewing pleasure.[46] Comedians are meant to be funny rather than act funny, which is why in the comedian comedy they can only play themselves. The power to ad-lib, or be naturally funny, was important to the marketing of the comedian and his films. On the other hand, Hope was known for having one of the biggest crews of gag writers; they produced his syndicated columns, memoirs, and his jokes for all of his many media appearances.[47] As Seife notes, "Though Hope's delivery is such that these lines sound like they could be improvised, his words appear verbatim in the final draft of the film's screenplay."[48] Even the Hope and Crosby feud was manufactured by Paramount writers in homage to earlier feuding comedians, and others have suggested that the friendship that underscored the rivalry was manufactured as well.[49] The indivisibility of their real and on-screen personas was important for the Hope and Crosby movies, yet at the same time, that reality had to be uniquely tied to their extraordinary talent as comedians. Even at the time, the *New York Times* suggested that this clowning was subject to financial concerns, noting that on *Road to Rio*, the first film in which Hope and Crosby arranged for profit sharing with Paramount by coproducing it themselves, the on-set ribbing was much less rampant.[50] Nevertheless, this promise of spontaneity and real-life kidding was part of the legacy Hope and Crosby bequeathed on cameos and their origin myths.

The Big Ones Don't Even Act: The Cameo and the Anti-narrative Impulse

The *Road* films were the original substance of the Hope-Crosby partnership, but their union grew to have significance beyond the series as it was promoted in radio, print, and in other movies through cameos. While Hope never appeared in any Crosby movies (although Lamour does turn up among a large group in a rather small airplane to sing along with Bing in *Here Comes the Groom*), Crosby was a fixture in Hope films, making six appearances in total beginning in the 1940s. His association with Hope continued even after the *Road* partnership dissolved, with Crosby making his last cameo, laughing helplessly as Hope goes to his presumed execution in *Cancel My Reservation* (1972). (The rivalry often took a macabre turn; this is the third Hope execution scene in which Bing's cameo is invoked.) These cameos were not identified as such until *Alias Jesse James* (1959), three years after Todd had established the links between cameos, celebrities, and small roles. The comedic playfulness of Crosby's appearances would come to be as influential on the model of the cameo as Todd's definition of the concept, which preserved the laudatory lineage of star appearances seen in *Show People* or *Sunset Boulevard*. The first Hope film that Crosby appears in, dating to the time of their second film in the *Road* series, *Road to Morocco* (1942), was *My Favorite Blonde*, a chase film where Hope is a suspected murderer. Dragging Madeleine Carroll along with him, he ends up at a union picnic, where he asks a bystander for a light. That bystander turns to out to be Bing Crosby, a fact that Hope's character first recognizes and then rejects in a protracted double take. Just like a spectator, Hope enacts the recognition of his partner, who appeared without introduction. Like other cameos of the time, this appearance allowed the audience to do the work of identification. Crosby's cameo and Bob's ability to recognize him indicate a willingness to disrupt the diegesis of the comedy film, transforming it into a characteristic comedian comedy.

The cameos continued. Crosby swoops in as a fellow swashbuckler to take Bob's girl in the finale of *The Princess and the Pirate* (1944). He steps in as a foiled executioner in *My Favorite Brunette* (1947); he drops in as a purported "character actor" in *Son of Paleface* (1956) and a sharpshooter in *Alias Jesse James* (1959), and he laughs at Hope in a dream in *Cancel My Reservation* (1972). Although the cameos may have been initiated to promote the films the duo made together, their growth as a signature of the pair clearly influenced the makeup of the series in the 1940s, as *Road to Rio* (1947) and *Road to Bali* featured increasing numbers of cameos by other actors. Owing to the precedents set by the Crosby trade, cameos became an important signifier of the *Road* series' brand of inside Hollywood jokes. Even when Crosby was absent, his visibility is invoked: Hope is warned that the rifles of a shooting squad will make what is described as a "bing" sound in *Monsieur Beaucaire*, leading Hope to some snide wordplay and his typical camera aside, while Bing's hit songs are the subject of jokes in *They Got Me Covered* (1943), *Where There's Life* (1947), and *Caught in the Draft* (1941).[51] As Hope says to the audience as Crosby croons over the radio in *They Got Me Covered*, "That guy keeps haunting me." These hauntings are like invisible cameos, carrying "the residue of various film roles."[52] Crosby's cameos were such a part of Hope's comedic identity that in *Son of Paleface*, he begins the film by mentioning that "this old character actor" will not be appearing. However, this voice-over accompanies a cutaway from the opening action at turn-of-the-century Yale to an image of Bing himself driving nonchalantly in a modern car, foiling Hope's attempt at mastering the situation. Cameos continually evade Hope's control; they are made to appear impromptu and unauthorized, exemplifying the feud between the two as Crosby appears taunting Hope in moments of failure or attempting to upset Hope's success. Yet, behind the aura of impromptu ribbing promoted in the film's uneasy documentary space was an extrafilmic narrative of mischievous cooperation. In the press book for *My Favorite Blonde* (1942), the first Crosby cameo was characterized as having its origins in a gag where Hope tried to sneak him on set under the director's nose, a joke the director turned on the duo by putting Bing to work.

Each cameo by Crosby in a Hope movie served to remind the viewer of the team of Hope and Crosby and their *Road* series.[53] Partnerships, new and lasting, were represented by cameos that kept the duo visible to audiences as a pair. In this way, cameos worked as usual in the marketing of a studio product. When the two appeared together in a cameo in Cecil B. DeMille's *The Greatest Show on Earth* in 1952, Crosby and Hope were among a crowd eagerly watching a circus performance from Dorothy Lamour, their regular *Road* costar. However, the Hope-Crosby pairing was more important than promoting studio affiliation, instead reflecting on the partnership itself as a media phenomenon that extended to other media and to other studios. Crosby appeared in a cameo in *The Princess and the Pirate* in 1944, a film produced by Goldwyn and Hope's one freelance film for that year as permitted in his contract. His appearance came despite the fact that the film was not only a production outside of Paramount but also one that was not directly benefiting from promoting the Paramount-produced *Road* movies.[54] What makes this cameo a particular punchline is not only that Crosby appears in a Hope film, but also that Crosby appears in a Goldwyn picture. As if to underscore this cross-studio appearance, Hope sets up the cameo by pointing out that Crosby is a bit player from Paramount, ending with the line, "This is the last picture I do for Goldwyn!" This was already the second Hope-Crosby cameo, yet in a special letter to critics, Goldwyn's publicist begged reviewers to keep this cameo a secret from audiences by refraining from mentioning it in their columns.[55] Crosby had already become a regular in Hope films, so his appearance in *The Princess and the Pirate* is surprising only because it flies in the face of studio allegiances. Only industry-savvy audiences who knew how jealously studios guarded their actors could be expected to be shocked at this cameo trade. Such cameos play to a sophisticated audience familiar with both the star's persona and the conditions of a film's production. Bob and Bing were still very much working in Paramount's interest, as this cameo promoted their partnership, which Paramount continued to profit from, and their freedom outside the studio was limited to a single major role per year. Yet this cameo allowed Hope and Crosby to assert to an industry-savvy audience that they were their own men. To audiences, these cameos reflected the triumph of unalienated labor, as actors worked openly for their own gain and personal reputation, throwing off the waning control of the studios and rejecting their interchangeability as stars.[56] While still confined to limiting contracts in the 1940s, Hope and Crosby were nevertheless publicly weaning themselves and their personas from the studio system.

The Hope-Crosby cameo trades developed into sequences that were more and more disruptive to narrative. In *My Favorite Blonde*, the first trade, the Crosby cameo was written into the script very late, appearing nowhere in the shooting script that was finalized a month before he appeared before the cameras.[57] Unlike many later cameos, his cameo was shot during regular production rather than after the main production was completed. Because Crosby was fully incorporated into the scene, appearing in a long shot that includes not only images of the milling extras but also other components of the union hall set, he had to be on set during shooting. Even so, the cameo was completed in less than an hour of shooting time. Two versions of the scene were shot: one with Bing and one without.[58] In this initial case, the cameo's disruption of the narrative was minimal. Yet, unlike earlier Hollywood-set cameos, where stars appeared in predictable settings such as studio lots or ritzy Los Angeles restaurants, Crosby appears in the unglamorous setting of a union picnic. Crosby's diegetically indeterminate role had one foot in the story and one foot planted in the real world of Hollywood. Many reviewers seemed taken aback by the cameo role, relying on laborious descriptions of the action to explain the laugh produced by the intersection of narrative and documentary space.[59] Writing about Crosby's follow-up cameo in *My Favorite Brunette*, one enthusiastic reviewer provided a shot-by-shot account of the exchange.[60] Other writers had more faith that, by the time of this second installment, audiences could juggle the cameo's meaning. As *Variety* noted, "Hope's impatient executioner turns out to be—you guessed it—Bing Crosby."[61] Hope and Crosby's comedy appealed directly to fan culture, and because fans had absorbed the cameo into their lexicon, Hope was in on the joke this time too. The on-screen Hope quickly transformed from the bumpkin who fails to recognize Crosby in *My Favorite Blonde* to the much-abused friend waiting on Bing's predictable mean-spirited interruptions. Like Hope, audiences quickly became tuned in to diegetic disruption.

Once audiences were trained to recognize Crosby's cameos, these small roles shrugged off any pretense to belonging to the narrative. The reasons for this were twofold: on the one hand, the breaks and starts made for comedic disruption; on the other hand, the pretense also allowed for efficient production of the cameos. Divorced from the narrative, these cameos allowed actors to report for shooting at any time convenient to them, using cutaways, reaction shots, and the ubiquitous driving sequence to create loosely diegetic scenarios that could be assembled using rear projection and other process shots after production had wrapped. Cameos were shot as process shots, for example, with rear projection in a car that allowed them to be cut into almost any scene with the use of some location footage thrown up on standing transportation sets. The car conceit was common. Crosby appeared in just such a cameo in *Son of Paleface*, where he is driving a car in a complete aside from the nineteenth-century setting. Likewise, *Mad World* opted to set the cameos of Jack Benny and Jerry Lewis in two highway driving sequences that required just a half hour of the star's time on set.[62] When Bob and Bing appear in the Dean Martin and Jerry Lewis comedy *Scared Stiff* in 1953, it is in a final cutaway to a previously unseen dungeon where the two are imprisoned, presumably as a result of an earlier, unsuccessful attempt on behalf of the heroine to enlist a goofy duo's help (fig. 24). Likewise, Martin and Lewis appear in *Road to Bali* in a silhouetted dream sequence that could have been shot anywhere. In *Alias Jesse James* in 1959, most of the cameos by western stars from Gary Cooper to the Lone Ranger were shot in the film's postproduction period. As the star's presence rather than his role in the narrative became the focal point for the cameo, the cameo's style was defined by the conditions of star convenience. Because cameos were not tied to narrative continuity, any open set became suitable for shooting, and any incongruous settings were disguised by close-ups. The cameo became more disruptive as a result of the pressures put on its production by the stars it celebrated.

Hope may have been the driving comedic force behind the *Road* movies, but Crosby's mellow star image influenced the cameos that publicized their partnership. In the 1940s, Crosby's persona was of the effortless crooner, whose public image was perpetually casual. The images that circulated of Crosby showed him dressed down and off-duty at the race track or with his family.[63] As Raubicheck points out, Crosby's image was so laid-back that Paramount felt the need to produce a campaign emphasizing his hardworking nature in anticipation of *Going My Way* in 1944, a drama for which he eventually won an Oscar for his role as an offbeat priest.[64] Crosby had been named as "the laziest man in Hollywood" in the preceding years, and his somewhat sleepy delivery as well as his style of crooning made his acting seem almost damnably

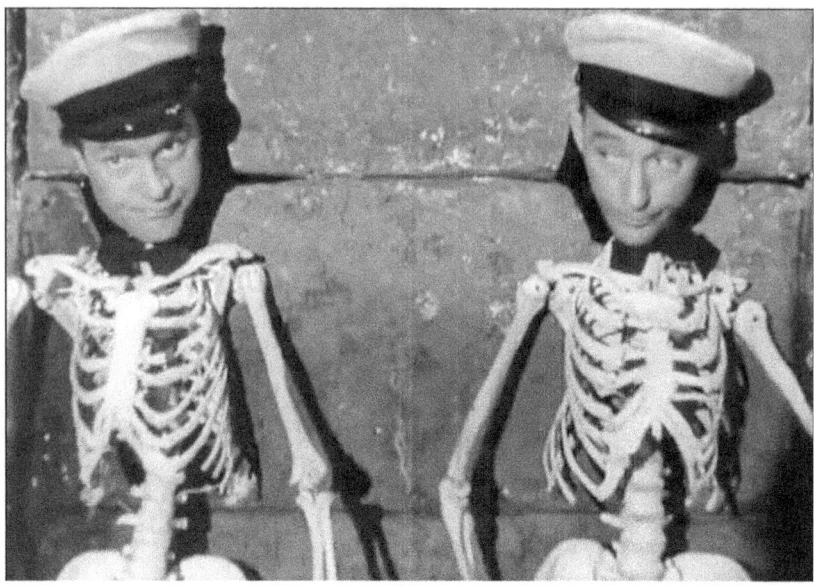

Figure 24. Crosby and Hope get the last laugh with their closing cameo in Martin and Lewis's *Scared Stiff* (1953).

effortless.⁶⁵ This assessment of his performance style persists: Cohan writes that Crosby's delivery in the *Road* series is "a performance so low-key it barely seems like he is acting."⁶⁶ The performances of Crosby and Hope were publicized as off the cuff and impromptu, drawing on their individual reputations for casual performance and direct address. For this reason, the cameos that Crosby presented were taken as advertised: as two jokers playing around on set, as their publicists made sure they were known to do. Improvisation and ad-libbing were an important part of the Hope and Crosby identity, and as the cameos became their trademark, the cameo became stamped with their brand of playful and effortless disruption.

Cameos, of course, did appear to be easy work. Certainly they were easy in terms of time demanded: Dorothy Lamour recounts how much she liked working on wartime roll-call productions such as *Stage Door Canteen* (1943), where "you came in, did your cameo, and left."⁶⁷ For stars, there was none of the waiting that defined extra work.⁶⁸ Once the cameo's disruptive nature was established, such roles became less and less demanding in terms of time dedicated on set, often shot after production was completed in process shots or tightly framed close-ups. On the other hand, the casual, easygoing relationships that Hope and Crosby had established as a representation of their working life meant that cameos were recounted as spontaneous, and, because they were as effortless as the comedians' own personalities, as easy as breathing. How hard was it to stand up and be visible as yourself? In the early days of the Hope and Crosby cameo trades, the emphasis was on the humbleness of the actor descended to a small part.

As performance, the Hope-Crosby cameo trades appealed to the audience's appetite for access to stars' lives beyond classical narratives. The competition and petty ribbing may have seemed out of place for the biggest box office draws of the 1940s and 1950s; certainly they didn't belong to the gracious Bette Davis or even Humphrey Bogart, but the laid-back nonchalance with which they purported to joke about not only their contracts but also their status as labor established Hope and Crosby as ordinary workers underneath all that extraordinary talent. Especially within the comedian comedy, the cameo exposes some of the contradictions between documentary and narrative space to the audience in a way that, like the polished backstage musical, invokes the film set as a work environment while concealing all but the most casual labor.[69] The archetype of the ordinary star with the singular talent has, according to Dyer, continued to be relevant to the making of celebrity,[70] even as audiences recognize that the ordinary star is yet another carefully constructed presentation. The desire to unmask the real person has driven much of the fascination with and demand for celebrities' increasingly intimate revelations. The Hope-Crosby cameo trades prefigure the tactics of "predictable spontaneity"[71] that are part of the visibility celebrities favored in supposedly candid environments such as interviews and talk shows. Yet, preserving the comedian comedy's "myth of the spontaneous clown,"[72] they conversely strove to show that their talent made their labor carefree and that the work of performance was not just easy but effortless.

In the *Road* movies, cameos reinforced extrafilmic relationships that savvy audiences recognized from fan magazines and past films. Hope's and Crosby's friends and colleagues Humphrey Bogart, Bob Crosby, Dean Martin and Jerry Lewis, Jane Russell and Jerry Colonna were among the many cameoists. These cameos disrupted the diegesis, consciously bringing in extradiegetic references to showbiz in a way that nostalgic cameos only hinted at. With the exception of Bogart, who appeared not in person but rather in a clip from *The African Queen* (1951) that was cut into the footage of a jungle-weary Hope and Crosby in Bali, these cameos feature artists with whom the duo worked on other films and broadcasts. Russell appears as Hope's romantic interest in the *Paleface* comedy-westerns, while Jerry Colonna was a longtime fixture of Hope's radio and television broadcasts who appears in several *Road* movies. Each of these cameos presents a diegetic break in the film, often combining references to other Hope films. Jane Russell is from a snake-charming basket in *Road to Bali* dressed in her saloon-girl costume from *Paleface*. Jerry Colonna, a Hope radio regular, appears in a "wild spot"[73] as the leader of a cavalry troop in *Road to Rio*, where scenes of him riding at full speed in an anonymous wilderness and with an unclear purpose were intercut with the main action. Bob Crosby's cameo turns up in the bush among the wandering Hope and Crosby in *Road to Bali*, suddenly shooting a gun at Crosby's say-so, who explains "I promised him a shot in the film." The same film contains a Martin and Lewis cameo where they intrude on the dreams of Dorothy Lamour, a "contractually agreed" favor returned by Hope and Crosby in their own Paramount buddy comedy, *Scared Stiff* (1953).[74] Other planned cameos were likewise narratively disruptive and more relevant to the world of Hollywood than that of the film: real-life upstart Sinatra stealing Crosby's limelight on the Brazil-bound ship in *Road to Rio*, or William Holden reprising his Asia-set roles of the 1950s in *The Road to Hong Kong*. Yet, some semblance of narrative had to be maintained; amid this sea of callouts, Crosby's cameos were the crowning disruption, and so limited to less intrusive points at the very ending or beginning of Hope's films.

Historically, comedy has been considered a low art, concerned with the mundane interactions of the ordinary class. For Neale and Krutnik, comedy is "founded on the transgression of decorum and verisimilitude, on deviations from any social or aesthetic rule, norm, model, convention or law."[75] According to this view, comedy revels in upturning the conventions of social interaction. The cameo acts out against the norms of classical Hollywood while playing out some of the internal contradictions of that form. Hollywood's claims to verisimilitude rely on the audience accepting its conventions, whether they are sets that make one place appear to be another or performances that profess one person as someone totally different. The cameo exposes the audience's devotion to a film's narrative space and its established rules. When Bing's brother Bob strolls across the soundstage version of the tropics in *Road to Bali* and claims he has dropped by simply to be visible, his appearance is funny. However, the punchline is not merely that Bob Crosby isn't supposed to be wandering around in the deepest darkest jungle, but that of course there is no reason why he can't be there—on set, in Hollywood—except by the logic established for the audience by the narrative's own conventions. Cameos call attention to the conventions of classical cinema and the rules established for the medium that govern who can appear on-screen and where.

While reviewers were excited to see nostalgic or glamorous cameos, not everyone liked the incorporation of cameos in the *Road* series. *Variety* claimed that "guest star appearances ... serve no other purpose than to get a laugh,"[76] while others warned that gags about Hollywood have a "strong local appeal that may puzzle the cowpokes on the Wyoming range."[77] Disruptive cameos were dismissed as "sudden irrelevant appearances."[78] What exasperated many of these reviewers, but drove audiences wild, were exactly the intertextual strategies of convergence that allow audiences to participate as viewers. As one reviewer wrote,

> If at some far future date historians should unearth a time-capsule containing this most recent of the Hope-Crosby junkets they would probably be able to make neither head nor tail of it, for that genial duo deals in an increasingly more rarefied form of strictly contemporary humor ... numerous lines and situations whose full enjoyment requires a knowledge of the pair's past pictures, off-screen activities, professional rivals, the personnel and format of their respective radio shows, and various other related subjects.[79]

Irreverent cameos by the likes of Bob Crosby and Jane Russell were an extension of the "gaggery"[80] that Hope and Crosby films traded in, and they required a complicit viewer who was fluent in the "strictly contemporary."[81] While to reviewers these were sloppy performances whose flat characters relied on star personas that they acknowledged were "so familiar to the audience that they automatically evoke a fuller image than the screen presents,"[82] to audiences the chance to fill in the character was itself a participative thrill. As a critic at the *New Yorker* had to concede, such cameos "obviously struck the audience as hilarious."[83] These cameos fit securely into the genre of comedian comedy, referring to the recognizable persona of the comedian and his cohorts outside of the film.

Trades and Tag Teams: Establishing an Entertainment Network

Cameos helped establish Hope and Crosby as a unit soon after their initial appearance as a duo in 1940, and their performances within the comedian comedy genre established them as men who couldn't help but be themselves. The cameos helped establish their reputation as kidders on- and off-set, bolstered by accompanying press releases that insisted the cameos were set up on the fly, taking advantage of good friends who happened to be on the lot. In this way, the logic of convenience by which early cameos were assembled, by now transparent to viewers who had become increasingly savvy about the business of film production, became a part of the marketing of each film. However, instead of assembling those who were present on-set by order of the studio or by deference to social obligations, the cameos that were arranged for Hope's movies represented friendship groups that were also entertainment units on radio, movies, and later television. Hope's cameo trades of the 1950s and 1960s included Jack Benny, Vincent Price, and Cecil B. DeMille, and he was scheduled to do walk-ons on *Gunsmoke* (1955–75) and *Tales of Wells Fargo* (1957–62) alongside the western TV stars who appeared in *Alias Jesse James*.[84] Jerry Colonna, a recurring and not-entirely-photogenic performer on his radio show since the mid-1930s who would be carried with the Hope entourage into television, had repeat cameos in Hope's films. Colonna's inclusion indicates the triumph of Hope's personal magnetism over studio diktat, whose doubts were expressed in his removal from secondary billing.[85] This narrative of personal power was continued in the story of Hope's role in Crosby's supposedly impromptu appearance in *My Favorite Blonde*. In a planned article from 1959 about the Hope cameo tradition's latest iteration in *Alias Jesse James* to be titled "Friendship in Show Business," Paramount publicity agents suggested Hope discuss how these cameos were done completely free of charge for old friends. Even some of the cameos mentioned in the draft seem more imagined than real, creating a pedigree of cameos from Bogey to Sinatra to Crosby, all done for free and out of the goodness of their hearts. In the *Son of Paleface* press book, it was mentioned as a point of pride that "one of the highest paid figures in the entertainment world" was "playing a bit part so small that any self-respecting extra from Central Casting would turn up his nose at it."[86] Publicity surrounding these cameos emphasized that personal kidding rather than contractual obligations steered these events.

Asserting that these cameos were unplanned, not only in terms of the production but also in terms of the budget, publicists spread the fiction that these small roles were uncompensated. No friendship it seemed was stronger than the friendship in which money was not an issue. As the *Life* article draft erroneously states, "All the western guys in *Alias Jesse James* were happy to do this for nothing. It all started way back in the early days of talkies when Hope got Bogart to do a guest spot for nothing in his movie then Crosby, then Jack Benny then Jerry Lewis, etc."[87] This is almost certainly untrue. Not only does the Bogart cameo date only to 1952 with *Road to Bali*, but also while Gary Cooper shot *Alias Jesse James* with no reported compensation, many of the other actors received other guarantees that made the small amount of work profitable.[88] When Todd offered cars, jewelry, and paintings to the cameoists in *Around the World*, he was following a tradition of gifts in kind, tax-deductible presents, and marketing trades that had perhaps begun with Hope. Dorothy Lamour was content to appear in Crosby's *Here Comes the Groom* (1951) in the type of small part she had rejected in the final *Road* movie as "only a cameo . . . a couple of pages of dialogue that an extra could have handled"[89] because "the money was certainly right."[90] Biographer Marx recounts that Bing asked for $25,000 for the *My Favorite Brunette* cameo, an amount that came out of coproducer Hope's pocket and became a tax deduction for Crosby when he donated it to his alma mater. To be fair, in some situations it does seem that Hope was promoting his own associates at the expense of the studio; for example, Paramount's producers were somewhat unconvinced that Jerry Colonna should be paid $7,500 for his single day of work on *Road to Rio*, where his previous work at Disney had been at a rate of only $2,500 a day.[91] Whether or not performers were compensated, these cameos were marketed entirely as visible declarations of friendship and support, made without the usual contractual and financial considerations. Unlike the studios, who could be confident in their control of actors on salary, buddies and partners did not ask one another for cash.

The Hope-Crosby cameo trades in the 1940s and 1950s strongly influenced the general function of cameos in film. While they existed alongside the developing nostalgic cameo, and perhaps influenced the explosion of ensemble cameo movies in the 1950s and 1960s, they carved a comedic niche for the cameo that not only called on documentary space to supplement narrative but that also entirely broke with it. The comedian comedy around which Hope and Crosby wove their cameos in solo projects and in the *Road* movies set a precedent for cameos as not just recognizable, but as fragments that stand outside of the diegesis. Likewise, the projection of an easygoing and spontaneous performance style reflected on the reception of the cameo. Because this is how they were marketed, these comedian cameos of the 1940s and 1950s were seen as informal trades among friends. Where Todd boasted about the small pay for which stars appeared in his cameo-filled *Around the World in 80 Days* in 1956 and the two following years of the film's promotion, Hope followed suit by claiming his friends did it all for nothing in 1959. Yet, while Todd emphasized the perfectness of the characters for his roles, Hope's friends were cast, or rather happened to waltz over to the set, merely because they were friends. These cameos were not so much about skill, but about spontaneity, luck, chance, and most of all, about happy-go-lucky palling around.

As another entertainment unit who doubled as friendship group, members of the Rat Pack found the cameo a useful technique for reinforcing their image. In the final moments of their last pairing in *Road to Hong Kong*, where Bing and Bob ended up moonside with Joan Collins, Frank Sinatra and Dean Martin drop in with cocktail shaker in hand to whisk her away. The girl-chasing Hope and Crosby had met their match in "the Italians," as the pair is identified. Where Hope and Crosby had left off in the mid-1950s with their previous *Road* film, Sinatra and his Rat Pack had picked up with their series of films starring their favorite friends. Sinatra and Crosby had their own crooner rivalry as the young buck and the old standby that played out on their television specials of the 1950s.[92] Martin had previously trod the same diegetically disruptive territory as Hope and Crosby in the hit madcap comedian comedies he made during his partnership with Jerry Lewis.[93] As a duo, Martin and Lewis eschewed cameo appearances in their own films, except at the behest of Hope and Crosby, perhaps because cameos were such a Hope-Crosby signature during the height of the duo's popularity from 1948 to 1956. When Martin graduated to the Rat Pack, however, cameos became part of the group's visual vocabulary, in their own coproduced films that included guest stars by stars big and small, and also in their solo work, such as Martin in Sinatra's *Come Blow Your Horn* (1963). The Rat Pack, as a friendship group in which hedonism and ease was the unifying factor, adopted all of the friendly spontaneity established by Hope and Crosby as integral to the cameo without the complete disruptiveness of the comedian comedy. Yet, without the framework of the comedian comedy genre, these cameos tread a fine line between lazy and likeness.

Ocean's 11 was the first of the Rat Pack series of films made in the 1960s. These films were coproduced by the major Rat Pack players, a group of actors and performers that included Martin and Sammy Davis Jr. as its core members. The Rat Pack was centered on Frank Sinatra and his nightclub acts at the Sands in Las Vegas, a casino in which he was a part owner.[94] The Rat Pack was known for celebrating postwar hedonism and masculine freedom, and their act made sure that audience knew that they were having a good time as expressed through sexual innuendo and playful drunkenness.[95] The Rat Pack films were mythologized as an extension of that carousing lifestyle, a star-studded free-for-all that included Rat Pack members playing former army buddies who band together to rob a Vegas casino, for more or less altruistic reasons. Sinatra was the ringleader, Martin was a lounge singer, and other Rat Pack members and hangers-on appeared throughout the film. Like the Hope-Crosby films, press coverage of the event emphasized that pranks abounded on set.[96] As one critic suggested at the time of the film's release, their "natural born enthusiasm carried over into the making of the film. At one point Dean asked Frank, 'You will give me a chance to read the script before we're done shooting it, won't you?'" Other contemporary accounts asserted that the actors wrote their own jokes.[97] The film was perceived as fast and easy, "an insider's joke"[98] or "a genial group effort by a bunch of real-life pals,"[99] and the "most expensive home movie ever."[100] Yet, at least one of those writing for the audience for *Ocean's 11* clearly expected viewers to have a more tempered view of what is and is not impromptu. Rather than being as dazzled as reporters witnessing Hope and Crosby quips of over a decade before, one reviewer slyly referred to the writers as those who crafted these "spontaneous-sounding ad-libs."[101] The movie was framed as a marriage of convenience, where the group needed to be in Vegas to fulfill their nightclub obligations, so the film was set where they were working. However, the workload of shows and filming was serious.[102] Sinatra adopted the Crosby stance toward acting, with a "cavalier 'natural' air, seldom bothering to suffer more than two takes of a scene."[103]

Amid a sudden glut of cameo films and actors playing themselves, these efforts to define larger roles based purely on star persona in the Hope and Crosby model were poorly received. A mere six years later in 1966, reviews for *Ocean's 11*'s debut on television touted Sinatra and his rat pack as the furthest thing from hip, sneering at the days "when they thought they were of national importance."[104] While the main roles belong to core Rat Pack members, more peripherally associated performers such as Shirley MacLaine and Vegas regular Red Skelton appear in pure cameos.[105] A role for some-time Rat Packer Tony Curtis was also publicized during the film's production, but it did not materialize. In fact, in preproduction the same cameos were assigned to a few different actors. As the producer, Sinatra's contract allowed him to cast the minor roles with whomever he wanted without approval from Warner Brothers, the major studio attached to the film's distribution.[106] Friends were included, but big names were also important. Like in the Hope and Crosby trades, cameos were clearly as much business as friendship. Both of these unflattering cameos, picturing MacLaine as a drunk who doesn't want to be left out of the picture and Skelton as a gambler who tries to throw his fame around at the casino, adopted the sparring attitude of the Hope cameo trades. These had begun as bit roles such as Dealer, Client, and Drunk Girl that were then expanded around a star performer.[107] The unflattering nature of the Skelton and MacLaine cameos indicate that the desirability of being associated with the Rat Pack aura had overtaken any remaining considerations of propriety once mandated by studio contracts. In fact, once MacLaine was cast in the part, Drunk Girl became sexier, bawdier, and, with the addition of her final line, "This is where you leave me, huh?" suddenly surprised that she was not included in the rest of the film. A far cry from the virtuous, waitressing Barbara Stanwyck in *Hollywood Canteen* or Kim Novak, who cheerfully allows herself to be mistaken for a shopgirl in *Pepe*, MacLaine appears in a cameo that demonstrates the absence of typical studio protection not only in her acceptance of a bit part but also by revealing a vulgar and vulnerable side of the star. While *Ocean's 11* was largely seen as self-serving and forgettable, driving audience ennui at the concept of stars playing stars, nevertheless, it adopted a subtly new stance toward the cameo's kind of disruptiveness.

Taking It Too Easy: A Cameo Backlash

Films such as *Pepe*, *Mad World*, and *Greatest Story Ever Told* were the victims of a palpable cameo backlash that began in the 1960s. While critics reviewing *Road* films of the 1940s had objected to the cameo's disruptive power, by the 1960s they objected to the cameo as a tired tool of star visibility. Cameo trades were seen as excessive; Crosby's "just plain embarrassing"[108] appearance in *Pepe* was Crosby's third cameo of 1960, including cameos in *Alias Jesse James* and the Marilyn Monroe film *Let's Make Love* (1960) where he was a very exclusive musical coach for the hapless Yves Montand. At the root of this rejection of the cameo was a question about acting as labor. Merely being oneself was no longer considered much of a performance, especially when there was little challenge to the audience's powers of recognition and the disruptive poke at the industry was purely for the financial benefit of the actor. These cameos were a reflection of a decadent industry that was no longer in touch with fans. By establishing the cameo as a glimpse of the actor at leisure, the cameo had distanced itself from labor that audiences could understand. No longer did the cameo resonate with the generational aspirations for luxury and ease that Hope and Crosby and the Rat Pack epitomized, nor did fans want to celebrate labor freed from the clutches of the studio system as their own victory. Cameos were a well-worn tool for celebrating the famous. Hope and Crosby had set out to position themselves as fans of the industry kidding along with the spectator, but by the end of the *Road* series, audiences wanted more from cameos and actors. Where their cameos had stood as evidence that acting was easy for those who lived and breathed comedy, reviews of *Ocean's 11* showed that audiences were questioning not only the cameos, but how real the talent was, too.[109]

As cameos were disconnected from work behind the scenes, fans became disenchanted with the so-called insider view they presented. In the 1930s, publicists had turned away from the glamorous languor of stars who lived in castles and ancient estates to cultivate a more down-to-earth image. The cameo in the wake of Hope and Crosby created an image that revealed too much about the practical side of Hollywood, exposing contractual obligations and marketing strategies as part of their humor. At the same time, Hope and Crosby and the Rat Pack embraced the hedonism that, though tempered with a manic energy, was nevertheless divorced from ordinary life. As these stars moved into demanding careers that spanned many media and a nonstop schedule of tapings, shoots, and live performances, they nevertheless cultivated an aura of "easy living."[110] To supplement this impression, the comedian comedy genre positioned comedians as actors who couldn't help being funny wherever they were, whether they were wisecracking between takes or, like Buster Keaton, rolling down the stairs at cocktail parties. Studios, their publicists claimed, merely caught this talent on film.[111] Yet, the hypermasculine comedy duos that cameos marketed in the 1950s employed cameos as the punchline for put-downs and rivalries.[112] The fiercely jeering comedic cameos that Hope and his cohorts adopted in the late 1950s purported to present stars in their most basic form and reveal them as talentless hacks. Cameos were called on to show audiences what they least wanted to see. At the same time, although cameos were carefully orchestrated, the marketing that portrayed cameos as happenstance occurrences made these roles seem opportunistic. Without an image to cultivate that was separate from the personal self, the star was not seen as performing the labor that was integral to stardom. Audiences who had seen cameos as a cue to unravel the mythmaking behind the celebrity persona were left with little to do. Cameos had claimed to strip away the mystery, leaving nothing for the fan as detective to solve.

Movie reviews in the 1960s reflected negative audience reactions to cameo casting following the cameo fad of the decade previous. A change in the attitudes of reviewers as they narrated cameos to potential audiences conveyed a general fatigue with the cameo. Reviewers were happy to point out cameos that they saw as sloppy work or transparent marketing attempts. Cameos were seen as "box office bait."[113] One reviewer of *Ocean's 11* snarkily noted the cameo of "Shirley MacLaine in an unpublicized appearance that will be well-publicized,"[114] and indeed the self-produced Rat Pack films were "designed to maximize financial independence"[115] of its stars. While audiences were eager for improvisational qualities in their actors that allowed them to see through the star persona, these reviews show a changing tide. Reviewers as audience stand-ins were no longer claiming that cameos provided access to anything other than the manufactured star persona. What had begun as a way of activating cult appreciation and participative viewing was no longer effective or enticing, as the idea that films such as *Ocean's 11* were "the most expensive home movie ever" dwelled not on the idea of actors at leisure but the extraordinary expense. Others perceived the cameo as an act of convenience. As David Niven claimed about the making of *Around the World in 80 Days*, the period of cameo casting, sometimes completed only hours before shooting, "was not improvisation but facile opportunism"[116] based on availability and willingness to act at the Todd price. Todd bragged in *Life* that Sinatra was paid off with a Thunderbird and $100 for 2 days' work, joking that the amount was a little more than the union minimum because "it's good for their egos to get over the day-player's contract pay."[117]

Hoping to emphasize what little pay the stars received in order to spread the kind of goodwill that Hope's publicists tried to harness in his 1959 *Life* proposal, Todd instead exposed to audiences just what went into cameos, and they noticed.

While in the first half of the century it was studios who saw the financial benefits of using salary stars as often as possible, stars who had control of their own appearances likewise saw the cameo as a way to maximize their earnings. Despite the fact that stars hung their hats on the idea that other stars wanted to appear with them for the sake of friendship, cameos were carefully remunerated during this period. Some of the most frequent cameoists were people who controlled their own image through their own production companies, such as Frank Sinatra, who couldn't say no to a cameo in the 1950s. Obviously, cameos were sometimes undertaken as ways to be paid creatively and in kind without having the studio or tax authorities take a cut of the profits, with cars, plane and event tickets, jewelry, and art objects.[118] The cameo fad also served the creative accounting of many newly independent stars. The trade that Todd offered for the cameoists was likely unflattering—most stars received the minimum day player's rate of around $100 and a car or a painting of their choice, a gift in kind that the studio couldn't easily take its cut of.[119] This practice of paying off cameos with nominal sums equivalent to union mandated rates and more substantial gifts would continue in *Pepe*, where Maurice Chevalier received a vacation in Las Vegas for his screen time. For *It's a Mad, Mad, Mad, Mad World*, a private box at the Dodgers stadium was given to Carl Reiner, and a publicity exchange such as director Stanley Kramer's appearance on Jerry Lewis's talk show was traded for Lewis's half hour of work as the Mean Man[120] (fig. 25). George Sidney did a similar trade with Donna Reed's *Pepe* cameo by appearing on her TV show. Even in *The List of Adrian Messenger* (1963), which featured what are arguably cameos by five stars, Robert Mitchum was forced by his production company to refuse the offer of payment in the form of a gift of a painting.[121] This gift, offered with instructions that it was to be donated to a museum, would have served as a deductible, his biographer claims, much in the same way that Crosby donated his payments for his Hope cameos.[122] On the other hand, David Niven claims that in *Around the World in 80 Days* the "older and fading stars who could use the cash"[123] were paid generously. Audiences were more than aware of this kind of dealing: a 1962 article published around the time of the release of the final *Road* film provided a typology of small roles and detailed the pay received by cameoists, more or less accurately, as Todd's gift to Noel Coward of a Pierre Bonnard, for example, became the slightly more sensational Picasso.[124] There was also the beginning of cameo regulars—Jimmy Durante, for example, appears in *Mad World* too, while Frank Sinatra, present in *Around the World* and *Pepe*, sat it out. Given the fact that publicists had associated free cameos with freewheeling cameos, the gradual revelation that these were paid appearances was not to be taken lightly by audiences.

As a result, in the 1960s, cameos were pointed out as signs of rampant commercialism and cynical marketing. The *Mirror* claimed the *Pepe* cameos from 1960 were advertising, pure and simple, writing "many cameo bits are little more than meaningless walk-ons and some no more than out-and-out plugs, such as Donna Reed's promotion for her TV show, the front marquee and casino of the Sands in Las Vegas, and the promotion of Acapulco's plush spas."[125] On the other hand, the cameos in *Mad World* in 1963 were regaled as "bits that rise high in comic stature."[126] These cameos were not free from their own cynical manufacture, as the cameo for Jerry Lewis, for example, was originally scripted for what *Mad World* writer William Rose noted should be "some comedian who's so busy he can only give you one shot, you know, Jack Paar, somebody like that."[127] However, while Donna Reed in *Pepe* is interrupted on the way to work on her show, as she sweetly informs us, Jerry Lewis in *Mad World* is playing the typical Lewis madcap character, squealing and making funny faces. Rather than tell us he is Jerry,

Figure 25. A driving cameo featuring Jerry Lewis in *It's a Mad, Mad, Mad, Mad World* (1963).

or promise he is Jerry, he is acting as Jerry. His diegetic disruption is appropriate because it is what he does best: comedy. Donna Reed's performance neither plays with the limits of star persona nor presents any participative payoff: she is present merely to be recognized in a kind of cameo that was no longer standout. Beginning as a mark of verisimilitude, the disruptiveness of the cameo had come to be its most important attribute.

The dismissal of Bing Crosby's "embarrassing" cameo in *Pepe* can likewise be seen as a reflection of the growing expectation of disruption, especially in comparison to the earlier excitement at his cameo trades. While Crosby's brief sing-along appeared alongside *Pepe*'s other such disappointingly misleading credits as the Voice of Judy Garland, his performance can't be said to be any smaller or less taxing than his appearance as a wordless driver in *Son of Paleface*. Nor was this the first time Crosby's name was used to market movies he was barely in: while Crosby was never credited in the Hope films, he was definitely not absent from their marketing, even in his miniscule parts. Pepe, playing the bumpkin, doesn't recognize Crosby or his famous song. Unlike Hope's endearingly wily simpletons, Pepe is too painfully unaware of pop culture for audiences to even have the pleasure of defining themselves against him as knowing fans enacting cult appreciation. Like Reed's cameo, Crosby's appearance is only minimally disruptive, abandoning the breaks with the conventions of filmmaking that Crosby's cameos had had when paired with Hope's commentary, or even the disruptive jolt of Lamour's coincidental appearance on Crosby's plane. Clearly, cameos were at their best when they were disruptive of the diegesis, coming to heads with narrative norms in a way that made them funny.

Bad or Bumpy: Cameos, Comedy, and the New Hollywood

Cult films, says Mathijs, are often bad films, with bumpy plots composed of cult moments that are the result of accident and coincidence.[128] Cameos, as they break with diegesis in favor of visibility, are consciously "bumpy."[129] Their powerful appeal to audiences delivers a challenge to classical narratives and the norms of conventional filmmaking. The lackluster cameos in *Pepe* and other ensemble cameo films of the 1960s were uninteresting to savvy viewers, who saw cameos as cues to engage their fan knowledge. These tired cameos did not offer viewers an opportunity to collect new information or engage their repertoire of knowledge. While reviewers were delighted with the resurrection of old stars in the 1930s, by 1963, reviews of *Mad World* indicate fatigue with the sheer number of cameos that tried to trade visibility and the privilege of celebrity encounter for plot and story.[130] Readers of movie reviews were fully aware that the carefree and spontaneous attitudes of cameoists were manufactured. While Crosby's studied casualness had been a trademark of his star persona, when this attitude was adopted by other cameoists as in *Mad World*, such roles were described as sly actorly shirking of the work of performance in favor of the simple act of being famous. As these reviews suggested, viewers needed new challenges to their achievement as practiced untanglers of cameos. A film such as *The List of Adrian Messenger* could be seen as a new kind of cameo puzzle, where viewers were enlisted to recognize disguised actors who were ostensibly playing small roles. The failure of *Adrian Messenger* is perhaps owing to its inability to adhere to its own guarantee, as the famous actors, such as Frank Sinatra, did not even play the small roles to which they attached their faces in a final credit-sequence unmasking (fig. 26; fig. 27).

Figures 26 and 27. Newspaper ads for *The List of Adrian Messenger* (1963) and *Mad World* promised challenges to fans' powers of recognition but didn't always deliver.

If the influence of comedian comedies meant the cameo was identified with spontaneity at its best and laziness at its worst, it also proved that the diegetic disruption of the cameo belongs to the comedy in a way that it does not in the drama. The litmus test for celebrity cameos in drama was *The Greatest Story Ever Told* (1965), where the diegetic disruption was "shattering";[131] in comedian comedy, it found its natural home. *The Greatest Story Ever Told*, the story of Christ's crucifixion—an example of a narrative where one would think the character spaces are so deeply inhabited by centuries of tradition that not even the brief star power of John Wayne can overcome them—succumbed to criticism of the "conscious intermingling of theatrical personalities with sincere dramatic intentions."[132] These cameos were seen as interruptions, when "right at a point of piercing anguish, up pops the brawny John Wayne in the costume of a Roman centurion. Inevitably, viewers whisper, 'That's John Wayne!'"[133] Dramas couldn't hold the diegetic disruption that was now implicit within the cameo. Instead, in comedy they found their natural home.

While comedy would continue to be the home for the cameo, transformations in other genres also affected its trajectory. What it meant to be oneself on-screen changed in the 1960s, as the Production Code loosened restrictions around depictions of violence and sexuality with the release of *Who's Afraid of Virginia Woolf?* (1966).[134] Many directors of the "road show blockbuster era" in which the cameo film had had its heyday were retiring, as well as the old studio producers.[135] In the 1970s, there was a spate of Hollywood-set dramas glaringly without cameos, such as *Gable and Lombard* (1976) and *The Day of the Locust* (1975), while cameos were revived to bolster lackluster spoof comedies such as *Won Ton Ton, the Dog Who Saved Hollywood* (1976). Films of the New Hollywood evoked nostalgia through a new kind of realism and naturalism in acting.[136] Realism was not exemplified by witnesses of the past; instead, movies in the 1970s were marketed to a younger demographic who were less interested in nostalgic cameos or their parents' heroes.[137] Just like studio affiliations before them, unserious friendship groups such as the Rat Pack and comedy duos of Hope and Crosby's ilk were being left behind by celebrities who were invested in expressing their performances as labor. Television appearances and talk shows had overtaken the cameo's claims to reveal to the audience the celebrity as he really was in the flesh. Cameos needed to promise to surprise and engage the audience by disrupting classical Hollywood forms and the boundaries of star persona before they could again be perceived as exciting challenges to the audience's powers of recognition.

4

THE AMBASSADORS

Cameos Transformed through Television

In 2000, Matthew Perry, one of the stars of the hit NBC sitcom *Friends* (1994–2004), appeared as a mild-mannered dentist caught up in a gangster's revenge alongside action star Bruce Willis in the buddy comedy *The Whole Nine Yards* (2000). The film was released in February and spent three weeks at box office number one. In late April, just as the film was released to second-run theaters, Willis appeared in several episodes of *Friends* as a new love interest. This crossover of comedy duos into other projects is familiar territory in the history of cameos. In an interview with Willis that coincided with the film's release, *People* magazine published an account that claimed the upcoming cameo was "just for fun."[1] Whether fun or not, this cameo had multiple benefits for actors and studios involved. At the time, *Friends* was one of the most-watched shows on television, and an appearance there would be a potential boon to Willis, whose flagging career had received a recent boost with the 1999 thriller *The Sixth Sense*. Indeed, Willis even won an Emmy for this role. The cameo continued to pay dividends: the pair would work together again a few years later in a sequel, *The Whole Ten Yards* (2004). In fact, while the performances and plotlines themselves may have been long forgotten, almost two decades later, this cameo and the story of its genesis has taken on a life of its own. In the version of events aggregated as clickbait and celebrity gossip on the internet, the *Friends* appearance was the subject of a wager where Willis pitted his fee for the small role against the possibility that the film would be the highest grossing release on its first weekend. This anecdote seems more like a good story than a reasonable bet: was Willis rooting for Perry's first major movie role to crash and burn? was he so pessimistic about his return to box-office success that he would lay down money against his own performance? Yet, the story prevails: the cameo has outlived the film, the television show, and the characters the actors played, continuing to knit the two together across media as friends and colleagues, with a nod to the fast and loose cameo deals of the Rat Pack.

In his *Friends* appearance, Willis didn't play himself, but his movie star persona overshadowed his role in the sitcom, even though his cameo was a recurring role that ran across three episodes. Like cinema, television as narrative negotiates audience attention between background and foreground characters as minor and major roles. However, the unique duration of the television series, as it extends over many hours and weeks, and its reception in the home as regular domestic entertainment, means that the viewer's relationship to the character-spaces represented on the show is more fully developed than that of the ninety-minute movie. Cameo roles can last an entire episode in guest spots as guest stars, where that episode represents less than the narrative space a cameo would occupy in a movie.

Almost as old as television itself, the cameo in a fictional television series was a common alternative to the television talk show circuit for entertainers with upcoming releases of films or albums. While celebrities appeared regularly in variety and talk shows, television cameos offered a crossover media space where the cameo's function of creating visibility could be fully expressed as advertisement, exposing audiences to celebrities challenged to perform in a new, more intimate visual medium. Even longer guest spots on television functioned like cinematic cameos, where the sustained disruption by an extended cameo appearance was absorbed by the long-running narratives of a television series. In the 1950s, cameos on television quickly became an important way to market both studio films and stars from other media like music in trades that reflected an increasingly integrated mediascape. Yet, there were no publicity claims that stars had spontaneously dropped in on a television production; the increased access to on-set spaces through television formats like game shows and live audiences made at-home viewers aware of the elaborate systems of the television industry in a way that was obscured in cinema. Like radio before it, television created a multimedia environment where celebrities were welcomed as stars and ambassadors from another medium rather than characters. By the 1960s, audiences had become bored with the so-called spontaneity of cameos on the cinema screen, preferring total suspension of disbelief over the diegetic flimsiness created by the self-conscious barrage of well-known faces. Television was quickly identified as an appropriate place for stars to walk the line between persona and performance.

Thanks to television, cameos became the links that tied together different media rather than consolidating star images. When comedic film cameos reared their heads again in spoof comedies of the late 1970s and 1980s, cameos were rarely about affirming personal relationships. Instead, they often created absurdist and anarchic juxtapositions that placed stars in situations that were ridiculously outside of the bounds of their star image. Rejecting both the naturalness of the casual cameo and the admiring views of the studio age, these cameos exposed the constructed star image in the name of sending up not only the film industry but also the growing multimedia grasp of Hollywood from sports to journalism to finance. Television's expansion into the multichannel format with its need for constant content, much of which is supplied as celebrity-driven infotainment, embroiled audiences more and more deeply into star images. Responding to the interests of the media-savvy viewer, cameos have come to reflect and critique star image-making rather than promise unmediated or natural views of unscripted celebrity. Yet as twenty-four-hour TV and the internet have transformed access to celebrity lives in a way that mirrors the changes of the 1950s, cameos have again ricocheted to present friendship groups. Rather than affirming those claims through casual cameos, these bad cameos seem to outdo celebrity gossip by disrupting celebrity image with the kind of boundary-pushing absurd situations seen in spoof comedies while embracing a wider range of pop culture figures into their networks. This chapter will explore a cross section of television cameos in sitcoms from the 1950s to the 2000s, examining a transition in the cameo's role from confirming to undermining star images as audience demands changed while still keeping stars and their multimedia networks visible.

In movies, the cameo fulfills the desire of producers and stars to affirm their status through visibility and of fans eagerly to affirm that recognition. Although television has a vastly different mode of reception and distribution from cinema, centered on presentation in the private sphere of the home, both television and film are nevertheless visual media that because of their similarity as entertainment have historically competed for audience attention. Very early on, television networks adopted many of the same marketing strategies as film studios to draw attention to their programs. In the 1950s, as television came into its own, cameos were in heavy use in movies, and they quickly became adopted into television's visual lexicon. Film and television worked together to make cameos a recognized trope that increased visibility and recognition in both media.

The cameo on television has its own history that bears examination. Much as movie cameos in the 1950s offered glimpses of stars in the real world in an attempt to make movies special in the poststudio television era, television began in the 1950s with a similar strategy of casting movie stars in small roles. The TV cameo emerged from the intimacy afforded by live performances and home viewing. The precedents of early television performance continue to be reflected in the reception of the television cameo as an intimate, spontaneous, self-reflexive, surprising, and often disruptive glimpse of a celebrity persona. These traits of the television cameo can be traced through key developments in television from the 1950s, as the emerging television industry negotiated the role of movie stars on television as stars, characters, and advertisers. Benefiting from the precedents for unpredictability set by television's history of live performances and off-casting, as well as the flow of programming that Raymond Williams describes as routinely juxtaposing narrative and documentary space,[2] celebrities on television presented yet another side of their persona for inspection by the curious viewer.

The hierarchy of stardom has influenced what kind of stars have appeared on television. As star-studded anthology dramas became less common, expensive movie stars retreated from television in the early 1960s. Guest star roles within fictional narratives were instead filled by aspiring stars from other media, such as musicians who reflected the interests of the desirable youth market. In the 1970s, a reappraisal of the desires of television viewers that resulted in network sitcoms emphasizing the changing work and home life of Americans meant their narratives were rarely troubled by famous faces. As a result, cameos ebbed once again, only to return as the inheritor of self-reflexivity and narrative complexity in the 1990s and 2000s. As older cameo-laden series were rebroadcast to fill in the twenty-four-hour schedule of the increasingly dense multichannel spectrum, and old cameos were repackaged as trivia worthy of note on accompanying television programs and video special features, the cameo as self-reflexive disruption and ham-fisted promotional tactic became a subject of ironic commentary and imitation. In the early twenty-first century, the reimagined cameo reflects movie stars who have long since mastered the performance conventions of television and savvy viewers who are no longer fooled by the intimate glimpses afforded by the cameo's production. Insulated by the promise that cameos never present celebrities as they really are, the cameo instead offers the recognizing viewer a sense of complicity as they share in the joke. That joke is on viewers who think that TV could ever reveal what celebrities are really like.

Stars on the Small Screen in the 1950s

In the United States, television viewing has been in competition with film-going since shortly after networks began regular daytime broadcasts in 1948.[3] As Amanda Lotz points out, because television was not pay-per-use, it quickly acquired a vast audience, especially among women working in the home and within the domestic sphere of the television set. However, television viewers paid in different ways, for the set, the service, and then as the consumers of goods that were the subject of televised advertising.[4] As networks experimented with different formats in the 1950s, they determined that ordinary, domestic figures and the routine of regular watching were what kept families in front of the television screen rather than in their local movie theater.[5] Home viewing was valued for its predictable schedule, characters, and narrative arc.

While radio networks traded on their relationships with film studios for movie-star hosts and broadcasting radio adaptations of popular movies, the movie industry was on less friendly terms with television.[6] Fears of overexposure meant movie stars were largely forbidden to appear, with an exception for walk-ons that promoted a newly released film.[7] Although the movie business was a major precedent, many television stars initially came from the radio. Like radio, television programs were sponsored by oft-mentioned corporations that sold products such as cigarettes or cosmetics.[8] The variety show format borrowed from radio and vaudeville was initially the most common type of television programming, where a host featured many different acts that included guest stars of varied brilliance, united by a shared time slot rather than a narrative.[9] Vaudeville MCs who had won little success on radio, often because of an incompatible slapstick style, were happy to break into the new visual medium, bringing with them vaudeville's characteristic self-reflexivity to the new format. In the 1940s, such anarchic comedy had been shooed off cinema screens as too irreverent, or, mellowed under the care of crossover stars like Bob Hope, allowed in limited doses like the casual cameo. Television was not the movies. From the beginning, television hosts set themselves up as outsiders; hosts like Milton Berle and Jack Benny established their exclusion from the glamorous world of stardom with routines where they coveted the success of other stars, or made self-deprecating statements about the artificiality of the sponsor arrangement.[10] Denise Mann suggests this ironic distance between star and stardom helped create an environment where hosts could be trusted by audiences as go-betweens with the advertisers.[11] The perceived freedom of hosts to speak honestly about their sponsors softened the commercial message and established the intimate address of television.

While movie cameos promised off-duty glimpses of stars, television created a more constant stream of depictions of real life in the sitcom. Sitcoms purported to parallel the real lives of families such as the Nelsons in *The Adventures of Ozzie and Harriet* (1952–66) or the Ricardos in *I Love Lucy* (1951–57). Coverage of these shows was thick with statements about how authentically these soundstage representations of their lives mimicked their at-home behaviors.[12] Having a regular cast in sitcoms was seen as a way to keep costs low; as Lynn Spigel writes, they were "cheaper than guest stars."[13] Drawing on the self-reflexivity established in a much more aggressive, self-mocking fashion by variety show hosts, early sitcoms reflected the identity of their leads by casting them as performers. Like Hollywood-set films that presented Hollywood stars for promotional purposes, these sitcoms could thus portray other off-duty performers as well as provide the framework for variety-show-like performances. Even once studios lifted their ban on television appearances in the mid-1950s, the intense schedule required for recurring roles on television, as well as the complete ownership of the image that sponsors placed on television actors, meant that even lesser movie actors on contract could simply not be a part of the regular cast.[14] However, they could appear as the friends and acquaintances of their sitcom colleagues. Such appearances not only benefited their studio's most recent film but also exposed the star's persona through the more candid environment of the sitcom.

As casual cameos in cinema became seen as repetitive and predictable in the 1950s, television offered a way to counter the perceived out-of-touchness of movie stars. In her examination of movie stars on television in the 1950s, Christine Becker shows how movie stars distanced themselves from inapproachable glamour via television. Movie stars countered a backlash against lavish lifestyles described in the newly liberated gossip magazines of the 1960s with press that described them as homebodies and housewives. Cameo roles that purported to show them as they really were as supporting evidence for their down-to-earthness.[15] When *I Love Lucy* moved to Hollywood for a season in 1955, movie stars such as John Wayne and Charles Boyer regularly appeared as normal folks at the mercy of rabid fans that included Lucy herself[16] (fig. 28). As Becker writes, by "knowingly mocking their constructed star images and the essence of fandom, they came across as down-to-earth, unpretentious people, presumably further endearing themselves to audiences as a consequence."[17] Like film cameos, these television roles were used to market other films produced by the same production company. These *I Love Lucy* cameos featured a parade of stars with upcoming MGM releases in the 1955 season.[18] However, by appearing on television, these stars addressed their audiences in an intimate space that promised to convey the authenticity that audiences were beginning to feel film cameos lacked.

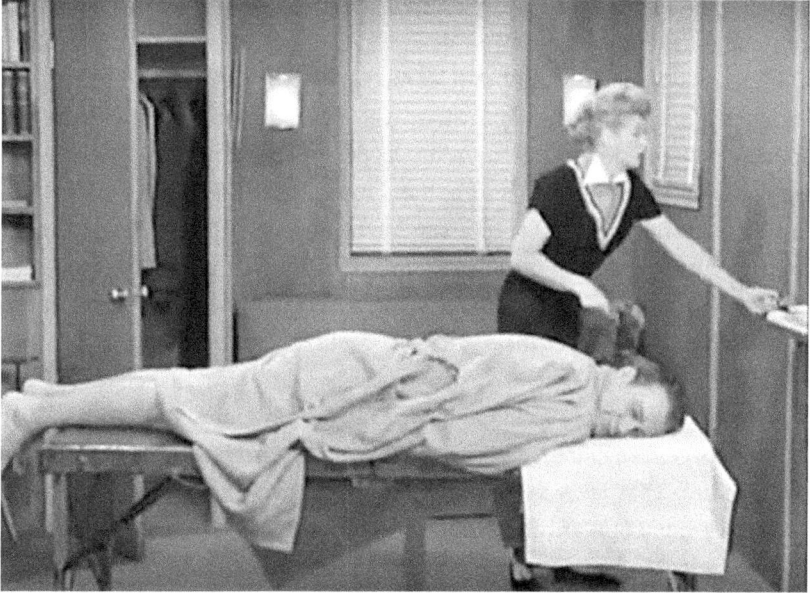

Figure 28. Lucy gets herself in trouble with John Wayne on *I Love Lucy* (1951–57).

Nevertheless, there was a concrete divide between movie star and television star that continued to make guest star appearances or cameos by movie stars spectacular events. Like the studios resurrecting former stars for nostalgic cameos, television in the 1950s had also mined the past for its recognizable faces, presenting aging stars or character actors as top-tier talent. This strategy had a lasting effect on the television star's subservient position in the star hierarchy, and movie stars who were seen on television feared that they would likewise be grouped with the has-beens.[19] Even prestige productions like anthology dramas, where stars were either hosts or played one-off roles, were often seen as a last resort for actors unhappy in Hollywood's calcified typecasting.[20] In response, advertising for television programs emphasized quality of performance and story above and beyond star power.[21] Authenticity became a watchword for television, as a "value superior to the quality of constructed glamour."[22] Television soon had its own constellation of stars, though without the lasting name recognition that movie stars of the period command today. While these television stars may have been recognizable in their own right, they succeeded perhaps too well at adapting to the domestic setting of the television where they owed their popularity to being supposedly unremarkable. Although celebrities availed themselves of the opportunity to appear on television sets, TV stars did not make the transition to movies in the same way, especially in cameos. When a late-career Bob Hope welcomed stars from the TV western genre cameo trade in *Alias Jesse James*, they were cast as a group and without any specific names listed in the shooting script or requests to the CBS network for particular television stars. Like the ranks of studio actors in Golden Age Hollywood, they were easy to assemble in number. Donna Reed's cameo appearance in *Pepe* was given much more exposition to establish her credentials as a television star than the settings of opulent hotels or department stores where the viewer meets more recognizable movie stars, appearing dutifully in a studio office to pick up a well-labeled script that cued the producer she encountered to name her and her eponymous show. Because of the supposed transparency of their medium, television stars lack the extraordinariness that Dyer asserts sets film stars apart, failing to inspire the compulsion to compare and contrast their constructed persona that drives the fan. Television personalities remained subordinated to the hierarchy that placed the film star at its pinnacle, making any cameo appearance a noteworthy event.

From Guest Stars to Cameos

Cameos on television take advantage of the television series' extended character system to introduce performances that are often longer than their movie counterparts. Because of the entrenched character spaces of recurring characters in a television series, even an episode-long supporting performance could be considered cameo. Action star Bruce Willis's cameo on *Friends*, for example, was part of a three-episode story arc where he appeared as both the object of a May–December romance and a protective father foiling another pairing. Big stars can be absorbed into little roles on television thanks to the labyrinthine character system of a series, which features a continuity of characters in different stories each week, while serials present continuity of action through a long-running story.[23] Unlike films, series and serials take as their premise the continued exploration of what Matt Hills calls hyperdiegesis, "a vast and detailed narrative space, only a fraction of which is every directly seen or encountered within the text."[24] The endlessly unfolding hyperdiegesis can be expanded in series and serials to build a complex character system populated mostly by minor character-spaces but anchored by a few major characters.

The cameo is uniquely suited to the series. Cameos are rare in soap operas, the most common example of a serial in twentieth-century television,[25] because, as daytime fare aimed at women, their narratives are meant to be easy to follow and therefore avoid disruption.[26] Anthology programs were also unlikely sites for cameos because, as neither series nor serials, they had a character system that functioned like a film with each episode featuring new characters and a stand-alone diegesis unrelated to stories that came before, as in the case of the long-running *Alfred Hitchcock Presents* (1955–65). Character spaces in an anthology fail to expand with each episode, and any cameos would need to be as brief as their filmic counterparts so as not to overwhelm the nascent character-system. Variety shows regularly featured celebrity guests yet lacked any kind of hyperdiegesis. Only series such as the sitcom had a character-system complex enough to carry the disruptive cameo while maintaining continuity of plot. The established character system of conniving Lucy and exasperated Ricky in *I Love Lucy* can handle the interloping of film heartthrob William Holden, just as, decades later, the jealous Ross is not overshadowed by the intrusion of Bruce Willis on *Friends*.[27] In fact, Greg Smith suggests that guest stars are integral to the long-running sitcom.[28] The character space that television stars build during their tenure on a series can be so well-rounded that it overshadows the star persona; television actors are often better known by their character names, and it is in this guise they appear in crossover episodes or spinoffs.[29] While viewers enjoyed the regular appearance of familiar faces from within a well-worn character system, new character spaces are needed to create "more plot than a small group of core characters can dependably produce."[30] Guest stars allow regular cast members to be presented with new problems, and to react in new ways, revealing an ever-deepening character space.[31] Cameos could serve an important narrative function in the sitcom by providing a foil against which recurring characters came into conflict.

Television has paved the way for the deconstruction of the star image in a way that the casual cameo only hinted at. With the explosion of television in the early 1950s, viewers were accosted with narrative, both fictional and documentary, for hours each day. As Williams writes in 1974, "drama as an experience is now an intrinsic part of everyday life."[32] Williams suggested that flow was the central experience of watching television, where audiences were interested not in individual programs but in the experience of watching a stream of images from commercials to news magazines to sitcoms and dramas.[33] This flow created a continuous experience of narrative.[34] As Lotz points out, Williams's flow is an experience of television that predates control devices such as home taping, remote control, or modern video-on-demand, which have worked together to create a customizable televisual experience. Flow is a concept that is nevertheless valuable when discussing stars on television. Television showed not just a star's recent releases and current profile, but it rebroadcast older films in reruns and dug up forgotten trivia for game shows. The star on television existed in many times and places at once, linked through the constant flow of images.[35] While a story of triumph was built around Gloria Swanson's return to Paramount for *Sunset Boulevard* in 1950, only a few years later television's reliance on studio archives for content meant that viewers had access to stars like Swanson, Buster Keaton, or the Three Stooges and their career highs many nights of the week. Old stars were not special but de rigueur. Flow linked together the movie star's succession of career moves, whether they were forgotten faces or current headliners, illustrating the assembled nature of star identity. The contradictions and continuities of star image became more visible through the flow of television than in the discrete units of cinema.

The opposition between glamorous movie star and ordinary familiar television personality is an established dichotomy in studies of television.[36] While casual cameos in movies promised only momentary reveals of the person behind the actor, much of television programming like sitcoms and variety shows explicitly made the real star its subject. As a visual medium, television allowed viewers to observe stars in an informal way that radio could not. Stars came by this informality naturally. Holmes points out that in the 1950s the experience of performing for the multiple cameras and live audiences of a television studio was new to even the most practiced movie star.[37] Unlike in radio, whose star-studded variety programs at least claimed to broadcast from stages and nightclubs such the imaginary Orchid Room of Louella Parsons's famous *Hollywood Hotel* (1935–38) radio program, variety shows often interviewed stars in consciously informal environments, which, like the sitcom, featured sets that borrowed sofas, armchairs, and the ubiquitous ashtray from the living room.[38] In this ostensibly documentary space, the brief glimpses of the real star that movie cameos supposedly authorized became the subject of a more extended scrutiny by the television viewer.

While enabling close and intimate observation of movie stars, television also provided incentive for the savvy viewer to collect and retain fan knowledge. If the movie cameo had rewarded audiences engaged with sleuthing out details about the real behaviors of celebrities, television provided even more opportunities for studying famous people. Pitting ordinary contestants against panels of stars, a whole genre of game shows "rewarded contestants for their knowledge of star psychology and their ability to put it to use."[39] Becker notes how mid-1950s game shows like *Personality Puzzle* and *Masquerade Party* challenged contestants to identify celebrities based on biographical trivia.[40] Ordinary people and stars were presented as interchangeable in series such as *This Is Your Life* (1952–61), which assembled the biography of its weekly subject through surprise interviews with people from his or her past and alternated between ordinary and star subjects.[41] Subjected to the same conditions as regular contestants, celebrities and their reactions could be judged and affirmed as authentic as, "caught off-guard, they seemed as vulnerable and ordinary as anyone discovering they are on national television."[42] Television provided new opportunities for the viewer to view the star image as an assemblage of constituent parts experienced through flow, enticing audiences to sift through the views of celebrity and assess their authenticity. At the same time, the cameo fatigue of the 1960s seen in reaction to celebrity cameos in films such as *The Greatest Story Ever Told* and *Pepe* is perhaps more understandable given the increasing number of perspectives on celebrity the competing medium of television provided.

Youth Audiences and Musical Cameos

While television courted movie stars with increasing intensity in the 1950s, that decade saw the high point of their participation in television programming. In fact, movie stars began to disappear from television again in the early 1960s following a shift from New York studios to Hollywood that placed television production under the indirect control of film studios.[43] While this shift was initially to take advantage of Hollywood's existing infrastructure of sets, studios, and skilled workers, including actors, it had the effect of reinforcing the segmentation between movie and television stars. Those studios that had promised cheap productions to the networks used casting to differentiate between the economical television and prestige film products.[44] The benefits of off-casting and live television available in television's more experimental early stages were no longer on offer. Rather than an exciting new medium for performers, the budget-conscious television programs became associated with lowbrow fare, where the much-maligned wasteland of lazy programming was matched by the "sloppy aesthetics of television watching."[45] Just as soap operas aimed for the viewership of the distracted housewife, the rest of the household's viewers were believed to be too distracted by food, games, or family members to concentrate on complex narratives. The quiz show scandals in the mid-1950s, where sponsors were revealed to have influenced the outcome of these games in keeping with audience sympathies or to maintain suspense over several shows, undermined audiences' faith in authenticity, and stars' willingness to participate in this genre.[46] Many movie stars, who had been attracted by rising paychecks from television, were too expensive for this new profit model, and the star-studded musical spectaculars that were a monthly occurrence on television in the late 1950s had not proved to attract any more viewers than the regular, weekly sitcom fare, despite their higher price tag.[47] Briefly ushered into television, movie stars were on their way out again.

Questions of prestige and profit separated movie stars from television stars in the 1960s. However, this shift allowed the cameo once again to stand out as a special event rather than a normal occurrence. While movie stars were less likely to perform starring roles in televised dramas, this did not exclude them from smaller roles and cameos. Small appearances from single, mostly second-tier stars were an affordable alternative to cost-conscious production companies. Comedic series such as *Gilligan's Island* (1964–67) and *Batman* (1966–68) featured guest appearances with almost every episode, many of these drawn from the pool of older stars and character actors. *Batman*, for example, began its run of guest stars with the aging Jerry Lewis as himself and later featured failing director Otto Preminger as Mr. Freeze.[48] While these remembered faces were sure to draw recognition from viewers, as in films, they were increasingly irrelevant to the largely teenage audience of baby boomers. Appealing to younger viewers was a growing concern. Teen characters saw increased attention in long-running sitcoms such as *Ozzie and Harriet*, where Ricky Nelson emerged as a singing star.[49] Perhaps owing to this early success, music and musical performers were seen as one of the keys to television's younger audiences.[50] Just as short appearances from movie stars had been used to market movies in the 1950s, cameos from musical acts were injected into hundreds of sitcoms from the 1960s, from *The Flintstones* (1960–66) to *I Dream of Jeannie* (1965–70). While the idea of tailoring television shows to one demographic or another was largely anathema to networks who wanted to appeal to as many potential viewers as possible, cameos allowed for segments of an episode to acknowledge the desires of the youth market through multimedia relationships.[51]

Musical acts, both local and otherwise, used the cameo in the 1960s as a platform for potential visibility akin to the variety show, where one remarkable appearance had the potential to make stars recognizable. Like Hollywood stars seen in their natural habitat on studio lots, musicians often appeared in the background in bar or nightclub settings.[52] However, just as some early talk shows established casual codes for guest interviews with sets reminiscent of home interiors,[53] some sitcom episodes featured an intimate living-room performance for a number of marginally appreciative spectators, such as the Seeds' "psychedelic freak out"[54] on *The Mothers-in-Law* (1967–69) in 1968 or singer-songwriter Harry Nilsson's "low-key"[55] crooning in *The Ghost and Mrs. Muir* (1968–70) in the same year. Bad acting from these musicians abounded: the laconic Nilsson seems somewhat shell-shocked on set as he takes refuge from a soundstage storm among the characters of the high-strung sitcom world. Unlike variety show performances, frequently cable-free electric guitars and poor lip-synching suggest the promise of a live musical performance was less important than the unusual opportunity to see the musician interacting with the quotidian environment of the sitcom. While some TV appearances featured established stars such as Neil Diamond on detective series *Mannix* (1967–75) in 1967,[56] or the not-exactly youth-oriented Sammy Davis Jr. on teen-centric *The Patty Duke Show* (1965–68) in 1965,[57] in keeping with the cost-cutting impulses of the television production of the time, many of these cameos featured emerging Los Angeles musicians such as the Standells' stint on *The Munsters* (1964–66) in 1965.[58]

Like cameos that interchangeably cast stars for their aura of star power rather than their specific star persona, many of these groups seem to stand in for the icons of contemporary music rather than being representative of current fame. Sometimes these representations were conscious: on the "Far Out Munsters" episode, the Standells played the Beatles' hit *I Wanna Hold Your Hand*.[59] Yet unlike the introduction of ingenue Eleanor White among a bevy of famous stars in *Hollywood Boulevard* (1938), there is no aura of glamour to borrow from; instead, on television it is entirely the potential for visibility that counts. All the same, these musician cameos were often reduced to musical performance and little else. While the prevalence of music-focused television shows such as *The Monkees* (1966–68) and *The Partridge Family* (1970–74) demonstrate cooperation between the music and television industries in the late 1960s, cameos by musical acts were undoubtedly another cross-promotion tactic. Harry Nilsson, for example, was advised to do such personal appearances by his record company in order to publicize his latest album.[60] Networks did not seem concerned about presenting the same cameos as their competitors, or keeping the references in-house, as overexposure was not a concern when sales were made by endless repetition of the same hits on the radio. Singing duo Chad and Jeremy, with several sporadic hits under their belt by 1965, for example, appeared not only in variety shows but also in the final seasons of both CBS's *The Dick Van Dyke Show* (1961–66)[61] and ABC's *The Patty Duke Show*[62] on consecutive Wednesday episodes in January 1965, and again on both *Batman* and the western series *Laredo* (1965–67) in 1966.[63]

The brief interlude of the musician cameos was used as a strategy to broaden viewership, briefly acknowledging the youth audience while still acknowledging the dominant interest of older viewers. A balance between the two was difficult to meet. Even as tactics aimed at the youth market, many musician cameos were alarmingly off-key: Sammy Davis Jr. seems very out of place as the talk of a junior prom on *The Patty Duke Show* in 1965, especially when he was joined by a surprisingly aged Peter Lawford. Chad and Jeremy were the subject of several notices in *Variety* about attempts to develop television programs around them, not only because of their youth appeal but also for a wider audience as traditional "pop artists to appeal beyond the teen scene."[64] Just as film studios looked to television to test and groom potential stars in the 1950s, guest star roles were often used to test potential recurring roles.[65] The kind of shows developed for the duo reflect the desire to combine the interests of older and younger viewers as both the tired western genre and the edgy comedy of *The Smothers Brothers Comedy Hour* (1967–69) were invoked.[66] Cameos seem to have provided a happy compromise. Many of these cameos appeared on sitcoms such as *The Mothers-in-Law* that took the older generation's conflict with the values of the coming-of-age baby boomers as the subject of their comedy. The on-screen reaction to these living room performances often pitted young against old as the centuries-old ghost of *The Ghost and Mrs. Muir* expressed his displeasure with Nilsson through otherworldly tempests while the eponymous *Mothers-in-Law* are made "gassy" by the musicians (fig. 29; fig 30).

Figure 29. Harry Nilsson is unwelcome in the living room of his hosts in *The Ghost and Mrs. Muir* (1968–70) . . .

Figure 30. . . . while the Seeds are even more out of place on the living room set of *The Mothers-in-Law* (1967–69).

Even as cameos seemed to be increasingly youth-oriented, young audiences continued to feel overlooked by television narratives, disheartened by censorship and disillusioned by the commercialism that was an integral part of television's mission.[67] The neutered cameo, bracketed by the approval of older characters and limited by a song's performance, hardly offered promised disruption. Functional uses of the cameo as a strategy for testing future stars or marketing upcoming singles through multimedia partnerships between entertainment industries was similarly likely to raise the hackles of the consumption-wary youth generation.[68] Cameos sequestered youth subjects in a space that had been carved out as brief and extradiegetic, while what growing numbers of the audience wanted was more narrative inclusion.

Reruns, Replay and Reflexivity: The Cameo in the Multichannel Era

By the end of the 1960s, television sitcoms were seen as cheaply made, crassly commercial, and out of touch with popular needs, a state of affairs that community groups campaigned to rectify and regulators blamed on the conditions of television production.[69] The uneven acting styles and narrative disruption caused by television cameos that were blatant advertising spots no doubt contributed to the impression that television was low-quality entertainment while creating a backlash against cameos. Cameos as advertising were part of the strategy of production companies and networks to make television profitable. During the early 1970s, new financial interest and syndication or fin-syn regulations for television in the United States were aimed at curtailing some of the excessive demands networks had placed on studios to produce inexpensive television while demanding the profits made when those shows were sold into syndication as reruns.[70] Networks had outsourced production from the early 1950s when it became clear that the additional cost of television production meant that the radio model of sponsorship would not allow networks to finance new television shows.[71] According to Lotz, networks demanded a share of syndication profits from the production companies who made and retained the rights to the series they produced. This stranglehold on production had hurt independent producers who could not afford to give up the profits recouped in syndication, given that most programs were initially sold at a loss to the networks.[72] Eventually only established studios who had other revenue streams from the film business, as well as the existing infrastructure and vaults of supplementary footage, could reliably afford to shoulder the costs when a series was not popular enough to reach syndication.[73] As a result, producers made multiple programs as cheaply as possible in order to increase the chance of earning an ever-reduced share of syndication. Fin-syn regulations were supposed to encourage independent producers to take the time and money to produce quality shows that thus would be more likely to reach syndication and ensure a return on a more considerable investment.[74] At the same time, groups advocated for increased emphasis on community and special-interest television ushered in the Blue Sky period at the end of the 1960s, where American legislators sought to protect and improve the kind of television programming available to audiences.[75] Television was championed as a potential site for education and discussion on relevant social issues. Quality TV was supposed to meet this challenge, addressing important issues of the time such as women in the workplace and issues of race and class.[76] Shows such as *The Mary Tyler Moore Show* (1970–77), about a single woman working in network television, and its spinoffs were exemplary of this approach to television programming. Cameos in *MTM*, for example, were never at the expense of narrative; the show kept cameos largely within the extended family of crossovers or mainstream and medium-appropriate figures such as Walter Cronkite.[77] Maturing audiences and an emphasis on naturalistic settings meant that cameos by "pop rock guest stars"[78] diminished in the 1970s. The 1980s saw an emphasis on hour-long dramas and police procedurals such as *Hill Street Blues* (1981–87) and *L.A. Law* (1986–94) rather than sitcoms, where quality television emphasized multiepisode story arcs that were not conducive to the comedic disruption of the cameo.[79]

New cameos may not have been seen with great regularity on television in the 1970s and early 1980s, but old cameos began to resurface in the form of reruns and video releases. Reruns had been a regular fixture of television since 1950 when, in a bid to compete with studio offerings, independent producers encouraged networks to broadcast their shows in multiple programming slots.[80] Television fed off movie studio vaults of old films, recycling cast-off movies, public domain films, and eventually, old television series to fill "low-rated fringe time hours."[81] As Derek Kompare has shown, reruns were central to television programming in the 1970s and 1980s, as the explosion of new cable channels, local cable turned superstations via satellite link, and new twenty-four-hour schedules meant that programming was needed to fill dead time cheaply.[82] Cameos in older films were made recognizable again as viewers became familiar with vanished celebrities, either through repeat viewing or through commentary that accompanied these repeat screenings. Specialty cable channels repackaged sitcoms and films with broadcast introductions or compilation programs that provided commentary from stars, scholars, or experts on the film broadcast.[83] Cable networks such as AMC, originally known as American Movie Classics, founded in 1984, and TCM, or Turner Classic Movies, which followed a decade later in 1994, employed elderly movie stars such as Debbie Reynolds and Douglas Fairbanks Jr. as hosts commenting on films drawn from the dregs of forgotten archival holdings that were often only tangentially related to those that had made them famous.[84] These commentaries provoked viewers to interact with media on television in cultish ways that emphasized the overlooked detail and the forgotten form, activating them as "television heritage."[85] Beginning in 1985, Nickelodeon's *Nick at Nite*, which featured marathon showings of entire seasons of series, also compiled clips from old sitcoms such as *The Dick Van Dyke Show* thematically, accompanying documentary evidence from episodes dealing with new technology or social mores with wry commentary.[86] Among the commentaries, hosts particularly pointed out cameos that were made visible when condensed into a week's worth of viewing, such as the appearance of Dick Van Dyke's personal assistant in a handful of episodes over the show's six seasons.[87] New viewing techniques made possible by expanding multimedia partnerships made cameos stand out to be recognized in a way they had not been before. Other latter-day rediscoveries of cameos were enabled by home viewing technology that allowed the viewer to endlessly revisit murky scenes to look for familiar faces. Cameos became more visible on television to be collected, captured, and replayed at the viewer's whim.

The impact of subscription cable channels such as HBO brought a new era of competition to the television landscape in the 1980s. HBO, and its imitators, benefited from subscribers who paid directly for the service rather than relying on the approval of advertisers for their programming.[88] The initial cost of setting up satellite-enabled channels, as well as restrictions on the film content that they could broadcast, meant that inexpensive documentary-based reality television and sports programming was a mainstay of their programming for decades.[89] Yet, when HBO and Showtime went into production for themselves in the 1980s, they had unusual creative freedom. DeFino points to the groundbreaking experience of disruptive self-reflexive comedy in Showtime's Hollywood-set sitcom *It's Garry Shandling's Show* (1986–90) and HBO's follow-up featuring Shandling as a late-night TV host on *The Larry Sanders Show* (1992–98).[90] Yet self-reflexivity is as old as television itself: much of television has presented backstage narratives about TV writing and producing, from *I Love Lucy* to *The Dick Van Dyke Show*. However, DeFino claims that in this new kind of backstage sitcom emerging in the late 1980s, even the promised glimpses of celebrity personas were undermined by artifice, with "many of the cameos conveying a pervading sense of randomness that undermined believability even within a comic context."[91] On *It's Garry Shandling's Show*, randomness was created by Shandling's ironic performance style, which emphasized the cameo as a break from the show's already shaky diegesis. Each cameo began with Shandling answering the door on his sitcom set, introducing the intruder to the studio audience with a smug "Hey, everybody!" Shandling refused the sitcom's conventions of naturalism and authenticity, acknowledging that cameos were no less constructed than the sitcom's makeshift set.

When stars could be seen elsewhere on television in talk shows, rerun movies, music videos, and even emerging reality television, the cameo offered nothing special, and Shandling underscored that fact. Unlike Lucy, Patty, or Batman, who were invariably driven to distraction by the proximity of a famous face in the 1950s and 1960s, Shandling appeared fatigued by celebrity as he suffered through the awkward attention of each cameoist from Gilda Radner to Tom Petty. Guest stars in the past had episodes built around them; for example, Brits Chad and Jeremy popped in on thematically named if narratively incoherent "The Redcoats Are Coming" on *The Dick Van Dyke Show*, while Nilsson's episode of *The Ghost and Mrs. Muir* was "The Music Maker." However, *Shandling's Show* pointed to the constructedness of cameos by refusing to naturalize them within the narrative. Television had long positioned itself against insincere film publicity and opened up intimate depictions of its subjects to careful scrutiny, embracing disruptive cameos that displaced the glamour of the movies into the domestic setting of television.[92] However, in the *Shandling* universe, stars were no longer special or worthy of note, and their cameos were just another part of the Hollywood machine. Shandling's mid-1990s HBO comedy *The Larry Sanders Show*, set backstage at a talk show, used the weekly cameo of a famous guest to reveal not their normalcy but larger-than-life lifestyles that included Playboy centerfolds and invitations to the White House as merely part of an average day's work. The semifamous Sanders's jealousy for these celebrity heavyweights was driven by the fact that he craved the opportunities for visibility that they treated as simply normal.[93] Exploring and exposing the inauthenticity of the cameo became its newest function in the coming decades, serving to make the tired cameo relevant again.

Television created an environment where celebrities were convened together on the small screen, in talk shows and variety shows. In the late 1980s, the development of national sporting leagues saw professional athletes appear on these circuits with more regularity, bringing a new set of recognizable figures to the entertainment industry. Taking advantage of this media convergence, the 1980s saw the reintroduction of anarchic comedy in films that spoofed media in vignettes reminiscent of the loose narratives featuring the comedy duos of the 1940s and 1950s. Yet rather than building inside jokes or a set of larger-than-life friends, spoof cameos emphasized past performances rather than any suggesting the gathering of real-world celebrity intelligence. Cameoists play themselves, but what they are identified with is tied up in the other films or entertainment fields they have appeared in rather than any personal details. When Charlie Sheen and Martin Sheen pass each other in boats navigating a perilous tropical river in *Hot Shots Part Deux* (1993), we witness a convergence of the Vietnam battlefields of *Platoon* and *Apocalypse Now* rather than a father-son reunion. The cameoists in these comedies don't exist outside of other roles they have played; for example, Martin Sheen yells to his real-life son, "I loved you in *Wall Street!*" In *Airplane* (1980), a film produced by Zucker, Abrahams, and Zucker, who were responsible for a glut of spoof films in the 1980s and 1990s, Gloria Swanson's self-obsessed cameo references her 1950 role in *Sunset Boulevard* as faded silent film queen Norma Desmond. These cameos were aimed at audiences equipped with detailed knowledge of the scripts and scenarios of old and new movies thanks to home viewing and a reappraisal of what there was to know about celebrities. The emerging category of mediatized sports stars still needed some of the introduction of older cameo forms, like basketball player Kareem Abdul-Jabbar, who informs a fan that he is not an NBA star but simply an airline pilot in *Airplane*, or 1984 Olympic gold medalist gymnast Mary Lou Retton, who is identified in a voice-over before she appears as a celebrity guest in a film-within-a-film in the television-industry-set *Scrooged* (1988). In the slapstick comedy films that were spun off from recurring roles from the *Saturday Night Live* late night sketch show, which featured celebrity guest hosts, cameos from actress Heather Locklear in *Wayne's World* (1993) or model Twiggy in *The Blues Brothers* (1980) were used not to create a sense of friendships or real-world connections but to bring the convergence of the television environment to the big screen. These cameos did not purport to be any less manufactured than the comedic characters they interacted with on-screen.

In the 1990s, stars once again came to the rescue of beleaguered networks. Movie stars had eased viewers into television viewing in the 1950s, while musical groups had enticed younger viewers in the 1960s. In the late 1960s, fin-syn regulations that severed financial links between networks and producers of television had curtailed the kind of multimedia promotion for which cameos had once been useful. Of course, in the intervening decades, studios and networks inched back into cooperation as buyouts and mergers often placed them in different branches of the same huge corporations. Networks may not have eschewed cameos in the decades before the 1990s, but the number of highly promoted television cameos in the celebrity-saturated end of the twentieth century certainly made cameos a prominent part of television viewing. With hundreds of channels to choose from by the early 1990s, television programs needed to work for audiences; as Lotz writes, "content must do more than appear 'on television' to distinguish itself as having cultural relevance, because what appears on television might be seen by just a few viewers."[94] In this narrowcast environment, where specialty channels outnumbered the formerly dominant networks, television was no longer a mass medium but a viewing experience aimed at multiple niche audiences.[95] Networks battled narrowcasting by enticing regular viewers with "phenomenal television" that was heavily marketed in multiple environments.[96] Just as cameos had been used to bring viewers from television to movie theaters or the record store, cameos now encouraged viewers to flip the channel on the TV set.

Cameos were used as a part of the marketing tactic to broaden the narrowcast environment. Cameos appeared in premieres or season finales as well as during the sweeps period that were used to determine ratings, a factor which allowed advertisers to determine how many viewers their ads were actually reaching.[97] They often appeared at the end of episodes, using heavy promotion of the star appearance to entice new viewers from other niche markets to hang on until the last moment. Music-loving baby boomers had to sit through the latest frivolous exploits of Gen-Xers *Dharma and Greg* (1997–2002) for a glimpse of Bob Dylan in "Play Lady Play," for example.[98] As in response to the star-studded cameo films of the 1960s, critics expressed predictably negative reactions to this "cameo-at-all-costs"[99] strategy as marketing at the expense of narrative. While often well-advertised cameos simply dispatched with surprise in exchange for the chance to observe the star in a new environment, as when an internetwork George Clooney cameo on *Friends* simply transferred the handsome *ER* (1994–2009) doctor to the *Friends* set, others such as affable game-show host Alex Trebek as a mysterious suited man in *The X-Files* (1993–2002) accounted for the loss of intimacy by revealing a dark side to the celebrity persona.[100] HBO negotiated the cameo particularly well, providing cameos in a self-reflexive environment such as *The Larry Sanders Show*, *Entourage* (2004–11), or *Curb Your Enthusiasm* (2000–2011), which avoided this charge of making story secondary by making the cameo, and its reversal of expectations, not only the subject of the show itself but practically a house style.

Television cameos in the 1990s reflect a highly integrated multimedia entertainment industry spanning music, film, and television. Yet despite this integration, the sheer number of media platforms and often unstable mergers and buyouts created an environment where there was no simple imperative for related companies or networks to cross-market media products through cameos. For example, politician Jesse Jackson was one of the first cameoists on *The Fresh Prince of Bel-Air* (1990–96) in 1990,[101] concurrent with the launch of Jackson's own talk show under the same production company. Oprah and Jay Leno, each with shows from rival networks and producers, also appeared in cameos during November sweeps[102] (fig. 31). Cameos by these television personalities, in which they are presented as part of the media landscape that is integral to establishing continuity with the viewer's world, not only acknowledge their influence but also consolidate their visibility as indispensable parts of real life. Personal narratives also seem to have trumped industrial loyalties in the name of visibility in the case of superstar Brad Pitt's appearance as a Thanksgiving guest on the sitcom *Friends* on the eve of the release of *Ocean's Eleven* (2001).[103] This November appearance of the celebrity couple of Pitt and his wife, *Friends* star Jennifer Aniston, together as enemies on the show was no doubt meant to spike ratings on the NBC sitcom while providing publicity for the upcoming 20th Century Fox film. While the end of fin-syn regulations in the 1990s may have encouraged networks to purchase from their own studios, stifling creativity due to lack of competition, cooperation between rival corporations in search of visibility was also still evident.[104] These cameos reflect that there was no simple model of affiliation to media corporations that governed who would be made visible and where.

Older television stars have a unique place on television. While the appearance of older stars and character actors in nostalgic cameos was a worn tactic in the 1960s, older stars have been largely overlooked for cameos since that period as the audience for films has gotten younger.[105] Television cameos continue to embrace nostalgia. Plasketes notes how cameos in the 1990s mostly featured baby boomer stars, such as Mick Jagger in *The Simpsons* (1989–) and Bob Dylan in *Dharma and Greg*.[106] *The Brady Bunch* (1969–74) mom Florence Henderson is one such forgotten star with

Figure 31. Oprah on the set of *Fresh Prince of Bel-Air*, or vice versa, in 1992.

an afterlife in cameos, with appearances on *It's Garry Shandling's Show*, backstage television comedy *30 Rock* (2006–13) and cartoon *The Cleveland Show* (2009–13) to name a few.[107] *Batman*'s Adam West is another actor, who, despite a long-running role on the animated *Family Guy* (1999–) as inept bureaucrat Mayor West, is also a cameo regular on sitcoms *King of Queens* (1998–2007) and nerd-oriented *The Big Bang Theory* (2007–).[108] Viewing a movie star in the familiar environs of a setting that is closely united with a domestic space is a celebrity encounter that is still thrilling to viewers.

Mocking Celebrity Culture

Television in the twenty-first century has been able to entice movie stars to return to the medium. In the late 1990s, subscription cable courted producers with a limited but standout record of series such as *The Larry Sanders Show* and *Sex and the City* (1998–2004) with few checks on language or sexual content. Instated as autocratic, auteurist showrunners, these television producers would come to embody the moniker of quality television in the early 2000s with complex, serialized narratives that demand extended concentration.[109] Indeed, successful series such as *Game of Thrones* (2011–19) and *The Sopranos* (1999–2007) found their greatest profitability in the sale of DVD collections; these series have season-long narratives and extended character systems, emphasizing detail-oriented viewing and "complexity of plot and narrative unavailable to the shorter form feature film."[110] At the same time, viewers continue to diversify their viewing experiences on mobile, internet-connected devices enabling on-demand viewing that bears little resemblance to the television and its model of flow.[111] In the wake of this new stream of storytelling, the network year, where a number of new shows are premiered at the end of the summer following intensive, restricted development periods and rigid shooting schedules, has given way to year-round scheduling.[112] While on the one hand this break with a calendar has encouraged a "constant habit of viewing,"[113] as with anthology series in the 1950s, the moveable schedule and much-reduced commitment of time as well as the return of closed-ended series, not to mention the creative potential of these kind of narrative structures, has once again made television a desirable place for actors wary of overexposure or exposure in a lowbrow environment thought to be beneath a real star.

Cameos continue to be used to test potential cast members on television. Networks have drawn increasingly from the ranks of those who are more firmly established within the moviemaking A-list, such as Alec Baldwin in *30 Rock*, while cable channels HBO and FX have drawn top-tier stars Brad Pitt and Glenn Close. Each of these actors made their initial appearances as stars on television in cameos in the early 2000s: Pitt and Baldwin both made *Friends* appearances as potential love interests and Glenn Close had a cameo on *The West Wing* (1999–2006).[114] While Close, who is known for theater as much as for movies, may have been wooed as a highbrow "dream name" for *The Shield's* (2002–8) producers at FX, she was approachable because of her cameo.[115] Chloë Sevigny, regarded as an indie darling for her work in edgy independent films, went from cameoist on queer-friendly sitcom *Will and Grace* (1998–2004) to regular as a Mormon bigamist on HBO's *Big Love* (2006–11). Movie stars are appearing with frequency on television again, and not only in cameos. Stars who appear on television are often, as with Pitt or Close, in roles that require us to deal with a series' worth of character space that overtakes their star persona. While Colin Farrell and Matthew McConaughey appeared on closed-end subscription cable drama *True Detective* (2014–), Christina Ricci and Parker Posey appeared in recurring comedic roles on basic cable on AMC and CBS. The failure of television to procure personalities with the distinction of movie stars serves to reinforce the quality of these newly star-approved television productions, as the formerly hard division between the star hierarchies lends distinction to those instances in which movie stars now appear on television as recurring characters. As migration of actors between television and movie productions has become more fluid, celebrated movie actors have made the gradual transition to television through small roles. The cameo provides a gateway to the television experience.

On the other hand, television stars in movies are often reduced to appearances on diegetic television screens, such as host Jay Leno on a mock version of *The Tonight Show* (1992–2014) joking about the subject of political satire in *Wag the Dog* (1997) or interviewer Larry King ending *Enemy of the State* (1998) as the hero watches *Larry King Live* (1985–2010). Because these talk show hosts normally operate in the documentary space of a talk show, their commentaries on diegetic events such as presidential infidelities or surveillance scandals, framed in the domestic television screen, contribute verisimilitude to the diegesis of a film. Yet just as cameos by entertainment celebrities have transformed in the 1990s from trustworthy intimate views to self-parody, the cameo by a real-world television journalist has become so commonplace that it has begun to lose its impact as a marker of the real world. For example, comedy-horror TV film *Sharknado* (2013) featured NBC weatherman Al Roker reporting on the titular shark-infested tornado, and actress Naomi Watts appeared in political black-comedy *Vice* (2018) in brief vignettes as the opinionated newscaster for a CNN-like twenty-four-hour news network. Both cameos shatter the authority of the real-world journalist through juxtaposition. On the one hand, Roker's cameo shows the potential abuse of the power of the known newscaster by using him to give plausibility to an impossible weather event. On the other hand, the use of a well-known star, whose relationship to stardom and scriptedness is transparent, to play the small role of an unabashedly critical news anchor undermines the convention of the celebrity news host as objective source. Cameos continue to transform through the reversal of expectations of the celebrity persona as new forms of celebrity become conventional.

The boundaries of celebrity are increasingly defined by visibility, while visibility is available to many on television. As John Ellis points out, the experience of being filmed, a rare occurrence when television first began, has become a regular part of the twenty-first-century experience.[116] Audiences have firsthand experience of the modes of performance as actors in front of a camera. In this environment, cameos cannot promise the access they once did. While celebrities since Hope and Crosby have been undermining their star images to make themselves more ordinary, such a reveal has been so thoroughly absorbed into the cameo's function that it offers little to the viewer. The ubiquity of television cameos on network television in the 1990s made the claims that celebrities were people just like us, just as the rise in reality programming made ordinary people celebrities and promised little of the unknown for either the eager fan or curious viewer. The idea that a cameo is other than a performance, or that a movie star or ordinary person would not be fluent in its codes, is unthinkable. As a result, rather than cameos that present stars as people just like us, cameos often reveal stars as horrifyingly different. This trend is more visible on cable, where the trend toward less-censored language and storylines makes such roles more common than network television. In the mid-1990s, HBO's *The Larry Sanders Show* redeemed those celebrity faults revealed through cameos by comparing them with the invariably worse traits of antihero Larry Sanders, and subsequent Hollywood-set cable shows from many of the same writers featuring similar antiheroes have followed suit (fig. 32). In more recent years, HBO's *Curb Your Enthusiasm* (2000–) and FX's *Louie* (2010–15) have used the creative freedom and uncensored language of these platforms to showcase celebrities as liars and egoists whose public images cannot be trusted. In the cameos in these series, for example, actor Michael J. Fox tries to explain away his bad behavior as the symptoms of Parkinson's, a disease about which he has very publicly discussed the effects. In a *Louie* cameo that is more poignant in light of his suicide, usually upbeat comedian Robin Williams

Figure 32. Despite her glamorous appearance, Sharon Stone is too down-to-earth for talk show host Larry Sanders on *The Larry Sanders Show* (1992–98).

takes excessively cruel pleasure in putting down another comic.[117] Top-tier stars whose forays beyond cinema have usually taken them to the highbrow forum of the theater are also increasingly willing to appear in polar offcasting, such as a potty-mouthed Kate Winslet on *Extras* (2005–7)[118] (fig. 33). Such supposedly intimate views of the famous as cheap, rude, insensitive, and insecure are tempered by the knowledge that the cameo is a performance like any other, rewarding instead the viewer who recognizes that cameos are just another performance among many.

Rather than celebrating celebrities, cameos on television are increasingly used to mock celebrity culture. Addressing skepticism about celebrity images, especially star images marketed by film publicists, has been part of television's strategy for winning viewers since the 1950s. Yet, celebrity images, constantly exposed on the internet, have seemingly little left to admit to, except the process of construction itself. In the 2008 appearance of Coldplay singer Chris Martin on TV industry comedy *Extras*, the episode

Figure 33. Kate Winslet talks dirty behind the scenes in the backstage comedy *Extras* (2005–7).

follows the showrunner's horror as the producers insist that Martin inexplicably serenade a shift of factory workers to promote his new album.[119] The appearance of minor celebrity and former celebrity-trial witness Kato Kaelin as a rodeo entertainer in Zach Galifianakis's AMC TV series, *Baskets* (2016), where he is identified as he enters the rodeo ring as being "from the OJ trial," mocks manufactured celebrity of another kind.[120] Just as the multichannel revolution has opened up television to movie stars by creating an outlet for the detailed mise-en-scène of quality television, it has also lifted ordinary people to fame's heights as many more channels fill up the bulk of their time with cheap reality programming from news to game shows. Both question why viewers celebrate visibility, creating comedy as they disrupt the conventions surrounding who is worthy of recognition.

5

AUTHOR SIGNATURE

Directors On-Screen and the Celebratory Cameo

"Don't forget this man," the announcer for the theatrical trailer for Hitchcock's *Spellbound* (1945) admonishes, his voice-over accompanying the image of a busy hotel lobby caught in freeze-frame as a number of men in hats and suits emerge from a crammed elevator. The frame shows a jumble of bodies and mustachioed faces, catching the two men at the front of the crowd as they exit, one in a dark suit and smoking a cigar, already heading off-screen from center frame, and the second one just caught in focus, wearing a lighter suit and a similar hat (fig. 34). Which one should we remember and which one should we forget? The man we should be paying attention to, of course, is Alfred Hitchcock, who, as the announcer tells us, "has plenty to do with the terrifying mystery" of the movie to come, yet who is already leaving the scene as quickly as he arrived. While the attention of the trailer quickly turns to the invisible producer, David O. Selznick, the scene nevertheless begins with the image of Hitchcock as arresting hook. The director cameos of Hitchcock are an important part of the history of the cameo role, occurring as they do in many of his films. These brief appearances of Hitchcock as an extra in his own movies are an example of a recurring type, and maybe even the archetype, of the cameo, where the author delivers his signature with a flourish. Like the Renaissance artist appearing in his portraits of the powerful, or even the Vitagraph team of the early twentieth century, Hitchcock is presenting for recognition his role in image-making. As an artist-cameo, Hitchcock's cameos made a powerful bid for the importance of the director, not only establishing his visibility but also consolidating his reputation as a director in control of the minutiae of his filmmaking. As miniature roles, the cameo confirmed to his breathless critics that Hitchcock's hand was visible in even the tiniest details.

Before Hitchcock, recognizable director cameos in films of their own making are few and far between. Other than directors doubling as actors in the very early cinema, King Vidor appeared in his film *Show People* in 1929, and Chaplin played a brief cameo in *A Woman in Paris* in 1923. DeMille was a regular in other people's films. However, Hitchcock made himself visible and recognizable in his own films, where the name, the image, and the film product under his aegis were linked together from a very early point in his career. The cameo had no small hand in consolidating this reputation and establishing his recognition. In fact, the cameos in which Hitchcock indulged from his first films as a director were the model for the famous introductory skits that accompanied his television series of the 1950s and 1960s. The ever-present Hitchcock image, combined with his insistence in his press that he had a creative hand in all aspects of his films, was used to illustrate his presence. Like stars who did not belong in small roles, directors

Figure 34. Hitchcock in the background of *Spellbound* (1945).

did not belong in the background. Appearing as an extra, or in small comedic bits, Hitchcock confirmed his presence not only in front of the camera but also behind it at any given moment, in establishing shots that could have been handled by a second unit, but instead bear his imprint. The director cameo as a sign of unusual attention to detail is thus a signature of authorial control.

While Hitchcock's cameos may have tried to assert his visibility as the primary creative force of the film, and set the tone for other directors establishing themselves as auteurs, other behind-the-scenes roles also stood up in that period to be celebrated as authors. In the 1950s, as filmmaking established itself as an art worthy of contemplation, there were new reasons to take credit. Writers of scripts and music occasionally appeared in cameos that identified them within their work, such as Jay Livingston and Ray Evans in *Sunset Boulevard* or screenwriter Buck Henry in *The Graduate* (1967). Directors such as Cecil DeMille and Otto Preminger showed their hand not only by presenting their own image to be lauded but also by enveloping other famous figures within a world of their own invention. Woody Allen summons Marshall McLuhan to a ticket queue to respond to a pretentious moviegoer in *Annie Hall* (1977) and Martin Scorsese places the real boxer Jake LaMotta beside the fictionalized version of himself played by Robert DeNiro in the biopic *Raging Bull* (1980). Some of these appearances truly blend into the background, visible only to expert audiences. These cameos of celebrated figures who are otherwise not widely known, or as I call them, celebratory cameos, have a cultish appeal. Celebratory cameos, unlike celebrity cameos, feature figures that are not necessarily immediately or broadly recognizable but are nevertheless worthy of tribute. Rather than presenting already-visible celebrities, these cameos celebrate less visible groups, such as authors, directors, benefactors, muses, parents, or even old friends. Celebratory cameos divide the audience into two groups: the privileged insiders who can recognize the little-seen honoree, and those without the fan knowledge necessary to recognize the celebrated figure as more than an extra.

Celebratory cameos challenge the audience to recognize them, creating a game of recognition. Hitchcock's cameos made the director extremely visible as the author of his films, but by the end of his career, this signature often seemed to overshadow the films themselves in reviews and studio publicity. Director cameos continue to reward cinephiles eager to show their familiarity with the makers of movies. Yet, perhaps reluctant to repeat the turn of events where the Hitchcock cameo was more anticipated than the film, directors today seem more inclined to keep their cameos out of the spotlight, making sure they take only a minor part in the press around the film and its auteur. Rather than presenting their bodies as obvious author signatures, these directors prefer to conjure up a more nebulous collection of celebratory cameos that are often at least minimally disguised. These celebratory cameos require more careful attention to the touch of the master, his interests and approval, than the much-publicized Hitchcock cameos demanded. Yet, following his precedent, the celebratory cameo has become an undeniable sign of authority clearly planted by filmmakers mimicking the master and sought out in turn by those filmgoers seeking to play along with their favorite directors.

Hitchcock in His Own Image

Like artist portraits of the Renaissance or the Vitagraph cameos of the 1910s, director cameos reveal their role in the making of the image as a sign of power. Director cameos were a signature of sorts, establishing visibility for the otherwise largely invisible behind-the-scenes role. Unlike actor-directors who played larger roles in their own films, the director cameo is purely about the signature.[1] The consensus that these cameos are attributable to a signature draws on the precedent of artist-portraits in painting. Like these early examples, director cameos compete with the established intertwined systems of power and visibility, wresting attention away from actors and celebrities to assert an alternate visible locus of creative power. As Stam writes, "filmmakers have the perennial choice of revealing or concealing the effects by which they create illusions."[2] Director cameos privilege directors as the creative authority behind the filmmaking, because they are often the sole creator behind the filmic illusion who appears for recognition. When other authors such as screenwriters or composers appear for recognition, the authorial signature is refocused or dissipated.

Hitchcock's cameos, which appeared as early as his first thriller *The Lodger* (1926), are perhaps the most celebrated. The genealogy of Hitchcock's cameos has been linked to Chaplin's "flash appearances" in *Woman in Paris* (1923),[3] while other cameos contemporary to Hitchcock's first appearance come from more experimental European art cinema, such as the work of Luis Buñuel and Abel Gance.[4] François Truffaut, the champion of the *politique des auteurs* in the 1950s and 1960s, held up Hitchcock as an example of the kind of complete authorship that the filmmakers of the French New Wave sought to emulate.⁵ Bolstered by "his roost atop the pantheon of American auteurs,"⁶ Hitchcock established a vogue for the director cameo as a sign of authorial control that would influence American directors emerging in the shadow of the New Wave as the New Hollywood, so that "in the seventies, indeed, such signatures became almost de rigueur."⁷

The strength of these claims to authority is dependent on the extent of their visibility in popular culture and the audience's powers of recognition. The choice to insert a director cameo often goes hand in hand with other campaigns of visibility. Directors are much less identifiable than actors, for whom visibility is a profession. As such, directorial cameos do not necessarily call attention to themselves as a diegetic break, in instances such as Hitchcock's appearance among extras as in *Spellbound*, or simply falling short of celebrity visibility as when art house director Terrence Malick rings a killer's doorbell in *Badlands* (1973). Identifying directors can be a challenge, enticing the viewers into a game. Like games, they challenge passive viewers to demonstrate active mastery.⁸ This mastery is dependent on knowledge of cinema that extends beyond its most visible stars and may include attention to other, subcultural metatexts such as fan magazines and websites.⁹ In some cases, especially in that of directors such as Malick or David Cronenberg who work independently or outside of the mainstream, they require special knowledge of a person who is largely invisible in popular culture. As independents, such directors are often seen as eschewing the industrial prerogatives that could distance their films from the personal creative vision that is the quintessential goal of the auteur.¹⁰ While stylistic or thematic trends found in those works can be debated, the cameo is an established way of making the authorial signature undeniably visible in what Mathijs calls "active auteuring,"¹¹ binding together a director's body of work as a continuous supertext.¹² While authors use the cameo to signal their mastery, viewers who recognize this signature can also lay public claim to an element of distinction. Just as scholars and critics delight in sharing Hitchcock sightings, Mathijs recounts identifying other Cronenberg initiates in the theater based on their knowing laughter on his cameo appearance.¹³ Solving Hitchcock's puzzles is not only about proving that one is privy to knowledge about the director, but also that the spectator can think like the film's author, Hitchcock.¹⁴ The discerning eye that uncovers celebratory cameos hidden like extras in the background is a specialist eye. Celebratory cameos are not for every audience, but they are evidence of the director's presence signaled for those in the know.

Hitchcock was an unusually visible director, presenting an image that was tailored for recognizability, from his habitual sober suit to his "carefully designed"[15] speeches. Even before he established his "trademark of a tiny personal appearance,"[16] his body was used as a stamp of authorship, extending to his first use of a sketch of his profile as a signature in the 1920s (fig. 35). This signature would be his for the rest of his life, adopted with some modification across his multimedia empire of mystery magazines and television series.[17] His biographers attribute to him a preternatural campaign for visibility dating back to those days when he was first using this caricature, where he actively pursued name recognition to guarantee his continued desirability.[18] In his twenties, in 1926, he was first hailed as a great director with the success of his third film, and first thriller, *The Lodger*. While he has a brief appearance in that film, his cameos were first noted by the contemporary press in a longer, slightly comedic sequence in *Blackmail* (1929), where he is annoyed by a small boy on a train as he reads his newspaper. From the commentary on the cameos, it is clear that Hitchcock had already emerged as a public and visible figure.[19] In the 1930s, Hitchcock appeared intermittently as an extra in his own films, loitering in crowd scenes, with his scenes becoming more visible and more remarked on following his move to Hollywood in the 1940s. This visibility only increased with his television series in the 1950s, which began with a brief introduction and conclusion from Hitchcock. By the late 1970s, Hitchcock would become "the most universally recognized man in the world."[20] He appeared in cameos in many of his fifty-three films, ranging from barely distinguishable walk-ons to incongruous comedic bit parts that paired him with nurses, infants, and double basses.

Hitchcock and his cameos were beloved by the New Wave; Alain Resnais even featured a Hitchcock "cameo" in cardboard form in his impeccable art film *Last Year at Marienbad* (1961).[21] However, the broad humor of the most visible of Hitchcock's cameos links them more strongly with the comedic cameos in Hope films rather than the realist pretensions of Truffaut or Resnais. Although his influences may have been the visible appearances of Chaplin and Lang, it was only after his move in the 1940s to Hollywood where cameos were a part of a vernacular and often comedic tradition that Hitchcock's cameos were publicized as a marketing tactic and came to

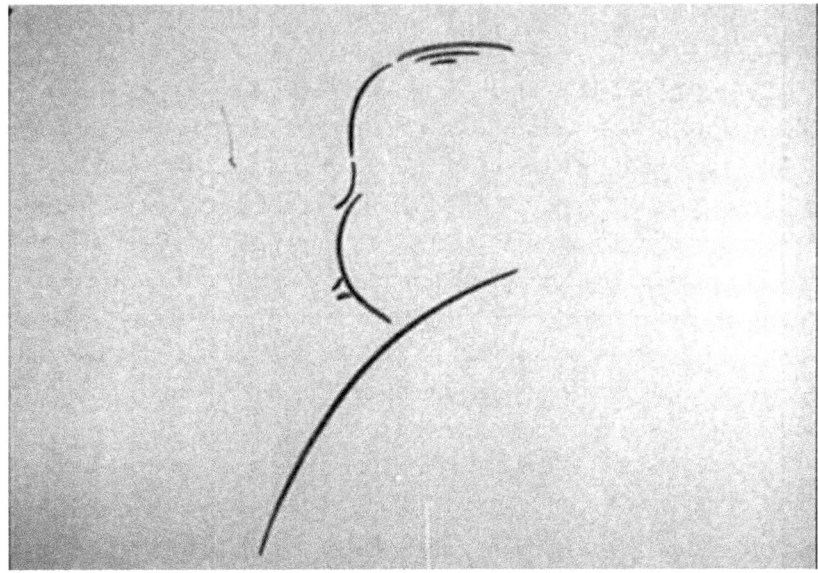

Figure 35. The sketched profile that opened *Alfred Hitchcock Presents* (1955–62).

regularly adopt the middlebrow wit that was so appealing to mass audiences. Hitchcock's cameos, despite being a signature of the personal creative control that would gain him champions in the international art cinema, owed their visibility to his employment within the Hollywood industry.

Like all cameos, Hitchcock's appearances introduce his public persona into the diegetic world, presenting him variously as a gourmand in *Lifeboat* (1944), a dog lover in *The Birds* (1963), and a bridge player in *Shadow of a Doubt* (1943) rather than the omniscient director of auteur theory. The question of where he belongs in the diegesis is what drives the disruptive pleasure of cameos, and Hitchcock's cameos in particular. Is Hitchcock the celebrity recognized in *Strangers on a Train* by the tennis star protagonist? Certainly, he would have been visible to the tennis star's companion, the murderer Bruno, who happens to be reading one of Hitchcock's mystery anthologies.[22] Yet, others have pointed out that many of Hitchcock's cameos often ostensibly put him at the mercy of his fictional world rather than in control of it. Like Chaplin's Tramp, Hitchcock is a kind of modern-day bumpkin, unaware of the highly dangerous situations into which he has naively blundered, "a figure on the margin of the fictional world."[23] Although he does remain a marginal background figure in *Mr. and Mrs. Smith* (1941), *Psycho* (1960), or *Frenzy* (1972), he is often caught up in the business of performance that borders on the slapstick, whether expressing indignation at being shut out of a bus in *North by Northwest* or jumping out of a wheelchair in *Topaz* (1969). These performances do not present a glimpse of a purportedly candid Hitchcock, as in the case of DeMille on set in *Star Spangled Rhythm* (1942) or Crosby demonstrating how to croon in *Let's Make Love*. Whereas DeMille and later Scorsese appear alongside cameras in directorial poses of control in many of their cameos, references within the cameos to Hitchcock as director have been deciphered by scholars only through what Miller calls a "too-close view."[24] Instead, the cameos demonstrate the author's power to play whatever role he chooses, writing himself in only to take himself out again just as quickly. As Cohen writes, "here is the one figure who is not an actor,"[25] yet he insists on taking that role too. Rather than weighed down with meaning, they are playful, emphasizing his ability to intertwine both documentary and narrative space.

Hitchcock's fondness for games is well documented, and they were a recurring theme in publicity for his films. In 1943 he "directed" a *Look* "Photocrime" editorial in which pictorial clues in a series of photographic illustrations revealed a murderer to the canny reader.[26] To publicize *Torn Curtain* (1966) twenty years later, he proposed a similar photo editorial where he would play all the characters in a murder investigation, acting out a riddle that the public could solve, or working in various trades while recording in candid camera style the reactions of all involved.[27] Film magazines used similar pictorial games of identification to condition viewers to pay attention to the star as a cinephilic detail, encouraging the development of a community of knowledgeable fans.[28] The game of seeking out Hitchcock's on-screen image conditioned fans in much the same way with Hitchcock in the role of star, and was positioned by critics as "a regular game played by devoted fans to watch for a brief glimpse of his august bulk at some unexpected point."[29] For these scholars, Hitchcock is seen as the man behind the curtain, planting cinematic clues of his mastery as he creates the "secret writing systems that traverse this work."[30]

The invitation to play along with Hitchcock's cameos has been irresistible to critics and scholars. If scholars and fans overlap in their attitudes and pursuits, nowhere is that more clear than in studies of Hitchcock.[31] Bellour thrills about his discovery in the cameo of *I Confess* (1953): "Again master at the game, Hitchcock passes across the screen, in a now famous image, silhouetted against the sky at the top of the steps (count them almost thirty-nine!)."[32] Miller reveals the return of the diet drug that Hitchcock advertises in his newspaper-ad cameo in *Lifeboat* in a flashing neon sign outside the apartment where *Rope* (1948) unfolds, but also dwells on the graphic riddles posed by the marks of a dolly on the apartment's carpet.[33] Some of these unveilings are more convincing than others. If Hitchcock presented his own image in each of his films, why not present other signs of his influence, from having his hero mistake the name of a spymaster for his own acronym "A-H" in *The 39 Steps* (1935)[34] to the "beloved brandy that appears, like his own cameo, in fifty-one of his fifty-three films"?[35] In *Find the Director and Other Hitchcock Games*, Leitch denies the cameo's thematic or aesthetic importance to situate it as a game undertaken purely for pleasure, treating the cameos "as moves in a game of hide and go seek."[36] When Hitchcock began his cameos, most cameos were announced within the film for proper identification; his appearances created the game of find-the-director that opened up documentary space within the narrative (fig. 36). Yet it is from the intentional quality of the cameos that the purposefulness of these flourishes can be extrapolated, making the cameos the most vital evidence of a game that is engaging the viewer. As Miller writes, "the recognized style is so because it courts recognizability and flatters recognition."[37] In recognition, one becomes like Hitchcock.

Hitchcock's authorial control was legendary even in his time; as one reviewer wrote, "He's known to plot his movies down to the last frame."[38] Widespread anecdotes of the autocratic author were part of a concerted effort to establish Hitchcock as an auteur.[39] Hitchcock's ethic became ideology in the hands of critics such as Truffaut, who extracted from Hitchcock the mantra, "For better or for worse, I must do the whole thing myself."[40] His disdain for actors, his distrust of writers, and his dislike for improvisation were subjects he frequently expounded on.[41] From his first years in Hollywood, his determination to re-create his precisely plotted frames led to shoots that went expensively past schedule.[42] His exacting visual demands drove him to insist on directing or at least attending the shoots of his own second units on films such as *North by Northwest* or *The Paradine Case* (1947), where he traveled to England to stipulate the relative color-value of the steam in a busy train station.[43] Hitchcock was known to involve himself in the script's creation in ways that ranged from supervision and the

Figure 36. Hitchcock is unmistakable in *Strangers on a Train* (1951).

delivery of copious notes to the obsessive one-on-one writer's conference of his later years.[44] As Charles Bennett, who adapted *The 39 Steps* among other Hitchcock productions of the 1930s and 1940s said about the ultimate attribution of credit, "It always has to be Hitch."[45] Yet, despite his insistence that Hitchcock derided his work as an author, Bennett himself appeared as a "companion"[46] to Hitchcock in his cameo in *The 39 Steps*. It speaks to the strength of the Hitchcock myth, as well as the role of visibility in the cameo's function, that this cameo had to be "revealed many years later"[47] to Bennett's biographer.[48] While scholars working against purely auteurist critique have suggested that his ability to consistently assemble brilliant production teams was Hitchcock's greatest achievement,[49] the popular and scholarly attention to Hitchcock's cameos alone suggests that he triumphed as the author worthy of being recognized. Whether or not Bennett appears, cameos and their attendant recognition were overwhelmingly reserved for Hitchcock alone.

The cameo presents Hitchcock's body as tool and proof of his authorship. Bellour suggests that the cameo serves just this purpose of "authorial signature,"[50] and Hitchcock appears in places that indicate his control of the progress of the narrative, holding all the cards as in *Shadow of a Doubt* (1943), or exiting to allow characters to enter important narrative sites as in *Marnie*, *The Birds*, or *Strangers on a Train*.[51] These cameos acknowledge the camera as the representative of his point of view, as he looks back at the camera "whose inscription he duplicates."[52] Miller, on the other hand, argues that the cameo shows Hitchcock infiltrating the lives of his characters, demonstrating physical as well as emotional proximity to their stories.[53] Many scholars suggest that Hitchcock's cameos point to important details that are otherwise imperceptible.[54] Hitchcock certainly was no stranger to using his body and his image in publicity, playing the sober deadpan on television, in interviews and events, or even disguising himself as other characters. Hitchcock promoted stories about his enormous girth in the American press in the 1930s to attract the attention of Hollywood studios.[55] These "ridiculous stunts"[56] included floating a wax effigy of himself in the Thames for the *Frenzy* trailer, playing a slightly batty twin brother in some introductions to the television series, or dressing as a woman for the cover of *Holiday* (1964).[57] Indeed, Hitchcock participated in the fictional lives of his characters in quite intimate ways. Hitchcock traced out the flight path of his defecting protagonists in *Torn Curtain* by taking a series of flights from Sweden into East Berlin during the height of the Cold War.[58] He even completed a trailer for *Frenzy* that showed him buying a red necktie that he insisted was to be used to strangle a woman to death in the manner of the film's antagonist.[59] While usually the cameo is the intrusion of the extradiegetic, in this case it seems that Hitchcock was perfectly willing to have his films intrude on his own sense of person.

Cameos and the Hitchcock Brand

Hitchcock established his brand early on in his career. Perhaps foreshadowing his use of the cameo, even his first film in 1926 began audaciously with an image of his autograph.[60] The press for *The Lodger*, released when his first directing credit was only eleven months behind him, predicted a future "when, as is surely coming, Alfred Hitchcock's name looms large on screens, programs, and advertisement[s] instead of that of the star artists."[61] Though Hitchcock was following in the steps of continental and American directors such as Lang, Murnau, and Griffith,[62] such a strategy represented "the first time in British film history that the director received even greater press than his stars."[63] Hitchcock courted such press from the beginning of his career; in 1925, Hitchcock made a speech to the British Film Institute about the importance of establishing the director brand.[64] He approved of the "self-promotional flair"[65] of directors such as DeMille, citing him at this time as a model for the visible director.[66] DeMille would go on to embrace cameos as part of his own successful quest for continued visibility in film and radio,[67] yet he appeared only in the films of other directors, and always identified by name. Hitchcock's cameos from their inception are unusually invisible for someone with the goal of recognition, beginning with his two appearances as an extra in *The Lodger*: in a crowd scene and seen from behind as newspapers are rolled through the press at the printer. Although it is convenient to have the first cameo appear in what Hitchcock identified at Truffaut's urging as "the first true 'Hitchcock movie,'"[68] they do not obviously present him for recognition, nor were they recognized in the press. Hitchcock suggested that these cameos were "strictly utilitarian; we had to fill the screen."[69] Nevertheless, as an extension of the Hitchcock strategy to be the most visible element of his films, the cameo puts to use the techniques of visibility most readily available to him in a way that would be developed throughout his career as a game not only of showing but of hiding as well.

Hitchcock's next cameo was in *Blackmail*, and it included an attention-grabbing struggle with a little boy that borders on slapstick; as Spoto writes, he is "visible, just, in *The Lodger*, but in *Blackmail* he makes a characteristic gag appearance which more or less requires him to be recognized."[70] Yet even the journalist who delicately pointed out this early appearance felt the need to respect it as a secret whose appearance should not be too easily revealed, dancing around the fact with the closing statement: "if the gentleman who has his hat knocked over his eyes by a precocious infant in the tube train scene is not 'A.H.,' it must be his double."[71] Of the many clippings preserved in Hitchcock's scrapbooks, this mention from a trade paper is the only one that identifies his cameo, and, although to be fair there were no more outbursts of this kind of physical comedy in Hitchcock's films, there is no mention of the cameos again until *The Lady Vanishes* in 1938. In fact, despite the impression conveyed that Hitchcock appears in "celebrated cameo appearances in virtually all of his films,"[72] Hitchcock makes only four or five cameos during the early period of his first seventeen films, and he doesn't begin his celebrated run of cameos until his move to America to film

Rebecca in 1940. Curiously enough, most of those early cameos are from the thriller films most commonly associated with Hitchcock's later work rather than his early romantic comedies, dramas, or even musicals. These identified cameos also appear in Hitchcock's most frequently screened early films.[73] That Hitchcock happened to sign those films, which would fit most easily into the genre and themes that would define him as an auteur, either strenuously affirms that theory or suggests that perhaps other Hitchcock appearances have been overlooked or lost to the wear and tear of almost a century. Hitchcock himself identifies in a cameo in another well-regarded film, *Rich and Strange*, which as yet has not been uncovered.[74]

Clearly the cameo had captured the imagination of David O. Selznick, the *Gone with the Wind* producer who brought Hitchcock to America, and his publicists. Beginning with *Rebecca*, Hitchcock's name became increasingly associated with the films he made, receiving above-the-title billing on his move to the United States.[75] While the Hitchcock image was first used in a trailer in his last British film, *Jamaica Inn* (1939), by his second US production, the cameo began to trickle more regularly into reviews. The press campaign for *Foreign Correspondent* (1940) focused on exploring the "Hitchcock cult,"[76] and, as apparent from its frequent appearance in reviews of the time, obviously discussed the cameo as part of the director's "unmistakable stamp."[77] The filming of an alternate cameo was used as a publicity stunt for *Life* magazine in *Mr. and Mrs. Smith*.[78] The cameo itself was used in the trailer for *Lifeboat* (1944), yet even that film, which presented a return to the kind of visual gag of over a decade previous with a before-and-after photograph of Hitchcock advertising a miracle slimming drug in a newspaper onboard the castaways' raft, was not overwhelmingly called attention to, even when reviewers pointed out other minute "touches of artificiality."[79] As Leitch points out, "the audience was expected by this point now not only to be familiar with Hitchcock's profile but to be interested in its changing shape as personal revelation."[80] While Leitch suggests that Hitchcock's American films of the 1940s were much less whimsical than his British offerings, the extent to which whimsy was allowed free rein in the cameo demonstrates that this route to undermining classical narrative was welcomed in Hollywood.[81] After all, unlike other reflections of Hitchcock's wit that could be jarring with classical composition, Hitchcock's appearances were gently disruptive, asserting that "the movie they are watching is only a movie, but this realization will not break the movie's spell."[82]

Most writers take the point of *Alfred Hitchcock Presents* (1955–62) and each episode's characteristic introduction as the moment at which America became familiar with the Hitchcock image,[83] yet it seems as though the cameo and its attendant publicity in fact created the context for these witty intros. Publicity materials, such as the trailer for *Spellbound* in 1945, repeatedly asserted Hitchcock as a star who audiences could and should recognize and remember. The cameo with which the trailer begins was not highlighting a new feature but an acknowledgment of this type of appearance as part of the director's long-standing "traditional whimsy."[84] Lobby cards for *Spellbound* featured ads touting the film: "You would see it just to see its two brilliant stars . . . and here are all three!" The cards featured an illustration of Hitchcock between Ingrid Bergman and Gregory Peck.[85] The Hitchcock persona that seems built around the anthology television format of the mid-1950s had already emerged.[86] In fact, the initial script for the *Spellbound* trailer had a dry introduction from the director reminiscent of the form that would be perfected for the introductions to *Alfred Hitchcock Presents*, beginning with the ubiquitous "I'm Alfred Hitchcock."[87]

The ubiquitous television appearance built on the challenges to studio authority and classical narrative that were common not only in Hitchcock's work but also in that of fellow television star Bob Hope. Like many shows in the popular anthology format hosted by film celebrities, each episode began with Hitch's "cynical comments on the story to be shown and even—something totally taboo at the time on television—saying slighting things about the sponsor."[88] By 1956, one year after the launch of his series, Hitchcock hosted a television variety show with Doris Day to promote *The Man Who Knew Too Much* (1956) and talked freely about his cameos, saying "I manage to sneak into one scene in each picture. People call it my trademark. And I'm just ham enough to get a kick out of it."[89] Rather than suggesting the cameo as act of mastery, here Hitchcock sided with the popular evaluation of the cameo in the 1950s as an antidiegetic act completed at the expense of studio norms, "sneaking" into his own pictures (fig. 37; fig. 38). Hitchcock's cameos were fun. This slighting attitude was in keeping with Hope's attacks on Paramount, emphasizing the disruptive powers of the director above and beyond the studio that housed him. Drawing further parallels with Hope's brash visible style of self-promotion, with his move to Universal, Hitchcock's picture joined that of Hope in pride of place in the studio's commissary, the only director to be so made visible.[90]

Figure 37. Hitchcock advertises "Reduco" in the classifieds section in *Lifeboat* (1944).

Figure 38. Hitchcock's cameo in *North by Northwest* (1959).

Nevertheless, television had an immediate effect on his visibility, and his cameos as well. *The Wrong Man* (1956) presented the true story of a man mistakenly accused of a robbery in the style of documentary reenactment, a decision that garnered it much praise among the *Cahiers du cinéma* critics, using actual locations and presenting real-life participants throughout its construction.[91] Although Hitchcock shot a cameo for this film, "he decided to suppress that in the name of total credibility,"[92] choosing instead to appear in an introductory speech reminiscent of his television series, where he emphasized the film's adherence to the facts. The distinct way in which this cameo is relegated to a thoroughly extradiegetic sequence in this film calls into relief the playfulness of his disruptive presence within the diegesis of his other films. The cameo maintained its importance even in this new medium. The television shows, like the mystery books that also bore his name, were a secondary part of his oeuvre; after all, he did not direct many of them, and his introduction seems to have been the larger part of his involvement.[93] Yet, he did intend to cameo in some of the shows, having the show's producer seek out backgrounds and busy situations that could "conceal" him in the crowd.[94] In fact, Hitchcock consolidated his film and television work, as in the case of *Psycho*, where he used his television crew to shoot the film and scheduled his on-set appearances for cameos and trailers at the same time as his television introductions.[95] Trailers, cameos, and introductions were all of a piece in establishing the Hitchcock visibility and the illusion of control even where his influence was much reduced. As he said in the radio spot for that film, "I'm Alfred Hitchcock. I am the same Alfred Hitchcock you saw on television last Sunday evening. I shall return next Sunday. Now that I am also on radio do you have the uneasy feeling that you're surrounded? You are."[96] When *Holiday* asserted in 1964 that Hitchcock was "the only motion-picture director who is recognized wherever he goes,"[97] the author blamed this turn of events on Hitchcock's cameos.

Hitchcock's cameos are surprisingly heterogeneous, and this formal inconsistency argues against their thematic importance. The roles vacillated between exposure and concealment throughout his career, with comedic flashes such as the clockmaker in *Rear Window* (1954) or the fleeting passerby outside an office window in *Psycho*. The extended sequence in *Blackmail*, for example, was followed by a walk-on in *Easy Virtue* (1928); the almost-unrecognizable Hitchcock in the background of *Rebecca* (1940) is matched with the lingering newspaper ad in *Lifeboat*. The height of his exposure came in *Torn Curtain*, where Hitchcock not only performed a small vignette with an uncomfortable infant, but also his appearance was accompanied by the tune used to introduce his television series. Yet for his follow-up cameo in *Frenzy* (1972), he is hidden among the crowd of the film's opening. If Hitchcock's cameos were not only a signature but also a clue within the film to moments of great importance, this plotting was not necessarily determined in advance. The cameos are rarely mentioned in shooting scripts, except when a clean office copy has clearly been reproduced at a later date from the finished product, as in the case of *Lifeboat*.[98] Although the *Lifeboat* cameo in a newspaper ad must have involved some advance planning, in-depth studies of the production of his films show no evidence of concerted preproduction attention toward the cameo except, for example, when the shooting of the cameo was part of a publicity campaign in *Mr. and Mrs. Smith*.[99] The unusual *Lifeboat* cameo was also used in the trailer as part of the film's publicity. In preparation for shooting *Marnie*, Hitchcock coached title lead Tippi Hedren extensively on her passage through the hotel corridor where Bellour's favorite and most enunciative cameo occurs, yet he never mentioned the intersection with his own role.[100] Another of Hitchcock's notes prepared by his assistant suggests adding the elaborate cameo with distressed baby in *Torn Curtain* to the script a few days before shooting began.[101] The cameo was conceived even later in *Topaz*, as evident in the penned query "Hitch's shot?" in margins of his assistant's copy of the film's shooting script.[102] This handwritten addendum to an already-finalized script suggests a late, tentative addition, and a moveable one. In this way, the cameos bolster arguments that Hitchcock's legendary planning was used as the basis for a surprising amount of improvisation, which included the cameo.[103]

Hitchcock described the cameo to Truffaut as a "superstition,"[104] one to which he often seemed to only grudgingly adhere when bolstered by the intervention of his assistants. Hitchcock was sometimes dismissive of the cameos, stating in 1950 that "I don't like these small appearances";[105] elsewhere in 1956, he conceded that he enjoyed them.[106] In certain films, he seems to have been very concerned with the details of the cameo's composition. Hitchcock planned his appearance in *Strangers on a Train* in three separate scenes in the film, two of which were eventually shot. The insertion of the distinctive double-bass appearance eventually required a reshoot in studio of several sequences of the opening scene that had already been captured on location in Connecticut.[107] This reworking of the cameo is so unusual that it almost seems a pretext for the kind of expensive reshoot that made studios apprehensive about Hitchcock pictures;[108] elsewhere, he seems less patient with the necessity of committing his image to film. In *North by Northwest*, Hitchcock's near-miss with a city bus, so dear to Yacowar as an emblem of Hitchcock's control, was completed in a single take that was marked by the script supervisor as unusable because of poor lighting, and even then was reshot twice with an extra in the role.[109] Hitchcock in fact cut himself out of *Topaz* and *The Wrong Man* (1956), only to be reinstated in the former by his concerned team who were worried about "Mr. Hitchcock's appearance."[110] The cameos were often composed in process shots as was typical of the period,[111] but Hitchcock also appeared in a surprising number of on-location cameos in crowd scenes where his appearance was not merely a simple afterthought. In the case of *North by Northwest*, the cameo is not only on location but also appears to coincide with what had been slated as second-unit shoots, transforming them into first-unit with the appearance of the director.[112] In his on-location cameo in Morocco from *The Man Who Knew Too Much*, Hitchcock's appearance in the background of this brief establishing shot, where much of the rest of the sequence had to be reconstructed in a Hollywood studio owing to difficult shooting conditions among frenzied crowds of extras, attests to his penchant for courting complexity in production.[113] Despite his claims in the 1960s that the cameos were "a rather troublesome gag,"[114] fan requests for information on his cameos in the case of *Psycho* and *The Birds* received answers drafted in the first person, where other inquiries received curt formulaic replies from his secretary[115] (fig. 39). His decade-long commitment to the television introductions and the increasing use of his persona for radio spots and trailers in the 1960s suggest that he saw their utility as part of the growing Hitchcock trademark, a brand that his team was careful to protect.

Hitchcock's visibility grew in the 1950s and 1960s, but the character of this visibility changed. Kapsis notes that in the 1960s Hitchcock was courting identification with the art house, going so far as to have publicists for *The Birds* discretely pay for a tributary monograph and a retrospective of his work produced by the Museum of Modern Art in New York.[116] The mildly antiestablishment wit that Hitchcock had with the television introductions was increasingly adopted in press for his films. For *Torn Curtain* in 1966, Hitchcock's typical radio spots played with the recognizable elements of marketing jargon in the way that he had played with publicity over his

Figure 39. Hitchcock responded to fan requests for more information about his dogs' appearance in this cameo from *The Birds* (1963).

obesity in the 1940s: "I have three messages to deliver to males fourteen to eighteen, nineteen to 29, and 30 and over."[117] Hitchcock's films saw little critical success following the release of *The Birds*, but reviewers overwhelmingly came to dwell on the cameos as the triumph of style over substance, dismissed as one of "the little effects he likes so much."[118] As a trademark the cameo began to overwhelm his visibility as director. As one reviewer wrote, his films are identifiable "because you spotted his familiar silhouette in one of the scenes, and not because *Family Plot* has any of the skillful storytelling or moral ambiguity associated with the Master of Suspense."[119] Hitchcock's silhouette had been inserted into press advertisements for his films with predictable regularity since *North by Northwest*, but what had begun with comical juxtaposition of his silhouette alongside the small figures of his beleaguered stars became increasingly ridiculous throughout the 1960s, as birds nested on his head or he pulled back offending curtains.[120] So familiar were audiences with Hitchcock's image that only pieces or parts of him needed to appear. His cameos in *Shadow of a Doubt* and *The Man Who Knew Too Much* as well as advertisements for *Marnie* show only his back, and for his final film, *Family Plot*, posters showed Hitchcock's head comically encased in a crystal ball[121] (fig. 40; fig. 41). Hitchcock's image, made famous by the cameo, had outlived its associations with mastery.

Figure 40. Even Hitchcock's back was familiar to audiences, as in this cameo from *The Man Who Knew Too Much* (1956) . . .

In his later films, the cameos became one of the defining modes in which audiences related to Hitchcock films. Even as he was trying to become nominated to the film canon, the cameos became a vernacular way to understand Hitchcock that limited that ascension. As a result, despite the regular reference to them in the press of the time, their presence in scholarly discussions of Hitchcock is often only a gateway to more complicated rituals of misdirection. Even given the sheer volume of writing on Hitchcock, the cameos are too accessible to be worthy of mastery. Within the attempts to gain high culture legitimacy in his own lifestyle, the cameos as celebrity culture dogged him. One writer described an uneventful appearance at a convocation where he was given a doctorate by contextualizing it "as if he were making a cameo appearance in one of his own movies."[122] Like the actors whose visibility he had so long emulated, he had become inseparable from his film roles. A Lincoln Center film gala in 1974 included a program about "The Screen Cameos," as did a 1976 tribute at Universal.[123] The game was all that was left, and it was a game that everyone was playing.

Figure 41. . . . and this cameo-driven familiarity with his body was used to advertise his films, as in this newspaper ad for *Marnie* (1964).

Celebratory Cameos in Hitchcock's Wake: Proof of Authorship

The Hitchcock cameo set a precedent that was acted on in the 1970s. A new generation of American directors steeped in the study of film history and theory created elaborate textual references not only to the art cinema and the highly regarded filmmakers of the New Wave but also to Hitchcock, who they admired. Hitchcock was emblematic of the "traditional" director cameo, and the directors of the New Hollywood followed in his wake. Francis Ford Coppola appeared in *Apocalypse Now*. Roman Polanski played a bit part in *Chinatown*. Terrence Malick knocked on a door in *Badlands*. "Scorsese Out-Hitches 'Hitch'!" was the verdict in a review of *Taxi Driver* (1976), recounting Scorsese's cameos in each of his films. Yet unlike Hitchcock, for whom the cameo became as defining an element of his oeuvre as its style and themes, these directors did not adhere religiously to the cameo doctrine. Other films by these directors, such as *The Godfather* or Polanski's *The Tenant* (1976), appear to contain no authorial appearances, although critics stand ready to spot as yet undiscovered cameos.[124] As in the case of Hitchcock, it was in the best-regarded films of their early careers that cameos were to be found. While press surrounding Hitchcock's cameos only grew as the Hitchcock brand became tied to the Hitchcock body by design, after the initial nods of their early films, little press was dedicated to the directors' cameos. While Scorsese appeared prominently in *Taxi Driver* as noted, and many of his films after, his cameos are rarely mentioned in reviews of his films.[125] Likewise, the popular press called attention to Polanski's role in *Chinatown* (1974) but not to subsequent appearances.[126] Cronenberg's cameos were named in an obscure fan magazine rather than popular press. Given the way in which the cameo "superstition" dogged Hitchcock while making him one of the most visible directors of the twentieth century, succeeding filmmakers inspired by the auteurist model have been less dogmatic about any cameo appearances. Sacrificing visibility, their cameos don't merely succumb to precedent, expectation, and the allure of ready-made publicity. More often overlooked than Hitchcock, they are less constrained by the parameters of the trademark appearance. Auteurs or otherwise, many directors continue to use the cameo to pay tribute to the concept of authorship as both fans and successors to the master.

Of the New Hollywood group, Scorsese seems to have adopted the most Hitchcock-like approach to cameo, joining the game when he shows up directing a nightclub's spotlights in *After Hours* (1985) and a television show in *The King of Comedy* (1983) or when he appears as a photographer in *Age of Innocence* (1994) and *Hugo* (2011) (fig. 42). Like Coppola's cameo as a documentary director in *Apocalypse Now* (1979), or the DeMille appearances of a few decades earlier, these appearances often explicitly reference Scorsese's responsibilities as director. Scorsese, who began his filmmaking career at New York University at the moment when the French critics were at the peak of their American influence, has characterized his work as homage to filmmakers who came before him, including Hitchcock.[127] Yet, although Scorsese appears in many of his films, there are many in which he does not, appearing obliquely in voice recordings, references to his past films, or other clues that are reminiscent of Hitchcockian games. It is hard not to see Hitchcock's initials in *After Hours*, which Scorsese asserts is his take on the Hitchcockian chase film;[128] elsewhere, Scorsese claims to have hidden thousands of "Xs" in *The Departed* (2006) in reference to Howard Hawks's *Scarface* (1932).[129] Hitchcock stepped back from the blatant self-aggrandizement of DeMille, whose name and image always appeared hand-in-hand, often in reference to projects coming soon to a theater near you, appearing on the set of his *Samson and Delilah* (1949), in *Sunset Boulevard*, or name-dropping *The Greatest Show on Earth* with a sandwich board in *Son of Paleface*. Scorsese retreats even more until he actively seems to hide. Although his cameos are a part of Scorsese's oeuvre, they are not tied to the circulation of his visibility as they are for Hitchcock. Whether he is as well-known as Hitchcock is difficult to say, but certainly he is less recognizable. Yet, like the Cronenberg cameos that Mathijs is so pleased to point out, Scorsese cameos truly separate the fan from the regular filmgoing audience with their pretense to recognition.

Like Hitchcock, Scorsese vacillates between visible cameos and barely appearing as an extra. Sometimes they are so brief they seem impossible to find, as attested by blurry fan screenshots of arms hanging from truck windows or figures moving across the screen that are labeled Scorsese cameos.[130] Often these attributed cameos can only have been confirmed from other clues, such as the closing title credit to Scorsese's dog who appears briefly in *The Color of Money* (1986) in the company of a man walking very quickly through a casino.[131] Appearances like this blink-and-you-miss-it supposed cameo exhibit enough anonymity that whether they are meant to be recognized by anyone is open to question. For Scorsese's early films before the days of home screenings and replay culture, only someone with the kind of obsessive repetition that adherents of the New Wave claimed marked their cinephilic viewing practice could have recognized him.[132] Perhaps a modest man does not imagine that kind of future for his work, but maybe someone aspiring to the title of auteur does. By 1986, home viewing was a reality, and that closing credit, such as the fan magazine that pointed Mathijs in Cronenberg's direction, could be read as a clue for viewers playing a cinematic game started by Hitchcock. While Hitchcock reserved cameos

Figure 42. Martin Scorsese has appeared twice in his own films in cameos as a photographer. This one is in *Hugo* (2011).

for himself, Scorsese presented multiple cameos in his films, including his screenwriters and the regular appearance of his father and mother. Playing a bartender in *The Color of Money*, Charles Scorsese interrupts a series of two-shots of the protagonists at his bar in an awkwardly framed shot that can only be accounted for by the need to feature Scorsese's father center frame. By allowing his parents the more leisurely visibility that Hitchcock typically reserved for himself, Scorsese's homage extends as he has said not only to his influences but also to his literal parentage.[133] Like other directors appearing in cameos in their movies, Scorsese consciously introduces more complex layers of recognition into the Hitchcock game.

Directors continue to appear in cinematic cameos, often in contexts that specifically reference cinephilic viewing. Sometimes directors appear in single cameos, but it is only when cameos are repeated over a series of films that they are transformed into cultish signals to the active viewer.[134] Just as the repetition of themes and style signals a director as an auteur, repetition makes the cameo more meaningful as a game for the audience. Directors of horror, a genre that thrives on social and generic disruption, seem in particular to have gravitated to the cameo as signature, perhaps in direct homage to Hitchcock. Since his horror films of the 1980s, Peter Jackson has appeared as an extra in almost every one of his films, often disguised behind elaborate costumes and makeup. Rather than thwarting recognition, however, these disguised cameos can be seen as a challenge aimed at a particular viewing audience. Fans of the science fiction and fantasy genres in which Jackson primarily works, most famously as director of the *Lord of the Rings* (2001–15) films, operate within a community of interactivity, seeking out such details with the intent of identifying and compiling details that can be creatively repurposed into their own fan narratives.[135] The intersection of documentary space in which Jackson is a dwarf or a monster is one such alternative narrative, identifying Jackson not only as a director but also as a fan working within fan modes of appreciation. Where fans of science fiction create an intertextual connection to the objects of their interest by "speaking of characters as if they had an existence apart from their textual manifestations,"[136] Jackson goes beyond that engagement by actually inserting himself within the text. Entering into the text more fully than most fans can ever hope to, he emerges from the real existence of documentary space into the fantasy of the textual world. Like Hitchcock, Jackson uses the cameo to assert his control over multiple roles in the film's creation, as he takes responsibility for dominant and alternative fan narratives at once. Much of the attention to Jackson's cameos emerges from online communities of fans and is evident from online entertainment blogs and news aggregators.[137]

Quentin Tarantino's cameos likewise indicate fandom while asserting mastery of the medium. Tarantino's films call on a "transhistorical cinematic mythology,"[138] containing encyclopedic references to film texts both cult and classic. Although Tarantino appears in his films in lengthy roles that would seem to overtake the character-space allotted the cameo, his cameos purely serve the purpose of evangelizing his brash personality. Like Hitchcock, his appearances are used to publicize his films as all-Tarantino projects.[139] While Scorsese's appearance in *Taxi Driver* as a vengeful husband is so nuanced with diegetic character that it is more bit part than cameo, Tarantino's small roles are disruptive, demanding attention that creates a "ripple in the narrative flow."[140] Like Hitchcock, Tarantino's roles run the gamut from the background work of the scalped Nazi in *Inglourious Basterds* (2009) to the long-winded Australian with the attention-grabbing accent in *Django Unchained* (2012). And, like Hitchcock, because Tarantino has established himself for recognition as the actor/director/producer/writer "post-auteur"[141] hybrid, he positions himself as worthy of recognition. Of course, Tarantino lays the clues for find-the-director on other levels as well, like both Scorsese and Hitchcock leaving the marks of his influence via other technologies that are all but invisible, such as the answering machine recording in *Jackie Brown*. The references in his films to both classic and forgotten moments in film history offer up games galore for those who wish to measure themselves against his wealth of cinephilic knowledge.[142] At the same time, by playing characters he wrote for himself, Tarantino appears to plan his cameos into his films in a way that is more in line with actor-directors such as Woody Allen than with the apparently spontaneous personal appearances of Scorsese and Hitchcock.

If the director cameo in the wake of Hitchcock signals the transformation from fan to master, cameos can also be used to represent the director's godlike ability to conjure an important personage. Woody Allen is an example of an actor/writer/director who has cast himself as the star of his own films and used the power of conjuring up other real-world people of import to demonstrate his prowess. Perhaps the most well-known cameo in this vein is Marshall McLuhan in *Annie Hall*, who appears to bolster Allen's reputation by taking his side in an argument in a movie theater queue. Where the mass of stars in the cameo-rich films of Todd or Kramer reflected their ability to command the Hollywood system in a way that had once been restricted to studios and their megalomaniac producers, Allen also invited celebrities to appear in his films in cameos. However, he courted highbrow cultural celebrities such as philosopher McLuhan or musician Itzhak Perlman for their approval and participation, and the distinction they lend to those who like Allen can recognize their position in culture.[143] Unlike director cameos, these small roles did not necessarily have to be a particular personage; in fact, Allen had hoped to get Fellini "or whatever director we get"[144] to appear in McLuhan's stead to discuss the film that those waiting in line were about to see. These celebratory cameos are signifiers of a certain cultural capital commanded by the director, an effect magnified because Allen in his unique role as actor-director can literally make them appear on command. Jean-Luc Godard completed a similar conjuring act when he featured famous cineaste Fritz Lang as the director of an unraveling epic in the Cinecittà-set backstage film *Contempt* (1963). Likewise, Scorsese conjured figures from his own preferred cultural milieu, featuring New Wave musicians such as Iggy Pop and The Clash in *The Color of Money* and *The King of Comedy*. In 2014, Jackson welcomed comedian Stephen Colbert on set to film as a dwarf half-hidden in crowded candle-lit cavern in *The Hobbit*, a fact that Colbert publicized on his talk show during the lead-up to the film's release.[145] The ability to incorporate celebrities into their films celebrates both filmmaker and cameoist as, if not friends, then sharing in a mutual appreciation at each other's level of distinction.

While director cameos expose the director as author, other potential authors appear less frequently. The prevalence of the director even before the birth of auteur theory is evident when one considers the shocking invisibility of the writer cameo, for example. If the director established himself as at the heart of the film's creation early on, underneath him, as one screenwriter accounted, "there were layers and layers and the lowest layer was the writer."[146] As Ames writes, "writers themselves often viewed their lot so negatively or with such embarrassment that they were unlikely to portray themselves in film scripts."[147] Because authors were less visible, when they did lobby to appear, their very presence needed to be accounted for. In the 1923 *Hollywood* script, the unidentified writer indicates that among the listed stars appearing in cameos were "Tom Geraghty, Frank Condon (authors)," who are credited with the story.[148] Whether or not this is an instance of an author writing himself into the script, without the kind of visibility that accompanied fellow cameoist Pola Negri or even "Dinky Dean," they needed to justify their inclusion. With the advent of sound, scenarists became screenwriters and their stock gradually began to climb.[149] Although screenwriting underwent a renaissance of reputation with the reevaluation of the art cinema in the 1960s, writers continued to be underappreciated.[150] However, writers never came to consistently make cameos. Their claim to authorship can sometimes be shaky; the politics of writing meant that multiple writers would work on any one project from conception to shooting.[151] Even those identified as auteurs within the studio system such as Wilder and Hecht may have worked on a script almost unrecognizable from that which was finally produced. Additionally, writers often sought to hide rather than acclaim their credits in the cameo-laden films of the studio era, as those films that reflected a glamourized industry reality such as backstage musicals were seen as "bad credits."[152] No doubt drawing from the idea that nothing could be more naturally easy than actors playing themselves, these stories were contemptuously deemed too facile to need a real writer to create them. Although writers may not have belonged on set in the way actors and directors do, they could have been accommodated in the process shots that so many cameos used. Writers presented an alternative author who rivaled the directors' control as auteur, and as an auteur, Hitchcock was famously dismissive of their role.[153]

Charles Bukowski's cameo in *Barfly*, a script he penned for Barbet Schroeder, illuminates some of the tensions present in celebrating alternative authors in a film industry that has internalized the director's power. Bukowski, who grew from underground poet to cult figure with his semi-autobiographical stories about being a hard-up drunk in an unlovable Los Angeles, already recognized the power of his ravaged face as a visual testament to his stories of decades-long alcoholism. Interviewed in *Rolling Stone* in 1976, Bukowski echoes Didi-Huberman's opinions on the reflective power of the photographic face,[154] saying, "I know the face is helping to sell books now. . . . The face on that cover is so horrific and pasty and completely gone beyond the barrier that it makes people stop and wanna find out what the hell kinda madman this guy is."[155] Cameos make use of the same kind of witnessing, where the subject of a biography appears momentarily to authenticate the story of their life. Such roles are played by the musician falsely accused of murder, Manny Balestrero, in *The Wrong Man*, or pool shark Fast Eddie Felson in *The Hustler*, or even the Margaret Thatcher advisor who consulted on the biopic *The Iron Lady* (2011). Appearing in the background of the bar where the antihero makes his home, Bukowski is little more than an extra. Yet the production history of the film emphasizes the importance ascribed to Bukowski's role as author of the film, with Schroeder claiming in the film's press book that he wanted to make a film that was as much a product of the famed writer as possible.[156] Like so many cameos of this kind, Bukowski's appearance was publicized in press stills for the film, yet for the uninitiated his appearance is almost invisible (fig. 43). In *Hollywood*, his fictionalized account of the making of the film, Bukowski claims that he ad-libbed a fantastic trick of long-distance beer-spitting during the filming that was cut out of the film as too attention-getting, much to his chagrin.[157] For the author, the attention lavished on the somewhat vapid actors and withheld from him as the creator was characterized as a constant injustice during the making of the film. As Bukowski mourned, "The writer made their hearts beat, gave them words to speak, made them live or die, anything he wanted. And where was the writer? Whoever photographed the writer?"[158] The brief cameo seems an ignoble tribute to Bukowski. Despite the insistence of honoring Bukowski's authorial touch, the film dared not

Figure 43. Bukowski sits down the bar from Faye Dunaway in *Barfly* (1987).

shake the conventions of Hollywood narrative form where stars may stand out but not authors.

While Bukowski's cameo was cut because it drew too much attention to an alternative author, other films have reinforced the writer as a key authorial figure through cameo appearances. Such is the case of comic book writer Stan Lee, who appears in most of the film adaptations of Marvel Comics, whether authored by him or otherwise. Certainly Lee's persona has much more popular recognition than the dependable directors or screenwriters for the formulaic big budget Marvel blockbusters, although this popular visibility is perhaps a direct result of his repeat cameos. Lee was a well-known figure in the comic book world, and as the original Marvel Comics editor, had pioneered the complex intertwined storylines of the Marvel Universe.[159] Lee's interaction with fans included comic book letter columns and even self-written appearances in his comics since the 1960s, making him a visible comic book legend.[160] As a cameoist, he is perhaps the truest inheritor of the Hitchcock style, as his roles are often comedic refusals to acknowledge his importance, as when, as a wedding guest celebrating one of the characters he created in *Fantastic Four: Rise of the Silver Surfer* (2004), he rebuts a doorman who refuses him entry with disbelief, stating, "Don't you know who I am?" Likewise, in the *Iron Man* series (2008–), bionic billionaire Tony Stark repeatedly mistakes Lee for other celebrity figures such as Hugh Hefner and Larry King. Like Hitchcock, whose lost cameo in *Rich and Strange* supposedly featured him responding with disbelief to an account of the lead character's story, Lee refuses to be absorbed by the Marvel universes and the storylines that he created. Since the rise of Marvel Studios beginning with the *X-Men* series in 2000, movie cameos have made Lee and the Marvel Universe a mainstream pop culture phenomenon, serving as an important part of Marvel's advertising. Ever-more-complete lists of Stan Lee cameos, or even of Marvel films lacking cameos, circulate on the internet in articles, videos, and forum posts from entertainment media and fans alike.[161] The question of whether or not Lee would cameo in *Guardians of the Galaxy* (2014) was gossip fodder equal to the news about the casting of the film's stars.[162] Lee's cameos remind viewers that Marvel Studios pictures are not simply fantasy action films, but that they belong to an existing, densely intertextual universe that Lee and Marvel Comics helped create. Lee's appearances guarantee the continuity of that supertext, for both diehard comics fans and newer fans attracted by the multimedia Marvel Universe phenomenon. By presenting Lee as an overlooked skeptic, Marvel Studios gives voice to fan fears about the mainstreaming of the franchise through an originary figure while also paying tribute to Lee as creator to reassure audiences that the Marvel franchise will not lose sight of its roots.

It is hard to underestimate the influence that *replay culture*, as Klinger calls it, has had on director cameos.[163] The opportunity to watch and rewatch scenes frame by frame has been marked as changing the nature of cinephilia, transforming games of memory to opportunities for obsessive reading.[164] Certainly replay culture has influenced not only what cameos are identified but also the extent to which they can be appreciated as games. Hitchcock's cameos were particularly vulnerable to memory. During a 1976 screening of cameos organized by Universal, Hitchcock's appearance as a clock repairman in *Rear Window* had to be omitted due to ongoing legal trouble about the rights to the film.[165] Bellour, writing about Hitchcock's cameos in 1977, confessed it had been over ten years since he had seen *Rope*, and that he was writing about the film from memory.[166] Many authors who discussed the cameos had not had the benefit of recent screenings of the films. Leitch, in 1991, noted that Truffaut and Maurice Yacowar disagreed over the appearance of a cameo in *Rope* and suggested yet another possibility: that Hitchcock seated himself in the background of the rather small apartment set dressed up as one of the very few elderly supporting actors, the famous Sir Cedric

Hardwicke[167] (fig. 44; fig. 45). That Leitch could make such a ridiculous suggestion emphasizes how much the identification of the cameo was a game of memory invested with a bit of bluffing that tested the limits of probability, and how deeply the introduction of home viewing changed the rules. In 1993, archival research into production records combined with the benefits of the freeze frame exposed a bizarre, otherwise "unreadable" cameo in *Saboteur* (1942), where Hitchcock is purportedly using sign language to pick up his secretary.[168] Those films caught in limbo for decades such as *Rear Window*, *Rope*, and *Under Capricorn* (1949) now join the rest of Hitchcock's work on DVD. It is into this environment of replay culture that Miller's too-close reading is born. When Yacowar presented his catalog of cameos, his reading of the early films was restricted to those cameos that Truffaut identified in his special screenings of the films when preparing to interview Hitchcock, and mentions almost exclusively those cameos that Truffaut inquired about. A cursory search of YouTube turns up several compilations of every cameo ever, from his often-discussed appearance in a newsroom in *The Lodger* to the walk-on in the easily overlooked romantic comedy from 1928, *Easy Virtue*.[169] While Leitch was no doubt mistaken in his identification of Hitchcock masquerading as Sir Cedric Hardwicke in *Rope*, sometimes it is difficult to ascertain what the limits of the game are. How can one definitively say that the motionless blue blob atop the steps of the Australian Government House in *Under Capricorn*, which circulates in my university library on a Korean DVD version with substandard definition, is Hitchcock? The game of recognition continues to drive paranoid readings of Hitchcock's films circulating them in formats that he never imagined. YouTubers have manipulated his films to point out exactly where he can be recognized, using digitally enabled masks and drawn-on arrows to point out his purported form among many others. The same care has been taken with compilations of the cameos of Scorsese, Tarantino, and Jackson as well as the celebratory cameos incurred by Allen, with omissions and new claims for the provenance of unidentifiable extras.[170] Some of these determined cameos seem to fall within the parameters of "overknowing"[171] that Ferguson identifies as a pitfall of Miller's "too-close reading," as we ascribe to the master what may or may not be there, but can almost never be confirmed or denied. The game continues.

Figure 44. The much-discussed *Rope* (1948) cameo: is it Hitchcock or isn't it?

Figure 45. Another cameo contender from *Rope*: is the red light in the background illuminating Hitchcock's famous profile?

CONCLUSION

Cameos have entered pop culture as an expression of celebrity culture aimed at audiences eager for access to the famous. The profusion of cameo roles in contemporary Hollywood, as well as their remediation on the internet, indicates just how centrally cameos reflect the phenomenon of celebrity culture and fan viewing. Who is seen in cameos has been influenced by cultural, industrial, and aesthetic factors that have evolved since the beginning of film narratives through shifts in media forms, industrial organization, and fan culture. Cameos affirm the power of visibility as both means and end for celebrities, focused as they are on acknowledging the audience's powers of recognition. Setting up fans to judge and assess celebrity personas and the extent of their realness, cameos help sustain a metacritical relationship to celebrity that has become the norm. Each cameo is a portrait that provides the chance for a fan to demonstrate his or her powers of recognition. Drawing on cinephilic reverie and cult viewing practices, cameos create an opportunity for fans to assert their mastery of fan knowledge in an act that while dependent on personal memory is manufactured for a mass audience. Such pop culture knowledge offers distinction, albeit, as Bourdieu acknowledges, of a kind that is rehabilitated only as the last resort of the disenfranchised because its component parts of popular and lowbrow entertainment are so accessible to the masses.[1] Cameos create distinction, but only insofar as fans perform the consumption that cameos are designed to encourage.

Cameos create a participatory space for viewers, where recognizing those singled out among extras and small roles allows fans to demonstrate their knowledge. As Klinger points out, fans assert their fluency in details and trivia to make claims for a mastery of the form equivalent to that of a film's author. Cameos are a detail that permit and encourage this level of engagement. Just as Renaissance members of the royal court would learn the visual symbols with which a king preferred to be portrayed to curry favor, fans track the appearances of directors, actors, and showrunners, and even extras, to demonstrate their familiarity with a film, television series, or celebrity. Each cameo promises an intimate portrait, as it hints at tributes, trades, and personal and industrial relationships. Yet cameos, although they may encourage cult viewing that focuses on the detail and situate the viewer as a master who sets himself apart from the masses, are a mass phenomenon and an established and mainstream phenomenon. Even when the Hope-Crosby trades of the 1940s first plucked disruptively at the ends of classical film narratives, the sheer amount of press coverage identifying cameos firmly placed their recognition within the grasp of mainstream viewers. Cult viewing, in this case, is not about a cult genre, but about a detailed and knowing kind of viewing that is firmly mainstream, especially as it has been enabled by on-demand viewing and internet-enabled recirculation through metatexts that discuss and explore cameos as a phenomenon.

Comparing Cameos: Sharing on the Internet

The internet has enabled not only new viewing practices, but as a site for fan discussion and video sharing, it has also provided the opportunity for cameos to be collected, compared, and discussed, assuming a new prominence as they are subjected to the scrutiny of endless replay. As a result of viewing environments that have allowed increasingly individualized access like TV broadcasting, home viewing, and on-demand viewing, cameos circulate on the internet as a media artifact ideal for endless collecting and sharing. Stories that would have existed only in the brief rounds of publicity that accompanied a film's release or a filmmaker retrospective find new life on internet aggregators of pop culture trivia. Online aggregators revel in enumerating cameos from film and television alike, in lists such as "The Complete History of Guest Stars on The Fresh Prince of Bel-Air" or "Top 10 Epic Movie Cameos," usually accompanied with a film still, or more likely, a computer-enabled screen grab of the cameo itself.[2] The disruptive elements that make cameos ideal for cult reception lend themselves to this kind of repurposing on the internet, as moments that stand apart from the original narrative are completely cut away from it as still images. Isolated, they are a perfect instance of Jenkins and colleagues' spreadable or viral media: reusable, transportable, referential.[3] On the internet, whether as stills or video clips, these cameos often circulate directly alongside extratextual information about their creation, offering audiences familiar with star images the chance to uncover more information. As I discussed in chapter 4, the Bruce Willis *Friends* cameo shows how many of these stories, while gathering momentum in a new medium, echo the claims made about cameo extravaganzas of the 1960s: trades done for friendship, in tribute, for free, and in fun.

Reflecting the increasingly random nature of celebrity, the replay-enabled television environment, the growth of detailed mise-en-scène in complex, big-budget productions, and the possibility of stars appearing on television sometimes in invisible roles have made cameos the subject of a new kind of game. If Ben Affleck could appear on *Curb Your Enthusiasm* as little more than an extra in a background shot, eager viewers were all the more likely to assume that a policeman on whom the camera lingered imperceptibly on the season finale of *Homeland* (2011–20) could be Matt Damon. (Careful frame-by-frame examination enabled by Netflix helps to ascertain that this claim is unlikely.) Speculation peaked enough above the level of idle to spur fans to share their suspicions on internet message boards and aggregator *Reddit*[4] (fig. 46). Damon had already been identified on the internet several years earlier as someone whose cameos were unpredictable "random onscreen favours for friends."[5] IFC, in a regular blog series on cameos, posted this account of Matt Damon's cameos to coincide with the theatrical release of the company's coproduction of *Che* (2008), which had featured Damon's most recent small role. This web of activity online shows how the cameo contributes to ancillary content supplementing the often indivisible environment of television shows and movies. Online debate, such as that around Damon, is common, as online message boards are used to "pick away at the ambiguities"[6] in a constant manner no longer regulated by the initial broadcasts or theatrical releases.[7] Television has a much larger audience on the internet than for its initial broadcast, whether through an on-demand service or broken down into clips on YouTube.[8] The cameo, as a disruptive, extradiegetic moment, already fragmented from the film as a cult artifact, is uniquely suited to this spreadable environment.

Cameos have found a new home as digital content circulated on the internet. Fan culture has a unique relationship with the internet as what Jodi Dean calls an "imaginary site of action and belonging"[9] where largely invisible subcultures have reached out to each other through listservs and message boards to communicate about their fan object and create a shared, niche cultural space.[10] Fan cultures have embraced the internet as a way to share knowledge, but also to harness that knowledge to create new cultural products such as fan fiction or video compilations created through digital manipulation of existing movies or television shows.[11] Inexpensive or free video editing software, and the availability of already-digitized media, has made compilation videos one of the most common formats on the video sharing site YouTube.[12] Because the clips are brief, they are rarely the focus of the attentions of copyright owners who routinely pull bootleg content from YouTube.[13] Cameo clips are uniquely suited to this environment, and indeed cameo clips circulate on YouTube, as Plasketes writes, like the "underground circulation of rare recorded performances."[14] Edited clips of cameos can be as short as a single cameo; however, usually they are strung together in a thematic compilation based on either the subject, the originating film, or the genre. Completism, a trait that Klinger identifies with replay culture, drives fans to compile every cameo by repeat cameoists such as Scorsese, Jackson, or Stan Lee, or even mogul Donald Trump, or every cameo in a certain film or television show such as Hollywood-set *Entourage*.[15] Some of these cameos are used to make arguments: the best cameo from a TV series, or even within a single movie.[16] Videos depicting the same subjects compete based on quality or completeness, as the compilation allows a customizable participation in the creative process of production, emulating the power of the original producer. Gurevitch identifies the phenomenon of web-enabled video clip circulation as a major site of audience reception that has influenced film editing. In the editing room, movies are tailored for their ultimate destination on internet platforms, where they enter the popular culture easily broken up into abbreviated lengths that are ideal for internet viewing.[17] Cameos seem ready-made to serve as "digital attractions."[18] Yet while cameos function extradiegetically, they are nevertheless steeped in an accumulated, intertextual context of film stardom that belies the simple spectacular appeal reminiscent of early cinema that Gurevitch attaches to these stripped moments. Cameos allow snippets of film and television to recirculate, divorced from their original diegetic contexts while expressing fan mastery of long-existing systems of stardom.

Alongside video compilations, message boards and blogs provide evidence of fan contributions to a body of text-based discussion of cameos on the internet. Interest in the cameo has spread beyond specific fan cultures to emerge as a pop culture phenomenon. Discussions of the twenty-five cameos you shouldn't miss are a common trivia-oriented article on aggregators and the pop-culture-oriented blogs of print media from *The Onion*'s AV Club to *The Guardian*.[19] Alongside these blog articles, user-generated content

Figure 46. Is this an uncredited Matt Damon cameo in *Homeland* (2011–20)?

on reference sites such as Wikipedia and *TV Tropes* make complex points about the cameo's function. Klinger suggests that collecting is an impulse toward mastery, where "as a savvy decoder of a text's mysteries, the viewer becomes something of an authority,"[20] comparable to the filmmaker—or showrunner—to whom the manipulation of such detail is originally ascribed. Participation in user-generated forums allows the opportunity for fans to be publicly and immediately recognized for their knowledge, affirming their mastery. Like viewers chuckling knowingly at cameos in a movie theater, forum users re-create these moments of public, shared recognition.

An examination of these public forums exposes a detailed and complex discussion of cameos. *TV Tropes* exposes detailed fan interest in the cameo as portrait by generating an exhaustive typology of the cameo supported by copious examples, exploring narrative function and industrial limitations. One section is dedicated to "Lawyer Friendly Cameos," which highlights in-character cameos that take pains to reference pop culture icons while not infringing on copyright, such as the appearances of an unnamed yet identifiably costumed Lone Ranger and Annie Oakley in *Alias Jesse James*.[21] The user-generated format means that there is dissent on what exactly a cameo comprises, but the recognition of disruptive and extradiegetic elements that I have defined here seem to stand. The interest in the cameo, and its tropes, rather than specific television universes, represents the kind of fan mastery of the conditions of production that Klinger identifies with the traffic in trivia. More open-ended discussion is evident on message board threads on networking sites such as *Listal* or *Reddit*,[22] where favorite cameos are compiled with simple entries such as celebrity name and show title. Other resources project authority with single editors and focused subject matter, such as the massive PDF list compiled by now-defunct site *1960s Garage Bands* of every TV and movie cameo by garage bands of the era sorted by both actual and fictional name.[23] While maintained by a single editor, this list nevertheless acknowledged additional contributors sourced from the internet's vast number of users, soliciting additions and corrections via email. The website discussed cameos in a Web 1.0 environment that predated *Reddit*'s decentralized discussion but set the stage for online projects to crowdsource information about mass media products. Large, user-generated lists can be seen as efforts toward completism, as in video compilations or the appendixes to Hitchcock studies, but the disparate sources of exemplary cameos and the sheer number of authors means that conflicting definitions coexist of what makes a cameo. In such an environment, the cameo thus provokes discussion about itself nearly endlessly, as fans argue about where exactly cameos sit on the boundary of documentary and narrative space.

The cameo has long been part of a production's marketing, included in press releases surrounding the release or broadcast of a film or television show. While retrospectives of cameos, such as those of well-known directors, have also historically been a subject of cultural commentary, internet forums that allow video sharing and discussion allow cameos to live on in a different context. Rather than description, viewers can find thousands of cameos clipped from their original contexts. Cameos continue to circulate long past their original release date, renewing interest in forgotten or lost cameos that belong to the category of cameos rather than related to whatever film is being re-released or promoted at the time. Cameos have been fully embraced as a pop cultural phenomenon that exists outside of the original release of a film. In video sharing, many different kinds of cameos live side by side: in "Every Donald Trump Cameo Ever," Trump's appearance on *Home Alone 2* (1992) comes in quick succession to his television appearance on *The Fresh Prince of Bel-Air*. Cameos can also be recirculated to make new meaning: the compilation of Trump cameos is almost certainly related to his campaign for president, exposing two decades worth of his popular image as a very, very rich man in a pithy way. Edited down for video sharing, the disruptive, extradiegetic cameo comes to its obvious conclusion, as a performance that exists separate from any film or series, designed instead to circulate in the real world.

Criticizing the Cameo

Cameos are portraits, composed to reveal ever-more-intimate snapshots to the curious viewer. Captured in this portrait is a moment where documentary space and narrative space collide in an act of recognition that engages the viewer in many ways. The portrait offers an encounter with the celebrity in a potentially documentary space that intersects with the diegesis of a film. It is disruptive and comedic, emphasizing the celebrity's unusual visibility. Like a game, it challenges the viewer to demonstrate his mastery of celebrity culture. Many different kinds of celebrity are recognized in cameos, from more typically visible actors or stars to the celebrated figures of sports figures, directors, and producers, and even erstwhile extras raised to the heights of recognition through repetition and replay. Auteur theories have raised some films and filmmakers to the cusp of highbrow culture, elevating their cameos from the marginal respect of cult viewing to legitimate reception. Yet cameos are quintessentially popular. Unlike the alchemical signals of the court portrait, the knowledge required to identify them is not jealously guarded, but increasingly made public.

Cameos are everywhere in movies, television, and trailers. Their brief duration and their multiple and sometimes conflicting claims for verisimilitude, tribute, affiliation, and comedic disruption make them uniquely suited to films that promote repeat and intensive viewing. Some cameos continue to uphold older attributes, such as tributes and nods to verisimilitude in appearances such as author John Green in the movie adaptation of his *The Fault in Our Stars* (2013) or reporter Walter Robinson's daughter in the journalism-focused thriller *Spotlight* (2015).[24] Politician cameos continue to reveal those in power as awfully ordinary in lighthearted portraits such as that of American vice president Joe Biden on *Parks and Recreation* (2009–15). While tributes continue to appear in drama, contemporary comedies have most frequently embraced the cameo in its most complex form. These films encourage a metacritical stance on celebrity as celebrities mock their own star images not through supposedly telling reveals of their down-to-earth personas, but by exposing their failures and failings. Cameos have become so common in comedies that rather than a surprise, they often appear in trailers as a kind of shorthand for madcap narrative disruption to come. For example, in the trailer for the comedic, live action film *Pixels* (2015), which was loosely based on 1980s video games, the creator of the original Pac-Man video game appears in a cameo as an arcade repairman who is eaten by game characters who have come to life. A trailer for mockumentary *Popstar: Never Stop Never Stopping* (2016) featured the explosive death of singer Seal within its thirty-second spot.[25] Contemporary comedies, such *The Hangover* and *Trainwreck*, have embraced the cameo's disruption of celebrity and film narrative, although *This Is the End* is perhaps the best example of the cameo's accumulated legacy. A horror comedy about a postapocalyptic house party, *This Is the End* is a twenty-first-century cameo spectacular, showcasing celebrities hobnobbing with celebrities and disrupting genre and celebrity personas in a fragmented, vignetted narrative that is tailor-made for bite-sized redistribution on the internet.

In *This Is the End*, viewers are introduced, via a Hollywood house party on the eve of the apocalypse, to celebrity friend after celebrity friend of laid-back comedian Seth Rogen, who is playing himself. The first half of the film is focused on Rogen as he wanders the mansion of heartthrob James Franco, where stars are assembled and the most recognizable celebrities are greeted by name, such as musician Rihanna or actor Paul Rudd. Celebrity cameos appear to assert authenticity in the style of typical Hollywood-set films: like real celebrities, Franco and Rogen have celebrity friends. However, sensationalist recreational drug use and dystopian events, including cannibalism and murder, refute any audience expectations that these cameos are glimpses of celebrities as they truly are. Rather than candid reveals, audiences are treated to over-the-top exaggerations and antithetical views of each celebrity image, laying to rest the idea that such visibility offers access to anything other than performance. At the same time, the performances are less than convincing, and audiences are encouraged by the half-heartedness of the action to parse where performance ends and the real fun begins. The intersection of documentary and diegetic space is exposed by actors who seem on the verge of laughing at themselves and those around them. The film even disrupts the cameo's typical disruption of the character systems of classical filmmaking, as character actor David Krumholtz, who, unlike typical cameoists, definitely belongs in the background, is apparently done the honor of playing himself as he sits unnamed among the inner circle on Franco's couch. These vignette-like cameos make the film ready made for fragmentation into video clips for internet-enabled sharing. Indeed, on YouTube the movie is trimmed down not to its major plot points but to its choicest cameos, including clips of beefy Channing Tatum briefly enslaved by a power-hungry Danny McBride and multiple fan edits of the mild-mannered TV star Michael Cera flipping out on acid as in "Michael Cera best scenes" or "Michael Cera every scene high def."[26] The celebrity-heavy mise-en-scène promotes repetitive viewing for detail. *This Is the End* claims to show young Hollywood having fun at the expense of classical film conventions but for the benefit of fans who appreciate the disruptive power of the cameo. In the manner of contemporary cameos, it repeatedly shows glimpses of celebrities not as they really are, but celebrities as they are obviously not.

If *This Is the End* mocks celebrity visibility, other cameos mock fans' powers of recognition. In Altman's celebrity-heavy art house thriller *The Player* (1992), for example, Tim Robbins's character accosts celebrities who have no desire to be visible, such as Malcolm McDowell as he leaves a hotel, or John Cusack as he has a business lunch. Conventionally, failure to recognize celebrities has been the mark of bumpkins from Chaplin in *A Film Johnnie* to Lucy in *I Love Lucy*. More recently, in *The Other Guys* (2010), Mark Wahlberg is a policeman who accidentally shoots baseball player Derek Jeter during the World Series when he fails to recognize the star player of the team he has been assigned to do security for. However, as the cameo critiques evolving celebrity cultures, bumpkins express their naivety not only with failed recognition but also overeagerness to express their fan knowledge. *Trainwreck* stars Bill Hader as a renowned sports medicine doctor frequently at the side of famous sports figures. In one scene at a suburban baby shower, he stands in a group of guys listing all of his famous patients. Each name gets a huge reaction from these ordinary joes, who exclaim and high-five each other at the mere mention of each celebrity. Their reaction to what is merely a catalog of names seems ridiculous, especially without any supporting anecdotes about the lifestyles or character traits of these celebrities that would make these encounters interesting. While these reactions to mere names may seem over the top, they echo the excitement that viewers express at the appearance of cameos, an expression that can be audible in a quiet theater, as Mathijs has noted. Pointing out the absurdity of the excitement of recognizing the names of very famous people, this scene comments on reactions to the cameo, where similar excitement is predicated on the recognition of their very visible appearances. In this critique, a new type of bumpkin is exposed for ridicule—the savvy fan himself.

Trainwreck is not alone in criticizing the conventions of the cameo and the fan's pride in his powers of recognition. Fake cameos expose the fan's desire to give detail to character spaces that are never meant to be expanded. In *Fargo* (1996), singer Prince was credited as one of the many dead bodies in the film, which was set in his home region. This cameo, it turned out, never happened. The directors simply named him in the credits, creating a tribute to someone who wasn't even in the film, thus intentionally misleading fans who sought out details about the film's production.[27] Because the body itself was not recognizable as Prince, only extradiegetic information clued in fans who hang on for the credit roll. By misleading fans who seek out information beyond what is delivered in the film's diegesis, the Coens return the emphasis to detailed viewing rather than the accumulation of information from ancillary content. As a challenge to fan mastery, the fake cameo sets apart knowing auteurs from the fans who follow them. Likewise, in the DVD commentary for *Talladega Nights: The Ballad of Ricky Bobby* (2006), the director and stars claim to point out an otherwise invisible Sean Penn cameo that cost over $3 million, spurring some confused fans into a wild-goose chase.[28] These fake cameos destabilize not only the value of fan mastery but also the promise of the cameo in making the celebrity visible for inspection.

Invisible cameos likewise critique how fans recognize cameos in a media environment increasingly enabled by ancillary comment and metacommentary. In *21 Jump Street* (2012), Johnny Depp is disguised as a biker bad guy so as to be totally unrecognizable as the movie star who got his break on the original television series. When he is unmasked in the film's penultimate scene, he reveals his identity by pulling off a fake nose, sunglasses, and a fake beard, moustache, and wig. At the same time, it is revealed that Depp's fellow henchman is Peter DeLuise, his costar from the original series. However, unlike Depp, DeLuise did not become unbelievably famous after leaving the show, and so needed no such prosthetic disguise to be in "deep cover." His cameo is as invisible as Depp's until, after Depp's reveal, he explains who he is. The recognition is focused purely on Depp, not for his appearance in the original but for his visible success since the original *21 Jump Street* (1987–91). The contrast between DeLuise's and Depp's cameos demonstrate that rather than mere tribute, the cameo is an exploration of visibility. In fact, after Depp rips the prosthetic nose and grizzled beard from his famous face, he complains bitterly about his disguise as a biker. The elaborate scarves, rings, and goatee he claims to have worn reluctantly while undercover are undoubtedly familiar to fans from interviews and gossip magazines as the trademark style of the real Johnny Depp. Depp's performance suggests that there is no end to this celebrity reveal, exposing that the information fans have gleaned about the real Depp is yet another disguise: that of the celebrity image.

How long viewers will be content with cameos that claim to let fans be privy to knowing criticism of celebrity culture is unclear. After all, Hope and Crosby did much the same thing before their light jibes at Paramount and the studio system were perceived as hopelessly stuffy. Picking up where Zucker, Abrahams, and Zucker left off with the anarchic spoof film in the mid-1990s, comedies like *Zoolander 2* (2016), where male model Zoolander encounters airheaded celebrities working as highly skilled intelligence operatives, or *This Is the End* have once again begun to flirt with the cameo extravaganza as a genre. In some ways, disguised cameos perfectly reflect the attributes of the contemporary cameo. In *Tropic Thunder*, the disguised Tom Cruise as a dancing Les Grossman is the epitome of the candid, off-cast celebrity cameo that is a touchstone of contemporary comedy, emphasizing extratextual knowledge, testing the limits of visibility, and presenting an off-cast glimpse of the celebrity that nevertheless makes no claims to reality. Fans are encouraged to rewatch the whole movie, paying special attention to the studio head for any clues that Grossman is Cruise. Yet, as cameos become increasingly critical of not only celebrity culture but also fan culture itself, and fake and absent cameos muddy the waters, viewers bombarded with multiple extratextual claims can only trust the cameo's intrinsic property of visibility. However, disguised cameos strip those roles of that visibility. Can we be sure who we are seeing? (fig. 47). After all, if we are thinking intertextually, we must acknowledge the other latex masks Cruise has worn in the *Mission: Impossible* (1996–) film series, where the seamless performance of one person as another is aided not simply by diegetic super-spy technology but also by the combination of more-or-less realistic latex masks, continuity editing, and real live actors standing in for each other. Even without Cruise's own filmic precedents, *The List of Adrian Messenger* performed a similar reveal, where a stand-in played most of the roles credited to masked actors,

Figure 47. A long shot of a dancing Tom Cruise as Les Grossman in *Tropic Thunder*.

except in the final coda where the four were unmasked. Depp's cameo, too, is remarkably well-disguised until the final scene where he shows his face. It would be only too easy to have an extra don the bandanna, heavy sunglasses, and obscuring facial hair to run around in the background waving guns at *21 Jump Street*'s heroes for the rest of the film. While this paranoid reading of the cameo is perhaps excessive, the cameo's industrial precedents, cultural history, and its current attributes of metacritique can only lead us to ask if viewers can really trust in cameos that are mostly invisible.

As a fascinatingly complex manifestation of celebrity culture, there are many facets of the cameo that remain unexplored. In this study, I have mapped some industrial imperatives that have marked the cameo, from the birth of the star system, the decline of the studio system, the desire of networks and studios to differentiate television and film products, the access to on-demand viewing, and the unique suitability of the brief cameo, to the circulation of video on the internet. Each of these restrictions is tied to the continued use of the cameo to make stars visible, reinforcing their desirability as commodities. Work remains in tracking the history of sports figures as cameoists, especially during the explosion of sports stars in comedy farces of the 1980s from basketball's Kareem Abdul-Jabbar in *Airplane* (1980) to baseballer Reggie Jackson in *The Naked Gun* (1988), and their pivotal importance as quintessentially random cameoists in comedies such as *The Hangover*, *The Other Guys*, and *Trainwreck*. If viewers were supposed to be surprised by the presence of stars such as Alan Ladd or Humphrey Bogart in comedies of the 1940s and 1950s, today that mantle of surprise has been passed down to boxer Mike Tyson and basketball player Amar'e Stoudemire. The cameos of stars on animated movies and television series, which I have only briefly addressed, deserve to be investigated to explore how the industrial demands of voice work, coupled with the more indirect form of visibility offered owing to the visual styles of each illustrator, color what celebrities are likely to appear in cartoon form. The sheer number of stars of all kinds who have appeared in shows from ex-vice president Al Gore in *Futurama* (1999–2013) to talk show host "Jay Limo" in *Cars* (2006) suggests that animated cameos have a unique appeal, perhaps due to the restricted access of a mediated visibility. Lastly, detailed examination of ancillary content about cameos produced to supplement DVD releases and official websites of cameo-laden film and television series could shed light on how media industries have responded to and influenced fan engagement with cameos on the internet. Each of these projects would continue to shed light on the ongoing negotiation of how and why fans engage with celebrity culture.

The function of cameos has evolved several times in the last hundred years, and no doubt it will continue to be transformed. From portrait and mark of unusual performance, to marketing ploy that served to indicate the studio brand, the cameo became playful, disruptive, and self-referential as the studio system broke up and television introduced candid, intimate portrayals of celebrity into the routines of everyday life. The sheer number of cameos, as well as increasing familiarity with the remuneration of celebrities for such roles, in the 1960s alienated viewers who were seeking the intimate glimpse of celebrity as their true self. Auteur theories that established film as a highbrow art as well as popular entertainment made other producers seek the visibility that had been relegated to star performers. The self-referential cameo underwent another transformation in the 1990s, as the glimpse of the ordinary celebrity gave way to a critique of visibility, as celebrity cameos presented stars in unflattering light that, rather than suggesting the reveal of true persona, emphasized how celebrity is constructed for fans as what is made visible. The cameo currently sits in a space of metacritique, as the convention of the cameo is mocked and parodied through lost, invisible, and missing cameos. No doubt the cameo will continue to transform, reflecting the ongoing negotiation of celebrity culture by viewers eager to really know the media producers they admire. Engaging viewers in cinephilic attention to detail as they negotiate a cameo's relationship to documentary space and thus to viewers' own real lives, cameos create a personal moment of reflection that is nevertheless engineered for a mass audience. If, as Braudy suggests, recognition allows this mass audience to exert a modicum of control over their world as they participate in the selection of celebrities through the continued affirmation of their visibility, then bite-size, digitally circulated cameos allow fans endless opportunities to exert this power. Mining movies past and present for cameos, and identifying, examining, and sharing these portraits on the public forum of the internet, fans use their knowledge of celebrity culture to assert that they, like stars, directors, producers, authors, and even the occasional extra, deserve recognition, too.

NOTES

Introduction

1. Ernest Mathijs, "Cronenberg Connected: Cameo Acting, Cult Stardom, and Supertexts," in *Cult Film Stardom: Offbeat Attractions and Processes of Cultification*, ed. Kate Egan and Sarah Thomas (New York: Palgrave Macmillan, 2013), 146.
2. Charles Wolfe, "Buster Keaton: Comic Invention and the Art of Moving Pictures," in *Idols of Modernity: Movie Stars of the 1920s*, ed. Patrice Petro (New Brunswick, NJ: Rutgers University Press, 2010), 42.
3. Larry Carroll, "'Tropic Thunder' Multitasker Ben Stiller Can't Discuss Tom Cruise's Cameo, But He Did Reveal Jack Black's Water-Buffalo Baby," MTV News, April 2, 2008, www.mtv.com/news/1584693/tropic-thunder-multitasker-ben-stiller-cant-discuss-tom-cruises-cameo-but-he-did-reveal-jack-blacks-water-buffalo-baby/; Andrea Mandell, "Secret Cameos of 'American Hustle' (Renner's Baby!)," *USA Today*, December 10, 2013, www.usatoday.com/story/life/people/2013/12/10/secret-cameos-of-american-hustle/3968715/; "Kentucky College Professor Has Cameo Role in New Spielberg Movie 'Lincoln,'" Levisa Lazer, accessed January 24, 2014, www.thelevisalazer.com/lifestyles/arts-a-entertainment/6474-kentucky-college-professor-has-cameo-role-in-new-spielberg-movie-qlincoln.
4. Vivian Sobchack, "Inscribing Ethical Space: Ten Propositions on Death, Representation, and Documentary," *Quarterly Review of Film Studies* 9, no. 4 (1984): 294.
5. Mary Anne Doane, "The Object of Theory," in *Rites of Realism: Essays on Corporeal Cinema*, ed. Ivone Margulies (Durham, NC: Duke University Press, 2003), 82.

6. Victor Burgin, *The Remembered Film* (London: Reaktion, 2004), 68.
7. Leo Braudy, *The Frenzy of Renown: Fame and Its History* (New York: Vintage Books, 1997), 553.
8. Nathalie Heinich, *De la visibilité: Excellence et singularité en régime médiatique* (Paris: Gallimard, 2012), 37.
9. Richard deCordova, *Picture Personalities: The Emergence of the Star System in America* (Urbana: University of Illinois Press, 2001), 19.
10. Joshua Gamson, *Claims to Fame: Celebrity in Contemporary America* (Berkeley: University of California Press, 1994), 163.
11. deCordova, *Picture Personalities*, 131.
12. Michel Foucault, *The History of Sexuality* (New York: Vintage Books, 1990), 60–61.
13. Jane Feuer, *The Hollywood Musical* (Bloomington: Indiana University Press, 1993), 43.
14. Richard Dyer, *Stars* (London: BFI, 1979), 89.
15. Ann Chisholm, "Missing Persons and Bodies of Evidence," *Camera Obscura* 15, no. 1 (n.d.): 128.
16. Gamson, *Claims to Fame*, 52.
17. Ephraim Katz, "Cameo," in *The Film Encyclopedia* (New York: HarperCollins, 1994).
18. Gamson, *Claims to Fame*, 62.
19. Rudy Behlmer and Tony Thomas, *Hollywood's Hollywood: The Movies about the Movies* (Secaucus, NJ: Citadel Press, 1975), 119.
20. "Brad Pitt Says He'll Only Cameo in 'Twelve Years a Slave,' Hopes 'World War Z' Will Have Socio-Political Themes," *The Playlist*, accessed January 23, 2014, http://blogs.indiewire.com/theplaylist/brad-pitt-says-hell-only-cameo-in-twelve-years-a-slave-hopes-world-war-z-will-have-socio-political-themes.
21. Graeme Turner, *Understanding Celebrity* (London: SAGE, 2004), 4, 84.
22. Braudy, *Frenzy of Renown*, 7.
23. W. Straw, "Scales of Presence: Bess Flowers and the Hollywood Extra," *Screen* 52, no. 1 (2011): 121–27.
24. Serge Regourd, *Les seconds rôles du cinéma français: Grandeur et décadence* (Paris: Archimbaud/Klincksieck, 2010), 144.
25. Paul Willemsen, "The Figure of the Extra," in *Actors and Extras*, ed. Paul Willemsen and Thomas Trummer (Brussels: Argos Centre for Art and Media, 2009), 9.

26. Willemsen, "Figure of the Extra," 12.
27. Willemsen, 12.
28. Willemsen, 10.
29. "Kentucky College Professor Has Cameo Role in New Spielberg Movie 'Lincoln'"; "Allentown Native Dane DeHaan Has a Cameo Role as a Union Soldier in Lincoln," *Morning Call*, accessed January 24, 2014, http://articles.mcall.com/2012-11-15/entertainment/mc-lincoln-spielberg-dane-dehaan-emmaus-20121115_1_daniel-day-lewis-cameo-union.
30. Kate Masur, "In Spielberg's 'Lincoln,' Passive Black Characters," *New York Times*, November 12, 2012, www.northwestern.edu/newscenter/stories/2012/11/opinion-masur-nyt.html.
31. Braudy, *Frenzy of Renown*, 328.
32. Timothy Corrigan, "Film and the Culture of Cult," in *The Cult Film Experience: Beyond All Reason*, ed. J. P Telotte (Austin: University of Texas Press, 1991), 33–34.
33. James Robert Parish, Michael R. Pitts, and Gregory W. Mank, *Hollywood on Hollywood* (Metuchen, NJ: Scarecrow Press, 1978); Alex Barris, *Hollywood According to Hollywood* (South Brunswick, NJ: A. S. Barnes, 1978).
34. Behlmer and Thomas, *Hollywood's Hollywood*.
35. Patrick Donald Anderson, *In Its Own Image: The Cinematic Vision of Hollywood* (New York: Arno Press, 1978).
36. Anderson, *In Its Own Image*, 62.
37. Anderson, 62.
38. Anderson, 62.
39. Christopher Ames, *Movies about the Movies: Hollywood Reflected* (Lexington: University Press of Kentucky, 1997), 16.
40. Ames, *Movies about the Movies*, 62.
41. Anderson, *In Its Own Image*, 62.
42. Steven Cohan, *Hollywood by Hollywood: The Backstudio Picture and the Mystique of Making Movies* (London: Oxford University Press, 2018), 26, www.oxfordscholarship.com/view/10.1093/oso/9780190865788.001.0001/oso-9780190865788-chapter-2.
43. Georges Didi-Huberman, *Peuples exposés, peuples figurants* (Paris: Éditions de Minuit, 2012), 17.
44. Regourd, *Les seconds rôles du cinéma français*, 45.
45. Willemsen, "Figure of the Extra," 12.

46. Willemsen, 14.
47. Straw, "Scales of Presence."
48. Sam Staggs, *Close-up on Sunset Boulevard: Billy Wilder, Norma Desmond, and the Dark Hollywood Dream* (New York: Macmillan, 2003), 153.
49. Doane, "Object of Theory," 82.
50. Burgin, *Remembered Film*, 70.
51. Braudy, *Frenzy of Renown*, 335.
52. Braudy, 590.
53. Dyer, *Stars*, 31.
54. Dyer, 42.
55. Anderson, *In Its Own Image*, 62.
56. deCordova, *Picture Personalities*.
57. Barry King, "The Star and the Commodity: Notes towards a Performance Theory of Stardom," *Cultural Studies* 1, no. 2 (1987): 152.
58. Turner, *Understanding Celebrity*, 37.
59. Barbara Klinger, "Becoming Cult: *The Big Lebowski*, Replay Culture, and Male Fans," *Screen* 51, no. 1 (2010): 1–20.
60. Gamson, *Claims to Fame*, 5.
61. Gamson, 49.
62. Gamson, 49.
63. Umberto Eco, "'Casablanca': Cult Movies and Intertextual Collage," *SubStance* 14, no. 2 (1985): 463.
64. Ernest Mathijs and Xavier Mendik, Introduction to *The Cult Film Reader*, ed. Ernest Mathijs and Xavier Mendik (New York: Open University Press/McGraw-Hill Education, 2008).
65. Thomas Elsaesser, "The Mind Game Film," in *Complex Storytelling in Contemporary World Cinema*, ed. Warren Buckland (Oxford: Wiley-Blackwell, 2008), 16.
66. Elsaesser, "Mind Game Film," 16.
67. Mathijs and Mendik, Introduction, 7.
68. Henry Jenkins, "Reception Theory and Audience Research: The Mystery of the Vampire's Kiss," in *Reinventing Film Studies*, ed. Christine Gledhill and Linda Williams (London: Arnold, 2000), http://web.mit.edu/cms/People/henry3/vampkiss.html.
69. Barbara Klinger, "Digressions at the Cinema: Reception and Mass Culture," *Cinema Journal* 28, no. 4 (1989): 15.
70. Klinger, "Digressions at the Cinema," 15.

71. Gamson, *Claims to Fame*, 180.
72. Barbara Klinger, *Beyond the Multiplex: Cinema, New Technologies, and the Home* (Berkeley: University of California Press, 2006), 88.
73. "Cameo, n.," in *OED Online* (Oxford University Press), accessed February 5, 2014, www.oed.com.proxy2.library.mcgill.ca/view/Entry/26687.
74. Edmund Crispin, *Frequent Hearses* (Harmondsworth, England: Penguin Books, 1987), 34.
75. Behlmer and Thomas, *Hollywood's Hollywood*, 106; Barris, *Hollywood According to Hollywood*, 225.
76. Roland Barthes, "The Face of Garbo," in *Mythologies* (New York: Noonday Press, 1972), 56–57.
77. P. David Marshall, *Celebrity and Power: Fame in Contemporary Culture* (Minneapolis: University of Minnesota Press, 1997), 82.
78. Braudy, *Frenzy of Renown*, image caption.
79. Gamson, *Claims to Fame*, 25.
80. Turner, *Understanding Celebrity*, 12.
81. Dyer, *Stars*, 42.
82. Gamson, *Claims to Fame*, 33.
83. Gamson, 116.
84. Gamson, 148.
85. Behlmer and Thomas, *Hollywood's Hollywood*, 1.
86. Behlmer and Thomas, 97.
87. Behlmer and Thomas, 101.
88. Anderson, *In Its Own Image*, 77.
89. Robert Stam, *Reflexivity in Film and Literature: From Don Quixote to Jean-Luc Godard* (Ann Arbor, MI: UMI Research Press, 1985), 32.
90. Pierre Bourdieu, *Distinction: A Social Critique of the Judgement of Taste* (Cambridge, MA: Harvard University Press, 1984), 2.
91. Bourdieu, *Distinction*, 176.
92. James Naremore, *Acting in the Cinema* (Berkeley: University of California Press, 1990), 15–16.
93. Harry M. Geduld, *Chapliniana: A Commentary on Charlie Chaplin's 81 Movies* (Bloomington: Indiana University Press, 1987), 45.
94. Ames, *Movies about the Movies*, 207.
95. Barris, *Hollywood According to Hollywood*, 148.
96. Art Cohn, *The Nine Lives of Michael Todd: The Story of One of the World's Most Fabulous Showmen* (Whitefish, MT: Kessinger Publishing, 2007), 279.

97. Michael Todd Jr. and S. T. McCarthy, *A Valuable Property: The Life Story of Michael Todd* (New York: Arbor House, 1983).
98. Henry Jenkins, Sam Ford, and Joshua Green, *Spreadable Media: Creating Value and Meaning in a Networked Culture* (New York: New York University Press, 2013), 203.

Chapter 1: Worthy of Recognition

1. Ernest Mathijs, "Cronenberg Connected: Cameo Acting, Cult Stardom, and Supertexts," in *Cult Film Stardom: Offbeat Attractions and Processes of Cultification*, ed. Kate Egan and Sarah Thomas (New York: Palgrave Macmillan, 2013), 46.
2. Emmanuel Levinas, *Totality and Infinity: An Essay on Exteriority* (New York: Springer, 1979), 197.
3. Shearer West, *Portraiture* (Oxford: Oxford University Press, 2004), 25.
4. Richard Brilliant, *Portraiture* (Cambridge, MA: Harvard University Press, 1991), 15.
5. Brilliant, *Portraiture*, 40.
6. Brilliant, 8.
7. Brilliant, 124.
8. Brilliant, 10.
9. West, *Portraiture*, 27.
10. Ann Jensen Adams, *Public Faces and Private Identities in Seventeenth-Century Holland: Portraiture and the Production of Community* (New York: Cambridge University Press, 2009), 185.
11. West, *Portraiture*, 139.
12. Jill Burke, "Patronage and Identity in Renaissance Florence: The Case of S. Maria a Lecceto," in *Fashioning Identities in Renaissance Art*, ed. Mary Rogers (Brookfield, VT: Ashgate, 2000), 52.
13. West, *Portraiture*, 78.
14. Adams, *Public Faces and Private Identities in Seventeenth-Century Holland*, 174.
15. Burke, "Patronage and Identity in Renaissance Florence," 54.
16. Adams, *Public Faces and Private Identities in Seventeenth-Century Holland*, 174.
17. Adams, 158.
18. Adams, 174.

19. Stephen Perkinson, *The Likeness of the King: A Prehistory of Portraiture in Late Medieval France* (Chicago: University of Chicago Press, 2009), 83.
20. Brilliant, *Portraiture*, 38.
21. Brilliant, 103.
22. Brilliant, 158.
23. West, *Portraiture*, 51.
24. West, 81.
25. West, 44.
26. Lorne Campbell, *Renaissance Portraits: European Portrait-Painting in the 14th, 15th, and 16th Centuries* (New Haven, CT: Yale University Press, 1990), 206.
27. Perkinson, *Likeness of the King*, 269.
28. West, *Portraiture*, 51.
29. Campbell, *Renaissance Portraits*, 205.
30. Campbell, 215.
31. Campbell, 6.
32. James David Draper and Metropolitan Museum of Art (New York), *Cameo Appearances* (New York: Metropolitan Museum of Art, 2008), 5.
33. Draper and Metropolitan Museum of Art, *Cameo Appearances*.
34. Draper and Metropolitan Museum of Art, 44.
35. Margaret Cameron Coss Flower, *Victorian Jewellery* (London: Cassell, 1967), 20.
36. Draper and Metropolitan Museum of Art, *Cameo Appearances*, 47.
37. Draper and Metropolitan Museum of Art, 69.
38. Draper and Metropolitan Museum of Art, 11.
39. Flower, *Victorian Jewellery*, 22.
40. Jean Arnold, "Cameo Appearances: The Discourse of Jewelry in Middlemarch," *Victorian Literature and Culture* 30, no. 1 (2002): 286.
41. Flower, *Victorian Jewellery*, 9.
42. Flower, 215.
43. Flower, 213.
44. Jennifer Green-Lewis, *Framing the Victorians: Photography and the Culture of Realism* (Ithaca, NY: Cornell University Press, 1996), 29.
45. Roland Barthes, *Camera Lucida, Camera Lucida: Reflections on Photography* (New York: Hill and Wang, 1981), 5.
46. Barthes, *Camera Lucida*, 7.
47. West, *Portraiture*, 190.

48. Barthes, *Camera Lucida*, 30.
49. Green-Lewis, *Framing the Victorians*, 74.
50. Barthes, *Camera Lucida*, 30.
51. Barthes, *Camera Lucida*, 66.
52. Green-Lewis, *Framing the Victorians*, 222.
53. Peter Hamilton, Roger Hargreaves, and National Portrait Gallery (Great Britain), *The Beautiful and the Damned: The Creation of Identity in Nineteenth-Century Photography* (Burlington, VT: Lund Humphries, 2001), 17.
54. Hamilton, Hargreaves, and National Portrait Gallery, *Beautiful and the Damned*, 40.
55. Hamilton, Hargreaves, and National Portrait Gallery, 47.
56. West, *Portraiture*, 190.
57. Hamilton, Hargreaves, and National Portrait Gallery, *Beautiful and the Damned*, 46.
58. Hamilton, Hargreaves, and National Portrait Gallery, 41.
59. West, *Portraiture*, 190.
60. West, *Portraiture*.
61. "Cameo Photographs," *Syracuse Journal*, November 29, 1946.
62. Charlotte Mary Yonge, *Cameos from English History* (London: Macmillan, 1880).
63. Mathijs, "Cronenberg Connected: Cameo Acting, Cult Stardom, and Supertexts," 46.
64. Leo Braudy, *The Frenzy of Renown: Fame and Its History* (New York: Vintage Books, 1997), 161, 170, 172.
65. Braudy, 285.
66. Braudy, 321.
67. Braudy, 381.
68. Miriam Hansen, *Babel and Babylon: Spectatorship in American Silent Film* (Cambridge, MA: Harvard University Press, 1991), 30.
69. Hansen, *Babel and Babylon*, 31.
70. Charles Musser, "Preclassical American Cinema: Its Changing Mode of Film Production," in *Silent Film*, ed. Richard Abel (London: Athlone, 1996), 89.
71. Anthony Slide and Alan Gevinson, *The Big V: A History of the Vitagraph Company* (Metuchen, NJ: Scarecrow Press, 1987), 15.
72. Richard deCordova, *Picture Personalities: The Emergence of the Star System in America* (Urbana: University of Illinois Press, 2001), 34.

73. deCordova, *Picture Personalities*, 34.
74. Hansen, *Babel and Babylon*, 66.
75. "Famous Players Ad," *Moving Picture World*, June 1916.
76. deCordova, *Picture Personalities*, 77.
77. Hansen, *Babel and Babylon*, 35.
78. Hansen, 102.
79. Hamilton, Hargreaves, and National Portrait Gallery, *Beautiful and the Damned*, 41.
80. Slide and Gevinson, *Big V*, 55; Richard Abel, "G.M. Anderson: 'Broncho Billy' among the Early 'Picture Personalities,'" in *Flickers of Desire: Movie Stars of the 1910s*, ed. Jennifer M. Bean (New Brunswick, NJ: Rutgers University Press, 2011), 36.
81. Richard Abel, *Encyclopedia of Early Cinema* (London: Routledge, 2005), 355.
82. Graeme Turner, *Understanding Celebrity* (London: SAGE, 2004), 12.
83. Marc Norman, *What Happens Next: A History of American Screenwriting* (New York: Crown Archetype, 2008), 26.
84. Hansen, *Babel and Babylon*, 28.
85. deCordova, *Picture Personalities*, 78.
86. P. David Marshall, *Celebrity and Power: Fame in Contemporary Culture* (Minneapolis: University of Minnesota Press, 1997), 82.
87. deCordova, *Picture Personalities*, 52.
88. Gaylyn Studlar, "The Perils of Pleasure? Fan Magazine Discourse as Women's Commodified Culture in the 1920s," in *Silent Film*, ed. Richard Abel (London: Athlone, 1996), 17.
89. deCordova, *Picture Personalities*, 52.
90. Nathalie Heinich, *De la visibilité: Excellence et singularité en régime médiatique* (Paris: Gallimard, 2012), 37.
91. Heinich, *De la visibilité*, 49.
92. Heinich, 43.
93. Richard Dyer, *Stars* (London: BFI, 1979), 42.
94. Kerry O. Ferris, "Seeing and Being Seen: The Moral Order of Celebrity Sightings," *Journal of Contemporary Ethnography* 33, no. 3 (2004): 253.
95. Joshua Gamson, *Claims to Fame: Celebrity in Contemporary America* (Berkeley: University of California Press, 1994), 168.
96. Marshall, *Celebrity and Power*, 82.
97. Marshall, *Celebrity and Power*, 104.

98. Anthony Slide, *Inside the Hollywood Fan Magazine: A History of Star Makers, Fabricators, and Gossip Mongers* (Jackson: University Press of Mississippi, 2010).
99. Slide, *Inside the Hollywood Fan Magazine*, 6.
100. Slide, 4.
101. Abel, "G. M. Anderson: 'Broncho Billy' among the Early 'Picture Personalities,'" 33.
102. Jennifer M. Bean, *Flickers of Desire: Movie Stars of the 1910s* (New Brunswick, NJ: Rutgers University Press, 2011).
103. Studlar, "Perils of Pleasure?," 270.
104. Gamson, *Claims to Fame*, 26.
105. Abel, "G. M. Anderson: 'Broncho Billy' among the Early 'Picture Personalities,'" 40.
106. Slide and Gevinson, *Big V*.
107. Gaylyn Studlar, "Theda Bara: Orientalism, Sexual Anarchy, and the Jewish Star," in *Flickers of Desire: Movie Stars of the 1910s*, ed. Jennifer M Bean (New Brunswick, NJ: Rutgers University Press, 2011), 125, http://site.ebrary.com/id/10589783.
108. Slide, *Inside the Hollywood Fan Magazine*, 60.
109. "A Quartette of Vitagraph Players," *Vitagraph Life Portrayals*, July 1911.
110. "Fenwick's Corner," *Oregonian*, May 20, 1906; "Patience," *Variety*, November 5, 1912; "Reviews," *Atlantic News-Telegraph*, October 21, 1916; Fred, "Film Reviews: Playing with Fire," *Variety*, April 28, 1916; O. M. Samuel, "New Orleans," *Variety*, May 5, 1926.
111. Walt, "Girl in the Kimono," *Variety*, July 2, 1910; Tbee, "Moving Pictures: Within the Cup," *Variety*, March 22, 1918; RJ Whitley, "A Talkie Triumph," *Daily Mirror*, June 24, 1929.
112. Sime, "New Acts Next Week: Irene Bercseny," *Variety*, January 9, 1914.
113. "Show Reviews: Prospects," *Variety*, October 12, 1920.
114. "Age of Innocence," *Variety*, October 23, 1934; "Flying Fortress," *Variety*, July 15, 1942; "For Better, For Worse," *Variety*, October 13, 1954.
115. Dyer, *Stars*, 42.
116. Walt, "Out of Town: The Wife Tamers," *Variety*, September 3, 1910.
117. Brent E. Walker, *Mack Sennett's Fun Factory: A History and Filmography of His Studio and His Keystone and Mack Sennett Comedies, with Biographies of Players and Personnel* (Jefferson, NC: McFarland, 2013), 563.
118. Herb, "Film Reviews: Wild Geese Calling," *Variety*, July 30, 1941.

119. "B. S. Moss' Cameo Gets Under Way," *Variety (Archive: 1905–2000)*, December 30, 1921; "Pictures: 'Blood and Sand' Flops in Pittsburgh," *Variety*, September 29, 1922; "San Francisco," *Variety*, October 11, 1923; Chester B. Bahn, "Syracuse, N.Y.," *Variety*, May 10, 1923; "Pictures: Loew's Cameo, Brooklyn," *Variety*, December 3, 1924; "Cameo Theatre," *Highland Democrat*, October 1, 1927.
120. "Pictures: 18 B'way Picture Houses," *Variety*, April 30, 1930; "Hollywood Chatter," *Variety*, April 3, 1929.
121. Evelyn F. Scott, *Hollywood: When Silents Were Golden* (New York: McGraw-Hill, 1972).
122. Slide, *Inside the Hollywood Fan Magazine*, 21.
123. Slide, 15.
124. Scott, *Hollywood: When Silents Were Golden*.
125. Neil Harris, *Humbug: The Art of P. T. Barnum* (Boston: Little, Brown, 1973), 141.
126. *The Big Four Family*, June 1915.
127. "Purely Personal Puffs," *Vitagraph Bulletin*, August 1915.
128. "The Goddess," *New York Evening Journal*, May 3, 1915.
129. Rudy Behlmer and Tony Thomas, *Hollywood's Hollywood: The Movies about the Movies* (Secaucus, NJ: Citadel Press, 1975), 1.
130. Vivian Sobchack, "Inscribing Ethical Space: Ten Propositions on Death, Representation, and Documentary," *Quarterly Review of Film Studies* 9, no. 4 (1984): 294.
131. Behlmer and Thomas, *Hollywood's Hollywood*, 97.
132. "Rock, Smith, and Blackton Were Pioneer Exhibitors," *Moving Picture World*, July 1916.
133. "Comments on the Films: A Vitagraph Romance," *Moving Picture World*, September 18, 1912.
134. Behlmer and Thomas, *Hollywood's Hollywood*.
135. Behlmer and Thomas, *Hollywood's Hollywood*, 97; Patrick Donald Anderson, *In Its Own Image: The Cinematic Vision of Hollywood* (New York: Arno Press, 1978), 62; "Comments on the Films: A Vitagraph Romance."
136. "A Vitagraph Romance," *Vitagraph Life Portrayals*, September 17, 1912.
137. Slide and Gevinson, *Big V*, 4.
138. Slide, *Inside the Hollywood Fan Magazine*, 21.
139. Slide and Gevinson, *Big V*, 21.
140. Slide and Gevinson, 5.

141. J. Stuart Blackton, "Heart to Heart Talks," *Vitagraph Bulletin*, August 1915, 4.
142. "Aunty's Romance," *Moving Picture World*, July 27, 1912.
143. Jacqueline Nacache, *L'acteur de cinéma* (Paris: Armand Colin, 2005), 87.
144. Gilles Deleuze, *Cinema 2: The Time Image* (Minneapolis: University of Minnesota Press, 1986), 17.
145. Deleuze, *Cinema 2*.
146. Mary Anne Doane, "The Close-Up: Scale and Detail in the Cinema," *Differences: A Journal of Feminist Cultural Studies* 14, no. 3 (2003): 108.
147. Marshall, *Celebrity and Power*, 15.
148. Alex Woloch, *The One vs. the Many: Minor Characters and the Space of the Protagonist in the Novel* (Princeton, NJ: Princeton University Press, 2009), 14.
149. Woloch, *The One vs. the Many*.

Chapter 2: Familiar Faces

1. "Aunty's Romance," *Moving Picture World*, July 27, 1912.
2. Kerry O. Ferris, "Seeing and Being Seen: The Moral Order of Celebrity Sightings," *Journal of Contemporary Ethnography* 33, no. 3 (2004): 242.
3. Leo Calvin Rosten, *Hollywood: The Movie Colony, the Movie Makers* (New York: Harcourt, Brace, 1941), 13.
4. Richard deCordova, *Picture Personalities: The Emergence of the Star System in America* (Urbana: University of Illinois Press, 2001), 140.
5. Christopher Ames, *Movies about the Movies: Hollywood Reflected* (Lexington: University Press of Kentucky, 1997), 207.
6. Jan Olsson, "Screen Bodies and Busybodies: Corporeal Constellations in the Era of Anonymity," *Film History* 25, no. 1–2 (2013): 192.
7. Robert Stam, *Reflexivity in Film and Literature: From Don Quixote to Jean-Luc Godard* (Ann Arbor, MI: UMI Research Press, 1985), 33.
8. Pierre Bourdieu, *Distinction: A Social Critique of the Judgement of Taste* (Cambridge, MA: Harvard University Press, 1984), 2.
9. Ames, *Movies about the Movies*, 207.
10. Alex Barris, *Hollywood According to Hollywood* (South Brunswick, NJ: A. S. Barnes, 1978), 148.
11. Richard Dyer, *Stars* (London: BFI, 1979), 21.

12. Charles Musser, "Preclassical American Cinema: Its Changing Mode of Film Production," in *Silent Film*, ed. Richard Abel (London: Athlone, 1996), 94.
13. Harry M. Geduld, *Chapliniana: A Commentary on Charlie Chaplin's 81 Movies* (Bloomington: Indiana University Press, 1987), 45; James Naremore, *Acting in the Cinema* (Berkeley: University of California Press, 1990), 15.
14. Harry M. Geduld, *Charlie Chaplin's Own Story* (Bloomington: Indiana University Press, 1985), 140.
15. "Juvenile Film Corporation Presents Joseph Monahan in His Great Imitation of Charlie Chaplin's Burlesque on Carmen," *Moving Picture World*, June 1916.
16. Naremore, *Acting in the Cinema*, 14.
17. Naremore, 14.
18. Geduld, *Chapliniana*, 18.
19. James L. Neibaur, *Early Charlie Chaplin: The Artist as Apprentice at Keystone Studios* (Lanham, MD: Scarecrow Press, 2011), 211.
20. Kevin Brownlow, *The Parade's Gone By* (New York: Knopf, 1968), 272.
21. Stam, *Reflexivity in Film and Literature*, 32.
22. Stam, 78.
23. Stam, 78.
24. Geduld, *Chapliniana*, 18.
25. Stam, *Reflexivity in Film and Literature*, 78.
26. Naremore, *Acting in the Cinema*, 16; David Robinson, *Chaplin: His Life and Art* (New York: McGraw-Hill, 1985), 137.
27. Geduld, *Chapliniana*, 134.
28. Naremore, *Acting in the Cinema*, 15.
29. Brownlow, *Parade's Gone By*, 43.
30. Naremore, *Acting in the Cinema*, 77.
31. Naremore, 3.
32. Ames, *Movies about the Movies*, 19.
33. Rosten, *Hollywood*, 8.
34. Patrick Donald Anderson, *In Its Own Image: The Cinematic Vision of Hollywood* (New York: Arno Press, 1978), 62.
35. Goldwyn Studios, "Special Souls for Sale Trailer," February 23, 1923.
36. Anderson, *In Its Own Image*, 62.

37. Heidi Kenaga, "Promoting Hollywood Extra Girl (1935)," *Screen* 52, no. 1 (2011): 78–81.
38. Rudy Behlmer and Tony Thomas, *Hollywood's Hollywood: The Movies about the Movies* (Secaucus, NJ: Citadel Press, 1975), 101.
39. Steven Cohan, *Hollywood by Hollywood: The Backstudio Picture and the Mystique of Making Movies* (London: Oxford University Press, 2018), 5.
40. Kenaga, "Promoting Hollywood Extra Girl (1935)."
41. Robinson, *Chaplin*, 160; Beth Day Romulo, *This Was Hollywood: An Affectionate History of Filmland's Golden Years*. (Garden City, NY: Doubleday, 1960), 109.
42. Goldwyn Studios, "Special Souls for Sale Trailer."
43. Behlmer and Thomas, *Hollywood's Hollywood*, 117.
44. "A Saturnine Svongali," *New York Times*, July 30, 1923.
45. Behlmer and Thomas, *Hollywood's Hollywood*, 120.
46. Rupert Hughes, "Synopsis of Souls for Sale" (c. 1922), USC Cinematic Arts Collection.
47. Joshua Gamson, *Claims to Fame: Celebrity in Contemporary America* (Berkeley: University of California Press, 1994), 180.
48. Dyer, *Stars*, 42.
49. Grace Kingsley, "Film Reveals Studio World: Souls for Sale," *Los Angeles Times*, January 7, 1923.
50. "Film Stars Volunteer Aid in Show World," *Variety*, April 11, 1928.
51. Academy of Motion Picture Arts and Sciences, "Program from AMPAS Screening of *Show People* in Honor of *The Artist*," 2012, Press Clippings, Margaret Herrick Library.
52. Goldwyn Studios, "Title Sheet for Souls for Sale," March 10, 1923, 6, USC Cinematic Arts Collection.
53. Goldwyn Studios, "Souls for Sale Silent Cutting Continuity," March 14, 1923, 5, USC Cinematic Arts Collection.
54. "A Saturnine Svongali."
55. Paramount, "Hollywood Scenario," n.d., 86, Paramount Pictures Scripts H-677, Margaret Herrick Library; Paramount, "Hollywood Continuity Script," n.d., 23, Paramount Scripts H-679, Margaret Herrick Library.
56. Paramount, "Hollywood Scenario," 71.
57. John Emerson and Anita Loos, "Polly Preferred Screen Adaptation and Continuity," November 15, 1926, 1, Show People (1928) S-1123, Margaret Herrick Library.

58. Gamson, *Claims to Fame*, 29.
59. Dyer, *Stars*, 43.
60. Anderson, *In Its Own Image*, 90; "Hollywood—Paramount—Eight Reels," *Motion Picture Daily*, July 14, 1923, Production Clippings, Margaret Herrick Library.
61. Hughes, "Synopsis of Souls for Sale," 6.
62. Emerson and Loos, "Polly Preferred Screen Adaptation and Continuity," 81.
63. Robinson, *Chaplin*.
64. Marion Davies, *The Times We Had: Life with William Randolph Hearst* (Indianapolis: Bobbs-Merrill, 1975), 89.
65. Paramount, "Hollywood Scenario," 170.
66. Behlmer and Thomas, *Hollywood's Hollywood*, 119.
67. Goldwyn Studios, "Title Sheet for Souls for Sale," 55.
68. Goldwyn Studios, "Special Souls for Sale Trailer."
69. Paramount, "Hollywood Scenario," 142.
70. Paramount, "Hollywood Continuity Script," 24.
71. Paramount, "Hollywood Scenario," 105.
72. Paramount, "Hollywood Continuity Script."
73. Naremore, *Acting in the Cinema*, 16.
74. Neil Harris, *Humbug: The Art of P. T. Barnum* (Boston: Little, Brown, 1973), 88.
75. Mary Anne Doane, "The Object of Theory," in *Rites of Realism: Essays on Corporeal Cinema*, ed. Ivone Margulies (Durham, NC: Duke University Press, 2003), 85.
76. Victor Burgin, *The Remembered Film* (London: Reaktion, 2004), 8.
77. Burgin, *Remembered Film*, 17.
78. E. W. Hammons to Mr. Ratterjohn, "Florence Lawrence," September 28, 1914, GC 1011, Box 2, Folder 14, Seaver Center for Western History Research.
79. Paul Willemsen, "The Figure of the Extra," in *Actors and Extras*, ed. Paul Willemsen and Thomas Trummer (Brussels: Argos Centre for Art and Media, 2009), 9.
80. Rosten, *Hollywood*, 332.
81. Buster Keaton and Charles Samuels, *My Wonderful World of Slapstick* (New York: Da Capo Press, 1982), 260.
82. Serge Regourd, *Les seconds rôles du cinéma français: Grandeur et décadence* (Paris: Archimbaud/Klincksieck, 2010), 78.

83. W. Straw, "Scales of Presence: Bess Flowers and the Hollywood Extra," *Screen* 52, no. 1 (2011): 121–27.
84. William C. deMille, *Hollywood Saga*, 2nd ed. (New York: E. P. Dutton, 1939), 134.
85. Brownlow, *Parade's Gone By*, 145.
86. Rosten, *Hollywood*, 246.
87. Anderson, *In Its Own Image* 80.
88. David O. Selznick, *Memo from David O. Selznick*. (New York: Viking Press, 1972), 96.
89. Anderson, *In Its Own Image*; "Hollywood Boulevard," *Variety Weekly*, September 23, 1936, Production Clippings, Margaret Herrick Library.
90. "Film Stars Volunteer Aid in Show World."
91. "Hollywood Boulevard," *Variety Daily*, July 31, 1936, Production Clippings, Margaret Herrick Library.
92. "Hollywood Boulevard," *Motion Picture Herald*, August 22, 1936, Production Clippings, Margaret Herrick Library.
93. Gamson, *Claims to Fame*, 29.
94. Gamson, 33.
95. "Hollywood Boulevard," August 22, 1936.
96. "Hollywood Boulevard," September 23, 1936.
97. Paramount, "Hollywood Boulevard Press Book," n.d., Press Books, Margaret Herrick Library.
98. Paramount, "Hollywood Boulevard Press Book."
99. Barbara Klinger, "Digressions at the Cinema: Reception and Mass Culture," *Cinema Journal* 28, no. 4 (1989): 14.
100. Paramount, "Hollywood Boulevard Script," May 8, 1936, A-12, Paramount Scripts 683, Margaret Herrick Library.
101. Robert J. Read, "Uncredited: Jack Mulhall and the Decline of Stardom," *Screen* 52, no. 1 (2011): 114–20.
102. Read, "Uncredited."
103. Tom Kemper, *Hidden Talent: The Emergence of Hollywood Agents* (Berkeley: University of California Press, 2009), 41.
104. Kemper, *Hidden Talent*, 126.
105. Kemper, 149.
106. Kemper, 125.
107. Kemper, 124.
108. Behlmer and Thomas, *Hollywood's Hollywood*, 296.

109. Grayson Cooke, "We Had Faces Then: Sunset Boulevard and the Sense of the Spectral," *Quarterly Review of Film and Video* 26, no. 2 (2009): 89–101.
110. Janet M. Todd, *Women and Film* (New York: Holmes and Meier, 1988), 111; Gloria Swanson, *Swanson on Swanson* (New York: Random House, 1980), 4.
111. Patrice Petro, *Idols of Modernity: Movie Stars of the 1920s* (New Brunswick, NJ: Rutgers University Press, 2010), 19.
112. Maurice Zolotow, *Billy Wilder in Hollywood* (New York: Putnam, 1977), 169.
113. Gene D. Phillips, *Some Like It Wilder: The Life and Controversial Films of Billy Wilder* (Lexington: University Press of Kentucky, 2010), 122.
114. Phil Koury, "DeMille Takes Direction," *New York Times*, May 29, 1949.
115. Sam Staggs, *Close-up on Sunset Boulevard: Billy Wilder, Norma Desmond, and the Dark Hollywood Dream* (New York: Macmillan, 2003), 117; Ed Sikov, *On Sunset Boulevard: The Life and Times of Billy Wilder* (New York: Hyperion, 1998), 96.
116. Staggs, *Close-up on Sunset Boulevard*, 122.
117. Billy Wilder, *Sunset Boulevard* (Berkeley: University of California Press, 1999), 44.
118. Wilder, *Sunset Boulevard*, 61.
119. Keaton and Samuels, *My Wonderful World of Slapstick*, 274.
120. Behlmer and Thomas, *Hollywood's Hollywood*, 244.
121. Staggs, *Close-up on Sunset Boulevard*, 72.
122. Keaton and Samuels, *My Wonderful World of Slapstick*, 260.
123. Staggs, *Close-up on Sunset Boulevard*, 116.
124. Staggs, 104.
125. Phillips, *Some Like It Wilder*, 114.
126. Phillips, 114.
127. Staggs, *Close-up on Sunset Boulevard*, 72.
128. Staggs, 72, 102.
129. Staggs, 103.
130. Paramount, *Sunset Boulevard* Press Book, 1950, 14.
131. Paramount, *Sunset Boulevard* Press Book, 3; Staggs, *Close-up on Sunset Boulevard*, 96.
132. Paramount, *Sunset Boulevard Program*, 1950, 4.
133. Paramount, *Sunset Boulevard Program*, 17.

134. Richard Lamparski, *Whatever Became of . . . ? The Story of What Has Happened to More Famous Personalities* (New York: Crown Publishers, 1968), 145.
135. James Robert Parish, Michael R. Pitts, and Gregory W. Mank, *Hollywood on Hollywood* (Metuchen, NJ: Scarecrow Press, 1978), 211.
136. Behlmer and Thomas, *Hollywood's Hollywood*, 207.
137. United Artists, It's A Mad, Mad, Mad, Mad World 1970 Re-Release Press Book, 1970, 3.
138. Donald Spoto, *Stanley Kramer, Film Maker* (New York: Putnam, 1978), 19.
139. Vanessa R. Schwartz, *It's So French!: Hollywood, Paris, and the Making of Cosmopolitan Film Culture* (Chicago: University of Chicago Press, 2007).
140. "When the World Was Wider," *Life*, October 22, 1956, 81.
141. Art Cohn, *The Nine Lives of Michael Todd: The Story of One of the World's Most Fabulous Showmen* (Kessinger Publishing, 2007), 380.
142. Louella O. Parsons, *Tell It to Louella* (New York: Putnam, 1961), 259.
143. Ezra Goodman, "Rounding Up Stars in 80 Ways," *Life*, October 22, 1956.
144. Cohn, *Nine Lives of Michael Todd*, 379.
145. Schwartz, *It's So French!*, 171.
146. Cohn, *Nine Lives of Michael Todd*, 279.
147. Cohn, 379.
148. Goldwyn Studios, "Souls for Sale Silent Cutting Continuity," 32.
149. Edmund Crispin, *Frequent Hearses* (Harmondsworth, England: Penguin Books, 1987).
150. Schwartz, *It's So French!*, 176, 181.
151. "Many Film Precedents Set by 'Around the World in 80 Days,'" in Around the World in 80 Days 1968 Press Book, 1968, 6.
152. Cohn, *Nine Lives of Michael Todd*, 379.
153. Kemper, *Hidden Talent*, 40; David Niven, *The Moon's a Balloon* (New York: G. P. Putnam's Sons, 1972), 334.
154. Schwartz, *It's So French!*, 173.
155. Cohn, *Nine Lives of Michael Todd*, 379.
156. Michael Todd Jr. and S. T. McCarthy, *A Valuable Property: The Life Story of Michael Todd* (New York: Arbor House Publishing, 1983), 274.
157. Columbia Pictures, "Pepe Program," n.d., 15, Press Books, Margaret Herrick Library.

158. "It's a Mad Booklet" (Mar-King Publishing and Novelty Corp., n.d.), Linwood D. Gunn Papers, Folder 285, Margaret Herrick Library.
159. "It's a Mad Booklet," 6.
160. Spoto, *Stanley Kramer, Film Maker*, 255.
161. "It's a Mad Mad Mad Mad World Production Photographs," n.d., Box 66, Envelope 1, MW1392–1444; Box 67, Envelope 2; Box 68, Envelope 3, MWK340–342, Stanley Kramer Files, UCLA Special Collections.
162. Bosley Crowther, "Screen: 'The Greatest Story Ever Told'; Max von Sydow Stars in Biblical Film," *New York Times*, February 16, 1966.
163. "It's a Mad Booklet."
164. "It's a Mad Booklet," 31.
165. Roger Angell, "The Current Cinema: Poor Peon," *New Yorker*, December 31, 1960, www.newyorker.com/magazine/1960/12/31/poor-peon.
166. Philip K. Scheuer, "Cantinflas Carries Heavy 'Pepe' Load: Simple Peon Made Complex by Olla-Podrida of a Show," *Los Angeles Times*, December 28, 1960.

Chapter 3: Inside Laughs

1. Philip K. Scheuer, "Cantinflas Carries Heavy 'Pepe' Load: Simple Peon Made Complex by Olla-Podrida of a Show," *Los Angeles Times*, December 28, 1960.
2. "Brunette Funny Bob Hope," *Hollywood Reporter*, February 18, 1947, Production Code Administration Files My Favorite Brunette, Margaret Herrick Library.
3. Roger Angell, "The Current Cinema: Poor Peon," *New Yorker*, December 31, 1960, www.newyorker.com/magazine/1960/12/31/poor-peon.
4. Steve Seidman, *Comedian Comedy: A Tradition in Hollywood Film* (Ann Arbor, MI: UMI Research Press, 1981), 3, 6.
5. Timothy Corrigan, "Film and the Culture of Cult," in *The Cult Film Experience: Beyond All Reason*, ed. J. P Telotte (Austin: University of Texas Press, 1991), 31.
6. Umberto Eco, "'Casablanca': Cult Movies and Intertextual Collage," *SubStance* 14, no. 2 (1985): 463.
7. Walter Raubicheck, "Bing Crosby at Paramount: From Crooner to Actor," in *Going My Way: Bing Crosby and American Culture*, ed. Ruth Prigozy

and Walter Raubicheck (Rochester, NY: University of Rochester Press, 2007), 84.
8. James Naremore, *Acting in the Cinema* (Berkeley: University of California Press, 1990), 272.
9. A. P. Jacobs to I. Windisch, "Inter Office Memo: Bob Hope Idea," January 10, 1959, Marty Weiser Alias Jesse James 1959 Folder 14, Margaret Herrick Library; Dick Williams, "It's Cantinflas Who Puts Spark in Long Pepe," *Los Angeles Mirror*, December 28, 1961.
10. Jacqueline Nacache, *L'acteur de cinéma* (Paris: Armand Colin, 2005), 56.
11. Denise McKenna, "The Photoplay or the Pickaxe: Extras, Gender, and Labour in Early Hollywood," *Film History: An International Journal* 23, no. 1 (2011): 8.
12. P. David Marshall, *Celebrity and Power: Fame in Contemporary Culture* (Minneapolis: University of Minnesota Press, 1997), 91.
13. Adrienne Lai, "Glitter and Grain: Aura and Authenticity in the Celebrity Photographs of Juergen Teller," in *Framing Celebrity: New Directions in Celebrity Culture*, ed. Su Holmes and Sean Redmond (New York: Routledge, 2006), 227.
14. Lai, "Glitter and Grain." 215.
15. Joshua Gamson, *Claims to Fame: Celebrity in Contemporary America* (Berkeley: University of California Press, 1994), 30.
16. David Lusted, "The Glut of Personality," in *Stardom: Industry of Desire*, ed. Christine Gledhill (New York: Routledge, 1991), 253.
17. Gamson, *Claims to Fame*, 35.
18. Jane Feuer, *The Hollywood Musical* (Bloomington: Indiana University Press, 1993), 80.
19. Eco, "Casablanca," 462.
20. Ernest Mathijs and Xavier Mendik, Introduction to *The Cult Film Reader*, ed. Ernest Mathijs and Xavier Mendik (New York: Open University Press/McGraw-Hill Education, 2008), 144.
21. Barbara Klinger, "Digressions at the Cinema: Reception and Mass Culture," *Cinema Journal* 28, no. 4 (1989): 4.
22. Eco, "Casablanca," 463.
23. Paramount, "Hollywood Boulevard Press Book," n.d., Press Books, Margaret Herrick Library; "It's a Mad Booklet" (Mar-King Publishing and Novelty Corp., n.d.), Linwood D. Gunn Papers, Folder 285, Margaret Herrick Library.

24. Seidman, *Comedian Comedy*, 2.
25. Frank Krutnik and Steve Neale, *Popular Film and Television Comedy* (New York: Routledge, 2006), 31.
26. Nacache, *L'acteur de cinéma*, 14.
27. Krutnik and Neale, *Popular Film and Television Comedy*, 16; Kristine Brunovska Karnick and Henry Jenkins, *Classical Hollywood Comedy* (New York: Routledge, 2013), 157.
28. Karnick and Jenkins, *Classical Hollywood Comedy*, 85.
29. Krutnik and Neale, *Popular Film and Television Comedy*, 131.
30. Leo Calvin Rosten, *Hollywood: The Movie Colony, the Movie Makers* (New York: Harcourt, Brace, 1941), 80.
31. Thomas F. Brady, "Unemployment Rises as Production Drops—Roosevelt Kin Approve Films," *New York Times*, February 23, 1947.
32. Krutnik and Neale, *Popular Film and Television Comedy*, 187.
33. Karnick and Jenkins, *Classical Hollywood Comedy*, 154.
34. Frank Krutnik, "A Spanner in the Works? Genre, Narrative, and the Hollywood Comedian," in *Classical Hollywood Comedy*, ed. Kristine Brunovska Karnick and Henry Jenkins (New York: Routledge, 1995), 30.
35. Richard Zoglin, *Hope: Entertainer of the Century* (New York: Simon and Schuster, 2014), 7.
36. Lawrence J. Quirk, *Bob Hope: The Road Well-Traveled* (New York: Applause Books, 2000), 29.
37. Zoglin, *Hope*, 7.
38. "Bing, Bob, Dottie Doughtily Cruise to Rio," *Los Angeles Times*, January 1, 1948.
39. Ethan de Seife, *Tashlinesque: The Hollywood Comedies of Frank Tashlin* (Middletown, CT: Wesleyan University Press, 2012), 70.
40. Steven Cohan, "Almost Like Being at Home: Showbiz Culture and Hollywood Road Trips in the 1940s and 1950s," in *The Road Movie Book*, ed. Steven Cohan and Ina Rae Hark (New York: Routledge, 1997), 134.
41. Seidman, *Comedian Comedy*, 17.
42. David Bordwell, *The Way Hollywood Tells It: Story and Style in Modern Movies* (Berkeley: University of California Press, 2006), 8.
43. Neil Rau, "Visiting the Studios: Funniest Crosby and Hope Clowning Never Screened," *Los Angeles Examiner*, May 18, 1952; Paul Minoff, "The World Is Their Oyster," *Cue*, December 6, 1952.
44. Quirk, *Bob Hope*, 127.

45. Seidman, *Comedian Comedy*, 64.
46. Seidman, 48.
47. Zoglin, *Hope*, 130.
48. Seife, *Tashlinesque*, 85.
49. Cohan, "Almost Like Being at Home," 101.
50. Brady, "Unemployment Rises as Production Drops—Roosevelt Kin Approve Films."
51. Seidman, *Comedian Comedy*, 42.
52. Seidman, 48.
53. Cohan, "Almost Like Being at Home," 118.
54. Zoglin, *Hope*, 195.
55. George Glass to Reviewers, "From George Glass for Samuel Goldwyn to Reviewers," n.d., Production Clippings, Margaret Herrick Library.
56. Barry King, "The Star and the Commodity: Notes towards a Performance Theory of Stardom," *Cultural Studies* 1, no. 2 (1987): 145–61.
57. Don Hartman, Frank Butler, and Paramount, "My Favorite Blonde Shooting Script," November 10, 1941, Paramount Production Records My Favorite Blonde Folder 967, Margaret Herrick Library; Paramount, "My Favorite Blonde Script Supervisor's Notes," January 5, 1942, Paramount Production Files My Favorite Blonde Folder 8, Margaret Herrick Library.
58. Paramount Pictures Corporation, "My Favorite Blonde Script Supervisor's Notes," January 5, 1942, Paramount Production Files My Favorite Blonde Folder 8, Margaret Herrick Library.
59. Wolfe Kaufman, "Bob Hope's at His Best in My Favorite Blonde," *Chicago Sun*, June 20, 1942.
60. Redd Kann, "My Favorite Brunette," *Motion Picture Daily*, February 18, 1947.
61. "My Favorite Brunette," *Variety Weekly*, February 19, 1947.
62. Stanley Kramer Productions, "Daily Production Report," October 29, 1962, Stanley Kramer Box 62 Folder Mad World Production Reports Pre-Production, UCLA Special Collections; Eugene H. Frank to Stanley Kramer, "Re: Jerry Lewis," October 26, 1962, Stanley Kramer Box 61 Folder 4, UCLA Special Collections.
63. Gary Giddins, Introduction to *Going My Way: Bing Crosby and American Culture*, ed. Walter Raubicheck and Ruth Prigozy (Rochester, NY: University of Rochester Press, 2007), 5.

64. Raubicheck, "Bing Crosby at Paramount," 84.
65. Raubicheck, 90.
66. Cohan, "Almost Like Being at Home," 118.
67. Dorothy Lamour, *My Side of the Road* (Englewood Cliffs, NJ: Prentice-Hall, 1980), 120.
68. McKenna, "Photoplay or the Pickaxe," 8.
69. Feuer, *Hollywood Musical*, 11.
70. Richard Dyer, *Stars* (London: BFI, 1979), 42.
71. Gamson, *Claims to Fame*, 116.
72. Seidman, *Comedian Comedy*, 48.
73. "Hope and Crosby: New Road," *Newsweek*, January 26, 1948.
74. Shawn Levy, *King of Comedy: The Life and Art of Jerry Lewis* (New York: St. Martin's Press, 1997), 153, www.amazon.com/King-Comedy-Life-Jerry-Lewis/dp/0312168780.
75. Krutnik and Neale, *Popular Film and Television Comedy*, 86.
76. "Film Reviews: Road to Bali," *Variety*, November 19, 1952.
77. David Bongard, "Road to Bali," *Los Angeles Daily News*, December 26, 1952.
78. Margaret Hartford, "Hope, Crosby, Lamour Cutting Capers Again in 'Road' Film," *Hollywood Citizen-News*, December 26, 1952.
79. "Films: Road to Rio," *America*, January 10, 1948.
80. "Road to Rio," *Film Daily*, November 18, 1946, Press Clippings—Road to Rio, Margaret Herrick Library.
81. "Films: Road to Rio."
82. Bongard, "Road to Bali."
83. "The Princess and the Pirate," *New Yorker*, February 17, 1945.
84. Paramount, "Projected Outline on Alias Jesse James," November 1958, 3, Marty Weiser Alias Jesse James 1959 Folder 14, Margaret Herrick Library.
85. Paramount, "Road to Rio Main Title Billing Corrected," March 19, 1947, Paramount Pictures Production Records Road to Rio Billing #1, Margaret Herrick Library.
86. Paramount, "My Favorite Blonde Has Surprise in Store (Advance Feature)," My Favorite Blonde Press Book, 1943, 25.
87. Jacobs to Windisch, "Inter Office Memo: Bob Hope Idea."
88. Paramount, "Alias Jesse James Production Call Sheet," October 29, 1958, Paramount Pictures Production Records Folder 58, Margaret Herrick Library.
89. Lamour, *My Side of the Road*, 197.

90. Lamour, 140.
91. Paramount, "Authorization for Engagement of Artists by BC Enterprises, Inc. and Hope Enterprises Inc.—Jerry Colonna," February 25, 1947, Paramount Pictures Production Records Road to Rio Billing #1, Margaret Herrick Library.
92. Samuel L. Chell, "Rivalries: The Mutual Mentoring of Bing Crosby and Frank Sinatra," in *Going My Way: Bing Crosby and American Culture*, ed. Ruth Prigozy and Walter Raubicheck (Rochester, NY: University of Rochester Press, 2007), 118.
93. Seidman, *Comedian Comedy*, 23.
94. Chris Rojek, *Frank Sinatra* (Cambridge, MA: Polity, 2004), 50.
95. Rojek, *Frank Sinatra*, 26.
96. Mike Weatherford, *Cult Vegas: The Weirdest! The Wildest! The Swingin'est Town on Earth* (Las Vegas: Huntington Press, 2001), 24.
97. Philip K. Scheuer, "Las Vegas Swarms with Movie Stars: Heist Like Military Operation in Sinatra's 'Ocean's Eleven,'" *Los Angeles Times*, February 2, 1960.
98. Richard Griffiths, "'Ocean's 11' Fails to Awe N.Y. Critics," *Los Angeles Times*, August 30, 1960.
99. "Palship," *Newsweek*, August 8, 1960.
100. Bob Thomas, "Ocean's 11 Film Begun by Lawford," *Los Angeles Mirror*, January 18, 1960.
101. Philip K. Scheuer, "Sinatra Premieres 'Ocean's Eleven': Las Vegas Hotels Host Stars; Film Enjoyable, Slow-Starting," *Los Angeles Times*, August 5, 1960.
102. Rojek, *Frank Sinatra*, 147.
103. Rojek, 32.
104. "TV Preview: Sinatra's 'Rat Pack' in 'Ocean's 11,'" *Hartford Courant*, June 9, 1966.
105. Weatherford, *Cult Vegas*, 11; Rojek, *Frank Sinatra*, 136.
106. "Agreement between Dorchester Productions and Warner Bros.," November 8, 1957, Ocean's Eleven Legal Folder 63, Margaret Herrick Library.
107. "Ocean's Eleven Script Revision Final," February 16, 1960, 113, Scripts AMPAS Unpublished, Margaret Herrick Library; "Ocean's Eleven Script," January 4, 1960, 79, Lewis Milestone Ocean's Eleven Script Folder 60, Margaret Herrick Library; "Ocean's Eleven Script," 113.
108. Scheuer, "Cantinflas Carries Heavy 'Pepe' Load."

109. Griffiths, "'Ocean's 11' Fails to Awe N.Y. Critics"; Scheuer, "Sinatra Premieres 'Ocean's Eleven.'"
110. Rojek, *Frank Sinatra*, 26.
111. Seidman, *Comedian Comedy*, 48.
112. Cynthia J. Fuchs, "The Buddy Politic," in *Screening the Male: Exploring Masculinities in Hollywood Cinema*, ed. Steven Cohan and Ina Rae Hark (New York: Routledge, 1993), 198.
113. James Robert Parish, Michael R. Pitts, and Gregory W. Mank, *Hollywood on Hollywood* (Metuchen, NJ: Scarecrow Press, 1978), 211.
114. "Milestone Picture Is Funny and Flip," *Hollywood Reporter*, August 8, 1960.
115. Rojek, *Frank Sinatra*, 138.
116. David Niven, *The Moon's a Balloon* (New York: G. P. Putnam's Sons, 1972), 284.
117. Ezra Goodman, "Rounding Up Stars in 80 Ways," *Life*, October 22, 1956, 89.
118. Niven, *Moon's a Balloon*, 284.
119. Niven, 283.
120. Arthur Harvey and ABC to Stanley Kramer, "Re: Jerry Lewis Show," November 8, 1963, Stanley Kramer Box 64 Folder TV Shows Miscellaneous Mad World SEK, UCLA Special Collections; Lynn Stalmaster and Stalmaster-Lister Company, "Contract Request," June 13, 1962, Stanley Kramer Box 61 Folder 5 Actors Weekly Contracts, UCLA Special Collections.
121. Robert Mitchum to John Huston, September 21, 1962, John Huston Folder 266 List of Adrian Messenger correspondence, Margaret Herrick Library.
122. Mike Tomkies, *The Robert Mitchum Story* (New York: Ballantine Books, 1973), 194.
123. Niven, *Moon's a Balloon*, 283.
124. Bob Thomas, "Many Ask for Cameo Roles," *Daytona Beach Morning Journal*, October 27, 1962.
125. Williams, "It's Cantinflas Who Puts Spark in Long Pepe."
126. Archer Winsten, "'A Mad World' at Warner's Cinema," *New York Post*, November 19, 1963.
127. William Rose and Tania Rose, "It's A Mad, Mad, Mad, Mad World First Draft Screenplay," n.d., Scripts AMPAS Unpublished, Margaret Herrick Library.

128. Mathijs and Mendik, Introduction, 2.
129. Mathijs and Mendik, 7.
130. Bosley Crowther, "Wild Comedy about the Pursuit of Money: 'A Mad, Mad World' Opens at Warner," *New York Times*, November 19, 1963.
131. Bosley Crowther, "Screen: 'The Greatest Story Ever Told'; Max von Sydow Stars in Biblical Film," *New York Times*, February 16, 1966.
132. Crowther, "Screen: 'The Greatest Story Ever Told.'"
133. Crowther, "Screen: 'The Greatest Story Ever Told.'"
134. Peter Krämer, *The New Hollywood: From* Bonnie and Clyde *to* Star Wars (London: Wallflower, 2005), 47.
135. Krämer, *New Hollywood*, 81.
136. Christopher Ames, *Movies about the Movies: Hollywood Reflected* (Lexington: University Press of Kentucky, 1997), 12.
137. Krämer, *New Hollywood*, 38.

Chapter 4: The Ambassadors

1. Karen S. Schneider, "Gathering No Moss," *People*, May 15, 2000.
2. Raymond Williams, *Television Technology and Cultural Form* (New York: Routledge, 2003), http://public.eblib.com/choice/publicfullrecord.aspx?p=182593.
3. Lynn Spigel, *Make Room for TV: Television and the Family Ideal in Postwar America* (Chicago: University of Chicago Press, 1992), 76.
4. Amanda D. Lotz, *The Television Will Be Revolutionized*, 2nd ed. (New York: New York University Press, 2014), 32.
5. Christine Becker, "Televising Film Stardom in the 1950s," *Framework: The Journal of Cinema and Media* 46, no. 2 (2005): 9.
6. Christine Becker, *It's the Pictures That Got Small: Hollywood Film Stars on 1950s Television* (Middletown, CT: Wesleyan University Press, 2009), 191.
7. Susan Murray, *Hitch Your Antenna to the Stars: Early Television and Broadcast Stardom* (New York: Routledge, 2005), 43.
8. Denise Mann, "The Spectacularization of Television in Early Variety Shows," in *Private Screenings: Television and the Female Consumer*, ed. Lynn Spigel and Denise Mann (Minneapolis: University of Minnesota Press, 1992), 55.
9. Spigel, *Make Room for TV*, 80.
10. Mann, "Spectacularization of Television in Early Variety Shows," 55.

11. Mann, 53.
12. Spigel, *Make Room for TV*, 157.
13. Spigel, 156.
14. Murray, *Hitch Your Antenna to the Stars*.
15. Mann, "Spectacularization of Television in Early Variety Shows," 48.
16. Becker, *It's the Pictures That Got Small*, 174; James V. Kern, "Lucy and John Wayne," *I Love Lucy*, October 10, 1955; James V. Kern, "Lucy Meets Charles Boyer," *I Love Lucy*, March 5, 1956.
17. Becker, "Televising Film Stardom in the 1950s," 15.
18. Becker, *It's the Pictures That Got Small*, 233.
19. Becker, 9.
20. Becker, 20.
21. Gary Edgerton, "High Concept, Small Screen: Reperceiving the Industrial and Stylistic Origins of the American Made-for-TV Movie," in *Connections: A Broadcast History Reader*, ed. Michelle Hilmes (Belmont, CA: Thomas/Wadsworth, 2003), 218.
22. Becker, "Televising Film Stardom in the 1950s," 9.
23. Williams, *Television Technology and Cultural Form*, 56.
24. Matt Hills, *Fan Cultures* (New York: Routledge, 2003), 104.
25. Dean J. DeFino, *The HBO Effect* (London: Bloomsbury Academic, 2013), 110.
26. DeFino, *HBO Effect*, 110; Greg M. Smith, *Beautiful TV: The Art and Argument of Ally McBeal* (Austin: University of Texas Press, 2007), 146.
27. Michael Lembeck, "The One with Two Parts: Part 2," *Friends*, February 23, 1995.
28. Smith, *Beautiful TV*, 146.
29. Becker, *It's the Pictures That Got Small*, 30.
30. Smith, *Beautiful TV*, 146.
31. Smith, 171.
32. Williams, *Television Technology and Cultural Form*, 53.
33. Williams, 96.
34. Williams, 56.
35. Becker, "Televising Film Stardom in the 1950s," 11.
36. James Bennett, "The Television Personality System: Televisual Stardom Revisited after Film Theory," *Screen* 49, no. 1 (2008): 32.
37. Susan Holmes, "'As They Really Are, and in Close-up': Film Stars on 1950s British Television," *Screen* 42, no. 2 (2001): 185.

38. Holmes, "As They Really Are, and in Close-up," 170.
39. Mary Desjardins, "Maureen O'Hara's 'Confidential' Life: Recycling Stars through Gossip and Moral Biography," in *Small Screens, Big Ideas: Television in the 1950s*, ed. Janet Thumin (London: I. B. Tauris, 2002), 120.
40. Becker, *It's the Pictures That Got Small*, 44.
41. Desjardins, "Maureen O'Hara's 'Confidential' Life," 120.
42. Desjardins, 120.
43. Becker, *It's the Pictures That Got Small*, 231.
44. Becker, 202.
45. Barbara Klinger, *Beyond the Multiplex: Cinema, New Technologies, and the Home* (Berkeley: University of California Press, 2006), 4.
46. Lotz, *Television Will Be Revolutionized*, 162.
47. Becker, *It's the Pictures That Got Small*, 216.
48. George Waggner, "Green Ice," *Batman*, November 9, 1966; "Hi Diddle Riddle," *Batman*, January 12, 1966.
49. Spigel, *Make Room for TV*, 178.
50. George Plasketes, *B-Sides, Undercurrents and Overtones: Peripheries to Popular in Music, 1960 to the Present* (Farnham, UK: Ashgate Publishing, 2013), 137.
51. Roberta Pearson, "Star Trek and Cult Television," in *Television as Digital Media*, ed. James Bennett and Niki Strange (Durham, NC: Duke University Press, 2011), 119.
52. Plasketes, *B-Sides, Undercurrents and Overtones*, 137.
53. Holmes, "As They Really Are, and in Close-Up," 171.
54. Plasketes, *B-Sides, Undercurrents and Overtones*, 138.
55. Alyn Shipton, *Nilsson: The Life of a Singer-Songwriter* (New York: Oxford University Press, 2013), 92.
56. John Meredyth Lucas, "The Many Deaths of Saint Christopher," *Mannix*, October 7, 1967.
57. Richard Kinon, "Will the Real Sammy Davis Please Hang Up?," *The Patty Duke Show*, March 3, 1965.
58. Plasketes, *B-Sides, Undercurrents and Overtones*, 137.
59. Joseph Pevney, "Far Out Munsters," *The Munsters*, March 18, 1965.
60. Shipton, *Nilsson*, 71.
61. Jerry Paris, "The Redcoats Are Coming," *The Dick Van Dyke Show*, February 10, 1965.

62. Bill Colleran, "Patty Pits Wits, Two Brits Hits," *The Patty Duke Show*, February 17, 1965.
63. James B. Clark, "The Cat's Meow," *Batman*, December 14, 1966.
64. "Radio-Television: Chad and Jeremy Figure in Spinoff of 'Laredo,'" *Variety*, December 8, 1965.
65. Smith, *Beautiful TV*, 147.
66. Pearson, "Star Trek and Cult Television," 118.
67. Aniko Bodroghkozy, *Groove Tube: Sixties Television and the Youth Rebellion* (Durham, NC: Duke University Press, 2001), 47.
68. Bodroghkozy, *Groove Tube*, 47.
69. Megan Mullen, *Television in the Multichannel Age: A Brief History of Cable Television* (Malden, MA: Wiley-Blackwell, 2008), 7.
70. Lotz, *Television Will Be Revolutionized*, 82.
71. Lotz, 156.
72. Lotz, 83.
73. Lotz, 85.
74. Phil Williams, "Feeding Off the Past: The Evolution of the Television Rerun," *Journal of Popular Film and Television* 21, no. 4 (1994): 240.
75. Williams, "Feeding Off the Past," 235; DeFino, *HBO Effect*, 32.
76. DeFino, *HBO Effect*, 9.
77. Plasketes, *B-Sides, Undercurrents and Overtones*, 168; Jay Sandrich, "Ted Baxter Meets Walter Cronkite," *The Mary Tyler Moore Show*, February 9, 1974.
78. Plasketes, *B-Sides, Undercurrents and Overtones*, 168.
79. Williams, "Feeding Off the Past," 243; DeFino, *HBO Effect*, 9.
80. Williams, "Feeding Off the Past," 243.
81. Derek Kompare, "I've Seen This One Before: The Construction of 'Classic TV' on Cable Television," in *Small Screens, Big Ideas: Television in the 1950s*, ed. Janet Thumin (London: I. B. Tauris, 2002), 21.
82. Kompare, "I've Seen This One Before," 19.
83. Kompare, 21.
84. Klinger, *Beyond the Multiplex*, 83.
85. Kompare, "I've Seen This One Before," 21.
86. Mullen, *Television in the Multichannel Age*, 155.
87. Kompare, "I've Seen This One Before," 30.
88. Lotz, *Television Will Be Revolutionized*, 217.
89. Lotz, 160.

90. DeFino, *HBO Effect*, 82.
91. DeFino, 137.
92. Becker, *It's the Pictures That Got Small*, 9.
93. Todd Holland, "Broadcast Nudes," *The Larry Sanders Show* (HBO, August 4, 1993); Todd Holland, "The Mr. Sharon Stone Show," *The Larry Sanders Show* (HBO, August 10, 1994).
94. Lotz, *Television Will Be Revolutionized*, 38.
95. Lotz, 36.
96. Lotz, 38.
97. Plasketes, *B-Sides, Undercurrents and Overtones*, 142.
98. Robert Berlinger, "Play Lady Play," *Dharma and Greg*, October 12, 1999.
99. Plasketes, *B-Sides, Undercurrents and Overtones*, 142.
100. Rob Bowman, "Jose Chung's 'From Outer Space,'" *The X-Files*, April 12, 1996.
101. Shelley Jensen, "Hare Today . . . ," *Fresh Prince of Bel-Air*, April 8, 1996.
102. "The Complete History of Guest Stars on 'The Fresh Prince of Bel-Air,'" Complex CA, accessed April 11, 2016, http://ca.complex.com/music/2012/09/the-complete-history-of-guest-stars-on-the-fresh-prince-of-bel-air/; Werner Walian, "I, Stank Hole in One," *The Fresh Prince of Bel-Air*, May 6, 1996; Shelley Jensen, "A Night at the Oprah," *The Fresh Prince of Bel-Air*, November 9, 1992.
103. Gary Halvorson, "The One with the Rumor," *Friends*, November 22, 2001.
104. Lotz, *Television Will Be Revolutionized*, 87.
105. DeFino, *HBO Effect*, 63.
106. Plasketes, *B-Sides, Undercurrents and Overtones*, 148.
107. Linda Mendoza, "My Whole Life Is Thunder," *30 Rock* (NBC, December 6, 2012); Alan Rafkin, "The Schumakers Go to Hollywood," *It's Garry Shandling's Show*, November 20, 1987; Steve Robertson, "The Men in Me," *The Cleveland Show*, March 25, 2012.
108. Rob Schiller, "Shear Torture," *King of Queens*, October 24, 2005; Mark Cendrowski, "The Celebration Experimentation," *The Big Bang Theory*, February 25, 2016.
109. Brett Martin, *Difficult Men: Behind the Scenes of a Creative Revolution; From* The Sopranos *and* The Wire *to* Mad Men *and* Breaking Bad (London: Penguin Books, 2014), 252.
110. DeFino, *HBO Effect*, 8.
111. Lotz, *Television Will Be Revolutionized*, 28.

112. Lotz, 105.
113. Lotz, 105.
114. Gary Halvorson, "The One in Massapequa," *Friends*, March 28, 2002; Jessica Yu, "The Supremes," *The West Wing*, March 24, 2004.
115. Martin, *Difficult Men*, 227.
116. John Ellis, "New Responses to Fake Footage," in *Relocating Television: Television in the Digital Context*, ed. Jostein Gripsrud (New York: Routledge, 2010), 186.
117. Alec Berg, "Larry vs. Michael J. Fox," *Curb Your Enthusiasm*, September 11, 2011; Louis C. K, "Barney/Never," *Louie* (HBO, August 2, 2012).
118. Ricky Gervais and Stephen Merchant, "Kate Winslet," *Extras*, August 4, 2005.
119. Ricky Gervais and Stephen Merchant, "Chris Martin," *Extras*, October 5, 2006.
120. Jonathan Krisel, "Renoir," *Baskets*, January 21, 2016.

Chapter 5: Author Signature

1. Thomas M. Leitch, *Find the Director and Other Hitchcock Games* (Athens: University of Georgia Press, 1991), 4.
2. Robert Stam, *Reflexivity in Film and Literature: From Don Quixote to Jean-Luc Godard* (Ann Arbor, MI: UMI Research Press, 1985), 126.
3. Robert E. Kapsis, *Hitchcock: The Making of a Reputation* (Chicago: University of Chicago Press, 1992), 21.
4. Stam, *Reflexivity in Film and Literature*, 130; Kevin Brownlow, *The Parade's Gone By* (New York: Knopf, 1968), 529.
5. John Orr, *Hitchcock and Twentieth-Century Cinema* (London: Wallflower Press, 2005), 57.
6. Thomas M. Leitch, "Hitchcock and His Writers," in *Authorship in Film Adaptation*, ed. Jack Boozer (Austin: University of Texas Press, 2009), 74.
7. Stam, *Reflexivity in Film and Literature*, 130.
8. Chris Crawford, *The Art of Computer Game Design* (New York: Osborne/McGraw-Hill, 1984), 99; Stephen Kline, Nick Dyer-Witheford, and Greig De Peuter, *Digital Play the Interaction of Technology, Culture, and Marketing* (Montreal: McGill-Queen's University Press, 2005), 14.
9. Ernest Mathijs, "Cronenberg Connected: Cameo Acting, Cult Stardom, and Supertexts," in *Cult Film Stardom: Offbeat Attractions and Processes*

of Cultification, ed. Kate Egan and Sarah Thomas (New York: Palgrave Macmillan, 2013), 147.
10. Michel Marie, *The French New Wave: An Artistic School*, trans. Richard Neupert (Malden, MA: Wiley-Blackwell, 2002), 76.
11. Mathijs, "Cronenberg Connected: Cameo Acting, Cult Stardom, and Supertexts," 147.
12. Mathijs, 144.
13. Mathijs, 149.
14. D. A. Miller, "Hitchcock's Understyle: A Too-Close View of Rope," *Representations*, no. 121 (2013): 26.
15. PR, Universal to Fred Thomas, Rank Organization, "Re: Speeches," June 29, 1966, Hitchcock Folder 935, Torn Curtain—speeches, Margaret Herrick Library.
16. Donald Spoto, *The Dark Side of Genius: The Life of Alfred Hitchcock* (New York: Da Capo Press, 1999), 95.
17. John Russell Taylor, *Hitch: The Life and Times of Alfred Hitchcock* (New York: Pantheon Books, 1978), 230.
18. Spoto, *Dark Side of Genius*, 95; Jan Olsson, *Hitchcock à la Carte* (Durham, NC: Duke University Press, 2015), 31.
19. Taylor, *Hitch*, 102.
20. Taylor, 17.
21. Orr, *Hitchcock and Twentieth-Century Cinema*, 133.
22. Miller, "Hitchcock's Hidden Pictures," 107.
23. Leitch, *Find the Director and Other Hitchcock Games*, 5.
24. Miller, "Hitchcock's Understyle," 24.
25. Tom Cohen, *Hitchcock's Cryptonymies* (Minneapolis: University of Minnesota Press, 2005), 242.
26. Look, "Look Photocrime: The Murder of Monty Woolley Directed by Alfred Hitchcock," c. 1943, Hitchcock Folder 353, Margaret Herrick Library.
27. Alfred Hitchcock and Ernest Lehman, "Transcript of Tapes," November 2, 1973, Hitchcock Folder 138 Family Plot—script 1973, Margaret Herrick Library.
28. Michael Cowan, "Learning to Love the Movies: Puzzles, Participation, and Cinephilia in Interwar European Film Magazines," *Film History: An International Journal* 27, no. 4 (2015): 11.
29. "Face to Face with Alfred Hitchcock," *Hollywood Studio*, January 1970.
30. Cohen, *Hitchcock's Cryptonymies*, xi.

31. Matt Hills, *Fan Cultures* (New York: Routledge, 2003), xvii.
32. Raymond Bellour, "Hitchcock, The Enunciator," *Camera Obscura* 1, no. 2 (1977): 73.
33. Miller, "Hitchcock's Understyle."
34. Cohen, *Hitchcock's Cryptonymies*, 134.
35. Spoto, *Dark Side of Genius*, 267.
36. Leitch, *Find the Director and Other Hitchcock Games*, 8.
37. Miller, "Hitchcock's Understyle," 5.
38. John Coleman, "Seeing Red," *New Statesman*, July 10, 1964, Hitchcock Folder 479 Marnie (pub.—TV), Margaret Herrick Library.
39. Charles Barr, *English Hitchcock* (Moffat, UK: Cameron and Hollis, 1999), 12; Bill Krohn, *Hitchcock at Work*, new ed. (London: Phaidon Press, 2003).
40. François Truffaut and Alfred Hitchcock, *Hitchcock* (New York: Simon and Schuster, 1967), 319.
41. Universal Studios Press Department, "Transcript of Closed Circuit Press Conference at NBC (Richard Schickel Interviews), NBC Studios, Burbank," March 23, 1976, 31, 37, Hitchcock Folder 200 Family Plot Hitchcock, Alfred 1973–1977 (publicity), Margaret Herrick Library; Leitch, "Hitchcock and His Writers," 81.
42. Taylor, *Hitch*, 294.
43. Alfred J. Hitchcock, "The Paradine Case London and Cumberland Locations," May 18, 1946, Folder 558 The Paradine Case Miscellaneous, Margaret Herrick Library; Krohn, *Hitchcock at Work*, 16; MGM, "North by Northwest Shooting Schedule Revised," August 18, 1954, Hitchcock Folder 547 North by Northwest schedule, Margaret Herrick Library.
44. Spoto, *Dark Side of Genius*, 324.
45. Patrick McGilligan, *Backstory: Interviews with Screenwriters of Hollywood's Golden Age* (Berkeley: University of California Press, 1986), 30.
46. Barr, *English Hitchcock*, 235.
47. Barr, 235.
48. John Belton, "Charles Bennett and the Typical Hitchcock Scenario," *Film History* 9, no. 3 (1997): 320.
49. Tony Lee Moral, *Hitchcock and the Making of Marnie* (Lanham, MD: Scarecrow Press, 2002), xv; Leitch, "Hitchcock and His Writers," 81.
50. Bellour, "Hitchcock, The Enunciator," 73.
51. Bellour, 78.

52. Bellour, 73.
53. Miller, "Hitchcock's Hidden Pictures."
54. Miller, "Hitchcock's Hidden Pictures"; Cohen, *Hitchcock's Cryptonymies*; Maurice Yacowar, *Hitchcock's British Films* (Detroit: Wayne State University Press, 2010); Krohn, *Hitchcock at Work*, 37.
55. Kapsis, *Hitchcock*, 20.
56. Taylor, *Hitch*, 308.
57. John D. Weaver, "The Man behind the Body," *Holiday*, September 1964; Bob Faber, "Regular Trailer Revised," December 3, 1971, Hitchcock Folder 267 Frenzy Script 1971–1972, Margaret Herrick Library; Andrew A. Erish, "Reclaiming Alfred Hitchcock Presents," *Quarterly Review of Film and Video* 26, no. 5 (2009): 385–92.
58. Truffaut and Hitchcock, *Hitchcock*, 309.
59. Leitch, *Find the Director and Other Hitchcock Games*, 5.
60. Barr, *English Hitchcock*, 27.
61. "The Films: Good Things of the Week," *The Star*, January 19, 1927, Hitchcock Folder 1621 Scrapbooks, Margaret Herrick Library.
62. Kapsis, *Hitchcock*, 17.
63. Spoto, *Dark Side of Genius*, 95.
64. Spoto, *Dark Side of Genius*.
65. Scott Simmon, "Cecil B. DeMille's Hollywood," *Film Quarterly* 59, no. 4 (2006): 189.
66. Spoto, *Dark Side of Genius*, 73.
67. Simmon, "Cecil B. DeMille's Hollywood," 189.
68. Truffaut and Hitchcock, *Hitchcock*, 43.
69. Truffaut and Hitchcock, *Hitchcock*, 49.
70. Taylor, *Hitch*, 102.
71. "Blackmail," *Daily Film Renter*, June 24, 1929, Hitchcock Folder 1617 Scrapbooks, Margaret Herrick Library.
72. Leitch, *Find the Director and Other Hitchcock Games*, 2.
73. Yacowar, *Hitchcock's British Films*, 1.
74. Yacowar, 243.
75. Taylor, *Hitch*, 198.
76. Rose Pelswick, "McCrea-Day Picture Presented at the Rivoli," *New York Journal and American*, August 28, 1940, Hitchcock Folder 1623 Scrapbooks, Margaret Herrick Library.

77. Bosley Crowther, "The Screen: Foreign Correspondent," *New York Times*, August 28, 1940, Hitchcock Folder 1623 Scrapbooks, Margaret Herrick Library; "New Hitchcock Film Thriller of the Year," *New York World Telegram*, August 28, 1940, Hitchcock Folder 1623 Scrapbooks, Margaret Herrick Library.
78. Krohn, *Hitchcock at Work*, 34.
79. Archer Winsten, "Alfred Hitchcock's 'Lifeboat' Opens at the Astor Theatre," *New York Post*, January 13, 1944, Hitchcock Folder 1622 Scrapbooks, Margaret Herrick Library.
80. Leitch, *Find the Director and Other Hitchcock Games*, 3.
81. Leitch, 107.
82. Leitch, 3.
83. Leitch, 1.
84. "Hitchcock's Hand Steers Lifeboat Safely through Film's Troubled Sea," *Newsweek*, January 17, 1944, Hitchcock Folder 1622 Mr and Mrs Smith Scrapbook, Margaret Herrick Library.
85. "'You Would See It Just to See Its Two Brilliant Stars' Advertisement," December 1941, Hitchcock Folder 656 Suspicion (misc) Lobby Reproductions for theaters, Margaret Herrick Library.
86. Erish, "Reclaiming Alfred Hitchcock Presents."
87. Mel Dinelli, "Trailer Material for Spellbound," September 3, 1945, Hitchcock Folder 650 Spellbound (script), Margaret Herrick Library.
88. Taylor, *Hitch*, 230.
89. "American Heart Fund 'Close to Your Heart' 15-Minute Transcribed Program by American Heart Association," February 1, 1956, Hitchcock Folder 394 The Man Who Knew Too Much, Margaret Herrick Library.
90. Weaver, "Man behind the Body," 64.
91. Orr, *Hitchcock and Twentieth-Century Cinema*, 47.
92. Taylor, *Hitch*, 309.
93. Taylor, 229.
94. Joan Harrison and Shamley Productions to Alfred Hitchcock, March 18, 1958, Hitchcock Folder 1274 Alfred Hitchcock Presents (correspondence), Margaret Herrick Library.
95. Erish, "Reclaiming Alfred Hitchcock Presents"; Revue Studios, "Daily Production Report Revue Studios Psycho," January 28, 1960, Hitchcock Folder 601 Psycho (prod.), Margaret Herrick Library; Revue Studios,

"Revue Advance Schedule," November 30, 1959, Hitchcock Folder 600 Psycho (prod.), Margaret Herrick Library.

96. "Psycho Lobby/Radio Spots," n.d., Hitchcock Folder 101 The Birds—radio spots 1963, Margaret Herrick Library.
97. Weaver, "Man behind the Body."
98. Jo Swerling, "Lifeboat Screenplay Revised Final," July 29, 1943, Hitchcock Folder 353 Lifeboat, Margaret Herrick Library.
99. Moral, *Hitchcock and the Making of Marnie*; Walter Raubicheck and Walter Srebnick, *Scripting Hitchcock:* Psycho, The Birds, *and* Marnie (Urbana: University of Illinois Press, 2011); Krohn, *Hitchcock at Work*, 34.
100. Tippi Hedren and Alfred Hitchcock, "Marnie Tapes Transcript Conversation Tippi Hedren, Hitchcock Tape 1," October 23, 1963, 2, Hitchcock Folder 458 T. Hedren, Margaret Herrick Library.
101. Alfred Hitchcock and Peggy Robertson, "Mr. Hitchcock's Notes on Screenplay Dated Sept 27 1965," October 12, 1965, 1, Hitchcock Folder 651 Torn Curtain (script), Margaret Herrick Library.
102. Samuel Taylor, "Topaz First-Draft Screenplay with Changes up to Feb 11 1969, Peggy Robertson's Script," n.d., 63, Hitchcock Folder 692, Margaret Herrick Library.
103. Leitch, "Hitchcock and His Writers," 79.
104. Truffaut and Hitchcock, *Hitchcock*, 61.
105. Spoto, *Dark Side of Genius*, 534.
106. "American Heart Fund 'Close to Your Heart' 15-Minute Transcribed Program by American Heart Association."
107. Krohn, *Hitchcock at Work*, 123.
108. Leonard J. Leff, *Hitchcock and Selznick: The Rich and Strange Collaboration of Alfred Hitchcock and David O. Selznick in Hollywood* (Berkeley: University of California Press, 1999), 92.
109. "Daily Scene Report North by Northwest," September 4, 1959, Hitchcock Folder 531, Margaret Herrick Library.
110. Peggy Robertson, "Mr. Hitchcock's Secret Cuts," July 7, 1969, Hitchcock Folder 738 Topaz (cutting), Margaret Herrick Library.
111. Paramount, "First Unit Shooting Schedule To Catch a Thief," June 7, 1954, Hitchcock Folder 63 To Catch a Thief (production), Margaret Herrick Library.

112. MGM, "North by Northwest Shooting Schedule Revised"; "Continuity Notes Into Thin Air," May 20, 1955, Hitchcock Folder 374 Man Who Knew Too Much, Margaret Herrick Library.
113. "Continuity Notes into Thin Air," sc 86; "Shooting Schedule Studio Portion Only," June 29, 1955, sc 87, Hitchcock Folder 396 The Man Who Knew Too Much, Margaret Herrick Library.
114. Truffaut and Hitchcock, *Hitchcock*, 61.
115. Suzanne Gauthier to Patrick G. Busch, August 15, 1963, Hitchcock Folder 51 The Birds—fan queries 1963, Margaret Herrick Library; Alfred J. Hitchcock to Mrs. Samuel Hart, Jr., August 25, 1960, Hitchcock Folder 592 Psycho Fan Mail, Margaret Herrick Library.
116. Robert E. Kapsis, "Reputation Building and the Film Art World: The Case of Alfred Hitchcock," *TSQ Sociological Quarterly* 30, no. 1 (1989): 24.
117. "Torn Curtain 1 Minute Radio Spot #1," n.d., Hitchcock Folder 911 Torn Curtain (post production), Margaret Herrick Library.
118. Monroe Freedman, "Topaz," *The Nation*, January 12, 1970, Hitchcock Folder 797 Topaz (reviews), Margaret Herrick Library.
119. Richard Corliss, "Let Us Not Praise Famous Men," *New York Times Magazine*, April 16, 1976, Hitchcock Folder 222 Family Plot reviews 1976, Margaret Herrick Library.
120. "North by Northwest Ad.," *Variety*, July 24, 1959, Hitchcock Folder 545 North by Northwest (publicity), Margaret Herrick Library.
121. Universal Studios, "Family Plot Brochure," 1976, Hitchcock Folder 218 Family Plot—publicity 1976, Margaret Herrick Library; "Hitchcock's Back: Advertisement of the Month," *ADAM: The Professional Journal of Creative Advertising and Marketing*, 1964.
122. Guy Flatley, "I Tried to Be Discrete with That Nude Corpse," *New York Times*, June 22, 1972, Hitchcock Folder 313 Frenzy Publicity, Margaret Herrick Library.
123. Truffaut and Hitchcock, *Hitchcock*, 345; PR, MCA to Frank Wright, MCA, "Interoffice Memorandum: Reel of Mr. Hitchcock's Appearances in 9 Motion Pictures," May 14, 1976, Hitchcock Folder 1456 General (A Hitchcock—misc), Margaret Herrick Library.
124. Philip French, "The 10 Best Movie Cameos," *The Guardian*, July 25, 2010, www.theguardian.com/culture/2010/jul/25/philip-french-10-best-movie-cameos.

125. Vincent Canby, "Review/Film: The Age of Innocence; Grand Passions and Good Manners," *New York Times*, September 17, 1993, sec. Movies, www.nytimes.com/1993/09/17/movies/review-film-the-age-of-innocence-grand-passions-and-good-manners.html; Manohla Dargis, "Martin Scorsese's 'Hugo,' with Ben Kingsley and Sacha Baron Cohen," *New York Times*, November 22, 2011, www.nytimes.com/2011/11/23/movies/martin-scorseses-hugo-with-ben-kingsley-and-sacha-baron-cohen-review.html; Vincent Canby, "After Hours (1985)," *New York Times*, September 13, 1985, www.nytimes.com/movie/review?res=9C07E7DD153AF930A2575AC0A963948260; Vincent Canby, "Mean Streets (1973)," *New York Times*, October 3, 1973, www.nytimes.com/movie/review?res=EE05E7DF1739E56EBC4B53DFB6678388669EDE.

126. Vincent Canby, "Chinatown (1974)," *New York Times*, June 21, 1974, www.nytimes.com/movie/review?res=EE05E7DF1739E460BC4951DFB066838F669EDE.

127. Richard Schickel, *Conversations with Scorsese*, updated, expanded ed. (New York: Knopf, 2013), 157.

128. Schickel, *Conversations with Scorsese*, 157.

129. Schickel, 237.

130. Erik Davis, "See Every Martin Scorsese Cameo, from 'Boxcar Bertha' to 'The Wolf of Wall Street,'" Movies.com, January 28, 2014, www.movies.com/movie-news/martin-scorsese-cameos/14777?wssac=164&wssaffid=news.

131. Davis, "See Every Martin Scorsese Cameo."

132. Christian Keathley, *Cinephilia and History; or, The Wind in the Trees* (Bloomington: Indiana University Press, 2006), 7.

133. Schickel, *Conversations with Scorsese*, 144.

134. Mathijs, "Cronenberg Connected," 148.

135. Henry Jenkins, "Reception Theory and Audience Research: The Mystery of the Vampire's Kiss," in *Reinventing Film Studies*, ed. Christine Gledhill and Linda Williams (London: Arnold, 2000), http://web.mit.edu/cms/People/henry3/vampkiss.html.

136. Henry Jenkins, *Textual Poachers: Television Fans and Participatory Culture* (New York: Routledge, 1992), 18.

137. "Peter Jackson Reveals His Unrecognizable Cameo in 'The Hobbit,'" *Ace Showbiz*, December 15, 2012, www.aceshowbiz.com/news/view/00056384.html; "Peter Jackson Dishes on Stephen Colbert's 'Hobbit'

Cameo," *Entertain This!* (blog), December 17, 2014, http://entertainthis.usatoday.com/2014/12/17/peter-jackson-dishes-on-stephen-colberts-hobbit-cameo/; *Peter Jackson Movie Cameos*, 2009, www.youtube.com/watch?v=tvgwXAky1t8&feature=youtube_gdata_player; Jennifer Brayton, "Fic Frodo Slash Frodo: Fandoms and The Lord of the Rings," in *From Hobbits to Hollywood Essays on Peter Jackson's Lord of the Rings*, ed. Peter Jackson, Ernest Mathijs, and Murray Pomerance (Amsterdam: Rodopi, 2006), 143.
138. Caetlin Benson-Allott, "Grindhouse: An Experiment in the Death of Cinema," *Film Quarterly* 62, no. 1 (2008): 20.
139. Alice Vincent and Tristram Fane Saunders, "Quentin Tarantino: His 10 Best Cameo Roles," *The Telegraph*, December 10, 2015, www.telegraph.co.uk/film/hateful-eight/quentin-tarantino-best-cameo-roles/.
140. Yacowar, *Hitchcock's British Films*, 217.
141. "Watching Movies with Quentin Tarantino," *New York Times*, September 15, 2000, www.nytimes.com/2000/09/15/arts/15WATC.html.
142. Joshua Wucher, "'Let's Get Into Character': Role-Playing in Quentin Tarantino's Postmodern Sandbox," *Journal of Popular Culture* 48, no. 6 (2015): 1287–305.
143. Pierre Bourdieu, *Distinction: A Social Critique of the Judgement of Taste* (Cambridge, MA: Harvard University Press, 1984), 16.
144. Woody Allen, "Annie Hall Script," n.d., 19, AMPAS Script Collection, Margaret Herrick Library.
145. "Peter Jackson Dishes on Stephen Colbert's 'Hobbit' Cameo."
146. McGilligan, *Backstory*, 205.
147. Christopher Ames, *Movies about the Movies: Hollywood Reflected* (Lexington: University Press of Kentucky, 1997), 165.
148. Paramount, "Hollywood Continuity Script," n.d., 20, Paramount Scripts H-679, Margaret Herrick Library.
149. Evelyn F. Scott, *Hollywood: When Silents Were Golden* (New York: McGraw-Hill, 1972).
150. Leitch, "Hitchcock and His Writers," 79.
151. Moral, *Hitchcock and the Making of Marnie*, 110.
152. McGilligan, *Backstory*, 165.
153. Leitch, "Hitchcock and His Writers," 81.
154. Georges Didi-Huberman, *Peuples exposés, peuples figurants* (Paris: Éditions de Minuit, 2012), 54.

155. Glenn Esterly, "Buk: The Pock-Marked Poetry of Charles Bukowski," *Rolling Stone*, June 17, 1976, 33.
156. Cannon Films, "Barfly Press Kit," n.d., 7, Charles Bukowski Papers, Barfly, Box 9, USC Special Collections.
157. Charles Bukowski, *Hollywood* (Santa Rosa: Ecco, 1989), 214.
158. Bukowski, *Hollywood*, 155.
159. Sean Howe, *Marvel Comics: The Untold Story* (New York: HarperCollins, 2012), 9.
160. Chris Sims, "Stan Lee's 10 Greatest Comics," *Looper*, accessed September 26, 2019, www.looper.com/108933/thats-whats-stan-lees-10-greatest-comics/.
161. luke colomer, "Marvel Movies with No Stan Lee Cameo," IMDb, July 10, 2013, www.imdb.com/list/ls053928812/; "Every Stan Lee Marvel Cameo," *Insider*, September 2016, www.thisisinsider.com/stan-lee-marvel-movie-cameos-2016-9; "Every Stan Lee Cameo in the Marvel Cinematic Universe," *Consequence of Sound*, November 2018, https://consequenceofsound.net/2018/11/every-stan-lee-cameo-mcu/.
162. Bryan Enk, "Anti-Excelsior! Stan Lee Won't Cameo in 'Guardians of the Galaxy,'" *Yahoo*, January 22, 2014, www.yahoo.com/movies/bp/anti-excelsior-stan-lee-won-t-cameo-guardians-203703788.html; "Stan Lee Will Have a Cameo in Guardians of the Galaxy after All," *Cinema Blend*, March 2014, www.cinemablend.com/new/Stan-Lee-Have-Cameo-Guardians-Galaxy-All-42750.html.
163. Barbara Klinger, "Becoming Cult: The Big Lebowski, Replay Culture and Male Fans," *Screen* 51, no. 1 (2010): 1–20.
164. Victor Burgin, *The Remembered Film* (London: Reaktion, 2004), 8.
165. PR, MCA to Frank Wright, MCA, "Interoffice Memorandum: Reel of Mr. Hitchcock's Appearances in 9 Motion Pictures"; Taylor, *Hitch*, 222.
166. Bellour, "Hitchcock, The Enunciator," 73.
167. Leitch, *Find the Director and Other Hitchcock Games*, 3.
168. Krohn, *Hitchcock at Work*, 48.
169. "Alfred Hitchcock's Movie Cameos," *Listal*, accessed April 3, 2014, www.listal.com/list/hitchcocks-cameos; Will Erickson, *Every Hitchcock Cameo Ever* (YouTube, 2012), www.youtube.com/watch?v=okLiLsncyi0&feature=youtube_gdata_player; Morgan T. Rhys, *Every Alfred Hitchcock Cameo* (YouTube), accessed September 9, 2014, www.youtube.com/watch?v=_YbaOkiMiRQ.
170. "Peter Jackson Dishes on Stephen Colbert's 'Hobbit' Cameo."

171. Frances Ferguson, "Now It's Personal: D. A. Miller and Too-Close Reading," *Critical Inquiry* 41, no. 3 (2015): 535.

Conclusion

1. Pierre Bourdieu, *Distinction: A Social Critique of the Judgement of Taste* (Cambridge, MA: Harvard University Press, 1984), 61.
2. "The Complete History of Guest Stars on 'The Fresh Prince of Bel-Air,'" *Complex CA*, accessed April 11, 2016, http://ca.complex.com/music/2012/09/the-complete-history-of-guest-stars-on-the-fresh-prince-of-bel-air/; WatchMojo, *Top 10 Epic Movie Cameos* (YouTube, 2013), www.youtube.com/watch?v=x-IstfVHLJw&feature=youtube_gdata_player.
3. Henry Jenkins, Sam Ford, and Joshua Green, *Spreadable Media: Creating Value and Meaning in a Networked Culture* (New York: New York University Press, 2013), 203.
4. "I See You There Matt Damon, Hiding in Plain Sight," Reddit, January 18, 2012, www.reddit.com/r/homeland/comments/olosx/i_see_you_there_matt_damon_hiding_in_plain_sight/; Jethro Nededog, "'Homeland' Finale: It's a Battle of Wills for Carrie and Brody (Video)," *Hollywood Reporter*, December 18, 2011, www.hollywoodreporter.com/live-feed/showtime-homeland-finale-recap-275147; David Steinberg, "Officer Krupke," *Curb Your Enthusiasm* (HBO, November 8, 2009); Michael Cuesta, "Marine One," *Homeland* (Showtime, December 18, 2011).
5. Stephen Saito, "The Curious Cameography of Matt Damon," IFC, January 8, 2009, http:/2009/01/the-curious-cameography-of-mat.
6. Suzanne Scott, "Battlestar Galactica Fans and Ancillary Content," in *How to Watch Television*, ed. Ethan Thompson and Jason Mittell (New York: New York University Press, 2013), 322.
7. Barbara Klinger, *Beyond the Multiplex: Cinema, New Technologies, and the Home* (Berkeley: University of California Press, 2006), 72.
8. Amanda D. Lotz, *The Television Will Be Revolutionized*, 2nd ed. (New York: New York University Press, 2014), 63.
9. Jodi Dean, "Communicative Capitalism: Circulation and the Foreclosure of Politics," *Cultural Politics* 1, no. 1 (2005): 67.
10. Matt Hills, *Fan Cultures* (New York: Routledge, 2003), 142.
11. Henry Jenkins, *Convergence Culture: Where Old and New Media Collide* (New York: New York University Press, 2006), 114.

12. Louisa Stein, "Gossip Girl: Transmedia Technologies," in *How to Watch Television*, ed. Ethan Thompson and Jason Mittell (New York: New York University Press, 2013), 342.
13. Lucas Hilderbrand, "YouTube: Where Cultural Memory and Copyright Converge," *Film Quarterly* 61, no. 1 (2007): 48–57.
14. George Plasketes, *B-Sides, Undercurrents and Overtones: Peripheries to Popular in Music, 1960 to the Present* (Farnham, UK: Ashgate Publishing, 2013), 147.
15. CH2, *Every Donald Trump Cameo Ever*, 2015, www.youtube.com/watch?v=yosAVMB47-Y; Slate Magazine, *Every Single Entourage Cameo*, 2015, www.youtube.com/watch?v=jteNDkI2WqY.
16. razgandeanu, *The Expendables—Sylvester Stallone, Arnold Schwarzenegger, and Bruce Willis—Best Scene Ever*, 2010, www.youtube.com/watch?v=hrMmiUSVRRI&feature=youtube_gdata_player; Ono Ramírez, *TOP 20 Guest Stars in Friends*, 2014, www.youtube.com/watch?v=7GbOUIFa87g.
17. Leon Gurevitch, "The Cinemas of Transactions: The Exchangeable Currency of the Digital Attraction," *Television and New Media* 11, no. 5 (2010): 367–85.
18. Gurevitch, "Cinemas of Transactions."
19. Donna Bowman et al., "The Friends of Friends: 17 Gimmicky Cameos Intended to Boost TV Ratings," Inventory, A.V. Club, April 7, 2008, www.avclub.com/article/the-friends-of-ifriendsi-17-gimmicky-cameos-intend-2243; Philip French, "The 10 Best Movie Cameos," *The Guardian*, July 25, 2010, www.theguardian.com/culture/2010/jul/25/philip-french-10-best-movie-cameos.
20. Klinger, *Beyond the Multiplex*, 160.
21. "Lawyer-Friendly Cameo," TV Tropes, accessed May 31, 2016, http://tvtropes.org/pmwiki/pmwiki.php/Main/LawyerFriendlyCameo.
22. "Cameos," Reddit, accessed May 13, 2016, www.reddit.com/r/cameos/; "Death by Cameo," TV Tropes, accessed September 6, 2014, tvtropes.org/pmwiki/pmwiki.php/Main/DeathByCameo.
23. Mike Dugo, "TV/Film Cameos," 1960s Garage Bands, accessed May 13, 2016, www.60sgaragebands.com/tvfilmcameos.html.
24. "Globe Reporters Tell Their 'Spotlight' Stories," *Boston Globe*, November 29, 2014, www.bostonglobe.com/arts/movies/2014/11/29/spotlightfilm-intro/d8Tp3MQ4Y0OQA3JZgABkeO/story.html.

25. Devan Coggan, "Popstar Trailer: Seal Gets Attacked by Wolves," *Entertainment Weekly*, May 18, 2016, www.ew.com/article/2016/05/18/popstar-trailer-seal-attacked-wolves.
26. Brandon Jones, *"This Is The End": Every Michael Cera Scene High Def!*, 2013, www.youtube.com/watch?v=R5y0UCMZWLM; BadfishKoo, *Michael Cera This Is The End Best Scenes*, 2013, www.youtube.com/watch?v=qIKPJlKHKxg.
27. Todd Van Luling, "5 Stories You Didn't Know about 'Fargo,' as Told by the Movie's Main Villain," *Huffington Post*, March 18, 2015, www.huffingtonpost.com/2015/03/17/fargo-movie-trivia-interview_n_6880346.html.
28. "What Movie Has the Best Audio Commentary?," Reddit, February 5, 2016, www.reddit.com/r/AskReddit/comments/44ai2l/what_movie_has_the_best_audio_commentary/.

WORKS CITED

Abel, Richard. *Encyclopedia of Early Cinema*. London: Routledge, 2005.
———. "G. M. Anderson: 'Broncho Billy' among the Early 'Picture Personalities.'" In *Flickers of Desire: Movie Stars of the 1910s*, edited by Jennifer M. Bean, 22–42. New Brunswick, NJ: Rutgers University Press, 2011.
Academy of Motion Picture Arts and Sciences. "Program for the AMPAS Screening of *Show People* in Honor of *The Artist* at the AMPAS Samuel Goldwyn Theater." November 1, 2012. Production Clippings Show People. Margaret Herrick Library.
"Ad: A Soul Adrift (The Cameo Girl)." *Variety*, January 18, 1919.
Adams, Ann Jensen. *Public Faces and Private Identities in Seventeenth-Century Holland: Portraiture and the Production of Community*. New York: Cambridge University Press, 2009.
"Age of Innocence." *Variety*, October 23, 1934.
"Agreement between Dorchester Productions and Warner Bros.," November 8, 1957. Ocean's Eleven Legal Folder 63. Margaret Herrick Library.
"Alfred Hitchcock's Movie Cameos." *Listal*. Accessed April 3, 2014. www.listal.com/list/hitchcocks-cameos.
Allen, Woody. "Annie Hall Script," n.d. AMPAS Script Collection. Margaret Herrick Library.
"Allentown Native Dane DeHaan Has a Cameo Role as a Union Soldier in Lincoln." *Morning Call*. Accessed January 24, 2014. http://articles.mcall.com/2012-11-15/entertainment/mc-lincoln-spielberg-dane-dehaan-emmaus-20121115_1_daniel-day-lewis-cameo-union.
"American Heart Fund 'Close to Your Heart' 15-Minute Transcribed Program by American Heart Association," February 1, 1956. Hitchcock Folder 394 The Man Who Knew Too Much. Margaret Herrick Library.
Ames, Christopher. *Movies about the Movies: Hollywood Reflected*. Lexington: University Press of Kentucky, 1997.

Anderson, Patrick Donald. *In Its Own Image: The Cinematic Vision of Hollywood.* New York: Arno Press, 1978.

Angell, Roger. "The Current Cinema: Poor Peon." *New Yorker*, December 31, 1960. www.newyorker.com/magazine/1960/12/31/poor-peon.

Arnold, Jean. "Cameo Appearances: The Discourse of Jewelry in Middlemarch." *Victorian Literature and Culture* 30, no. 1 (2002): 265–88.

"Aunty's Romance." *Moving Picture World*, July 27, 1912.

"B. S. Moss' Cameo Gets Under Way." *Variety*, December 30, 1921.

Bahn, Chester B. "Syracuse, N.Y." *Variety*, May 10, 1923.

Barr, Charles. *English Hitchcock.* Moffat, UK: Cameron and Hollis, 1999.

Barris, Alex. *Hollywood According to Hollywood.* South Brunswick, NJ: A. S. Barnes, 1978.

Barthes, Roland. *Camera Lucida: Reflections on Photography.* New York: Hill and Wang, 1981.

Bazin, Andre. *What Is Cinema?* Translated by Hugh Gray. 4th ed. Berkeley: University of California Press, 1968.

Bean, Jennifer M. *Flickers of Desire: Movie Stars of the 1910s.* New Brunswick, NJ: Rutgers University Press, 2011.

Becker, Christine. *It's the Pictures That Got Small: Hollywood Film Stars on 1950s Television.* Middletown, CT: Wesleyan University Press, 2009.

———. "Televising Film Stardom in the 1950s." *Framework: The Journal of Cinema and Media* 46, no. 2 (2005): 5–21.

Behlmer, Rudy, and Tony Thomas. *Hollywood's Hollywood: The Movies about the Movies.* Secaucus, NJ: Citadel Press, 1975.

Bellour, Raymond. "Hitchcock, the Enunciator." *Camera Obscura* 1, no. 2 (1977): 67–92.

Belton, John. "Charles Bennett and the Typical Hitchcock Scenario." *Film History* 9, no. 3 (1997): 320–32.

Bennett, James. "The Television Personality System: Televisual Stardom Revisited after Film Theory." *Screen* 49, no. 1 (2008): 32–50.

Benson-Allott, Caetlin. "Grindhouse: An Experiment in the Death of Cinema." *Film Quarterly* 62, no. 1 (2008): 20–24.

"Best Cameo Appearance in a Tv Series?" *Reddit*, December 7, 2015. Accessed May 15, 2016. www.reddit.com/r/television/comments/2oib51/best_cameo_appearance_in_a_tv_series/.

The Big Four Family, June 1915.

"Bing, Bob, Dottie Doughtily Cruise to Rio." *Los Angeles Times.* January 1, 1948.

"Blackmail." *Daily Film Renter*, June 24, 1929. Hitchcock Folder 1617 Scrapbooks. Margaret Herrick Library.

Blackton, J. Stuart. "Heart to Heart Talks." *Vitagraph Bulletin*, August 1915.

Bodroghkozy, Aniko. *Groove Tube: Sixties Television and the Youth Rebellion*. Durham, NC: Duke University Press, 2001.

Bongard, David. "Road to Bali." *Los Angeles Daily News*, December 26, 1952.

Bordwell, David. *The Way Hollywood Tells It: Story and Style in Modern Movies*. Berkeley: University of California Press, 2006.

Bourdieu, Pierre. *Distinction: A Social Critique of the Judgement of Taste*. Cambridge, MA: Harvard University Press, 1984.

Bowman, Donna et al. "The Friends of Friends: 17 Gimmicky Cameos Intended to Boost TV Ratings." AV Club, September 9, 2008. Accessed May 13, 2016. www.avclub.com/article/the-friends-of-ifriendsi-17-gimmicky-cameos-intend-2243.

"Brad Pitt Says He'll Only Cameo In 'Twelve Years a Slave,' Hopes 'World War Z' Will Have Socio-Political Themes." *Playlist*. Accessed January 23, 2014. http://blogs.indiewire.com/theplaylist/brad-pitt-says-hell-only-cameo-in-twelve-years-a-slave-hopes-world-war-z-will-have-socio-political-themes.

Brady, Thomas F. "Unemployment Rises as Production Drops—Roosevelt Kin Approve Films." *New York Times*, February 23, 1947.

Braudy, Leo. *The Frenzy of Renown: Fame and Its History*. New York: Vintage Books, 1997.

Brayton, Jennifer. "Fic Frodo Slash Frodo: Fandoms and *The Lord of the Rings*." In *From Hobbits to Hollywood: Essays on Peter Jackson's* Lord of the Rings, edited by Peter Jackson, Ernest Mathijs, and Murray Pomerance. Amsterdam: Rodopi, 2006.

Brilliant, Richard. *Portraiture*. Cambridge, MA: Harvard University Press, 1991.

Brownlow, Kevin. *The Parade's Gone By*. New York: Knopf, 1968.

"Brunette Funny Bob Hope," *Hollywood Reporter*, February 18, 1947. Margaret Herrick Library, Production Code Administration Files My Favorite Brunette.

Bukowski, Charles. *Hollywood*. Santa Rosa: Ecco, 1989.

Burgin, Victor. *The Remembered Film*. London: Reaktion, 2004.

Burke, Jill. "Patronage and Identity in Renaissance Florence: The Case of S. Maria a Lecceto." In *Fashioning Identities in Renaissance Art*, edited by Mary Rogers, 51–59. Brookfield, VT: Ashgate, 2000.

"Cameo, N." OED Online. Oxford University Press. Accessed February 5, 2014. www.oed.com.proxy2.library.mcgill.ca/view/Entry/26687.

"Cameo Photographs." *Syracuse Journal*, November 29, 1946.
"Cameo Theatre." *Highland Democrat*, October 1, 1927.
"Cameos." *Reddit*. Accessed May 13, 2016. https://www.reddit.com/r/cameos/.
Campbell, Lorne. *Renaissance Portraits: European Portrait-Painting in the 14th, 15th, and 16th Centuries*. New Haven, CT: Yale University Press, 1990.
Canby, Vincent. "After Hours (1985)." *New York Times*, September 13, 1985. www.nytimes.com/movie/review?res=9C07E7DD153AF930A2575AC0A963948260.
———. "Chinatown (1974)." *New York Times*, June 21, 1974. http://www.nytimes.com/movie/review?res=EE05E7DF1739E460BC4951DFB066838F669EDE.
———. "Mean Streets (1973)." *New York Times*, October 3, 1973. www.nytimes.com/movie/review?res=EE05E7DF1739E56EBC4B53DFB6678388669EDE.
———. "Review/Film: The Age of Innocence; Grand Passions and Good Manners." *New York Times*, September 17, 1993, sec. Movies. www.nytimes.com/1993/09/17/movies/review-film-the-age-of-innocence-grand-passions-and-good-manners.html.
Cannon Films. "Barfly Press Kit," n.d. Charles Bukowski Papers, Barfly, Box 9. USC Special Collections.
Carroll, Larry. "'Tropic Thunder' Multitasker Ben Stiller Can't Discuss Tom Cruise's Cameo, But He Did Reveal Jack Black's Water-Buffalo Baby." *MTV News*, April 2, 2008. Accessed September 3, 2014. www.mtv.com/news/1584693/tropic-thunder-multitasker-ben-stiller-cant-discuss-tom-cruises-cameo-but-he-did-reveal-jack-blacks-water-buffalo-baby/.
Chell, Samuel L. "Rivalries: The Mutual Mentoring of Bing Crosby and Frank Sinatra." In *Going My Way: Bing Crosby and American Culture*, edited by Ruth Prigozy and Walter Raubicheck, 115–22. Rochester, NY: University of Rochester Press, 2007.
Chisholm, Ann. "Missing Persons and Bodies of Evidence." *Camera Obscura* 15, no. 1 (n.d.): 123–61.
Coggan, Devan. "Popstar Trailer: Seal Gets Attacked by Wolves." *Entertainment Weekly*, May 18, 2016. Accessed June 7, 2016. www.ew.com/article/2016/05/18/popstar-trailer-seal-attacked-wolves.
Cohan, Steven. "Almost Like Being at Home: Showbiz Culture and Hollywood Road Trips in the 1940s and 1950s." In *The Road Movie Book*, edited by Steven Cohan and Ina Rae Hark, 113–42. New York: Routledge, 1997.
———. *Hollywood by Hollywood: The Backstudio Picture and the Mystique of Making Movies*. London: Oxford University Press, 2018.

Cohen, Tom. *Hitchcock's Cryptonymies*. Minneapolis: University of Minnesota Press, 2005.
Cohn, Art. *The Nine Lives of Michael Todd: The Story of One of the World's Most Fabulous Showmen*. Kessinger Publishing, 2007.
Coleman, John. "Seeing Red." *New Statesman*, July 10 1964. Hitchcock Folder 479 Marnie (pub.—TV). Margaret Herrick Library.
Columbia Pictures. "Pepe Program," n.d. Press Books. Margaret Herrick Library.
"Comments on the Films: A Vitagraph Romance." *Moving Picture World*, September 18, 1912.
"The Complete History of Guest Stars on 'The Fresh Prince of Bel-Air.'" *Complex CA*. Accessed April 11, 2016. http://ca.complex.com/music/2012/09/the-complete-history-of-guest-stars-on-the-fresh-prince-of-bel-air/.
"Continuity Notes into Thin Air," May 20, 1955. Hitchcock Folder 374 Man Who Knew Too Much. Margaret Herrick Library.
Cooke, Grayson. "We Had Faces Then: Sunset Boulevard and the Sense of the Spectral." *Quarterly Review of Film and Video* 26, no. 2 (2009): 89–101.
Corliss, Richard. "Let Us Not Praise Famous Men." *New Times Magazine*, April 16, 1976. Hitchcock Folder 222 Family Plot reviews 1976. Margaret Herrick Library.
Corrigan, Timothy. "Film and the Culture of Cult." In *The Cult Film Experience: Beyond All Reason*, edited by J. P. Telotte, 26–37. Austin: University of Texas Press, 1991.
Crispin, Edmund. *Frequent Hearses*. Harmondsworth, England: Penguin Books, 1987.
Cowan, Michael. "Learning to Love the Movies: Puzzles, Participation, and Cinephilia in Interwar European Film Magazines." *Film History: An International Journal* 27, no. 4 (2015): 1–45.
Crawford, Chris. *The Art of Computer Game Design*. New York: Osborne/McGraw-Hill, 1984.
Crowther, Bosley. "The Screen: Foreign Correspondent." *New York Times*, August 28, 1940. Hitchcock Folder 1623 Scrapbooks. Margaret Herrick Library.
———. "Screen: 'The Greatest Story Ever Told': Max von Sydow Stars in Biblical Film." *New York Times*, February 16, 1966.
———. "Wild Comedy about the Pursuit of Money: 'A Mad, Mad World' Opens at Warner." *New York Times*, November 19, 1963.

"Daily Scene Report North by Northwest," September 4, 1959. Hitchcock Folder 531. Margaret Herrick Library.

Dardis, Tom, and Buster Keaton. *Keaton: The Man Who Wouldn't Lie Down.* New York: Limelight Editions, 2004.

Dargis, Manohla. "Martin Scorsese's 'Hugo,' with Ben Kingsley and Sacha Baron Cohen." *New York Times,* November 22, 2011. www.nytimes.com/2011/11/23/movies/martin-scorseses-hugo-with-ben-kingsley-and-sacha-baron-cohen-review.html.

Davies, Marion. *The Times We Had: Life with William Randolph Hearst.* Indianapolis: Bobbs-Merrill, 1975.

Davis, Erik. "See Every Martin Scorsese Cameo, from 'Boxcar Bertha' to 'The Wolf of Wall Street.'" *Movies.com,* January 28, 2014. www.movies.com/movie-news/martin-scorsese-cameos/14777?wssac=164&wssaffid=news.

Dean, Jodi. "Communicative Capitalism: Circulation and the Foreclosure of Politics." *Cultural Politics* 1, no. 1 (2005): 51–73.

"Death by Cameo." *TV Tropes.* Accessed September 7, 2014. http://tvtropes.org/pmwiki/pmwiki.php/Main/DeathByCameo.

deCordova, Richard. *Picture Personalities: The Emergence of the Star System in America.* Urbana: University of Illinois Press, 2001.

DeFino, Dean J. *The HBO Effect.* London: Bloomsbury Academic, 2013.

Deleuze, Gilles. *Cinema 2: The Time Image.* Minneapolis: University of Minnesota, 1986.

Demille, William C. *Hollywood Saga.* 2nd ed. New York: E. P. Dutton, 1939.

Desjardins, Mary. "Maureen O'Hara's 'Confidential' Life: Recycling Stars through Gossip and Moral Biography." In *Small Screens, Big Ideas: Television in the 1950s,* edited by Janet Thumin, 118–30. London: I. B. Tauris, 2002.

Didi-Huberman, Georges. *Peuples exposés, peuples figurants.* Paris: Éditions de Minuit, 2012.

Dinelli, Mel. "Trailer Material for Spellbound," September 3, 1945. Hitchcock Folder 650 Spellbound (script). Margaret Herrick Library.

Doane, Mary Ann. "The Close-Up: Scale and Detail in the Cinema." *Differences: A Journal of Feminist Cultural Studies* 14, no. 3 (2003): 89–111.

———. "The Object of Theory." In *Rites of Realism: Essays on Corporeal Cinema,* edited by Ivone Margulies, 80–92. Durham, NC: Duke University Press, 2003.

Dowling, Nikki. "The Wonderful World of Celebrity Bets." *CNN,* October 12, 2009. Accessed June 20, 2016. http://edition.cnn.com/2009/SHOWBIZ/10/21/frisky.world.celeb.bets/.

Draper, James David, and Metropolitan Museum of Art (New York). *Cameo Appearances*. New York: Metropolitan Museum of Art, 2008.

Dugo, Mike. "TV/Film Cameos." *1960s Garage Bands*. Accessed May 13, 2016. www.60sgaragebands.com/tvfilmcameos.html.

Dyer, Richard. *Stars*. London: BFI, 1979.

Eco, Umberto. "'Casablanca': Cult Movies and Intertextual Collage." *SubStance* 14, no. 2 (1985): 3–12.

Edgerton, Gary. "High Concept, Small Screen: Reperceiving the Industrial and Stylistic Origins of the American Made-for-TV Movie." In *Connections: A Broadcast History Reader*, edited by Michelle Hilmes, 209–30. Belmont, CA: Thomas/Wadsworth, 2003.

Ellis, John. "New Responses to Fake Footage." In *Relocating Television: Television in the Digital Context*, edited by Jostein Gripsrud, 183–91. New York: Routledge, 2010.

Elsaesser, Thomas. "Cinephilia or the Uses of Disenchantment." In *Cinephilia: Movies, Love and Memory*, edited by Marijke de Valck and Malte Hagener, 27–44. Amsterdam: Amsterdam University Press, 2005.

———. "The Mind Game Film." In *Complex Storytelling in Contemporary World Cinema*, edited by Warren Buckland, 13–41. Oxford: Wiley-Blackwell, 2008.

Emerson, John, and Anita Loos. "Polly Preferred Screen Adaptation and Continuity," November 15, 1926. Show People (1928) S-1123. Margaret Herrick Library.

Erish, Andrew A. "Reclaiming Alfred Hitchcock Presents." *Quarterly Review of Film and Video* 26, no. 5 (2009): 385–92.

Esterly, Glenn. "Buk: The Pock-Marked Poetry of Charles Bukowski." *Rolling Stone*, June 17, 1976.

Evans, Elizabeth. *Transmedia Television: Audiences, New Media, and Daily Life*. London: Routledge, 2011.

"Every Stan Lee Marvel Cameo." *Insider*, September 2016. Accessed November 16, 2016. www.thisisinsider.com/stan-lee-marvel-movie-cameos-2016-9.

"Every Stan Lee Cameo in the Marvel Cinematic Universe." *Consequence of Sound*, November 2018. Accessed September 24, 2019. https://consequenceofsound.net/2018/11/every-stan-lee-cameo-mcu/.

Faber, Bob. "Regular Trailer Revised," December 3, 1971. Hitchcock Folder 267 Frenzy Script 1971–1972. Margaret Herrick Library.

"Face to Face with Alfred Hitchcock." *Hollywood Studio*, January 1970.

"Family Plot Ad." *Los Angeles Times*, April 8, 1976. Hitchcock Folder 218 Family Plot. Margaret Herrick Library.

"Famous Players Ad." *Moving Picture World*, June 1916.

"Fenwick's Corner." *Oregonian*, May 20, 1906.

Ferguson, Frances. "Now It's Personal: D. A. Miller and Too-Close Reading." *Critical Inquiry* 41, no. 3 (2015): 521–40.

Ferris, Kerry O. "Seeing and Being Seen: The Moral Order of Celebrity Sightings." *Journal of Contemporary Ethnography* 33, no. 3 (2004): 236–64.

Feuer, Jane. *The Hollywood Musical*. Bloomington: Indiana University Press, 1993.

"Film Reviews: Road to Bali." *Variety*, November 19, 1952.

"Film Stars Volunteer Aid in Show World." *Variety*, April 11, 1928.

"The Films: Good Things of the Week." *Star*, January 19, 1927. Hitchcock Folder 1621 Scrapbooks. Margaret Herrick Library.

"Films: Road to Rio." *America*, January 10, 1948.

Flatley, Guy. "I Tried to Be Discrete with That Nude Corpse." *New York Times*, June 22, 1972. Hitchcock Folder 313 Frenzy Publicity. Margaret Herrick Library.

Flower, Margaret Cameron Coss. *Victorian Jewellery*. London: Cassell, 1967.

"Flying Fortress." *Variety*, July 15, 1942.

"For Better, For Worse." *Variety*, October 13, 1954.

Frank, Eugene H. Letter to Stanley Kramer. "Re: Jerry Lewis," October 26, 1962. Stanley Kramer Box 61 Folder 4. UCLA Special Collections.

Fred. "Film Reviews: Playing with Fire." *Variety*, April 28, 1916.

Freedman, Monroe. "Topaz." *The Nation*, January 12, 1970. Hitchcock Folder 797 Topaz (reviews). Margaret Herrick Library.

French, Philip. "The 10 Best Movie Cameos." *The Guardian*, July 25, 2010. www.theguardian.com/culture/2010/jul/25/philip-french-10-best-movie-cameos.

Fuchs, Cynthia. "The Buddy Politic." In *Screening the Male: Exploring Masculinities in Hollywood Cinema*, edited by Steven Cohan and Ina Rae Hark, 194–210. New York: Routledge, 1993.

Gamson, Joshua. *Claims to Fame: Celebrity in Contemporary America*. Berkeley: University of California Press, 1994.

Gauthier, Suzanne. Letter to Patrick G. Busch, August 15, 1963. Hitchcock Folder 51 The Birds—fan queries 1963. Margaret Herrick Library.

Geduld, Harry M. *Chapliniana: A Commentary on Charlie Chaplin's 81 Movies*. Bloomington: Indiana University Press, 1987.

———. *Charlie Chaplin's Own Story*. Bloomington: Indiana University Press, 1985.

Giddins, Gary. Introduction to *Going My Way: Bing Crosby and American Culture*, edited by Walter Raubicheck and Ruth Prigozy, 1–10. Rochester, NY: University of Rochester Press, 2007.

Glass, George. Letter to Reviewers. "From George Glass for Samuel Goldwyn to Reviewers," undated. Production Clippings. Margaret Herrick Library.

"Globe Reporters Tell Their 'Spotlight' Stories." *Boston Globe*. Accessed June 7, 2016. www.bostonglobe.com/arts/movies/2014/11/29/spotlightfilm-intro/d8Tp3MQ4Y0OQA3JZgABkeO/story.html.

"The Goddess." *New York Evening Journal*, May 3, 1915.

Goldwyn Studios. "Souls for Sale Silent Cutting Continuity," March 14, 1923. USC Cinematic Arts Collection.

———. "Special Souls for Sale Trailer," February 23, 1923.

———. "Title Sheet for Souls for Sale," March 10, 1923. USC Cinematic Arts Collection.

Goodman, Ezra. "Rounding Up Stars in 80 Ways." *Life*, October 22, 1956.

Green-Lewis, Jennifer. *Framing the Victorians: Photography and the Culture of Realism*. Ithaca, NY: Cornell University Press, 1996.

Griffiths, Richard. "'Ocean's 11' Fails to Awe N.Y. Critics." *Los Angeles Times*, August 30, 1960.

Gurevitch, Leon. "The Cinemas of Transactions: The Exchangeable Currency of the Digital Attraction." *Television and New Media* 11, no. 5 (2010): 367–85.

Hamilton, Peter, Roger Hargreaves, and National Portrait Gallery (Great Britain). *The Beautiful and the Damned: The Creation of Identity in Nineteenth-Century Photography*. Burlington, VT: Lund Humphries, 2001.

Hammons, E. W. Letter to Mr. Ratterjohn. "Florence Lawrence," September 28, 1914. GC 1011, Box 2, Folder 14. Seaver Center for Western History Research.

Hansen, Miriam. *Babel and Babylon Spectatorship in American Silent Film*. Cambridge, MA: Harvard University Press, 1991.

Harris, Neil. *Humbug: The Art of P. T. Barnum*. Boston: Little, Brown, 1973.

Harrison, Joan, and Shamley Productions. Letter to Alfred Hitchcock, March 18, 1958. Hitchcock Folder 1274 Alfred Hitchcock Presents (correspondence). Margaret Herrick Library.

Hartford, Margaret. "Hope, Crosby, Lamour Cutting Capers Again in 'Road' Film." *Hollywood Citizen-News*. December 26, 1952.

Hartman, Don, Frank Butler, and Paramount. "My Favorite Blonde Shooting Script," November 10, 1941. Paramount Production Records My Favorite Blonde Folder 967. Margaret Herrick Library.

Harvey, Arthur, and ABC. Letter to Stanley Kramer. "Re: Jerry Lewis Show," November 8, 1963. Stanley Kramer Box 64 Folder TV Shows Miscellaneous Mad World SEK. UCLA Special Collections.

Hastie, Amelie. *Cupboards of Curiosity: Women, Recollection, and Film History.* Durham, NC: Duke University Press, 2007.

Heinich, Nathalie. *De la visibilité: Excellence et singularité en régime médiatique.* Paris: Gallimard, 2012.

Hedren, Tippi, and Alfred Hitchcock. "Marnie Tapes Transcript Conversation Tippi Hedren, Hitchcock Tape 1," October 23, 1963. Hitchcock Folder 458 T. Hedren. Margaret Herrick Library.

Herb. "Film Reviews: Wild Geese Calling." *Variety*, July 30, 1941.

Hilderbrand, Lucas. *Inherent Vice: Bootleg Histories of Videotape and Copyright.* Durham, NC: Duke University Press, 2009.

———. "YouTube: Where Cultural Memory and Copyright Converge." *Film Quarterly* 61, no. 1 (2007): 48–57.

Hills, Matt. *Fan Cultures*. New York: Routledge, 2003.

Hitchcock, Alfred J. Letter to Mrs. Samuel Hart Jr., August 25, 1960. Hitchcock Folder 592 Psycho Fan Mail. Margaret Herrick Library.

———. "The Paradine Case London and Cumberland Locations," May 18, 1946. Folder 558 The Paradine Case Miscellaneous. Margaret Herrick Library.

Hitchcock, Alfred, and Ernest Lehman. "Transcript of Tapes," November 2, 1973. Hitchcock Folder 138 Family Plot—script 1973. Margaret Herrick Library.

Hitchcock, Alfred, and Peggy Robertson. "Mr. Hitchcock's Notes on Screenplay Dated Sept 27 1965," October 12, 1965. Hitchcock Folder 651 Torn Curtain (script). Margaret Herrick Library.

"Hitchcock's Back: Advertisement of the Month." *Professional Journal of Creative Advertising and Marketing.* 1964. Hitchcock Folder 477 Marnie. Margaret Herrick Library.

"Hitchcock's Hand Steers Lifeboat Safely through Film's Troubled Sea." *Newsweek*, January 17, 1944. Hitchcock Folder 1622 Mr. and Mrs. Smith Scrapbook. Margaret Herrick Library.

"Hollywood—Paramount—Eight Reels." *Motion Picture Daily*, July 14, 1923. Production Clippings. Margaret Herrick Library.

"Hollywood Boulevard." *Variety Daily*, July 31, 1936. Production Clippings. Margaret Herrick Library.

"Hollywood Boulevard." *Motion Picture Herald*, August 22, 1936. Production Clippings. Margaret Herrick Library.

"Hollywood Boulevard." *Variety Weekly*, September 23, 1936. Production Clippings. Margaret Herrick Library.

"Hollywood Boulevard lobby card." *MovieStillsDB*. Accessed July 29, 2016. www.moviestillsdb.com/movies/hollywood-boulevard-i27757/MySRpj.

"Hollywood Chatter." *Variety*, April 3, 1929.

Holmes, Susan. "'As They Really Are, and in Close-Up': Film Stars on 1950s British Television." *Screen* 42, no. 2 (2001): 167–87.

"Hope and Crosby: New Road." *Newsweek*, Jan. 26, 1948.

Howe, Sean. *Marvel Comics: The Untold Story*. New York: HarperCollins, 2012.

Hughes, Rupert. "Synopsis of Souls for Sale," c. 1922. USC Cinematic Arts Collection.

"I See You There Matt Damon, Hiding in Plain Sight." *Reddit*, January 18, 2012. Accessed June 5, 2016. www.reddit.com/r/homeland/comments/olosx/i_see_you_there_matt_damon_hiding_in_plain_sight/.

"It's a Mad Booklet." Mar-King Publishing and Novelty Corp., n.d. Linwood D. Gunn Papers, Folder 285. Margaret Herrick Library.

"It's a Mad, Mad, Mad, Mad World Ad." *Spokesman Review*, June 4, 1965. Press Clippings. Margaret Herrick Library.

"It's a Mad Mad Mad Mad World Production Photographs," n.d. Stanley Kramer Files. UCLA Special Collections.

Jacobs, A. P. Letter to I. Windisch. "Inter Office Memo: Bob Hope Idea," January 10, 1959. Marty Weiser Alias Jesse James 1959 Folder 14. Margaret Herrick Library.

Jenkins, Henry. *Convergence Culture: Where Old and New Media Collide*. New York: New York University Press, 2006.

———. "Reception Theory and Audience Research: The Mystery of the Vampire's Kiss." In *Reinventing Film Studies*, edited by Christine Gledhill and Linda Williams. London: Arnold, 2000. Accessed February 25, 2016. http://web.mit.edu/cms/People/henry3/vampkiss.html.

———. *Textual Poachers: Television Fans and Participatory Culture*. New York: Routledge, 1992.

Jenkins, Henry, Sam Ford, and Joshua Green. *Spreadable Media: Creating Value and Meaning in a Networked Culture*. New York: New York University Press, 2013.

"Juvenile Film Corporation Presents Joseph Monahan in His Great Imitation of Charlie Chaplin's Burlesque on Carmen," *Moving Picture World*, June 1916.

Kann, Redd. "My Favorite Brunette." *Motion Picture Daily*, February 18, 1947.

Kapsis, Robert E. *Hitchcock: The Making of a Reputation*. Chicago: University of Chicago Press, 1992.

———. "Reputation Building and the Film Art World: The Case of Alfred Hitchcock." *TSQ Sociological Quarterly* 30, no. 1 (1989): 15–35.

Karnick, Kristine Brunovska, and Henry Jenkins. *Classical Hollywood Comedy*. New York: Routledge, 2013.

Kaufman, Wolfe. "Bob Hope's at His Best in My Favorite Blonde." *Chicago Sun*, June 20, 1942.

Keathley, Christian. *Cinephilia and History; or, The Wind in the Trees*. Bloomington: Indiana University Press, 2006.

Keaton, Buster, and Charles Samuels. *My Wonderful World of Slapstick*. New York: Da Capo Press, 1982.

Kemper, Tom. *Hidden Talent: The Emergence of Hollywood Agents*. Berkeley: University of California Press, 2009.

Kenaga, Heidi. "Promoting Hollywood Extra Girl (1935)." *Screen* 52, no. 1 (2011): 78–81.

"Kentucky College Professor Has Cameo Role in New Spielberg Movie 'Lincoln.'" *Levisa Lazer*. Accessed January 24, 2014. www.thelevisalazer.com/lifestyles/arts-a-entertainment/6474-kentucky-college-professor-has-cameo-role-in-new-spielberg-movie-qlincoln.

King, Barry. "The Star and the Commodity: Notes Towards a Performance Theory of Stardom." *Cultural Studies* 1, no. 2 (1987): 145–61.

King, Susan. "Funny Business." *Los Angeles Times*, October 29, 2012. Production Clippings. Margaret Herrick Library.

Kingsley, Grace. "Film Reveals Studio World: Souls for Sale." *Los Angeles Times*, January 7, 1923.

Klevan, Andrew. *Film Performance: From Achievement to Appreciation*. London: Wallflower Press, 2005.

Kline, Stephen, Nick Dyer-Witheford, and Greig De Peuter. *Digital Play: The Interaction of Technology, Culture, and Marketing*. Montreal: McGill-Queen's University Press, 2005.

Klinger, Barbara. "Becoming Cult: *The Big Lebowski*, Replay Culture, and Male Fans." *Screen* 51, no. 1 (2010): 1–20.

———. *Beyond the Multiplex: Cinema, New Technologies, and the Home*. Berkeley: University of California Press, 2006.

———. "Digressions at the Cinema: Reception and Mass Culture." *Cinema Journal* 28, no. 4 (1989): 3–19.

Kompare, Derek. "I've Seen This One Before: The Construction of 'Classic TV' on Cable Television." In *Small Screens, Big Ideas: Television in the 1950s*, edited by Janet Thumin, 19–34. London I. B. Tauris, 2002.

Koury, Phil. "DeMille Takes Direction." *New York Times*, May 29, 1949.

Krämer, Peter. *The New Hollywood: From Bonnie and Clyde to Star Wars*. London: Wallflower, 2005.

Krohn, Bill. *Hitchcock at Work*. New ed. London: Phaidon Press, 2003.

Krutnik, Frank. "A Spanner in the Works? Genre, Narrative, and the Hollywood Comedian." In *Classical Hollywood Comedy*, edited by Kristine Brunovska Karnick and Henry Jenkins, 17–38. New York: Routledge, 1995.

Krutnik, Frank, and Steve Neale. *Popular Film and Television Comedy*. New York: Routledge, 2006.

Lai, Adrienne. "Glitter and Grain: Aura and Authenticity in the Celebrity Photographs of Juergen Teller." In *Framing Celebrity: New Directions in Celebrity Culture*, edited by Su Holmes and Sean Redmond, 215–30. New York: Routledge, 2012.

Lamour, Dorothy. *My Side of the Road*. Englewood Cliffs, NJ: Prentice-Hall, 1980.

Lamparski, Richard. *Whatever Became Of . . . ? The Story of What Has Happened to More Famous Personalities*. New York: Crown, 1968.

"Lawyer-Friendly Cameo." *TV Tropes*. Accessed May 31, 2016. http://tvtropes.org/pmwiki/pmwiki.php/Main/LawyerFriendlyCameo.

Leff, Leonard J. *Hitchcock and Selznick: The Rich and Strange Collaboration of Alfred Hitchcock and David O. Selznick in Hollywood*. Berkeley: University of California Press, 1999.

Leitch, Thomas M. *Find the Director and Other Hitchcock Games*. Athens: University of Georgia Press, 1991.

———. "Hitchcock and His Writers." In *Authorship in Film Adaptation*, edited by Jack Boozer, 63–84. Austin: University of Texas Press, 2009.

Levy, Shawn. *King of Comedy: The Life and Art of Jerry Lewis*. New York: St. Martin's Press. 1997.

"The List of Adrian Messenger Ad," c. 1963. John Huston Folder 267 The List of Adrian Messenger (1963)—general. Margaret Herrick Library.

Look. "Look Photocrime: The Murder of Monty Woolley Directed by Alfred Hitchcock," c. 1943. Hitchcock Folder 353. Margaret Herrick Library.

Lotz, Amanda D. *The Television Will Be Revolutionized*. 2nd ed. New York: New York University Press, 2014.

Levinas, Emmanuel. *Totality and Infinity: An Essay on Exteriority*. New York: Springer, 1979.
luke colomer. "Marvel Movies with No Stan Lee Cameo." *IMDb*. July 10, 2013. Accessed January 14, 2015. www.imdb.com/list/ls053928812/.
Lusted, David. "The Glut of Personality." In *Stardom: Industry of Desire*, edited by Christine Gledhill, 251–58. New York: Routledge, 1991.
Mandell, Andrea. "Secret Cameos of 'American Hustle' (Renner's Baby!)." *USA Today*, December 10, 2013. Accessed September 3, 2014. www.usatoday.com/story/life/people/2013/12/10/secret-cameos-of-american-hustle/3968715/.
Mann, Denise. "The Spectacularization of Television in Early Variety Shows." In *Private Screenings: Television and the Female Consumer*, edited by Lynn Spigel and Denise Mann. Minneapolis: University of Minnesota Press, 1992.
"Many Film Precedents Set by 'Around the World in 80 Days.'" In Around the World in 80 Days 1968 Press Book, 6, 1968.
Marie, Michel. *The French New Wave: An Artistic School*. Translated by Richard Neupert. Malden, MA: Wiley-Blackwell, 2002.
Marshall, P. David. *Celebrity and Power: Fame in Contemporary Culture*. Minneapolis: University of Minnesota Press, 1997.
Martin, Brett. *Difficult Men: Behind the Scenes of a Creative Revolution; From* The Sopranos *and* The Wire *to* Mad Men *and* Breaking Bad. London: Penguin, 2014.
Masur, Kate. "In Spielberg's 'Lincoln,' Passive Black Characters." *New York Times*, November 12, 2012.
Mathijs, Ernest. "Cronenberg Connected: Cameo Acting, Cult Stardom, and Supertexts." In *Cult Film Stardom: Offbeat Attractions and Processes of Cultification*, edited by Kate Egan and Sarah Thomas. New York: Palgrave Macmillan, 2013.
Mathijs, Ernest, and Xavier Mendik. Introduction to *The Cult Film Reader*, edited by Ernest Mathijs and Xavier Mendik. New York: Open University Press/McGraw-Hill Education, 2008.
McGilligan, Patrick. *Backstory: Interviews with Screenwriters of Hollywood's Golden Age*. Berkeley: University of California Press, 1986.
McKenna, Denise. "The Photoplay or the Pickaxe: Extras, Gender, and Labour in Early Hollywood." *Film History: An International Journal* 23, no. 1 (2011): 5–19.
MGM. "North by Northwest Shooting Schedule Revised," August 18, 1954. Hitchcock Folder 547 North by Northwest schedule. Margaret Herrick Library.
"Milestone Picture Is Funny and Flip." *Hollywood Reporter*, August 8, 1960.

Miller, D. A. "Hitchcock's Hidden Pictures." *Critical Inquiry* 37, no. 1 (2010): 106–30.

———. "Hitchcock's Understyle: A Too-Close View of Rope." *Representations*, no. 121 (2013): 1–30.

Milty. "Film Reviews: Cancel My Reservation." *Variety*, September 20, 1972.

Minoff, Paul. "The World Is Their Oyster." *Cue*, December 6, 1952.

Mitchum, Robert. Letter to John Huston, September 21, 1962. John Huston Folder 266 List of Adrian Messenger correspondence. Margaret Herrick Library.

Moral, Tony Lee. *Hitchcock and the Making of Marnie*. Lanham, MD: Scarecrow Press, 2002.

Morrison, James. *Hollywood Reborn: Movie Stars of the 1970s*. New Brunswick, NJ: Rutgers University Press, 2010.

Mullen, Megan. *Television in the Multichannel Age: A Brief History of Cable Television*. Malden, MA: Wiley-Blackwell, 2008.

Murray, Susan. *Hitch Your Antenna to the Stars: Early Television and Broadcast Stardom*. New York: Routledge, 2005.

———. "Lessons from Uncle Miltie: Ethnic Masculinity and Early Television's Vaudeo Star." In *Small Screens, Big Ideas: Television in the 1950s*, edited by Janet Thumin, 66–87. London: I. B. Tauris, 2002.

Musser, Charles. "Preclassical American Cinema: Its Changing Mode of Film Production." In *Silent Film*, edited by Richard Abel, 85–108. London: Athlone, 1996.

"My Favorite Brunette." *Variety Weekly*, February 19, 1947.

Nacache, Jacqueline. *L'acteur de cinéma*. Paris: Armand Colin, 2005.

Naremore, James. *Acting in the Cinema*. Berkeley: University of California Press, 1990.

"Nate Silver, Joe Scarborough Bet on Election and More Wild Wagers (Photos)." *Daily Beast*, November 4, 2012. www.thedailybeast.com/galleries/2012/11/04/nate-silver-joe-scarborough-bet-on-election-more-wild-wagers-photos.html.

Nededog, Jethro. "'Homeland' Finale: It's a Battle of Wills for Carrie and Brody (Video)." *Hollywood Reporter*, December 18, 2011. www.hollywoodreporter.com/live-feed/showtime-homeland-finale-recap-275147.

Neibaur, James L. *Early Charlie Chaplin: The Artist as Apprentice at Keystone Studios*. Lanham, MD: Scarecrow Press, 2011.

"New Hitchcock Film Thriller of the Year." *New York World Telegram*, August 28, 1940. Hitchcock Folder 1623 Scrapbooks. Margaret Herrick Library.

Niven, David. *The Moon's a Balloon*. New York: G. P. Putnam's Sons, 1972.

Norman, Marc. *What Happens Next: A History of American Screenwriting*. New York: Crown Archetype, 2008.

"North by Northwest Ad." *Variety*, July 24, 1959. Hitchcock Folder 545 North by Northwest (publicity). Margaret Herrick Library.

"Ocean's Eleven Script," January 4, 1960. Lewis Milestone Ocean's Eleven Script Folder 60. Margaret Herrick Library.

"Ocean's Eleven Script Revision Final," February 16, 1960. Scripts AMPAS Unpublished. Margaret Herrick Library.

Olsson, Jan. *Hitchcock à la Carte*. Durham, NC: Duke University Press, 2015.

———. "Screen Bodies and Busybodies: Corporeal Constellations in the Era of Anonymity." *Film History* 25, no. 1–2 (2013): 188–204.

Orr, John. *Hitchcock and Twentieth-Century Cinema*. London: Wallflower Press, 2005.

"Palship." *Newsweek*, August 8, 1960.

Paramount. "Alias Jesse James Production Call Sheet," October 29, 1958. Paramount Pictures Production Records Folder 58. Margaret Herrick Library.

———. "Authorization for Engagement of Artists by BC Enterprises, Inc. and Hope Enterprises Inc.—Jerry Colonna," February 25, 1947. Paramount Pictures Production Records Road to Rio Billing #1. Margaret Herrick Library.

———. "First Unit Shooting Schedule to Catch a Thief," June 7, 1954. Hitchcock Folder 63 To Catch a Thief (production). Margaret Herrick Library.

———. "Hollywood Boulevard Press Book," n.d. Press Books. Margaret Herrick Library.

———. "Hollywood Boulevard Script," May 8, 1936. Paramount Scripts 683. Margaret Herrick Library.

———. "Hollywood Continuity Script," n.d. Paramount Scripts H-679. Margaret Herrick Library.

———. "Hollywood Scenario," n.d. Paramount Pictures Scripts H-677. Margaret Herrick Library.

———. "A Most Unusual Motion Picture," Sunset Boulevard Press Book, n.d. USC Cinematic Arts Library.

———. "My Favorite Blonde Has Surprise in Store (Advance Feature)." My Favorite Blonde Press Book, 1943, 25.

———. "My Favorite Blonde Script Supervisor's Notes," January 5, 1942. Paramount Production Records My Favorite Blonde Folder 8. Margaret Herrick Library.

———. "Road to Rio Main Title Billing Corrected," March 19, 1947. Paramount Pictures Production Records Road to Rio Billing #1. Margaret Herrick Library.

———. Sunset Boulevard Press Book, 1950.
———. Sunset Boulevard Program, 1950.
Parish, James Robert, Michael R. Pitts, and Gregory W. Mank. *Hollywood on Hollywood*. Metuchen, NJ: Scarecrow Press, 1978.
"Patience." *Variety*, November 5, 1912.
Parsons, Louella O. *Tell It to Louella*. New York: Putnam, 1961.
Pearson, Roberta. "Star Trek and Cult Television." In *Television as Digital Media*, edited by James Bennett and Niki Strange, 100–130. Durham, NC: Duke University Press, 2011.
Pelswick, Rose. "McCrea-Day Picture Presented at the Rivoli." *New York Journal and American*, August 28, 1940. Hitchcock Folder 1623 Scrapbooks. Margaret Herrick Library.
Perkinson, Stephen. *The Likeness of the King: A Prehistory of Portraiture in Late Medieval France*. Chicago: University of Chicago Press, 2009.
"Peter Jackson Dishes on Stephen Colbert's 'Hobbit' Cameo." *Entertain This!*, December 17, 2014. Accessed January 21, 2016. http://entertainthis.usatoday.com/2014/12/17/peter-jackson-dishes-on-stephen-colberts-hobbit-cameo/.
"Peter Jackson Reveals His Unrecognizable Cameo in 'The Hobbit.'" *Ace Showbiz*, December 15, 2012. Accessed January 21, 2016. www.aceshowbiz.com/news/view/00056384.html.
Petro, Patrice. *Idols of Modernity: Movie Stars of the 1920s*. New Brunswick, NJ: Rutgers University Press, 2010.
Phillips, Gene D. *Some Like It Wilder: The Life and Controversial Films of Billy Wilder*. Lexington: University Press of Kentucky, 2010.
"Pictures: 18 B'Way Picture Houses." *Variety*, April 30, 1930.
"Pictures: 'Blood and Sand' Flops in Pittsburgh." *Variety*, September 29, 1922.
"Pictures: Loew's Cameo, Brooklyn." *Variety*, December 3, 1924.
Plasketes, George. *B-Sides, Undercurrents and Overtones: Peripheries to Popular in Music, 1960 to the Present*. Farnham, UK: Ashgate, 2013.
PR, MCA. Letter to Frank Wright, MCA. "Interoffice Memorandum: Reel of Mr. Hitchcock's Appearances in 9 Motion Pictures," May 14, 1976. Hitchcock Folder 1456 General (A Hitchcock—misc.). Margaret Herrick Library.
PR, Universal. Letter to Fred Thomas, Rank Organization. "Re: Speeches," June 29, 1966. Hitchcock Folder 935, Torn Curtain—speeches. Margaret Herrick Library.
"The Princess and the Pirate." *New Yorker*, February 17, 1945.
"Psycho Lobby/Radio Spots," n.d. Hitchcock Folder 101 The Birds—radio spots 1963. Margaret Herrick Library.

"Purely Personal Puffs." *Vitagraph Bulletin*, August 1915.
"A Quartette of Vitagraph Players." *Vitagraph Life Portrayals*, July 1911.
Quirk, Lawrence J. *Bob Hope: The Road Well-Traveled*. New York: Applause Books, 2000.
"Radio-Television: Chad and Jeremy Figure in Spinoff of 'Laredo.'" *Variety*, December 8, 1965.
Rau, Neil. "Visiting the Studios: Funniest Crosby and Hope Clowning Never Screened." *Los Angeles Examiner*, May 18, 1952.
Raubicheck, Walter. "Bing Crosby at Paramount: From Crooner to Actor." In *Going My Way: Bing Crosby and American Culture*, edited by Ruth Prigozy and Walter Raubicheck. Rochester, NY: University of Rochester Press, 2007.
Raubicheck, Walter, and Walter Srebnick. *Scripting Hitchcock: Psycho, The Birds, and Marnie*. Urbana: University of Illinois Press, 2011.
Read, Robert J. "Uncredited: Jack Mulhall and the Decline of Stardom." *Screen* 52, no. 1 (2011): 114–20.
Regourd, Serge. *Les seconds rôles du cinéma français: Grandeur et décadence*. Paris: Archimbaud/Klincksieck, 2010.
"Reviews." *Atlantic News-Telegraph*, October 21, 1916.
Revue Studios. "Daily Production Report Revue Studios Psycho," January 28, 1960. Hitchcock Folder 601 Psycho (prod.). Margaret Herrick Library.
———. "Revue Advance Schedule," November 30, 1959. Hitchcock Folder 600 Psycho (prod.). Margaret Herrick Library.
"Road to Rio." *Film Daily*, November 18, 1946. Press Clippings—Road to Rio. Margaret Herrick Library.
Robertson, Peggy. "Mr. Hitchcock's Secret Cuts," July 7, 1969. Hitchcock Folder 738 Topaz (cutting). Margaret Herrick Library.
Robinson, David. *Chaplin: His Life and Art*. New York: McGraw-Hill, 1985.
"Rock, Smith and Blackton Were Pioneer Exhibitors." *Moving Picture World*, July 1916.
Rojek, Chris. *Frank Sinatra*. Cambridge, MA: Polity, 2004.
Romulo, Beth Day. *This Was Hollywood: An Affectionate History of Filmland's Golden Years*. Garden City, NY: Doubleday, 1960.
Rose, William, and Tania Rose. "It's A Mad Mad Mad Mad World First Draft Screenplay," n.d. Scripts AMPAS Unpublished. Margaret Herrick Library.
Rosten, Leo Calvin. *Hollywood: The Movie Colony, the Movie Makers*. New York: Harcourt, Brace, 1941.

Saito, Stephen. "The Curious Cameography of Matt Damon." *IFC*, January 8, 2009. Accessed February 2, 2016. www.ifc.com/2009/01/the-curious-cameography-of-mat.

Samuel, O. M. "New Orleans." *Variety*, May 5, 1926.

"San Francisco." *Variety*, October 11, 1923.

Sarris, Andrew. "Notes on the Auteur Theory in 1962." In *Film Theory and Criticism: Introductory Readings*, edited by Leo Braudy and Marshall Cohen, 561–64. 5th ed. New York: Oxford University Press, 1999.

"A Saturnine Svongali." *New York Times*, July 30, 1923.

Scheuer, Philip K. "Cantinflas Carries Heavy 'Pepe' Load: Simple Peon Made Complex by Olla-Podrida of a Show." *Los Angeles Times*, December 28, 1960.

———. "Las Vegas Swarms with Movie Stars: Heist Like Military Operation in Sinatra's 'Ocean's Eleven.'" *Los Angeles Times*, February 2, 1960.

———. "Sinatra Premieres 'Ocean's Eleven': Las Vegas Hotels Host Stars; Film Enjoyable, Slow-Starting." *Los Angeles Times*, August 5, 1960.

Schickel, Richard. *Conversations with Scorsese*. Updated, expanded ed. New York: Knopf, 2013.

Schneider, Karen S. "Gathering No Moss." *People*, May 15, 2000.

Schwartz, Vanessa R. *It's So French!: Hollywood, Paris, and the Making of Cosmopolitan Film Culture*. Chicago: University of Chicago Press, 2007.

Scott, Evelyn F. *Hollywood, When Silents Were Golden*. New York: McGraw-Hill, 1972.

Scott, Suzanne. "Battlestar Galactica Fans and Ancillary Content." In *How to Watch Television*, edited by Ethan Thompson and Jason Mittell, 320–30. New York: New York University Press, 2013.

Seidman, Steve. *Comedian Comedy: A Tradition in Hollywood Film*. Ann Arbor, MI: UMI Research Press, 1981.

Seife, Ethan de. *Tashlinesque: The Hollywood Comedies of Frank Tashlin*. Middletown, CT: Wesleyan University Press, 2012.

Selznick, David O. *Memo from David O. Selznick*. New York: Viking Press, 1972.

Shipton, Alyn. *Nilsson: The Life of a Singer-Songwriter*. New York: Oxford University Press, 2013.

"Show Reviews: Prospects." *Variety*, October 12, 1920.

"Shooting Schedule Studio Portion Only," June 29, 1955. Hitchcock Folder 396 The Man Who Knew Too Much. Margaret Herrick Library.

Sikov, Ed. *On Sunset Boulevard: The Life and Times of Billy Wilder*. New York: Hyperion, 1998.

Sime. "New Acts Next Week: Irene Bercseny." *Variety*, January 9, 1914.

Simmon, Scott. "Cecil B. DeMille's Hollywood." *Film Quarterly* 59, no. 4 (2006): 51–52.

Sims, Chris. "Stan Lee's 10 Greatest Comics." *Looper*. www.looper.com/108933/thats-whats-stan-lees-10-greatest-comics/.

Siskel, Gene. "The Movies: Topaz." *Chicago Tribune*, January 19, 1970. Hitchcock Folder 797 Topaz (reviews). Margaret Herrick Library.

Slide, Anthony. *Inside the Hollywood Fan Magazine: A History of Star Makers, Fabricators, and Gossip Mongers*. Jackson: University Press of Mississippi, 2010.

Slide, Anthony, and Alan Gevinson. *The Big V: A History of the Vitagraph Company*. Metuchen, NJ: Scarecrow Press, 1987.

Smith, Greg M. *Beautiful TV: The Art and Argument of Ally McBeal*. Austin: University of Texas Press, 2007.

Sobchack, Vivian. "Inscribing Ethical Space: Ten Propositions on Death, Representation, and Documentary." *Quarterly Review of Film Studies* 9, no. 4 (1984): 283–300.

Spigel, Lynn. *Make Room for TV: Television and the Family Ideal in Postwar America*. Chicago: University of Chicago Press, 1992.

Spoto, Donald. *The Dark Side of Genius: The Life of Alfred Hitchcock*. New York: Da Capo Press, 1999.

———. *Stanley Kramer, Film Maker*. New York: Putnam, 1978.

Staggs, Sam. *Close-up on Sunset Boulevard: Billy Wilder, Norma Desmond, and the Dark Hollywood Dream*. New York: Macmillan, 2003.

Stalmaster, Lynn, and Stalmaster-Lister Company. "Contract Request," June 13, 1962. Stanley Kramer Box 61 Folder 5 Actors Weekly Contracts. UCLA Special Collections.

Stam, Robert. *Reflexivity in Film and Literature: From Don Quixote to Jean-Luc Godard*. Ann Arbor, MI: UMI Research Press, 1985.

Stanley Kramer Productions. "Daily Production Report," October 29, 1962. Stanley Kramer Box 62 Folder Mad World Production Reports Pre-Production. UCLA Special Collections.

Stein, Louisa. "Gossip Girl: Transmedia Technologies." In *How to Watch Television*, edited by Ethan Thompson and Jason Mittell, 338–46. New York: New York University Press, 2013.

Stewart, Susan. *On Longing: Narratives of the Miniature, the Gigantic, the Souvenir, the Collection*. Baltimore: Johns Hopkins University Press, 1984.
Straw, Will. "Scales of Presence: Bess Flowers and the Hollywood Extra." *Screen* 52, no. 1 (2011): 121–27.
Studlar, Gaylyn. "The Perils of Pleasure? Fan Magazine Discourse as Women's Commodified Culture in the 1920s." In *Silent Film*, edited by Richard Abel, 263–98. London: Athlone, 1996.
———. "Theda Bara: Orientalism, Sexual Anarchy, and the Jewish Star." In *Flickers of Desire: Movie Stars of the 1910s*, edited by Jennifer M. Bean, 113–36. New Brunswick, NJ: Rutgers University Press, 2011.
Swanson, Gloria. *Swanson on Swanson*. New York: Random House, 1980.
Swerling, Jo. "Lifeboat Screenplay Revised Final," July 29, 1943. Hitchcock Folder 353 Lifeboat. Margaret Herrick Library.
Taylor, John Russell. *Hitch: The Life and Times of Alfred Hitchcock*. 1st US ed. New York: Pantheon, 1978.
Taylor, Samuel. "Topaz First-Draft Screenplay with Changes up to Feb 11 1969, Peggy Robertson's Script," n.d. Hitchcock Folder 692. Margaret Herrick Library.
Tbee. "Moving Pictures: Within the Cup." *Variety*, March 22, 1918.
Thomas, Bob. "Many Ask for Cameo Roles." *Daytona Beach Morning Journal*, October 27, 1962.
———. "Ocean's 11 Film Begun by Lawford." *Los Angeles Mirror*, January 18, 1960.
Todd, Janet M. *Women and Film*. New York: Holmes and Meier, 1988.
Todd, Michael, Jr., and S. T. McCarthy. *A Valuable Property: The Life Story of Michael Todd*. New York: Arbor House, 1983.
Tomkies, Mike. *The Robert Mitchum Story*. New York: Ballantine Books, 1973.
"Torn Curtain 1 Minute Radio Spot #1," n.d. Hitchcock Folder 911 Torn Curtain (post production). Margaret Herrick Library.
Truffaut, François, and Alfred Hitchcock. *Hitchcock*. New York: Simon and Schuster, 1967.
Turner, Graeme. *Understanding Celebrity*. London: SAGE, 2004.
"TV Preview: Sinatra's 'Rat Pack' in 'Ocean's 11.'" *Hartford Courant*, June 9, 1966.
United Artists. It's A Mad Mad Mad Mad World 1970 Re-Release Press Book, 1970.
Universal Studios. "Family Plot Brochure," 1976. Hitchcock Folder 218 Family Plot—publicity 1976. Margaret Herrick Library.

Universal Studios Press Department. "Transcript of Closed Circuit Press Conference at NBC (Richard Schickel Interviews), NBC Studios, Burbank," March 23, 1976. Hitchcock Folder 200 Family Plot Hitchcock, Alfred 1973–1977 (publicity). Margaret Herrick Library.

Van Luling, Todd. "5 Stories You Didn't Know about 'Fargo,' as Told by the Movie's Main Villain." *Huffington Post*. March 18, 2015. www.huffingtonpost.com/2015/03/17/fargo-movie-trivia-interview_n_6880346.html.

Vieira, Mark A. *Irving Thalberg: Boy Wonder to Producer Prince*. Berkeley: University of California Press, 2009.

Vincent, Alice, and Tristram Fane Saunders. "Quentin Tarantino: His 10 Best Cameo Roles." *Telegraph*, December 10, 2015. www.telegraph.co.uk/film/hateful-eight/quentin-tarantino-best-cameo-roles/.

"A Vitagraph Romance." *Vitagraph Life Portrayals*, September 17, 1912.

Walker, Brent E. *Mack Sennett's Fun Factory: A History and Filmography of His Studio and His Keystone and Mack Sennett Comedies, with Biographies of Players and Personnel*. Jefferson, NC: McFarland, 2013.

Walker, Tim. "Meryl Streep Film *The Iron Lady* Is Criticised by Margaret Thatcher's Biographer." *Telegraph*, December 16, 2011. www.telegraph.co.uk/culture/film/film-news/8959033/Meryl-Streep-film-The-Iron-Lady-is-criticised-by-Margaret-Thatchers-biographer.html.

Walt. "Girl in the Kimono." *Variety*, July 2, 1910.

———. "Out of Town: The Wife Tamers." *Variety*, September 3, 1910.

"Watching Movies with Quentin Tarantino." *New York Times*, September 15, 2000. www.nytimes.com/2000/09/15/arts/15WATC.html.

Weatherford, Mike. *Cult Vegas: The Weirdest! The Wildest! The Swingin'est Town on Earth*. Las Vegas: Huntington Press, 2001.

Weaver, John D. "The Man behind the Body." *Holiday*, September 1964.

West, Shearer. *Portraiture*. Oxford: Oxford University Press, 2004.

Whitley, RJ. "A Talkie Triumph." *Daily Mirror*, June 24, 1929.

"What Movie Has the Best Audio Commentary?" *Reddit*, February 5, 2016. Accessed June 7, 2016. www.reddit.com/r/AskReddit/comments/44ai2l/what_movie_has_the_best_audio_commentary/.

"When the World Was Wider." *Life*, October 22, 1956.

Wilder, Billy. *Sunset Boulevard*. Berkeley: University of California Press, 1999.

Willemsen, Paul. "The Figure of the Extra." In *Actors and Extras*, edited by Paul Willemsen and Thomas Trummer, 9–36. Brussels: Argos Centre for Art and Media, 2009.

Williams, Dick. "It's Cantinflas Who Puts Spark in Long Pepe." *Los Angeles Mirror*, December 28, 1961.
Williams, Phil. "Feeding Off the Past: The Evolution of the Television Rerun." *Journal of Popular Film and Television* 21, no. 4 (1994): 162.
Williams, Raymond. *Television Technology and Cultural Form*. New York: Routledge, 2003. http://public.eblib.com/choice/publicfullrecord.aspx?p=182593.
Winsten, Archer. "Alfred Hitchcock's 'Lifeboat' Opens at the Astor Theatre." *New York Post*, January 13, 1944. Hitchcock Folder 1622 Scrapbooks. Margaret Herrick Library.
———. "'A Mad World' at Warner's Cinema." *New York Post*, November 19, 1963.
Wojcik, Pamela Robertson. "Typecasting." *Criticism* 45, no. 2 (2003): 223–49.
Wolfe, Charles. "Buster Keaton: Comic Invention and the Art of Moving Pictures." In *Idols of Modernity: Movie Stars of the 1920s*, edited by Patrice Petro, 41–64. New Brunswick, NJ: Rutgers University Press, 2010.
Woloch, Alex. *The One vs. the Many: Minor Characters and the Space of the Protagonist in the Novel*. Princeton, NJ: Princeton University Press, 2009.
Wood, Robin. *Hitchcock's Films Revisited*. New York: Columbia University Press, 1989.
Wucher, Joshua. "'Let's Get into Character': Role-Playing in Quentin Tarantino's Postmodern Sandbox." *Journal of Popular Culture* 48, no. 6 (2015): 1287–305.
Yacowar, Maurice. *Hitchcock's British Films*. Detroit: Wayne State University Press, 2010.
Yonge, Charlotte Mary. *Cameos from English History*. London: Macmillan, 1880.
"'You Would See It Just to See Its Two Brilliant Stars' Advertisement," December 1941. Hitchcock Folder 656 Suspicion (misc) Lobby Reproductions for theaters. Margaret Herrick Library.
Zoglin, Richard. *Hope: Entertainer of the Century*. New York: Simon and Schuster, 2014.
Zolotow, Maurice. *Billy Wilder in Hollywood*. New York: Putnam, 1977.

Film and Television Cited

12 Years a Slave. Dir. Steve McQueen. Fox Searchlight, 2013.
21 Jump Street. Fox, 1987–91.
21 Jump Street. Dirs. Phil Lord and Christopher Miller. Columbia/MGM, 2012.
30 Rock. NBC, 2006–13.
A Film Johnnie. Dir. George Nichols. Keystone Studios, 1914.

A Man's Man. Dir. James Cruze. MGM, 1929.
"A Night at the Oprah." *The Fresh Prince of Bel-Air*. NBC, November 9, 1992.
A Star Is Born. Dir. William A. Wellman. United Artists, 1937.
A Star Is Born. Dir. George Cukor. Warner Bros., 1954.
A Trip to the Moon. Dir. George Méliès. Star Film Company, 1902.
A Woman of Paris. Dir. Charles Chaplin. United Artists, 1923.
After Hours. Dir. Martin Scorsese. Warner Bros., 1985.
Age of Innocence. Dir. Martin Scorsese. Columbia, 1993.
Airplane. Dirs. Jim Abrahams, David Zucker, and Jerry Zucker. Paramount, 1980.
Alfred Hitchcock Presents. CBS/NBC, 1955–65.
Alias Jesse James. Dir. Norman Z. McLeod. United Artists, 1959.
Annie Hall. Dir. Woody Allen. United Artists, 1977.
Apocalypse Now. Dir. Francis Ford Coppola. United Artists, 1979.
Around the World in 80 Days. Dir. Michael Anderson. United Artists, 1956.
Badlands. Dir. Terrence Malick. Warner Bros., 1973.
Barfly. Dir. Barbet Schroeder. Cannon Film Distributors, 1987.
"Barney/Never." *Louie*. HBO, August 2, 2012.
Baskets. FX, 2016–.
Big Love. HBO, 2006–11.
Blackmail. Dir. Alfred Hitchcock. British International Pictures, 1929.
The Blues Brothers. Dir. John Landis. Universal Pictures, 1980.
Bojack Horseman. Netflix, 2014–.
Cancel My Reservation. Dir. Paul Bogart. Warner Bros., 1972.
Cars. Dir. John Lasseter. Buena Vista Pictures, 2006.
Caught in the Draft. Dir. David Butler. Paramount, 1941.
Che. Dir. Steven Soderbergh. Warner Bros./IFC, 2007.
Chinatown. Dir. Roman Polanski. Paramount, 1974.
"Chris Martin." *Extras*. BBC/HBO, October 5, 2006.
Come Blow Your Horn. Dir. Bud Yorkin. Paramount, 1963.
Contempt. Dir. Jean-Luc Godard. Rome Paris Films, 1963.
Curb Your Enthusiasm. HBO, 2000–11.
Dharma and Greg. ABC, 1997–2002.
Django Unchained. Dir. Quentin Tarantino. Weinstein Company/Sony, 2012.
Easy Virtue. Dir. Alfred Hitchcock. Woolf and Freedman Film Service, 1928.
Enemy of the State. Dir. Tony Scott. Walt Disney Studios, 1998.
Entourage. HBO, 2004–11.
ER. NBC, 1994–2009.

Extras. BBC/HBO, 2005–7.
Family Guy. Fox, 1999–.
Family Plot. Dir. Alfred Hitchcock. Universal, 1976.
Fantastic Four: Rise of the Silver Surfer. Dir. Tim Story. 20th Century Fox, 2007.
"Far Out Munsters." *The Munsters*. CBS, March 18, 1965.
Fargo. Dir. Joel and Ethan Cohen. Gramercy Pictures, 1996.
Follow the Boys. Dir. A. Edward Sutherland. Universal, 1944.
Foreign Correspondent. Dir. Alfred Hitchcock. United Artists, 1940.
Four Star Playhouse. CBS, 1952–56.
Frenzy. Dir. Alfred Hitchcock. Universal, 1972.
Futurama. Fox/Comedy Central, 1999–2013.
Gable and Lombard. Dir. Sidney J. Furie. Universal, 1976.
Game of Thrones. HBO. 2011–19.
Gilligan's Island. CBS, 1964–67.
"Green Ice." *Batman*. ABC, November 9, 1966.
Going My Way. Dir. Leo McCarey. Paramount, 1944.
Gunsmoke. CBS, 1955–75.
"Hare Today . . ." *Fresh Prince of Bel-Air*. NBC, April 8, 1996.
Here Comes the Groom. Dir. Frank Capra. Paramount, 1951.
"Hi Diddle Riddle." *Batman*. ABC, January 12, 1966.
Hill Street Blues. NBC, 1981–87.
His Regeneration. Dir. Gilbert M. Anderson. Essanay Studios, 1915.
Hollywood. Dir. James Cruze. Paramount, 1923.
Hollywood Boulevard. Dir. Robert Florey. Paramount, 1936.
Hollywood Canteen. Dir. Delmer Daves. Warner Bros., 1944.
Hollywood Hotel. CBS, 1935–38.
Hollywood Hotel. Dir. Busby Berkeley. Warner Bros., 1937.
Hollywood Story. Dir. William Castle. Universal International, 1951.
Home Alone 2: Lost in New York. Dir. Chris Columbus. 20th Century Fox, 1992.
How Motion Pictures Are Made. Keystone Studios, 1914.
Hot Fuzz. Dir. Edgar Wright. Universal Pictures, 2007. DVD: Universal Studios Home Entertainment, 2007.
Hot Shots Part Deux. Dir. Jim Abrahams. 20th Century Fox, 1993.
Hugo. Dir. Martin Scorsese. Paramount, 2011.
I Confess. Dir. Alfred Hitchcock. Warner Bros., 1953.
I Dream of Jeannie. NBC, 1965–70.
I Love Lucy. CBS, 1951–57.

"I, Stank Hole in One." *The Fresh Prince of Bel-Air*. NBC, May 6, 1996.
I'm Not There. Dir. Todd Haynes. The Weinstein Company, 2007.
Inez from Hollywood. Dir. Alfred E. Green. First National Pictures, 1924.
Inglourious Basterds. Dir. Quentin Tarantino. Weinstein Company/Universal, 2009.
Iron Man. Dir. Jon Favreau. Marvel Studios/Paramount, 2008.
Iron Man 2. Dir. Jon Favreau. Marvel Studios/Paramount, 2010.
Iron Man 3. Dir. Shane Black. Marvel Studios/Walt Disney Studios, 2013.
It's A Mad, Mad, Mad, Mad World. Dir. Stanley Kramer. United Artists, 1963.
It's Garry Shandling's Show. Showtime, 1986–90.
Jack and Jill. Dir. Dennis Dugan. Columbia, 2011.
Jackie Brown. Dir. Quentin Tarantino. Miramax, 1997.
Jamaica Inn. Dir. Alfred Hitchcock. Mayflower Pictures, 1939.
"Jose Chung's 'From Outer Space.'" *The X-Files*. Fox, April 12, 1996.
"Kate Winslet." *Extras*. BBC/HBO, August 4, 2005.
Kid Auto Races at Venice. Dir. Henry Lehmann. Keystone Studios, 1914.
King Kong. Dir. Merian C. Cooper. RKO, 1933.
LA Law. NBC, 1986–94.
Laredo. NBC, 1965–67.
Larry King Live. CNN, 1985–2010.
"Larry vs. Michael J. Fox." *Curb Your Enthusiasm*. HBO, September 11, 2011.
Last Year at Marienbad. Dir. Alain Resnais. Cocinor, 1961.
Let's Make Love. Dir. George Cukor. 20th Century Fox, 1960.
Lifeboat. Dir. Alfred Hitchcock. 20th Century Fox, 1944.
Lincoln. Dir. Steven Spielberg. Walt Disney Studios, 2012.
Louie. FX, 2010–2015.
"Lucy Meets Charles Boyer." *I Love Lucy*. CBS, March 5, 1956.
"Lucy and John Wayne." *I Love Lucy*, CBS, October 10, 1955.
Mannix. CBS, 1967–75.
"Marine One." *Homeland*. Showtime, December 18, 2011.
Marnie. Dir. Alfred Hitchcock. Universal, 1964.
Masquerade Party. ABC/NBC/CBS, 1952–60.
Mission: Impossible. Dir. Brian De Palma. Paramount, 1996.
Mr. and Mrs. Smith. Dir. Alfred Hitchcock. RKO Radio Pictures, 1941.
"Mr. Sharon Stone." *The Larry Sanders Show*. HBO, August 10, 1994.
"My Whole Life Is Thunder." *30 Rock*. NBC, December 6, 2012.
My Favorite Blonde. Dir. Sidney Lanfield. Paramount, 1942.
My Favorite Brunette. Dir. Elliott Nugent. Paramount, 1947.

Mystery Science Theatre 3000. KTMA-TV/The Comedy Channel/Comedy Central/ Sci Fi Channel, 1988–99.
North by Northwest. Dir. Alfred Hitchcock. MGM, 1959.
Ocean's 11. Dir. Lewis Milestone. Warner Bros., 1960.
Ocean's Eleven. Dir. Steven Soderbergh. Warner Bros., 2001.
"Officer Krupke." *Curb Your Enthusiasm*. HBO, November 8, 2009.
Oklahoma! Dir. Cecil B. DeMille. RKO Radio Pictures, 1955.
Parks and Recreation. NBC, 200915.
"Patty Pits Wits, Two Brits Hits." *The Patty Duke Show*. ABC, February 17, 1965.
"Play Lady Play." *Dharma and Greg*. ABC, October 12, 1999.
Playhouse 90. CBS, 1956–60.
Pepe. Dir. George Sidney. Columbia, 1960.
Personality Puzzle. ABC, 1953.
Pixels. Dir. Chris Columbus. Columbia, 2015.
Popstar: Never Stop Never Stopping. Dirs. Akiva Schaffer and Jorma Taccone. Universal, 2016.
Psycho. Dir. Alfred Hitchcock. Paramount, 1960.
Raging Bull. Dir. Martin Scorsese. United Artists, 1980.
Rear Window. Dir. Alfred Hitchcock. Paramount, 1954.
Rebecca. Dir. Alfred Hitchcock. United Artists, 1940.
"Renoir." *Baskets*. FX, January 21, 2016.
Rich and Strange. Dir. Alfred Hitchcock. British International Pictures, 1931.
Road to Bali. Dir. Hal Walker. Paramount, 1952.
Road to Morocco. Dir. David Butler. Paramount, 1942.
Road to Rio. Dir. Norman Z. McLeod. Paramount, 1947.
Road to Singapore. Dir. Victor Scherzinger. Paramount, 1940.
Road to Utopia. Dir. Hal Walker. Paramount, 1946.
Rope. Dir. Alfred Hitchcock. Warner Bros., 1948.
Saboteur. Dir. Alfred Hitchcock. Universal, 1942.
Samson and Delilah. Dir. Cecil B. DeMille. Paramount, 1949.
Scared Stiff. Dir. George Marshall. Paramount, 1953.
Scarface. Dir. Howard Hawks. United Artists, 1932.
Scrooged. Dir. Richard Donner. Paramount, 1988.
Sex and the City. HBO, 1998–2004.
Shadow of a Doubt. Dir. Alfred Hitchcock. Universal, 1943.
"Shear Torture." *The King of Queens*. CBS, October 24, 2005.
Show People. Dir. King Vidor. MGM, 1928.

Son of Paleface. Dir. Frank Tashlin. Paramount, 1952.
Souls for Sale. Dir. Rupert Hughes. Goldwyn Pictures, 1923.
Spellbound. Dir. Alfred Hitchcock. United Artists, 1945.
Spotlight. Dir. Tom McCarthy. Open Road Films, 2015.
Stage Door Canteen. Dir. Frank Borzage. United Artists, 1943.
Stage Fright. Dir. Alfred Hitchcock. Warner Bros., 1950.
Star Spangled Rhythm. Dir. George Marshall. Paramount, 1942.
Strangers on a Train. Dir. Alfred Hitchcock. Warner Bros., 1951.
Tales of Wells Fargo. NBC, 1957–62.
Talladega Nights: The Legend of Ricky Bobby. Dir. Adam McKay. Columbia Pictures, 2006.
Tarzan. NBC, 1966–68.
Taxi Driver. Dir. Martin Scorsese. Columbia, 1976.
"Ted Baxter Meets Walter Cronkite." *The Mary Tyler Moore Show*. CBS, February 9, 1974.
The 39 Steps. Dir. Alfred Hitchcock. Gaumont British Distributors, 1935.
The Adventures of Ozzie and Harriet. ABC, 1952–66.
The African Queen. Dir. John Huston. United Artists, 1951.
The Aviator. Dir. Martin Scorsese. Warner Bros./Miramax, 2004.
The Barbara Stanwyck Show. NBC, 1960–61.
The Big Bang Theory. CBS, 2007–.
The Birds. Dir. Alfred Hitchcock. Universal, 1963.
The Brady Bunch. ABC, 1969–74.
"The Cat's Meow." *Batman*. ABC, December 14, 1966.
"The Celebration Experimentation." *The Big Bang Theory*. CBS, February 25, 2016.
The Champion. Dir. Charles Chaplin. Essanay Studios, 1915.
The Cleveland Show. Fox, 2009–13.
The Color of Money. Dir. Martin Scorsese. Buena Vista Distribution, 1986.
The Day of the Locust. Dir. Joel Schlesinger. Paramount, 1975.
The Departed. Dir. Martin Scorsese. Warner Bros., 2006.
The Dick Van Dyke Show. CBS, 1961–66.
The Expendables. Dir. Sylvester Stallone. Lionsgate, 2010.
The Fault in Our Stars. Dir. Josh Boone. 20th Century Fox, 2014.
The Flintstones. ABC, 1960–66.
The Fresh Prince of Bel-Air. NBC, 1990–96.
The Ghost and Mrs. Muir. NBC/ABC, 1968–70.
The Godfather. Dir. Francis Ford Coppola. Paramount, 1972.

The Graduate. Dir. Mike Nichols. AVCO Embassy Pictures, 1967.
The Greatest Show on Earth. Dir. Cecil B. DeMille. Paramount, 1952.
The Greatest Story Ever Told. Dir. George Stevens. United Artists, 1965.
The Hangover. Dir. Todd Phillips. Warner Bros., 2009.
The Hustler. Dir. Robert Rossen. 20th Century Fox, 1961.
The Iron Lady. Dir. Phyllida Lloyd. Pathé/Film4, 2011.
The King of Comedy. Dir. Martin Scorsese. 20th Century Fox, 1983.
The King of Queens. CBS, 1998–2007.
The Knockout. Dirs. Mack Sennett and Charles Avery. Keystone Studios, 1914.
The Lady Vanishes. Dir. Alfred Hitchcock. Gainsborough Pictures, 1938.
The Larry Sanders Show. HBO, 1992–98.
The List of Adrian Messenger. Dir. John Huston. Universal International, 1963.
The Lodger. Dir. Alfred Hitchcock. Woolf and Freedman Film Service, 1926.
The Lord of the Rings. Dir. Peter Jackson. New Line Cinema, 2001–.
The Man Who Knew Too Much. Dir. Alfred Hitchcock. Paramount, 1956.
"The Many Deaths of Saint Christopher." *Mannix*. CBS, October 7, 1967.
The Mary Tyler Moore Show. CBS, 1970–77.
"The Men in Me." *The Cleveland Show*. Fox, March 25, 2012.
The Monkees. NBC, 1966–68.
The Mothers-in-Law. NBC, 1967–69.
The Munsters. CBS, 1964–66.
The Naked Gun: From the Files of Police Squad! Dir. David Zucker. Paramount, 1988.
"The One in Massapequa." *Friends*. NBC, March 28, 2002.
"The One Where Ross Meets Elizabeth's Dad." *Friends*. NBC, April 27, 2000.
"The One with the Rumor." *Friends*. NBC, November 22, 2001.
"The One with Two Parts: Part 2." *Friends*. NBC, February 23, 1995.
The Other Guys. Dir. Adam McKay. Columbia Pictures, 2010.
The Paradine Case. Dir. Alfred Hitchcock. Selznick Releasing Organization, 1947.
The Partridge Family. ABC, 1970–74.
The Player. Dir. Robert Altman. Fine Line Features, 1992. DVD: Criterion Collection, 2016.
The Princess and the Pirate. Dir. David Butler. RKO Radio Pictures, 1944.
"The Redcoats Are Coming." *The Dick Van Dyke Show*. CBS, February 10, 1965.
The Road to Hong Kong. Dir. Norman Panama. United Artists, 1962.
The Rocky Horror Picture Show. Dir. Jim Sharman. 20th Century Fox, 1975.
"The Schumakers Go to Hollywood." *It's Garry Shandling's Show*. Showtime, November 20, 1987.

The Shield. FX, 2002–8.
The Simpsons. Fox, 1989–.
The Smothers Brothers Comedy Hour. CBS, 1967–69.
The Sopranos. HBO, 1999–2007.
The Star. Dir. Stuart Heisler. 20th Century Fox, 1952.
"The Supremes." *The West Wing.* NBC, March 24, 2004.
The Tenant. Dir. Roman Polanski. Paramount, 1976.
The Terminator. Dir. James Cameron. Orion Pictures, 1984.
The Tonight Show with Jay Leno. NBC, 1992–2014.
The Trouble with Harry. Dir. Alfred Hitchcock. Paramount, 1955.
The West Wing. NBC, 1999–2006.
The Whole Nine Yards. Dir. Jonathan Lynn. Warner Bros., 2000.
The Wrong Man. Dir. Alfred Hitchcock. Warner Bros., 1956.
The X-Files. Fox, 1993–2002.
They Got Me Covered. Dir. David Butler. RKO Radio Pictures, 1943.
This Is The End. Dirs. Seth Rogen and Evan Goldberg. Columbia, 2013.
This Is Your Life. NBC, 1952–61.
Topaz. Dir. Alfred Hitchcock. Universal, 1969.
Torn Curtain. Dir. Alfred Hitchcock. Universal, 1966.
Trainwreck. Dir. Judd Apatow. Universal, 2015.
Tropic Thunder. Dir. Ben Stiller. DreamWorks Pictures, 2008.
True Detective. HBO, 2014–.
Uncle Josh at the Moving Picture Show. Dir. Edwin S. Porter. Edison Manufacturing, 1902.
Under Capricorn. Dir. Alfred Hitchcock. Warner Bros., 1949. DVD: ssine k'oria, 2005.
Wag the Dog. Dir. Barry Levinson. New Line Cinema, 1997.
"Will the Real Sammy Davis Please Hang Up?" *The Patty Duke Show.* ABC, March 3, 1965.
Will and Grace. NBC, 1998–2006.
What Price Hollywood. Dir. George Cukor. RKO-Pathé, 1932.
Wayne's World. Dir. Penelope Spheeris. Paramount, 1992.
Where There's Life. Dir. Sidney Lanfield. Paramount, 1947.
Who's Afraid of Virginia Woolf? Dir. Mike Nichols. Warner Bros., 1966.
Won Ton Ton, The Dog Who Saved Hollywood. Dir. Michael Winner. Paramount, 1976.
Vice. Dir. Adam McKay. Annapurna Pictures, 2018.

X-Men. Dir. Bryan Singer. Marvel Entertainment/20th Century Fox, 2000.
Zoolander 2. Dir. Ben Stiller. Panorama Pictures, Paramount, 2016.

Online Media Cited

BadfishKoo. *Michael Cera: This Is The End Best Scenes*, 2013. YouTube. Accessed June 15, 2016. www.youtube.com/watch?v=qIKPJlKHKxg.

Brandon Jones. *"This Is The End": Every Michael Cera Scene High Def!*, 2013. YouTube. Accessed June 15, 2016. www.youtube.com/watch?v=R5y0UCMZWLM.

CH2. *Every Donald Trump Cameo Ever*, 2015. YouTube. Accessed June 15, 2016. www.youtube.com/watch?v=yosAVMB47-Y.

Morgan T. Rhys. "Every Alfred Hitchcock Cameo." *YouTube*. Accessed September 9, 2014. www.youtube.com/watch?v=_YbaOkiMiRQ.

Ono Ramírez. *TOP 20 Guest Stars in Friends*, 2014. YouTube. Accessed June 15, 2016. www.youtube.com/watch?v=7GbOUIFa87g.

razgandeanu. *The Expendables—Sylvester Stallone, Arnold Schwarzenegger, and Bruce Willis—Best Scene Ever*, 2010. YouTube. Accessed August 21, 2014. www.youtube.com/watch?v=hrMmiUSVRRI&feature=youtube_gdata_player.

Slate Magazine. *Every Single Entourage Cameo*, 2015. Accessed May 8 2015. www.youtube.com/watch?v=jteNDkI2WqY.

User323232. *Peter Jackson Movie Cameos*, 2009. YouTube. Accessed September 6, 2014. www.youtube.com/watch?v=tvgwXAky1t8&feature=youtube_gdata_player.

warnerarchive. *Tarzan: The Complete Second Season (Preview Clip)*, 2013. YouTube. Accessed June 15, 2016. www.youtube.com/watch?v=H_F5kVa2QWY.

WatchMojo.com. *Top 10 Epic Movie Cameos*, 2013. YouTube. Accessed May 8, 2015. www.youtube.com/watch?v=x-IstfVHLJw&feature=youtube_gdata_player.

Will Erickson. "Every Hitchcock Cameo Ever." *YouTube*. Accessed September 9, 2014. www.youtube.com/watch?v=okLiLsncyi0.

INDEX

12 Years a Slave, 7
20th Century Fox, 155
21 Jump Street, 204
21 Jump Street (film), 204, 206
30 Rock, 156–57
39 Steps, The, 171–72

ABC, 146
Abdul-Jabbar, Kareem, 153, 206
Adventures of Ozzie and Harriet, The, 138, 145
Affleck, Ben, 197
African Queen, The, 117
After Hours, 184–85
Age of Innocence, 184
Airplane!, 153, 206
Albert, Prince of Saxe-Coburg and Gotha, 37
Alfred Hitchcock Presents, 10, 141, 176
Alias Jesse James, 111–12, 115, 120–21, 125, 140, 199
Allen, Woody, 27, 165, 188
Altman, Robert, 203
AMC, 150, 158, 161
Anderson, Broncho Billy, 22, 69, 102
Aniston, Jennifer, 155
Annie Hall, 165, 188
Apocalypse Now, 153, 184
Arbuckle, "Fatty," 22, 64, 68–69
Arcimboldo, Giuseppe, 35
Around the World in 80 Days, 6, 22, 25, 64, 93–98, 100, 121–22, 126–28
Augustine, Saint, 42–43
Aviator, The, 8

Badlands, 167, 184
Baldwin, Alec, 157

Balestrero, Manny, 190
Bara, Theda, 47
Barfly, 12, 190
Barnes, T. Roy, 74
Barthes, Roland, 18, 39, 57
Baskets, 161
Batman, 145–46, 156
Ben-Hur, 92
Bennett, Charles, 172
Benny, Jack, 115, 120–21, 138
Bergman, Ingrid, 176
Berle, Milton, 138
Bernhardt, Sarah, 44
Biden, Joe, 201
Big Bang Theory, The, 156
Big Love, 158
Biograph Studios, 18, 44
Birds, The, 169, 173, 180–81
Blackmail, 48, 168, 174
Blackton, J. Stuart, 29, 51–53, 55–58, 63
Blues Brothers, The, 153
Boardman, Eleanor, 74
Bogart, Humphrey, 117, 120–21, 206
Bonaparte, Napoleon, 37
Bonnard, Pierre, 128
Botticelli, Sandro, 33
Bourdieu, Pierre, 21, 44, 66, 195
Boyer, Charles, 139
Brady Bunch, The, 155
Broken Blossoms, 92
Brown, Joe E., 98
Bukowski, Charles, 12, 190–91
Buñuel, Luis, 166
Burrows, Abe, 88
Byron, Lord, 19

Index

Cahiers du cinéma, 178
Cameos from English History, 41
Cameos of the Yellowstone, 49
Cancel My Reservation, 111–12
Cantinflas, 98, 101
Cantor, Eddie, 85
Capra, Frank, 89
Carradine, John, 96
Carroll, Madeleine, 111
Cars, 207
Caught in the Draft, 112
CBS, 140, 146, 158
Cera, Michael, 203
Chad and Jeremy (musical group), 146–47, 152
Chaplin, Charlie, 21–22, 25, 62, 67–70, 72, 77–78, 102, 164, 166, 168–69, 203
Che, 197
Chevalier, Maurice, 96, 127
Chinatown, 184
Clash, The (musical group), 188
Cleveland Show, The, 156
Clooney, George, 154
Close, Glenn, 157
Coen, Joel and Ethan, 204
Cohn, Art, 22
Colbert, Stephen, 188–89
Collins, Joan, 122
Colonna, Jerry, 117–18, 120–21
Color of Money, The, 185–86, 188
Come Blow Your Horn, 122
Conklin, Chester, 92
Contempt, 188
Cooper, Gary, 115, 121
Coppola, Francis Ford, 184
Coward, Noel, 128
Crawford, Joan, 86
Crispin, Edmund, 18, 22, 95
Cronenberg, David, 167, 184–85
Cronkite, Walter, 150
Crosby, Bing, 26, 85, 101–4, 107–25, 127, 129, 132, 170, 196, 205
Crosby, Bob, 117–19
Cross, David, 8
Cruise, Tom, 1–3, 7, 205
Curb Your Enthusiasm, 155, 159, 197
Curtis, Tony, 124
Cusack, John, 203

Damon, Matt, 197
Davies, Marion, 22, 61–62, 72–74, 76, 78–79

Davis, Bette, 92
Davis, Sammy Jr., 123, 146
Day, Doris, 176
Day of the Locust, The, 132
DeCordova, Richard, 4, 15, 43–44, 46, 65
Deleuze, Gilles, 59
DeLuise, Peter, 204
DeMille, Cecil B., 22, 77, 85, 86–88, 90, 93, 113, 120, 164–65, 170, 174, 184–85
DeNiro, Robert, 165
Departed, The, 185
Depp, Johnny, 204–6
Desmond, Norma, 87–89, 153
Dharma and Greg, 154–55
Diamond, Neil, 146
Dick Van Dyke Show, The, 146, 151–52
Didi-Huberman, Georges, 13, 190
Dietrich, Marlene, 18, 22, 94
Disney, 121
Django Unchained, 187
Doane, Mary Anne, 14, 59
Durante, Jimmy, 92, 128
Dürer, Albrecht, 11
Durfee, Minta, 68–69
Dyer, Richard, 6, 15–16, 20, 46–47, 117
Dylan, Bob, 154–55

Easy Virtue, 178, 193
Eco, Umberto, 16, 49, 103
Educational Pictures, 49
Elizabeth I, Queen of England, 34
Elsaesser, Thomas, 16
Enemy of the State, 158
Entourage, 155, 198
ER, 154
Essanay Studios, 22, 25, 67–69
Evans, Ray, 165
Extras, 160

Fairbanks, Douglas, 61, 76–77
Fairbanks, Douglas Jr., 150
Family Guy, 156
Family Plot, 181
Famous Mrs. Fair, The, 77
Famous Players Film Company, 44
Fantastic Four: Rise of the Silver Surfer, 12, 21, 191
Fargo, 204
Farnum, Franklyn, 90
Farrar, Geraldine, 44
Farrell, Colin, 158

Fault in Our Stars, The, 201
Fellini, Federico, 188
Felson, "Fast Eddie," 190
Film Johnnie, A, 21, 68, 71, 203
Flintstones, The, 145
Flowers, Bess, 14
Follow the Boys, 85
Foreign Correspondent, 175
Foucault, Michel, 4
Fox, Michael J., 159
Franco, James, 202–3
French New Wave, 167–68, 183, 185
Frenzy, 170, 173, 179
Frequent Hearses, 18, 95
Fresh Prince of Bel-Air, The, 155, 200
Friends, 133, 141, 154–55, 157, 196
Futurama, 207
FX, 157, 159

Gable and Lombard, 132
Gaffigan, Jim, 106
Galifianakis, Zach, 161
Game of Thrones, 157
Gance, Abel, 166
Garbo, Greta, 7
Garland, Judy, 92, 100, 105, 129
Ghost and Mrs. Muir, The, 145, 147, 152
Gilbert, John, 7, 22
Gilligan's Island, 145
Gish, Lillian, 105
Godard, Jean-Luc, 188
Goddess, The, 52
Godfather, The, 16, 184
Going My Way, 115
Goldwyn Pictures, 72, 76, 102, 113
Gore, Al, 207
Graduate, The, 165
Greatest Show on Earth, The, 93, 113, 185
Greatest Story Ever Told, The, 98, 124, 131, 144
Greed, 76–77
Green, Alfred, 77
Green, John, 201
Griffith, D. W., 51, 173
Guardians of the Galaxy, 192
Guinness, Alec, 96
Gunsmoke, 120

Hader, Bill, 203
Hale, Creighton, 83

Hangover, The, 21, 202, 206
Hardwicke, Cedric, 96
Hart, William S., 61, 77
Hawks, Howard, 185
HBO, 151–52, 154, 157–59
Hearst, William R., 61, 76
Hefner, Hugh, 191
Henderson, Florence, 155
Henry, Buck, 165
Henry VIII, King of England, 43
Here Comes the Groom, 111, 121
Hill Street Blues, 150
His New Job, 69
His Regeneration, 22, 69, 71
Hitchcock, Alfred, 8–12, 27, 48, 163–88, 190–93
Hobbit, The, 189
Holbein, Hans the Younger, 35, 43
Holden, William, 118, 141
Holiday, 173, 176
Hollywood (1923), 21, 64, 71–72, 75, 77–78, 81, 83, 189
Hollywood, Souls for Sales, 25
Hollywood Boulevard, 82–84, 90, 106, 146
Hollywood Canteen, 22, 85–86, 124
Hollywood Hotel, 85, 143
Hollywood Story, 92
Home Alone 2, 28, 200
Homeland, 197
Hope, Bob, 26, 102–4, 107–27, 129, 132, 138, 140, 168, 176, 196, 205
Hopper, Hedda, 87, 90
Horton, Edward Everett, 98
Hot Shots Part Deux, 153
How Motion Pictures Are Made, 68
Hughes, Rupert, 72
Hugo, 184
Hustler, The, 190

I Confess, 170
I Dream of Jeannie, 145
IFC, 197
I Love Lucy, 138–39, 141, 151, 203
I'm Not There, 8
Ince, Harry, 52
Independent Moving Pictures Company (IMP), 45
Inglourious Basterds, 187
In the Palace of the King, 76
Iron Lady, The, 190
Iron Man, 191

It's a Mad, Mad, Mad, Mad World, 25, 64, 92–93, 98–100, 106, 115, 124, 127–28, 130
It's Garry Shandling's Show, 151, 156

Jack and Jill, 10
Jackie Brown, 188
Jackson, Jesse, 155
Jackson, Peter, 12, 27, 186–87, 198
Jackson, Reggie, 206
Jagger, Mick, 155
Jamaica Inn (1939), 175
Jenkins, Henry, 16
Jeter, Derek, 203
Jolson, Al, 75
Joy, Leatrice, 61
Juvenile Film Corporation, 67

Kaelin, Kato, 161
Keaton, Buster, 2, 14, 69, 80, 87–90, 92, 94–95, 98–99, 125, 142
Kellerman, Annette, 48
Kennedy, Jacqueline, 7
Keystone Studios, 22, 25, 62, 67–69
Kid Auto Races at Venice, 67–68
King, Larry, 158, 192
King Kong (1933), 92
King of Comedy, The, 184, 188
King of Queens, 156
Klinger, Barbara, 15–17, 83, 192, 195, 198–200
Knickerbocker, Cholly, 76
Knockout, The, 69
Kramer, Stanley, 93, 127, 188
Krumholtz, David, 202

Ladd, Alan, 206
Lady Vanishes, The, 174
Laemmle, Carl, 18, 45
L.A. Law, 150
LaMotta, Jake, 165
Lamour, Dorothy, 102, 107, 109, 111, 113, 116, 118, 121
Lang, Fritz, 168, 173, 188
Laredo, 146
Larry King Live, 158
Larry Sanders Show, The, 151–52, 155, 157, 159
Lasky, Jesse, 78
Last Year at Marienbad, 168
Lawford, Peter, 147

Lawrence, Florence, 18, 45, 46, 80
Lee, Stan, 12, 21, 191–92, 198
Leno, Jay, 155, 158
Let's Make Love, 124, 170
Levinas, Emmanuel, 32
Lewis, Jerry, 26, 102, 106, 108, 115, 117–18, 121–22, 127–29, 145
Lifeboat, 169, 171, 175, 178–79
Lillie, Beatrice, 94–95
Lincoln, 2, 11
Lincoln, Elmo, 89
List of Adrian Messenger, The, 127, 130, 205
Livingston, Jay, 165
Locklear, Heather, 153
Lodger, The, 166, 168, 173–74, 193
Loos, Anita, 51
Lord of the Rings, The, 12, 187
Louie, 159
Lubitsch, Ernst, 77

MacLaine, Shirley, 124, 126
Macpherson, Jeannie, 77
Making Motion Pictures: A Day in the Vitagraph Studio, 13, 20, 53, 58
Malick, Terrence, 167, 184
Mannix, 146
Man's Man, A, 7
Man Who Knew Too Much, The, 176, 180–81
Marnie, 8, 173, 179, 181
Martin, Chris, 160–61
Martin, Dean, 26, 102, 106, 108, 115, 117–18, 122–23
Marvel Studios, 12, 21, 191–92
Marx Brothers, 106
Mary Tyler Moore Show, The, 150
Masquerade Party, 143
Mathijs, Ernest, 2, 30, 86, 95, 106, 129, 167, 185, 203
Mayo, Frank, 83
Mazurki, Mike, 96
McBride, Danny, 203
McConaughey, Matthew, 158
McDowell, Malcolm, 203
McLuhan, Marshall, 165, 188
Méliès, Georges, 95
Metro-Goldwyn-Mayer (MGM), 22, 61, 74, 76, 85, 90, 96, 139
Mission: Impossible, 205
Mitchum, Robert, 127
Monkees, The, 146

Monroe, Marilyn, 125
Monsieur Beaucaire, 112
Montand, Yves, 125
Moore, Colleen, 51
Mothers-in-Law, The, 145, 147
Motion Picture Patents Company, 46, 55
Motion Picture Story Magazine, 46–47
Moving Picture World, 53, 55, 57
Mr. and Mrs. Smith (1941), 170, 175, 179
MTM, 150
MTV Cribs, 7
Mulhall, Jack, 83
Munsters, The, 146
Murnau, F. W., 173
Murray, Mae, 61, 78
Mutual Film Corporation, 49
My Favorite Blonde, 111–12, 114, 120
My Favorite Brunette, 112, 114, 121

Naked Gun, The, 206
NBC, 155, 158
Negri, Pola, 189
Neilan, Marshall, 77
Nelson, Ricky, 145
New Hollywood, 132, 167, 184
New York Times, 72, 111
Niblo, Fred, 77
Nickelodeon, 151
Nilsson, Anna Q., 14, 88–89
Nilsson, Harry, 145–47, 152
Normand, Mabel, 21, 55
North by Northwest, 170–71, 180–81
Novak, Kim, 124

Ocean's 11 (1960), 2, 6, 21, 123–26
Ocean's Eleven (2001), 155
Oklahoma!, 93
Olson, Nancy, 87
Other Guys, The, 203, 206

Paar, Jack, 128
Pacino, Al, 10, 16
Paleface, The, 118
Paradine Case, The, 171
Paramount Pictures, 69, 71, 82, 85–86, 90, 102, 108–11, 113, 120–21, 142, 176, 205
Parks and Recreation, 201
Parsons, Louella, 76, 143
Partridge Family, The, 146
Patty Duke Show, The, 146
Peck, Gregory, 176

Penn, Sean, 204
Pepe, 25, 64, 92–93, 98, 100–102, 104, 124–25, 127–29, 140, 144
Perlman, Itzhak, 188
Perry, Matthew, 133
Personality Puzzle, 143
Petty, Tom, 152
Philip IV, King of Spain, 43
Photoplay, 46, 65
Picasso, Pablo, 35, 128
Pickford, Mary, 45, 47, 51, 55, 71–72, 76, 105
Pitt, Brad, 7, 155, 157
Pitts, Zasu, 74, 76, 98
Pixels, 202
Platoon, 153
Player, The, 203
Polanski, Roman, 184
Pop, Iggy, 188
Popstar: Never Stop Never Stopping, 202
Porter, Edwin S., 21
Portrait historié, 33–34
Posey, Parker, 158
Preminger, Otto, 145, 165
Price, Vincent, 120
Prince (musician), 204
Princess and the Pirate, The, 112–13
Psycho (1960), 170, 176, 180

Quirk, Lawrence, 108

Radner, Gilda, 152
Raft, George, 94
Raging Bull, 165
Rat Pack, 103, 122–26
Rear Window, 178, 192–93
Rebecca, 175, 178
Reddit, 197, 200
Reed, Donna, 127–29, 140
Reiner, Carl, 127
Resnais, Alain, 168
Retton, Mary Lou, 153
Reynolds, Debbie, 150
Ricci, Christina, 158
Rich and Strange, 175, 192
Riesner, "Dinky" Dean, 189
Rihanna, 202
Road series (Hope and Crosby films), 102, 107–13, 115–16, 118–19, 121–22, 124, 127
Road to Bali, 107, 112, 115, 118, 121

Index

Road to Hong Kong, The, 107, 109, 118, 122
Road to Morocco, 111
Road to Rio, 108–9, 111–12, 118, 121
Road to Singapore, 107
Road to Utopia, 109
Robbins, Tim, 203
Robinson, Walter, 201
Rock, William T., 29, 53, 55–56, 63
Rocky Horror Picture Show, The, 16
Rogen Seth, 202
Roker, Al, 158
Rope, 171, 192–93
Rose, William, 128
Rosten, Leo, 70, 80
Rudd, Paul, 202
Russell, Jane, 117–19

Samson and Delilah, 185
Sandler, Adam, 10
Saturday Night Live, 153
Scared Stiff, 115, 118
Scarface (1932), 185
Schroeder, Barbet, 190
Schwarzenegger, Arnold, 16
Scorsese, Charles, 186
Scorsese, Martin, 27, 165, 170, 184–88, 198
Scrooged, 153
Seal (musician), 202
Seeds, The (musical group), 145
Seidman, Steve, 106
Seinfeld, Jerry, 106
Selznick, David O., 81, 163, 175
Sennett, Mack, 68–69
Sevigny, Chloë, 158
Sex and the City, 157
Shadow of a Doubt, 169, 173, 181
Shandling, Garry, 151–52
Sharknado, 158
Sheen, Charlie, 153
Sheen, Martin, 153
Shield, The, 157
Show People, 22, 25, 61, 63, 71–74, 76, 78, 81, 83, 100, 105, 111, 164
Showtime, 151
Sidney, George, 93, 127
Simpsons, The, 155
Sinatra, Frank, 6, 18, 22, 85, 94, 118, 120, 122–23, 126–27
Sixth Sense, The, 133
Skelton, Red, 2, 3, 21, 124
Skolsky, Sid, 88, 90

Smith, Albert E., 29, 52–53, 55–58, 63
Smith, Lydia, 11
Smothers Brothers Comedy Hour, The, 147
Sobchack, Vivian, 3, 14, 53
Son of Paleface, 92, 112, 115, 118, 120, 129, 185
Sopranos, The, 157
Souls for Sale, 70, 71–75, 77, 81, 95
Spellbound, 8, 163, 167, 176
Spotlight, 201
Stage Door Canteen, 116
Standells, The (musical group), 146
Stanwyck, Barbara, 85, 124
Star, The, 92
Star Is Born, A, 81, 92
Star Spangled Rhythm, 170
Stefani, Gwen, 7–8
Stein, Gertrude, 35
Stewart, Susan, 36, 49, 59
Stoudemire, Amar'e, 207
Strangers on a Train, 8, 169, 173, 179
Straw, William, 8, 14, 80
Sunset Boulevard, 14, 85, 86–92, 111, 142, 153, 165, 185
Swanson, Gloria, 14, 75, 86–87, 90, 142, 153
Sweet, Blanche, 74, 76

Tales of Wells Fargo, 120
Talladega Nights: The Ballad of Ricky Bobby, 204
Tarantino, Quentin, 27, 187–88
Tatum, Channing, 203
Taxi Driver, 184, 187
Taylor, Elizabeth, 7, 96, 98
TCM, 150
Tenant, The, 184
Terminator, The, 16
They Got Me Covered, 112
This Is the End, 9–10, 202–3, 205
This Is Your Life, 143
Three Stooges, 98, 142
Todd, Michael, 18, 22–23, 93–96, 98, 121–22, 126, 128, 188
Tonight Show, The, 158
Topaz, 170, 179–80
Torn Curtain, 170, 173, 179–80
Trainwreck, 202–4, 206
Trebek, Alex, 154
Trip to the Moon, A, 95
Tropic Thunder, 1, 7, 205
True Detective, 158

Truffaut, François, 166, 171, 179, 192
Trump, Donald, 28, 198, 200
Turner, Florence, 47, 57–58, 64, 67
TV Tropes, 199
Twiggy, 153
Tyson, Mike, 21, 207

Uncle Josh at the Moving Picture Show, 21
Under Capricorn, 193
Universal Pictures, 45, 51, 92, 176, 182, 192

Van Dyke, Dick, 151
Van Eyck, Jan, 34–35
Variety, 50, 82–83, 114, 119, 147
Velázquez, Diego, 11, 34, 43
Verne, Jules, 93
Vice, 158
Victoria, Queen of England, 37
Vidor, King, 164
Vitagraph Life Portrayals, 47, 48, 52
Vitagraph Romance, A, 20–21, 29, 53, 55–58, 59, 67–68
Vitagraph Studios, 13, 20, 22, 24–25, 29, 31, 45–47, 51–58, 63–64, 66–67
Von Stroheim, Erich, 77, 80, 86–87, 90

Wag the Dog, 158
Wahlberg, Mark, 203
Wall Street, 153
Warner, H. B., 88–89
Warner Brothers, 85, 124
Watts, Naomi, 158
Wayne, John, 98, 132, 139
Wayne's World, 153

West, Adam, 156
West Wing, The, 157
What Price Hollywood, 81
Where There's Life, 112
White, Eleanor, 146
Whole Nine Yards, The, 133
Whole Ten Yards, The, 133
Who's Afraid of Virginia Woolf?, 132
Wife Tamers, The, 49
Wikipedia, 199
Wilder, Billy, 87
Will and Grace, 158
Williams, Kathlyn, 47, 74
Williams, Robin, 159
Willis, Bruce, 133, 141, 196
Wilson, Lois, 75
Winfrey, Oprah, 155
Winslet, Kate, 160
Woman in Paris, A, 164, 166
Won Ton Ton, the Dog Who Saved Hollywood, 132
Wray, Fay, 92
Wrong Man, The, 178, 180, 190
Wyman, Jane, 85

X-Files, The, 154
X-Men, 192

Yacowar, Maurice, 180, 192–93
Young, Clara Kimball, 55
Young, James, 55
YouTube, 28, 193, 197–98

Zoolander 2, 205
Zucker, Abrahams, and Zucker, 153, 205